The Essay Connection
Readings for Writers

Lynn Z. Bloom
Virginia Commonwealth University

D. C. Heath and Company
Lexington, Massachusetts   Toronto

Acknowledgments

James Agee, "Comedy's Greatest Era." Reprinted by permission of Grosset & Dunlap, Inc. from *Agee on Film*, Vol. 1, copyright © 1958 by The James Agee Trust.

Woody Allen, "Selections from the Allen Notebooks." Copyright © 1973 by Woody Allen. Reprinted from *Without Feathers*, by Woody Allen, by permission of Random House, Inc. and Woody Allen.

Hans C. von Baeyer, "The Wonder of Gravity." Parts of this essay will appear in a book to be published by McGraw Hill Book Co. in 1983. Reprinted by permission of the author.

Laird Bloom, "The Progressives' Pilgrim: A Review of Lillian D. Wald's *The House on Henry Street*." Reprinted by permission.

Bill Bradley, "Fame and Self-Identity." Copyright © 1976 by Bill Bradley. Reprinted by permission of TIME BOOKS, a Division of Quadrangle/The New York Times Book Co., Inc. from *Life on the Run* by Bill Bradley.

Robert Brustein, "Reflections on Horror Movies." From *The Third Theatre*, by Robert Brustein, Professor of English, Harvard University. Reprinted by permission of the author.

Rachel Carson, "The Grey Beginnings." From *The Sea Around Us* by Rachel L. Carson. Copyright © 1950, 1951, 1961 by Rachel L. Carson; renewed 1978 by Roger Christie. Reprinted by permission of Oxford University Press.

Bruce Catton, "Grant and Lee: A Study in Contrasts." From *The American Story*, Earl Schenck Miers, editor. © 1956 by Broadcast Music, Inc. Reprinted by permission.

Natalie Crouter, "Release from Captivity." From *Forbidden Diary: A Record of Wartime Internment, 1941–1945*, edited by Lynn Z. Bloom (New York: Burt Franklin, Inc., 1980) pp. 465–475.

Elizabeth David, "To Cook Spaghetti." From *A Book of Mediterranean Food* by Elizabeth David, Alfred A. Knopf, Inc., 1950, 1980.

Joan Didion, "On Keeping a Notebook," and "Marrying Absurd." Reprinted by permission of Farrar, Straus and Giroux, Inc. from *Slouching Towards Bethelehem* by Joan Didion. Copyright © 1966, 1967, 1968 by Joan Didion.

Annie Dillard, "The Death of a Moth" ("Transfiguration"). Reprinted by permission of the author and her agent Blanche C. Gregory, Inc. Copyright © 1976 by Annie Dillard.

Loren Eiseley, "The Brown Wasps." In *The Night Country*. Copyright © 1971 Loren Eiseley (New York: Charles Scribner's Sons, 1971). Reprinted with the permission of Charles Scribner's Sons.

Peter Elbow, "Freewriting." From *Writing Without Teachers* by Peter Elbow. Copyright © 1973 by Oxford University Press. Reprinted with permission.

Ralph Ellison, "Hidden Name and Complex Fate." Copyright © 1964 by Ralph Ellison. Reprinted from *Shadow and Act*, by Ralph Ellison, by permission of Random House, Inc.

Copyright © 1984 by D. C. Heath and Company.

Published simultaneously in Canada.

Printed in the United States of America.

International Standard Book Number: 0-669-04476-8

Library of Congress Catalog Card Number: 82-84681

Frances FitzGerald, "Ethnic Bias in Textbooks." From *America Revised* by Frances FitzGerald. © 1979 by Frances FitzGerald. First appeared in *The New Yorker*. By permission of Little, Brown and Company in association with the Atlantic Monthly Press.

Linda Flower, "Writing for an Audience." From *Problem-Solving Strategies for Writing* by Linda Flower, copyright © 1981 by Harcourt Brace Jovanovich, Inc. Reprinted by permission of Harcourt Brace Jovanovich, Inc.

Andrew Hacker, "E.R.A.—R.I.P." Copyright © 1980 by Harper's Magazine. All rights reserved. Reprinted from the September 1980 issue by special permission.

Marcella Hazan, "How to Cook Pasta." From *The Classic Italian Cook Book,* by Marcella Hazan. Copyright © 1973 by Marcella Hazan and Victor Hazan. Reprinted by permission of Alfred A. Knopf, Inc.

Robert Jastrow, "Man of Wisdom." Reprinted from *Until the Sun Dies* by Robert Jastrow, with permission of W.W. Norton & Company, Inc. Copyright © 1977 by Robert Jastrow.

Suzanne Britt Jordan, "That Lean and Hungry Look." Copyright 1978, by Newsweek, Inc. All rights reserved. Reprinted by permission.

Kristin King, "Ontonagon." Reprinted by permission.

Martin Luther King, Jr., "Letter from Birmingham Jail—April 16, 1963." From *Why We Can't Wait* by Martin Luther King, Jr. Copyright © 1963 by Martin Luther King, Jr. Reprinted by permission of Harper & Row, Publishers, Inc.

Lai Man Lee, "My Bracelet." Reprinted by permission.

John Leonard, "The Only Child." From *Private Lives in the Imperial City* by John Leonard (New York: Alfred A. Knopf, Inc., 1977).

Barry Lopez, "My Horse." Reprinted with permission from *The North American Review,* copyright © 1975 by the University of Northern Iowa.

Jennifer McBride, "The Rock Fantasy." Reprinted by permission.

John McPhee, "The Pine Barrens." Selection from "The Woods from the Hog Wallow" from *The Pine Barrens* by John McPhee. Copyright © 1967, 1968 by John McPhee. This material first appeared in *The New Yorker*. Reprinted by permission of Farrar, Straus and Giroux, Inc.

N. Scott Momaday, "A Kiowa Grandmother." Reprinted from *The Way to Rainy Mountain* by N. Scott Momaday, © 1969 by The University of New Mexico Press.

Donald M. Murray, "The Maker's Eye: Revising Your Own Manuscripts." Reprinted by permission of International Creative Management, Inc. Copyright © 1973 by Donald M. Murray.

George Orwell, "Shooting an Elephant." From *Shooting an Elephant and Other Essays* by George Orwell. Copyright 1950 by Sonia Brownell Orwell; copyright 1978 by Sonia Pitt-Rivers. Reprinted by permission of Harcourt Brace Jovanovich, Inc. and the estate of the late George Orwell and Martin Secker & Warburg Ltd. "Marrakech." From *Such, Such Were the Joys* by George Orwell; copyright 1945, 1952, 1953 by Sonia Brownell Orwell; renewed 1973 by Sonia Pitt-Rivers, 1980 by Sonia Brownell Orwell, 1981 by Mrs. George K. Perutz, Mrs. Miriam Gross, Dr. Michael Dickson, Executors of the Estates of Sonia Brownell Orwell. Reprinted by permission of Harcourt Brace Jovanovich, Inc., the estate of the late Sonia Brownell Orwell and Martin Secker & Warburg Ltd.

Timothy J. Payne, "On the Beach at Bar Harbor." Reprinted by permission.

Linda Peterson, "From Egocentric Speech to Public Discourse: Richard Wright Composes His Thoughts on *Black Boy*." Reprinted by permission of the author.

Claudia Roden, "Rishta/Fresh Noodles." From *A Book of Middle Eastern Food* by Claudia Roden, Alfred A. Knopf, Inc., 1972.

Richard Rodriguez, "None of This Is Fair." Copyright © 1977 by Richard Rodriguez. Reprinted by permission of Brandt & Brandt Literary Agents, Inc.

Irma Rombauer and **Marion Rombauer** Becker, "Cooking Pastas." From *The Joy of Cooking,* copyright © 1931, 1936, 1941, 1942, 1943, 1946, 1951, 1952, 1953, 1962, 1963, 1964, 1975, by Irma S. Rombauer and Marion Rombauer Becker. Used with permission of the publisher, The Bobbs-Merrill Company, Inc.

Berton Roueché, "The Neutral Spirit: A Portrait of Alcohol." Reprinted by permission of Harold Ober Associates Incorporated. Copyright © 1960 by Berton Roueché.

Carl Sagan, "The Cosmic Calendar." From *The Dragons of Eden: Speculations on the Evolution of Human Intelligence,* by Carl Sagan. Copyright © 1977 by Carl Sagan. Reprinted by permission of Random House, Inc.

Max Shulman, "Love Is a Fallacy." Copyright © 1951 by Max Shulman, © renewed 1979 by Max Shulman. Reprinted by permission of the Harold Matson Company, Inc.

Judy Syfers, "I Want a Wife." Reprinted by permission of the author.

Studs Terkel, "John Fuller, Mail Carrier." From *Working: People Talk About What They Do All Day and How They Feel About What They Do,* by Studs Terkel. Copyright © 1972, 1974 by Studs Terkel. Reprinted by permission of Pantheon Books, a Division of Random House, Inc.

Lewis Thomas, "On Magic in Medicine." Reprinted by permission from the *New England Journal of Medicine.* Vol. 285, pp. 1366–1368; 1971. "The Technology of Medicine." From *The Lives of a Cell: Notes of a Biology Watcher* by Lewis Thomas. Copyright © 1971 by Massachusetts Medical Society. Originally published in the *New England Journal of Medicine.* Reprinted by permission of Viking Penguin Inc.

James Thurber, "University Days." Copyright © 1933, 1961 James Thurber. From *My Life and Hard Times,* published by Harper and Row. Reprinted by permission.

Sheila Tobias, "Who's Afraid of Math, and Why?" Reprinted from *Overcoming Math Anxiety* by Sheila Tobias, by permission of W. W. Norton & Company, Inc. Copyright © 1978 by Sheila Tobias.

Mark Twain, "Uncle John's Farm." From pp. 95–113 in *Mark Twain's Autobiography,* Volume I by Mark Twain. Copyright 1924 by Clara Clemens Samossoud. Reprinted by permission of Harper & Row, Publishers, Inc.

Ann Upperco, "Learning to Drive." Reprinted by permission.

E. B. White, "Once More to the Lake." From *Essays of E. B. White* by E. B. White. Copyright 1941 by E. B. White. Reprinted by permission of Harper & Row, Publishers, Inc.

Richard Wright, "Why I Wrote *Black Boy*," First Draft and Final Draft. Reprinted by permission of Ellen Wright and the Collection of American Literature, Beinecke Rare Book and Manuscript Library, Yale University.

Minoru Yamasaki, "The Aesthetics and Practice of Architecture." From *Life in Architecture* by Minoru Yamasaki (New York: Weatherhill, 1979). Reprinted by permission of the publisher.

William Zinsser, "Style." From *On Writing Well* by William K. Zinsser (Harper & Row, 1980). Copyright © 1980 by William K. Zinsser. Reprinted by permission of the author.

Preface

Like the symbolic bridge on the cover of this book, *The Essay Connection* attempts to span the distance between reading and writing, to bring the two endeavors closer together. As E.B. White, master essayist, has observed, "The essayist . . . can pull on any sort of shirt, be any sort of person, according to his mood or his subject matter—philosopher, scold, jester, raconteur, confidant, pundit, devil's advocate, enthusiast." The essays here have been chosen to reveal writers of essays in their many voices, many modes. We hope that the texts of the essays themselves, and the related introductory material and study questions, will enable students (and their teachers) to recognize in published essays elements and processes that they can use in writing essays of their own.

The fifty-three essays in *The Essay Connection* are drawn from many sources, mostly lively contemporary writing on varied subjects, with a leavening of classics by such authors as Swift and Jefferson, whose ideas and style remain as fresh and provocative today as when they were written. Of particular importance are seven essays by undergraduate college students, which provide not only discussions of interesting subjects (learning to drive, a recognition of the author's racial identity) but also models that other students can emulate. This mixture of essays by professional writers and people in other disciplines (scientists, historians, social analysts, film critics) and students, majority and minority authors, men and women, provides a realistic representation of engaging, witty, and elegant writing of current interest.

The essays vary in length from one to a dozen pages, though most are from three to five pages. In difficulty they range from the easily accessible to the more complicated. They have been chosen to represent ten common essay types, from narration and process analysis to argumentation. The introductory section, "Discovering Yourself and Others," with selections from writers' notebooks (Joan Didion's genuine one and Woody Allen's parody) and Peter Elbow's discussion of freewriting, attempts to begin where most writers start the process—getting ideas and warming up.

The concluding section, on revising and editing, shows through examples as well as analysis how professional and student writers rewrite to accommodate their audience, purpose, and point of view. This could be read as a prelude to the entire book, or as a preface to any other section. Surely the various versions of the writings by Donald Murray, Richard Wright, and student Angela Bowman embody principles of good writing that most of the writers of the rest of the essays in the book used in arriving at the final versions published here.

The introductions to each of the sections define the particular type of writing under discussion by identifying its conspicuous characteristics—its purpose and uses, its typical form and tone. The consistent focus of *The Essay Connection* on writing processes leads also to a discussion of the rhetorical strategies an author can use to accomplish the purpose of each type, illustrated with reference to the selections that follow. These rhetorical strategies are summarized at the end of each section, and are followed by suggested writing topics especially appropriate for that type. For instance, the section on Division and Classification suggests that the writer use division to analyze the structure or functioning of the writer's family or college (among other possibilities), or that he or she classify types of cars, restaurants, music, or vacations.

The introduction and study questions for each individual essay are designed to help students focus on five salient aspects of the writing situation. Who wrote the essay? Why did the author write it? What type of essay is it? For what audience is the essay intended? What rhetorical strategies and techniques (such as organization, emphasis, level of language, tone) does the author use to accomplish his or her aims? (See pages xix-xx.) The individual introduction provides a brief biography of the author, an indication of the key characteristics of the essay in question, and—when the information is available—the author's commentary on the writing process employed. The study questions focus on Content, Strategies and Structures, Language, and Suggestions for Writing—though all of these questions are suitable for class discussion, as well. The Glossary on pp. 475–491 explains basic terminology that will be useful for such discussions, or for reference.

The Essay Connection has, in some ways, been in the making for the past quarter century, and I am particularly indebted to the candid commentaries of multitudes of writing students over the years whose preferences and perplexities have so significantly influenced both the shape and emphasis of this volume, and the process-oriented style of teaching that it reflects. I am likewise grateful for the thoughtful suggestions of writing teachers throughout the country who have commented on various versions of *The Essay Connection:* Lynn Beene, University of New Mexico; Ruth Brown, San Diego State University; Larry Carver, The University of Texas at Austin; Roberta Clipper-Sethi, Kean College of New Jersey; Charles R. Duke, Murray State University; Janet E. Eber, County College of Morris; Mark Edelstein, Palomar College; J. Vail Foy, Carthage College; Edgar Glenn, California State University, Chico; Sandra Hanson, Fiorello H. LaGuardia Community College; Walter Klarner, Johnson County Community College; John M. McCluskey, The University of Tennessee; Alvin W. Past, Bee County College; Edna H. Shaw, Mississippi Gulf Coast Junior College; Jeffrey Smitten, Texas Tech University; and Arthur Wagner, Macomb County Community College.

To Linda Peterson, Yale University, and Donald M. Murray, University of New Hampshire, who contributed original texts on revising, I am particularly grateful. I also owe special thanks to the students who contributed to this volume not only their essays but comments on how they wrote them: Angela Bowman, Kristin King, Lai Man Lee, Jennifer McBride, Tim Payne, and Ann Upperco, all of the College of William and Mary; and Laird Bloom, University of Michigan. Lana Whited, College of William and Mary, Mark Orton, Virginia Polytechnic Institute and State University, and Anne M. Bowman and J. Reynolds Kinzey, both of Virginia Commonwealth University, were capable research assistants. Ms. Bowman and Mr. Kinzey, both experienced college writing teachers, prepared the Instructor's Manual. Typists include the ever patient, unfailingly energetic Sharon Call, Jacqueline Giri, Cindy Drinkard, and Donna Stallings, all of Virginia Commonwealth University.

In its earliest incarnations, *The Essay Connection* was overseen at D.C. Heath and Company by Gordon Lester-Massman and Carol Ryan. Most of the editorial process was conducted under the watchful and sensitive care of Paul Smith, Holt Johnson, and Marie Auclair.

In the course of typing the entire Instructor's Manual, Laird Bloom (yes, he is my son) shared innumerable insights born of uncommonly good critical sense and the parodist's intolerance of the banal and the sentimental. My husband, Martin Bloom, shared not only his sensible views on what should stay in *The Essay Connection* and what should end up on the cutting room floor, but also the household tasks—and, most importantly, the word processor—during the writing of this book.

Lynn Z. Bloom
Virginia Commonwealth University

Contents

---

[1] Student essays are marked by the symbol ◆.

PART IV   Arguing: Directly and Indirectly

PART V   Revising and Editing

To Students:
Suggestions for Reading Essays

You will encounter essays in this book that, as E.B. White remarked,* philosophize, scold, jest, tell stories, argue, or plead, among the many things they can do. You'll be able to read essays more easily and understand them better if you bear in mind as you read some of the following questions concerning the essay's author, intended audience, type, purposes, and rhetorical strategies.

Who is the Author?

a. When did the author live? Where? Is the author's ethnic origin, gender, or regional background relevant to understanding this essay?

b. What is the author's educational background? Job experience? Do these, or other significant life experiences make him or her an authority on the subject of the essay?

c. Does the author have political, religious, economic, cultural or other biases that affect the essay's treatment of the subject? The author's credibility?

What are the Context and Audience of the Essay?

a. When was the essay first published? Is it dated, or still relevant?

b. Where (in what magazine, professional journal, or book, if at all) was the essay first published?

c. For what audience was the essay originally intended? How much did the author expect the original readers to know about the subject? To what extent did the author expect the original readers to share his point of view?

d. Why would the original audience have read this essay?

e. What similarities and differences exist between the essay's original audience and the student audience now reading it?

*See Preface, page v.

f. What are you as a student reader expected to gain from reading this essay?

What is the Type of Essay?

a. What type of essay is this—narration, definition, exposition, argument, or other? Does the essay exhibit characteristics of other types of essays as well?

b. Does the subject fit the essay form in which it is presented? Would other forms be equally apt? Why or why not?

What are the Purposes of the Essay?

a. Why did the author write the essay? To inform, describe, explain, argue, or for some other reason or combination of reasons?

b. Is the pupose explicitly stated anywhere in the essay? If so, where? Is this the thesis of the essay? Or is the thesis different?

c. If the purpose is not stated explicitly, how can you tell what the purpose is? Through examples? Emphasis? Tone? Other means?

d. Does the form of the essay suit the purpose? Would another form have been more appropriate?

What are the Strategies of the Essay?

a. What does the author do to make the essay interesting? Is he or she successful?

b. What organizational pattern (and sub-patterns, if any) does the author use? How do these patterns fit the subject? The author's purpose?

c. What emphasis do the organization and proportioning provide to reinforce the author's purpose?

d. What evidence, arguments, and illustrations does the author employ to illustrate or demonstrate the thesis?

e. On what level of language (formal, informal, slangy) and in what tone (serious, satiric, sincere, etc.) does the author write?

f. Have you enjoyed the essay, or found it stimulating or otherwise provocative? Why or why not?

PART I

Writing About People, Yourself and Others

1 Discovering Yourself and Others

Getting started for many people is the most difficult aspect of writing. It's a problem to start if you don't know what to write about. It's hard to start if you give writing a low priority and do everything else first, even a month's laundry. It's often difficult to start if you put off writing until the last minute. And it's hard to keep going, says Peter Elbow in "Freewriting" (pp. 18–21), if you edit while you're writing, if the editor is "constantly looking over the shoulder of the producer and constantly fiddling with what he's doing while he's in the middle of trying to do it."

Keeping a writer's diary or notebook can be a good way to get started—and even to keep going. Writing regularly in a notebook over an extended period of time, as Joan Didion describes in "On Keeping a Notebook" (pp. 4–11), even if it's only for ten minutes a day, can give you a lot to think about while you're writing, and a lot to expand on later. You could keep an account of what you do every day (6:30–7:30, running along the reservoir; 7:30–8:15, breakfast—two eggs, toast, and orange juice . . .), but if your life is routine that might get monotonous. Didion's discussion of the notebook entries she keeps as a professional writer offers other dimensions of what a provocative and potentially useful notebook might contain:

* sketches of people, either intrinsically interesting or engaged in intriguing activities
* fragments of conversation, whether thoroughly mundane or provocative
* unusual details—of clothing, objects (such as cars, houses), natural settings
* possibilities for conflict, exploration, adventure.

Sights, sounds, scents, textures refracted and remembered. Or forgotten, unless you put in enough explanatory details to remind yourself two weeks—or two years—later what you meant when you wrote it down.

Woody Allen's "Selections from the Allen Notebooks" (pp. 13–17) spoofs the psychological and symbolic pretentiousness of some literary notebooks: "Should I marry W.? Not if she won't tell me the other letters in her name. And what about her career? How can I ask a woman of her beauty to give up the Roller Derby?" But in actuality, in a writer's notebook you can be most candid, most off-guard, for there you're writing primarily for yourself. Just as you are when you're freewriting—writing rapidly, with or without a particular subject, without editing, while you're in the process of generating ideas. As you freewrite you can free associate, thinking of connections among like or unlike things or ideas. You can explore the implications of an issue, or your feelings about it. Anything goes into the notebook, but not everything stays in later drafts if you decide to turn some of your most focused discussion into an essay.

Another interesting way to get ideas for writing is to talk to people. Do they have an occupation, commonplace or unusual, or a special skill that readers would like to know about? From this perspective Studs Terkel interviewed scores of people, encouraging them to describe the dimensions of their jobs, the tough and the easy, the challenging and the boring aspects, the problems—and possibly, the solutions. Thus he introduces us to John Fuller (pp. 23–27), a forty-eight-year-old mail carrier fulfilling his life's ambition in, as Fuller says, "one of the most respected professions that is throughout the nation."

You can also write about people who have participated in memorable events—World Wars I or II, the Great Depression, the love-ins or peace protests of the '60s. Through an interview, character sketch, or portraits, you could present representatives of a particular philosophy of life, a vanishing culture, or a typically contemporary lifestyle from a particular school, economic group, or region of the country. John Leonard's portrait of his brother, ironically titled "The Only Child," (pp. 28–31) begins with his appearance ("he is big"), proceeds to his grin that isn't a smile but a tic, then to his room ("a slum, and it stinks"), and finally to the cause of his wasted condition, "speed kills slowly. . . . I would like to thank Timothy Leary and all the other sports of the 1960's who helped make this bad trip possible."

Whether you write about yourself or other people, focusing on what you've experienced and people you know provides good subjects to begin writing about. You can ask yourself, "What or who do I want to write about?" "Why does the subject interest me?" If the answer is, "It doesn't," you can easily switch to one that's more appealing. As you write you will almost automatically be using description, narration, comparison and contrast, and other rhetorical techniques to express yourself, even if you don't attach labels to them. We'll discuss these in the introductions to other sections of *The Essay Connection.*

JOAN DIDION

Novelist and essayist Didion (b. 1934) was born in Sacramento, California, educated at the University of California in Berkeley, and worked as associate feature editor for *Vogue* and as a columnist for *Life* in New York. She won *Vogue*'s Prix de Paris and a Bread Loaf Fellowship in fiction, and, with husband John Gregory Dunne, returned to her native California to collaborate on several screenplays: *Panic in Needle Park* (1971), *A Star is Born* (1976), and *True Confessions* (1981). Her novels are *Run River* (1963), *Play It as It Lays* (1971), and *A Book of Common Prayer* (1977); her highly acclaimed nonfiction includes *Slouching Towards Bethlehem* (1969), *The White Album* (1979), and *Salvador* (1983). Much of her writing deals with estrangement and alienation—of people from each other, from religion, from their roots in geography, family, and society (see "Marrying Absurd," below, pp. 268–71). In "On Keeping a Notebook" Didion explains her method of recording some of the sources for her other writings.

On Keeping a Notebook

1   'T hat woman Estelle,' " the note reads, " 'is partly the reason why George Sharp and I are separated today.' *Dirty crepe-de-Chine wrapper, hotel bar, Wilmington RR, 9:45 a.m. August Monday morning.''*

2   Since the note is in my notebook, it presumably has some meaning to me. I study it for a long while. At first I have only the most general notion of what I was doing on an August Monday morning in the bar of the hotel across from the Pennsylvania Railroad station in Wilmington, Delaware (waiting for a train? missing one? 1960? 1961? why Wilmington?), but I do remember being there. The woman in the dirty crepe-de-Chine wrapper had come down from her room for a beer, and the bartender had heard before the reason why George Sharp and she were separated today. "Sure," he said, and went on mopping the floor. "You told me." At the other end of the bar is a

girl. She is talking, pointedly, not to the man beside her but to a cat lying in the triangle of sunlight cast through the open door. She is wearing a plaid silk dress from Peck & Peck, and the hem is coming down.

Here is what it is: the girl has been on the Eastern Shore, and now she is going back to the city, leaving the man beside her, and all she can see ahead are the viscous summer sidewalks and the 3 a.m. long-distance calls that will make her lie awake and then sleep drugged through all the steaming mornings left in August (1960? 1961?). Because she must go directly from the train to lunch in New York, she wishes that she had a safety pin for the hem of the plaid silk dress, and she also wishes that she could forget about the hem and the lunch and stay in the cool bar that smells of disinfectant and malt and make friends with the woman in the crepe-de-Chine wrapper. She is afflicted by a little self-pity, and she wants to compare Estelles. That is what that was all about.

Why did I write it down? In order to remember, of course, but exactly what was it I wanted to remember? How much of it actually happened? Did any of it? Why do I keep a notebook at all? It is easy to deceive oneself on all those scores. The impulse to write things down is a peculiarly compulsive one, inexplicable to those who do not share it, useful only accidentally, only secondarily, in the way that any compulsion tries to justify itself. I suppose that it begins or does not begin in the cradle. Although I have felt compelled to write things down since I was five years old, I doubt that my daughter ever will, for she is a singularly blessed and accepting child, delighted with life exactly as life presents itself to her, unafraid to go to sleep and unafraid to wake up. Keepers of private notebooks are a different breed altogether, lonely and resistant rearrangers of things, anxious malcontents, children afflicted apparently at birth with some presentiment of loss.

My first notebook was a Big Five tablet, given to me by my mother with the sensible suggestion that I stop whining and learn to amuse myself by writing down my thoughts. She returned the tablet to me a few years ago; the first entry is an account of a woman who believed herself to be freezing to death in the Arctic night, only to find, when day broke, that she had stumbled onto the Sahara Desert, where she would die of the heat before lunch. I have no idea what turn of a five-year-old's mind could have prompted so insistently "ironic" and exotic a story, but it does reveal a certain predilection for the extreme which has dogged me into adult life; perhaps if I were analytically inclined I would find it a truer story than any I might have told about Donald Johnson's birthday party or the day my cousin Brenda put Kitty Litter in the aquarium.

6   So the point of my keeping a notebook has never been, nor is it now, to have an accurate factual record of what I have been doing or thinking. That would be a different impulse entirely, an instinct for reality which I sometimes envy but do not possess. At no point have I ever been able successfully to keep a diary; my approach to daily life ranges from the grossly negligent to the merely absent, and on those few occasions when I have tried dutifully to record a day's events, boredom has so overcome me that the results are mysterious at best. What is this business about "shopping, typing piece, dinner with E, depressed"? Shopping for what? Typing what piece? Who is E? Was this "E" depressed, or was I depressed? Who cares?

7   In fact I have abandoned altogether that kind of pointless entry; instead I tell what some would call lies. "That's simply not true," the members of my family frequently tell me when they come up against my memory of a shared event. "The party was *not* for you, the spider was *not* a black widow, *it wasn't that way at all*." Very likely they are right, for not only have I always had trouble distinguishing between what happened and what merely might have happened, but I remain unconvinced that the distinction, for my purposes, matters. The cracked crab that I recall having for lunch the day my father came home from Detroit in 1945 must certainly be embroidery, worked into the day's pattern to lend verisimilitude; I was ten years old and would not now remember the cracked crab. The day's events did not turn on cracked crab. And yet it is precisely that fictitious crab that makes me see the afternoon all over again, a home movie run all too often, the father bearing gifts, the child weeping, an exercise in family love and guilt. Or that is what it was to me. Similarly, perhaps it never did snow that August in Ver-

mont; perhaps there never were flurries in the night wind, and maybe no one else felt the ground hardening and summer already dead even as we pretended to bask in it, but that was how it felt to me, and it might as well have snowed, could have snowed, did snow.

How it felt to me: that is getting closer to the truth about a notebook. I sometimes delude myself about why I keep a notebook, imagine that some thrifty virtue derives from preserving everything observed. See enough and write it down, I tell myself, and then some morning when the world seems drained of wonder, some day when I am only going through the motions of doing what I am supposed to do, which is write— on that bankrupt morning I will simply open my notebook and there it will all be, a forgotten account with accumulated interest, paid passage back to the world out there: dialogue overheard in hotels and elevators and at the hat-check counter in Pavillon (one middle-aged man shows his hat check to another and says, "That's my old football number"); impressions of Bettina Aptheker and Benjamin Sonnenberg and Teddy ("Mr. Acapulco") Stauffer; careful *aperçus* about tennis bums and failed fashion models and Greek shipping heiresses, one of whom taught me a significant lesson (a lesson I could have learned from F. Scott Fitzgerald, but perhaps we all must meet the very rich for ourselves) by asking, when I arrived to interview her in her orchid-filled sitting room on the second day of a paralyzing New York blizzard, whether it was snowing outside.

I imagine, in other words, that the notebook is about other people. But of course it is not. I have no real business with what one stranger said to another at the hat-check counter in Pavillon; in fact I suspect that the line "That's my old football number" touched not my own imagination at all, but merely some memory of something once read, probably "The Eighty-Yard Run." Nor is my concern with a woman in a dirty crepe-de-Chine wrapper in a Wilmington bar. My stake is always, of course, in the unmentioned girl in the plaid silk dress. Remember what it was to be me: that is always the point.

It is a difficult point to admit. We are brought up in the ethic that others, any others, all others, are by definition more interesting than ourselves; taught to be diffident, just this side of self-effacing. ("You're the least important person in the room and don't forget it," Jessica Mitford's governess would hiss in her ear on the advent of any social occasion; I copied that into my notebook because it is only recently that I have been able to enter a room without hearing some such phrase in my inner ear.) Only the very young and the very old may recount their dreams at breakfast, dwell upon self, interrupt with memories of beach picnics and favorite Liberty lawn dresses and the rainbow trout in a creek near Colorado Springs. The rest of us are expected, rightly, to affect absorption in other people's favorite dresses, other people's trout.

11   And so we do. But our notebooks give us away, for however dutifully we record what we see around us, the common denominator of all we see is always, transparently, shamelessly, the implacable "I." We are not talking here about the kind of notebook that is patently for public consumption, a structural conceit for binding together a series of graceful *pensées;* we are talking about something private, about bits of the mind's string too short to use, an indiscriminate and erratic assemblage with meaning only for its maker.

12   And sometimes even the maker has difficulty with the meaning. There does not seem to be, for example, any point in my knowing for the rest of my life that, during 1964, 720 tons of soot fell on every square mile of New York City, yet there it is in my notebook, labeled "FACT." Nor do I really need to remember that Ambrose Bierce liked to spell Leland Stanford's name "£eland $tanford" or that "smart women almost always wear black in Cuba," a fashion hint without much potential for practical application. And does not the relevance of these notes seem marginal at best?:

> In the basement museum of the Inyo County Courthouse in Independence, California, sign pinned to a mandarin coat: "This MANDARIN COAT was often worn by Mrs. Minnie S. Brooks when giving lectures on her TEA-POT COLLECTION."
>
> Redhead getting out of car in front of Beverly Wilshire Hotel, chinchilla stole, Vuitton bags with tags reading:

MRS LOU FOX

HOTEL SAHARA

VEGAS

Well, perhaps not entirely marginal. As a matter of fact, 13
Mrs. Minnie S. Brooks and her MANDARIN COAT pull me back
into my own childhood, for although I never knew Mrs. Brooks
and did not visit Inyo County until I was thirty, I grew up in
just such a world, in houses cluttered with Indian relics and bits
of gold ore and ambergris and the souvenirs my Aunt Mercy
Farnsworth brought back from the Orient. It is a long way from
that world to Mrs. Lou Fox's world, where we all live now, and
is it not just as well to remember that? Might not Mrs. Minnie
S. Brooks help me to remember what I am? Might not Mrs. Lou
Fox help me to remember what I am not?

But sometimes the point is harder to discern. What exactly 14
did I have in mind when I noted down that it cost the father of
someone I know $650 a month to light the place on the Hudson
in which he lived before the Crash? What use was I planning
to make of this line by Jimmy Hoffa: "I may have my faults, but
being wrong ain't one of them"? And although I think it interesting to know where the girls who travel with the Syndicate
have their hair done when they find themselves on the West
Coast, will I ever make suitable use of it? Might I not be better
off just passing it on to John O'Hara? What is a recipe for sauerkraut doing in my notebook? What kind of magpie keeps this
notebook? *"He was born the night the Titanic went down."* That
seems a nice enough line, and I even recall who said it, but is
it not really a better line in life than it could ever be in fiction?

But of course that is exactly it: not that I should ever use 15
the line, but that I should remember the woman who said it and
the afternoon I heard it. We were on her terrace by the sea, and
we were finishing the wine left from lunch, trying to get what
sun there was, a California winter sun. The woman whose husband was born the night the *Titanic* went down wanted to rent
her house, wanted to go back to her children in Paris. I remember
wishing that I could afford the house, which cost $1,000 a month.
"Someday you will," she said lazily. "Someday it all comes."
There in the sun on her terrace it seemed easy to believe in
someday, but later I had a low-grade afternoon hangover and

ran over a black snake on the way to the supermarket and was flooded with inexplicable fear when I heard the checkout clerk explaining to the man ahead of me why she was finally divorcing her husband. "He left me no choice," she said over and over as she punched the register. "He has a little seven-month-old baby by her, he left me no choice." I would like to believe that my dread then was for the human condition, but of course it was for me, because I wanted a baby and did not then have one and because I wanted to own the house that cost $1,000 a month to rent and because I had a hangover.

16   It all comes back. Perhaps it is difficult to see the value in having one's self back in that kind of mood, but I do see it; I think we are well advised to keep on nodding terms with the people we used to be, whether we find them attractive company or not. Otherwise they turn up unannounced and surprise us, come hammering on the mind's door at 4 a.m. of a bad night and demand to know who deserted them, who betrayed them, who is going to make amends. We forget all too soon the things we thought we could never forget. We forget the loves and the betrayals alike, forget what we whispered and what we screamed, forget who we were. I have already lost touch with a couple of people I used to be; one of them, a seventeen-year-old, presents little threat, although it would be of some interest to me to know again what it feels like to sit on a river levee drinking vodka-and-orange-juice and listening to Les Paul and Mary Ford and their echoes sing "How High the Moon" on the car radio. (You see I still have the scenes, but I no longer perceive myself among those present, no longer could even improvise the dialogue.) The other one, a twenty-three-year-old, bothers me more. She was always a good deal of trouble, and I suspect she will reappear when I least want to see her, skirts too long, shy to the point of aggravation, always the injured party, full of recriminations and little hurts and stories I do not want to hear again, at once saddening me and angering me with her vulnerability and ignorance, an apparition all the more insistent for being so long banished.

17   It is a good idea, then, to keep in touch, and I suppose that keeping in touch is what notebooks are all about. And we are all on our own when it comes to keeping those lines open to ourselves: your notebook will never help me, nor mine you.

"So what's new in the whiskey business?" What could that possibly mean to you? To me it means a blonde in a Pucci bathing suit sitting with a couple of fat men by the pool at the Beverly Hills Hotel. Another man approaches, and they all regard one another in silence for a while. "So what's new in the whiskey business?" one of the fat men finally says by way of welcome, and the blonde stands up, arches one foot and dips it in the pool, looking all the while at the cabaña where Baby Pignatari is talking on the telephone. That is all there is to that, except that several years later I saw the blonde coming out of Saks Fifth Avenue in New York with her California complexion and a voluminous mink coat. In the harsh wind that day she looked old and irrevocably tired to me, and even the skins in the mink coat were not worked the way they were doing them that year, not the way she would have wanted them done, and there is the point of the story. For a while after that I did not like to look in the mirror, and my eyes would skim the newspapers and pick out only the deaths, the cancer victims, the premature coronaries, the suicides, and I stopped riding the Lexington Avenue IRT because I noticed for the first time that all the strangers I had seen for years—the man with the seeing-eye dog, the spinster who read the classified pages every day, the fat girl who always got off with me at Grand Central—looked older than they once had.

It all comes back. Even that recipe for sauerkraut: even that 18 brings it back. I was on Fire Island when I first made that sauerkraut, and it was raining, and we drank a lot of bourbon and ate the sauerkraut and went to bed at ten, and I listened to the rain and the Atlantic and felt safe. I made the sauerkraut again last night and it did not make me feel any safer, but that is, as they say, another story.

Content

1. What kind of a notebook does Didion keep? What distinctions does she make between her kind of notebook—a writer's notebook, and a diary—a day-by-day account of events in the diarist's life? If you have ever kept a diary or writer's notebook, answer from your own experience; see also the excerpt from Natalie Crouter's diary, "Release from Captivity," (pp.64–74).

2. What purposes do writers' notebooks serve?

3. Does a writer's notebook have to make sense to anyone but the writer? Explain your answer. How much interpretation should a writer provide of an event or detail whose significance is likely to fade over time, however clear it may have been when it occurred or when it is being written down?

Strategies/Structures

1. For what audience does one keep a writer's notebook?

2. For what audience is Didion writing the essay, "On Keeping a Notebook"? Is this the same audience for which she herself keeps a notebook?

3. What kind of authorial personality does Didion convey in this essay? Is it what you imagine a novelist would be like? Is the expression of personality consistent throughout the essay? Would you like to get to know Didion better on the basis of the personality she presents here?

4. What kind of authorial personality do your own writings express— as manifested through your choice of subjects, attitude toward your material, and the choice and formality or informality of your vocabulary? Let a classmate who doesn't know you very well read something you've written and see whether or not he or she gains an accurate view of your personality.

Language

1. Look up in your dictionary unfamiliar words in the following quotation, and then explain the meaning of the quotation: "We are not talking here about the kind of notebook that is patently for public consumption, a structural conceit for binding together a series of graceful *pensées;* we are talking about something private, about bits of the mind's string too short to use, an indiscriminate and erratic assemblage with meaning only for its maker."

For Writing

1. Keep a writer's notebook for a week or two, in which you write for fifteen minutes or so each day. Put into it items that you might use later in other writing—notes about people you meet whose appearance, clothing, jobs, hobbies, mannerisms, or ways of speaking are interesting or unusual; places you want to remember; odd names or colorful words or figures of speech; amusing or startling incidents.

2. Pick one entry from your writer's notebook and expand it into an essay.

▶───◀

WOODY ALLEN

Allen, born Allen Stewart Konigsberg in Brooklyn in 1935 and educated at "a school for emotionally disturbed teachers," started writing jokes in 1950 while still in high school. After a succession of television writing jobs, and stints as a night club comedian, he began a successful movie career as screenwriter, actor, and director. Among his ten films are *Bananas* (1970), *Play it Again, Sam* (1972), *Annie Hall* (1975), for which Allen won Academy Awards for directing and screenwriting, and *Manhattan* (1979). His parodies and other short essays and stories appear frequently in *The New Yorker* and are collected in *Getting Even* (1971), *Without Feathers* (1975), and *Side Effects* (1980). Allen's most familiar comic figure, said to closely resemble himself, is a well-intentioned intellectual but inept and highly neurotic New Yorker, unsuccessful in love and business, but, with the aid of psychoanalysis, continually trying to improve. It is this persona that emerges in "Selections from the Allen Notebooks," a complete work in which even the title parodies conventional writers' notebooks.

Selections from the Allen Notebooks

Following are excerpts from the hitherto secret private journal of Woody Allen, which will be published posthumously or after his death, whichever comes first.

G etting through the night is becoming harder and harder. Last evening, I had the uneasy feeling that some men were trying to break into my room to shampoo me. But why? I kept

1

imagining I saw shadowy forms, and at 3 A.M. the underwear I had draped over a chair resembled the Kaiser on roller skates. When I finally did fall asleep, I had that same hideous nightmare in which a woodchuck is trying to claim my prize at a raffle. Despair.

2   I believe my consumption has grown worse. Also my asthma. The wheezing comes and goes, and I get dizzy more and more frequently. I have taken to violent choking and fainting. My room is damp and I have perpetual chills and palpitations of the heart. I noticed, too, that I am out of napkins. Will it ever stop?

3   Idea for a story: A man awakens to find his parrot has been made Secretary of Agriculture. He is consumed with jealousy and shoots himself, but unfortunately the gun is the type with a little flag that pops out, with the word "Bang" on it. The flag pokes his eye out, and he lives—a chastened human being who, for the first time, enjoys the simple pleasures of life, like farming or sitting on an air hose.

4   Thought: Why does man kill? He kills for food. And not only food: frequently there must be a beverage.

5   Should I marry W.? Not if she won't tell me the other letters in her name. And what about her career? How can I ask a woman of her beauty to give up the Roller Derby? Decisions . . .

6   Once again I tried committing suicide—this time by wetting my nose and inserting it into the light socket. Unfortunately, there was a short in the wiring, and I merely caromed off the icebox. Still obsessed by thoughts of death, I brood constantly. I keep wondering if there is an afterlife, and if there is will they be able to break a twenty?

7   I ran into my brother today at a funeral. We had not seen one another for fifteen years, but as usual he produced a pig bladder from his pocket and began hitting me on the head with it. Time has helped me understand him better. I finally realize

his remark that I am "some loathsome vermin fit only for ex-termination" was said more out of compassion than anger. Let's face it: he was always much brighter than me—wittier, more cultured, better educated. Why he is still working at McDonald's is a mystery.

Idea for story: Some beavers take over Carnegie Hall and 8 perform *Wozzeck*.[1] (Strong theme. What will be the structure?)

Good Lord, why am I so guilty? Is it because I hated my 9 father? Probably it was the veal-parmigian' incident. Well, what *was* it doing in his wallet? If I had listened to him, I would be blocking hats for a living. I can hear him now; "To block hats—that is everything." I remember his reaction when I told him I wanted to write. "The only writing you'll do is in collaboration with an owl." I still have no idea what he meant. What a sad man! When my first play, *A Cyst for Gus*, was produced at the Lyceum, he attended opening night in tails and a gas mask.

Today I saw a red-and-yellow sunset and thought, How 10 insignificant I am! Of course, I thought that yesterday, too, and it rained. I was overcome with self-loathing and contemplated suicide again—this time by inhaling next to an insurance salesman.

Short story: A man awakens in the morning and finds 11 himself transformed into his own arch supports (This idea can work on many levels. Psychologically, it is the quintessence of Kruger, Freud's disciple who discovered sexuality in bacon.)

How wrong Emily Dickinson was! Hope is not "the thing 12 with feathers." The thing with feathers has turned out to be my nephew. I must take him to a specialist in Zurich.

I have decided to break off my engagement with W. She 13 doesn't understand my writing, and said last night that my

---

[1] An exotic, discordant opera by the modern composer Alban Berg.

Critique of Metaphysical Reality reminder her of *Airport*. We quarreled, and she brought up the subject of children again, but I convinced her they would be too young.

14   Do I believe in God? I did until Mother's accident. She fell on some meat loaf, and it penetrated her spleen. She lay in a coma for months, unable to do anything but sing "Granada" to an imaginary herring. Why was this woman in the prime of life so afflicted—because in her youth she dared to defy convention and got married with a brown paper bag on her head? And how can I believe in God when just last week I got my tongue caught in the roller of an electric typewriter? I am plagued by doubts. What if everything is an illusion and nothing exists? In that case, I definitely overpaid for my carpet. If only God would give me some clear sign! Like making a large deposit in my name at a Swiss bank.

15   Had coffee with Melnick today. He talked to me about his idea of having all government officials dress like hens.

16   Play idea: A character based on my father, but without quite so prominent a big toe. He is sent to the Sorbonne[2] to study the harmonica. In the end, he dies, never realizing his one dream—to sit up to his waist in gravy. (I see a brilliant second-act curtain, where two midgets come upon a severed head in a shipment of volleyballs.)

17   While taking my noon walk today, I had more morbid thoughts. What *is* it about death that bothers me so much? Probably the hours. Melnick says the soul is immortal and lives on after the body drops away, but if my soul exists without my body I am convinced all my clothes will be too loose-fitting. Oh, well . . .

18   Did not have to break off with W. after all, for as luck would have it, she ran off to Finland with a professional circus

---

[2] The renowned University of Paris.

geek. All for the best, I suppose, although I had another of those attacks where I start coughing out of my ears.

Last night, I burned all my plays and poetry. Ironically as 19 I was burning my masterpiece, *Dark Penguin*, the room caught fire, and I am now the object of a lawsuit by some men named Pinchunk and Schlosser. Kierkegaard was right.

Content

1. Identify some of Allen's main topics. Are these subjects common to keepers of diaries and notebooks?
2. Why is a focus on the self natural for a diarist? Why do we read diaries or notebooks? Has Allen's "Notebook" fulfilled the reader's usual purpose? Or do we read it essentially as a parody?

Strategies/Structures

1. What features of a writer's notebook does Allen parody?
2. Does it matter in this parody if the reader doesn't recognize all of the allusions—to people and places, for instance?
3. Given the unhappy, neurotic author's persona that Allen presents here, why do readers laugh at his "Notebooks"?
4. If you have seen any of Allen's movies, what similarities do you find between their characteristic humor and Allen's "Notebooks"?
5. What governs the order of the entries in the "Notebooks"? Would any other arrangement be equally appropriate?
6. Why would it be hard to parody Allen's "Notebooks"?

Language

1. Identify some instances of the formal and informal language Allen uses and show why the juxtaposition is funny.
2. The joke of Allen's second entry begins when he couples "consumption" and "asthma." What are these diseases, what connotations do they have, and why is joining them funny?

For Writing

Write a brief parody of a type of writing (diary, typical newspaper sports or wedding column, a Western or Gothic novel, or any other form you like), or of a particular author (Hemingway, Salinger, Faulkner, or another), or of a specific literary work. For instance, you might write a parody of a fairy tale or an Aesop's fable, as James Thurber did in *Fables for Our Time*.

PETER ELBOW

Elbow was born in New York in 1935 and educated at Williams College, Oxford University, Harvard, and Brandeis. Known for his innovative methods of teaching writing, Elbow has taught and directed writing programs at the Massachusetts Institute of Technology, Franconia College, and Evergreen State College. He is currently at SUNY, Stony Brook. Elbow's widely-respected book, *Writing Without Teachers* (1973), from which "Freewriting" is taken, is intended to help people teach themselves how to write with ease, control, and confidence. As he explains in "Freewriting," a writer's "only source of power" is his "voice"—a natural sound, texture, and rhythm "that will make a reader listen." Writing freely, without editing prematurely, can help the writer find that voice.

Freewriting

1   The most effective way I know to improve your writing is to do freewriting exercises regularly. At least three times a week. They are sometimes called "automatic writing," "babbling," or "jabbering" exercises. The idea is simply to write for ten minutes (later on, perhaps fifteen or twenty). Don't stop for anything. Go quickly without rushing. Never stop to look back, to cross something out, to wonder how to spell something, to wonder what word or thought to use, or to think about what you are doing. If you can't think of a word or a spelling, just use a squiggle or else write, "I can't think of it." Just put down something. The easiest thing is just to put down whatever is in your mind. If you get stuck it's fine to write "I can't think what to say, I can't think what to say" as many times as you want;

or repeat the last word you wrote over and over again; or anything else. The only requirement is that you *never* stop.

What happens to a freewritng exercise is important. It must   2
be a piece of writing which, even if someone reads it, doesn't
send any ripples back to you. It is like writing something and
putting it in a bottle in the sea. The teacherless class helps your
writing by providing maximum feedback. Freewritings help you
by providing no feedback at all. When I assign one, I invite the
writer to let me read it. But also tell him to keep it if he prefers.
I read it quickly and make no comments at all and I do not speak
with him about it. The main thing is that a freewriting must
never be evaluated in any way; in fact there must be no discussion or comment at all.

Here is an example of a fairly coherent exercise (sometimes   3
they are very incoherent, which is fine):

> I think I'll write what's on my mind, but the only thing
> on my mind right now is what to write for ten minutes.
> I've never done this before and I'm not prepared in any
> way—the sky is cloudy today, how's that? now I'm
> afraid I won't be able to think of what to write when I
> get to the end of the sentence—well, here I am at the
> end of the sentence—here I am again, again, again,
> again, at least I'm still writing—Now I ask is there some
> reason to be happy that I'm still writing—ah yes! Here
> comes the question again—What am I getting out of
> this? What point is there in it? It's almost obscene to al-
> ways ask it but I seem to question everything that way
> and I was gonna say something else pertaining to that
> but I got so busy writing down the first part that I forgot
> what I was leading into. This is kind of fun oh don't
> stop writing—cars and trucks speeding by somewhere
> out the window, pens clittering across peoples' papers.
> The sky is still cloudy—is it symbolic that I should be
> mentioning it? Huh? I dunno. Maybe I should try colors,
> blue, red, dirty words—wait a minute—no can't do that,
> orange, yellow, arm tired, green pink violet magenta lav-
> ender red brown black green—now that I can't think of
> any more colors—just about done—relief? maybe.

4   Freewriting may seem crazy but actually it makes simple sense. Think of the difference between speaking and writing. Writing has the advantage of permitting more editing. But that's its downfall too. Almost everybody interposes a massive and complicated series of editings between the time words start to be born into consciousness and when they finally come off the end of the pencil or typewriter onto the page. This is partly because schooling makes us obsessed with the "mistakes" we make in writing. Many people are constantly thinking about spelling and grammar as they try to write. I am always thinking about the awkwardness, wordiness, and general mushiness of my natural verbal product as I try to write down words.

5   But it's not just "mistakes" or "bad writing" we edit as we write. We also edit unacceptable thoughts and feelings, as we do in speaking. In writing there is more time to do it so the editing is heavier: when speaking, there's someone right there waiting for a reply and he'll get bored or think we're crazy if we don't come out with *something*. Most of the time in speaking, we settle for the catch-as-catch-can way in which the words tumble out. In writing, however, there's a chance to try to get them right. But the opportunity to get them right is a terrible burden: you can work for two hours trying to get a paragraph "right" and discover it's not right at all. And then give up.

6   Editing, *in itself*, is not the problem. Editing is usually necessary if we want to end up with something satisfactory. The problem is that editing goes on *at the same time* as producing. The editor is, as it were, constantly looking over the shoulder of the producer and constantly fiddling with what he's doing while he's in the middle of trying to do it. No wonder the producer gets nervous, jumpy, inhibited, and finally can't be coherent. It's an unnecessary burden to try to think of words and also worry at the same time whether they're the right words.

7   The main thing about freewriting is that it is *nonediting*. It is an exercise in bringing together the process of producing words and putting them down on the page. Practiced regularly, it undoes the ingrained habit of editing at the same time you are trying to produce. It will make writing less blocked because words will come more easily. You will use up more paper, but chew up fewer pencils.

Next time you write, notice how often you stop yourself 8
from writing down something you were going to write down.
Or else cross it out after it's written. "Naturally," you say, "it
wasn't any good." But think for a moment about the occasions
when you spoke well. Seldom was it because you first got the
beginning just right. Usually it was a matter of a halting or even
garbled beginning, but you kept going and your speech finally
became coherent and even powerful. There is a lesson here for
writing: trying to get the beginning just right is a formula for
failure—and probably a secret tactic to make yourself give up
writing. Make some words, whatever they are, and then grab
hold of that line and reel in as hard as you can. Afterwards you
can throw away lousy beginnings and make new ones. This is
the quickest way to get into good writing.

The habit of compulsive, premature editing doesn't just 9
make writing hard. It also makes writing dead. Your voice is
damped out by all the interruptions, changes, and hesitations
between the consciousness and the page. In your natural way
of producing words there is a sound, a texture, a rhythm—a
voice—which is the main source of power in your writing. I
don't know how it works, but this voice is the force that will
make a reader listen to you, the energy that drives the meanings
through his thick skull. Maybe you don't *like* your voice; maybe
people have made fun of it. But it's the only voice you've got.
It's your only source of power. You better get back into it, no
matter what you think of it. If you keep writing in it, it may
change into something you like better. But if you abandon it,
you'll likely never have a voice and never be heard.

Freewritings are vacuums. Gradually you will begin to carry 10
over into your regular writing some of the voice, force, and
connectedness that creep into those vacuums.

Content

1. What is freewriting (¶* 1)? What does Elbow recommend if the
writer gets stuck or can't think of anything to write about?

---

* The symbol ¶ is used for "paragraph" throughout this book.

2. What differences does Elbow find between the process of speaking and the process of writing (¶s 4, 5)?

3. Elbow identifies "compulsive, premature editing" as the main inhibitor of good writing (¶ 9). What does he mean by this? Do you think he's right? What other factors might inhibit you or others from writing well?

4. What does Elbow mean by "voice" (¶ 9)? How can you identify your natural voice in writing?

5. What advice does Elbow give for writing good introductory sentences and paragraphs (¶ 8)?

Strategies/Structures

1. Does Elbow's example of freewriting (¶ 3) make his point clearly? Does it resemble any freewriting you might have tried?

2. For what audience is "Freewriting" intended? Identify some words or phrases that Elbow uses to give confidence to his readers.

3. Why does Elbow use the simile that freewriting "is like writing something and putting it in a bottle in the sea" (¶ 2)?

Language

1. What is the tone of Elbow's "Freewriting"? How does this reinforce the relationship he is trying to establish with his readers?

2. Why doesn't Elbow define "editing" (¶ 6)? Is Elbow's meaning apparent in context? When you edit your writing, what do you do?

For Writing

Try freewriting for ten or fifteen minutes every day for a week, following Elbow's guidelines. Experiment by writing at different times of the day or evening and in different settings (such as your room, or the library) to determine under what circumstances it's easiest for you to write. Does the writing become easier as the week goes on? Does it become more focused? More interesting? Could any of your daily writings be expanded into essays, stories, or poetry? How can freewriting help you with the types of writing that you usally do? Is it more useful for some types than for others?

STUDS TERKEL

Louis Terkel, born (1912) in New York, later adopted the nickname "Studs" after James T. Farrell's Chicago Irish proletarian hero Studs Lonigan. Terkel earned advanced degrees at the University of Chicago and the University of Chicago Law School, and worked as an actor, disc jockey, news commentator, and talk show host. From his talk show have evolved extensive series of interviews with people, famous, infamous, and unknown, whose edited accounts of their occupations and experiences Terkel has collected in his bestselling books. Among his collections of transcribed interviews are *Division Street, America* (1966), *Hard Times: An Oral History of the Great Depression* (1970), *Working: People Talk About What They Do All Day and How They Feel About What They Do* (1974), and *American Dreams: Lost and Found* (1980). Even though he cannot invent what the subject says, the interviewer has considerable freedom in shaping the material. Terkel has said that he selects the ten percent of each interview that is "pure gold" to shape into a portrait. The interview with "John Fuller, Mail Carrier," from *Working*, captures what Terkel calls "the man of inchoate thought," the uncelebrated worker attempting to explain the essence of his job, its demands and difficulties, frustrations, and satisfactions. Through skilfully re-creating his subjects' speech, Terkel conveys the nuances of their emotions.

John Fuller, Mail Carrier

He has been a mail carrier since 1964, though he's worked in the post office for twenty-six years. "Back in '47 I was a clerk at the finance window. I had a break in the service and came back as a truckdriver. I was a little confined. Bein' a carrier gives me more street time where I'm meeting more of the public." He is forty-eight years old.

I'm doing a job that's my life ambition. When I was in school, you said in the yearbook what you're most likely to be. I did say mailman. First thing came to my mind. As a kid, when I   1 was coming up, I didn't have any idea this would wind up as my chosen profession. It has.

2   This is a profession that everyone has looked up to and respected. They always say, "Here comes the mailman"—pony express or something. This always brought a gleam to everybody's eye. Everyone likes to receive mail. I feel it is one of the most respected professions that is throughout the nation. You're doing a job for the public and a job for the country.

3   It's getting to a point where it's payin' now. Used to be they didn't pay 'em much. Everyone thought the mailman was making much more than he makes, "Aw, you got a good job, you're makin' lots of money." What it takes to live, you're barely scraping it, just barely getting along.

4   You find that most people in the post office have two jobs. Some of 'em have three jobs. I have had two most of the time. Now I only have one. My wife, she's working. If she wasn't, I don't know how we'd make it.

5   Now the top is eleven thousand dollars. This is just the last couple of years, they'd progressed to that status. For quite a while, the top was only in the seven thousand bracket. A mailman, breaking in, he makes somewhere along $3.60 an hour. This is subs. They progress somewhere about seven cents a year.

6   Everybody in the post office are moonlighting. We have a lot of men in the post office and their wives also in the post office. There are more women carriers today. And they're doing a bang-up job. It's a fabulous job for a woman. At the eleven-thousand-dollar bracket after eight years, it's a nice piece of change for a woman.

7   My day starts at four o'clock. I hit the floor. At five thirty I'm at work. We pull mail from the cases that the night clerks have thrown. I start casin', throwin' letters. At my station we have fifty-three carriers. Each one has a pigeonhole that his mail goes in. You are constantly pulling mail out of these pigeonholes.

8   I have one big office building downtown and a smaller one. Each firm is a case. As you work on a case, you get to know the people who get personal mail. You throw it to that firm. I have sixty different outfits in the building that I service. Downtown is much easier than the residential district. You could have about

540 separations in the residential. I know about ninety percent of the people in the office building. We are on a first name basis.

I make two trips a day. The mail is relayed by truck. I get over to the building, I unsack it and line it up according to various offices. Then I start my distribution, floor by floor. We have twenty-three floors in this building. I take the elevator up to the fifteenth, and as I go up, I drop the mail off on each floor. Then I walk down and make the distributions. Later, I get the upper floors. 9

The various people I meet in the building, we're constantly chatting, world affairs and everything. You don't have a chance to go off daydreaming. My day ends about two o'clock. During the day I might feel sluggish, but at quitting time you always feel happy. 10

I worked residential six months and flew back downtown. (Laughs.) Quite a bit more walking there. I had one district that covered thirty-two blocks. In a residential district you have relay boxes. It's a large brown box, which you probably see settin' on a corner next to the red, white, and blue box. You have a key that will open this. You have maybe three relay boxes in your district. You can run about twenty-five miles a day. If I had a pedometer, I'd be clocked around ten on this job. 11

Walking is good for you. It keeps you active. You more or less feel better. The bag's on my shoulder with me at all times. It varies from two pounds to thirty-five—which is the limit you're supposed to carry. The shoulder's not affected. Just keep goin', that's all. 12

Constantly you walk. You go home and put your feet in a hot basin after. That feels good. About twice a week, you give 'em a good soakin'. When I'm home, I keep 'em elevated, stay off 'em as much as possible, give 'em a lot of rest. I wear out on the average about three or five pairs of shoes a year. When I first started the bag, seemed like I was carryin' a ton. But as you go along, the bag isn't getting any lighter but you're getting accustomed to it. 13

When I come home, I walk in the door, turn the one-eyed monster TV on, take my uniform off, sit on the couch to watch a story, and usually go to sleep. (Laughs.) Around six, seven 14 o'clock, my wife comes home. "You tired?" "Somewhat." So I watch TV again with her and eat dinner. Nine thirty, ten o'clock, I'm ready for bed.

15   If you've got a second job, you get off at two, hustle and bustle off to that second job. You get off from there eight, nine o'clock and you rush home, you rush to bed. Sleep fast and get up and start all over again. I've had a second job up until last year. I tried to get away from walkin' on that one. To find something wherein I was stationary in one spot. But most of my part-time jobs have always been deliveries. I was on the move at all times. If I hadn't been on the move, I would probably be asleep on the job. Moving about on my feet kept me awake.

16   Most things a carrier would contend with is dogs. You think he won't bite, but as soon as you open the door the dog charges out past the patron and he clips you. This is a very hectic experience for the mailman. On a lot of residential streets, you have dog packs roaming, and a lot of times you don't know whether the dog is friendly or not. You try to make friends with him in order that you won't be attacked. In some cases, he'll walk your district with you. He'd walk this block with you. When you reach the corner, he'd turn back and go home. (Laughs.) You got a vicious dog, he chases after you.

17   (Sighs.) There's more dogs nowadays. Yes, they have dogs that's always out. Oh, I've been attacked. (Laughs.) I've had several instances where dogs have made me jump fences. One was over in a vacant lot. I was about a hundred yards from him. I was doing steps and coming down. I'm watching him, and he's evidently watching me. As I pass this lot, here he comes. It's a middle-class white area. The woman, she was walking down the street. She musta knew the dog. She called him by name and shooed at him. Shot mace at him. (Laughs.) She come up and said, "I'm sorry he's bothering you." She spoke to him and told him to go and he went off.

18   Most people have the mailman pretty well timed as to what time he'll be around. You have old lady pensioners. You have ADC. They're constantly waiting for checks. They're always waiting. If they miss you on this block, they will run around to the next block. "Mailman, you got my check?" (Laughs.) You

know it's not there 'cause you know what you have. "Look in the bag again. It might be mixed up with somebody else's mail." You look anyway to make 'em feel good. You know who are getting checks. Therefore you have to be ready for 'em. Interesting life.

I'll work until retirement. I have the years of service but I don't have the age. Last year they made a special package. We could get out at twenty-five years of service and fifty-five years of age. I need seven more years. Retirement pays anywhere from $250 to $300 a month. Not much. That's why quite a few of 'em didn't go.   19

With thirty years of service, you can go up to seventy years of age. If the retirement's right, I'll not be here. At retirement, I'll be looking for another job where it wouldn't be life and butter. This other job would be just a supplement. I'm thinkin' about goin' in business for myself. So when I reach my reclining years I wouldn't have to work so hard.   20

Ever talk about your day's work with your wife?   21

No. She has enough problems of her own.   22

Content

1. Through this interview Terkel aims to show a mail carrier's typical work day. What are its main features?
2. What are John Fuller's principal concerns in life? Are readers supposed to think he is a typical mail carrier?
3. Why does Terkel devote so much space to the occupational hazards of what might seem to readers to be a fairly safe job?

Strategies/Structures

1. This essay is organized to follow the chronology of Mr. Fuller's life, from childhood to retirement, but within this general framework other organizational patterns emerge. What are they?
2. Do you think these patterns represent Fuller's natural discourse or

would they have been more likely to emerge as a result of Terkel's careful editing?

Language

1. Terkel appears to be quoting his subject verbatim, including ungrammatical staements, and speeches in dialect. What is the effect of this technique?

For Writing

1. Write an essay in which you characterize a person in terms of his or her main occupation or hobby with which your audience is unfamiliar. What details and/or information do you have to include that you could omit if you were writing for an audience of specialists in the same field?

2. Write an interview in which the main character does most of the talking.

▶───────────────────────◀

JOHN LEONARD

Leonard, born in 1939 in Washington, D.C. and educated at Harvard (1956–58) and the University of California at Berkeley (B.A., 1962), is the author of several novels, among them *The Naked Martini* (1964), *Crybaby of the Western World* (1969), and *This Pen for Hire* (1973). Since 1967 he has been book reviewer and since 1971 book review editor for the *New York Times*. His thoughtful, elegantly written reviews and essays analyzing contemporary life, "Private Lives," collected in *Private Lives in the Imperial City* (1979), have gained critical acclaim and a wide audience. With wit, understatement, and insight, Leonard focuses on family relationships—among husbands and wives, and ex-wives; parents and children; brothers and sisters. As "The Only Child" indicates, Leonard is particularly concerned about the difficulty of sustaining meaningful human relationships in a society that is increasingly urbanized, mechanized, and insecure.

The Only Child

He is big. He always has been, over six feet, with that slump   1
of the shoulders and tuck in the neck big men in this
country often affect, as if to apologize for being above the democratic norm in size. (In high school and at college he played
varsity basketball. In high school he was senior class president.)
And he looks healthy enough, blue-eyed behind his beard, like
a trapper or a mountain man, acquainted with silences. He also
grins a lot.

Odd, then, to have noticed earlier—at the house, when he   2
took off his shabby coat to play Ping-Pong—that the white arms
were unmuscled. The coat may have been a comment. This,
after all, is southern California, where every man is an artist,
an advertiser of himself; where every surface is painted and
every object potted; where even the statues seem to wear socks.
The entire population ambles, in polyesters, toward a Taco Bell.
To wear a brown shabby cloth coat in southern California is to
admit something.

So he hasn't been getting much exercise. Nor would the   3
children have elected him president of any class. At the house
they avoided him. Or, since he was too big to be avoided entirely, they treated his presence as a kind of odor to pass through
hurriedly, to be safe on the other side. They behaved like cats.
Of course, he ignored them. But I think they were up to more
than just protecting themselves from his lack of curiosity. Children are expert readers of grins.

His grin is intermittent. The dimples twitch on and off;   4
between them, teeth are bared; above them, the blue eyes dis-
appear in a wince. This grin isn't connected to any humor the
children know about. It may be a tic. It could also be a function
of some metronome made on Mars. It registers inappropriate
intervals. We aren't listening to the same music.

This is the man who introduced me to the mysteries of   5
mathematical science, the man I could never beat at chess, the
man who wrote haiku and played with computers. Now there

is static in his head, as though the mind had drifted off its signal during sleep. He has an attention span of about thirty seconds.

6   I am to take him back to where he lives, in the car I have rented in order to pretend to be a Californian. We are headed for a rooming house in one of the beach cities along a coast of off-ramps and oil wells. It is a rooming house that thinks of itself as Spanish. The ruined-hacienda look requires a patio, a palm tree and several miles of corrugated tile. He does not expect me to come up to his room, but I insist. I have brought along a six-pack of beer.

7   The room is a slum, and it stinks. It is wall-to-wall beer cans, hundreds of them, under a film of ash. He lights cigarettes and leaves them burning on the windowsill or the edge of the dresser or the lip of the sink, while he thinks of something else—Gupta sculpture, maybe, or the Sephiroth Tree of the Kabbalah. The sink is filthy, and so is the toilet. Holes have been burnt in the sheet on the bed, where he sits. He likes to crush the beer cans after he has emptied them, then toss them aside.

8   He tells me that he is making a statement, that this room is a statement, that the landlord will understand the meaning of his statement. In a week or so, according to the pattern, they will evict him, and someone will find him another room, which he will turn into another statement, with the help of the welfare checks he receives on account of his disability, which is the static in his head.

9   There are no books, no newspapers or magazines, no pictures on the wall. There is a television set, which he watches all day long while drinking beer and smoking cigarettes. I am sufficiently familiar with the literature on schizophrenia to realize that this room is a statement he is making about himself. I am also sufficiently familiar with his history to understand that, along with his contempt for himself, there is an abiding arrogance. He refuses medication. They can't make him take it, any more than they can keep him in a hospital. He has harmed no one. One night, in one of these rooms, he will set himself on fire.

10   He talks. Or blurts: scraps from Oriental philosophers—Lao-tzu, I think—puns, incantations, obscenities, names from the past. There are conspiracies; I am part of one of them. He

grins, winces, slumps, is suddenly tired, wants me to get out almost as much as I want to get out, seems to have lapsed in a permanent parenthesis. Anyway, I have a busy schedule.

Well, speed kills slowly, and he fiddled too much with the 11 oxygen flow to his brain. He wanted ecstasy and revelation, the way we grew up wanting a bicycle, a car, a girlfriend. These belonged to us by right, as middle-class Americans. So, then, did salvation belong to us by right. I would like to thank Timothy Leary and all the other sports of the 1960's who helped make this bad trip possible. I wish R. D. Laing would explain to me, once again and slowly, how madness is a proof of grace. "The greatest magician," said Novalis, "would be the one who would cast over himself a spell so complete that he would take his own phantasmagorias as autonomous appearances."

One goes back to the rented car and pretending to be a 12 Californian as, perhaps, one had been pretending to be a brother. It is odd, at my age, suddenly to have become an only child.

Content

1. What are the possible meanings of Leonard's title? Why does he wait until the last paragraph (¶ 12) to speak directly on the point? What is the effect of this delay?

2. Why does Leonard, a New Yorker, say he is "pretending to be a Californian" (¶s 6, 12)? What does California connote to him?

3. What kind of "statement" does Leonard's brother think his littered, filthy room is making? Does Leonard interpret this "statement" in the same way?

4. What is Leonard's view of the counter-culture of the 1960s, as evidenced by the example of his brother, and by his references to Timothy Leary and R. D. Laing in paragraph 11?

5. Can Leonard expect readers who were little children in the 1960s to understand without further explanation the elements of the counter-culture, such as drug-taking and social nonconformity, to which he only alludes in the essay? For this essay, published a decade later, should Leonard have provided more explanation?

Strategies/Structures

1. Why does Leonard present details of his brother's illness gradually, instead of all at once? Why does he delay labeling the diagnosis until

three-fourths of the way through (¶ 9)? Leonard is not a doctor, but a professional writer. Is his medical diagnosis convincing? Why or why not?

2. Leonard uses many natural symbols. What does he intend to indicate by the fact that his brother "played varsity basketball" in high school and college (¶ 1)? That his brother "grins a lot" (¶ 1)? That his brother wore "a brown shabby cloth coat in southern California" (¶ 2)? That Leonard could never beat him at chess (¶ 5)? That his brother now "has an attention span of thirty seconds" (¶ 5)?

3. In what ways does Leonard's showing the brother in his chosen context—a filthy room (¶s 6-9) and in an alien context—"at the house" (¶s 2,3)—help to explain the brother's personality and illness?

4. What is Leonard's attitude toward his brother? Does he expect his readers to share this? Why does he expect readers to be interested in his brother?

Language

1. In this highly personal essay Leonard generally uses the first person singular pronoun. Why does he use the impersonal and formal third person, "one," in the last paragraph?

2. Why doesn't Leonard ever identify his brother by name? At what point is their blood relationship clear?

For Writing

1. Write a character sketch of someone you know well, placing that person in his or her typical setting. Indicate your approval or disapproval of your subject's values through the details you select in describing the setting.

2. Write a character sketch of the same person you wrote about in #1, but this time selecting a different setting and details to present the person in an entirely different light from the way he or she appeared in the first version.

Strategies For Writing— About People, Yourself and Others

1. Why do you want to write about this person? To gain understanding of the subject's motives, conflicts, or problems? To provide a character sketch or brief biography? To tell a story? To use some aspect of the person's life as a good or bad example? To explain the person's job or a memorable period of history or event he or she experienced?

2. Does your audience know your subject personally or by reputation? If so, how well? If not, what if anything do you need to tell them about the subject's age, occupation, cultural or ethnic heritage, geographic origin?

3. Will you organize your essay chronologically, according to the sequence of events in the life of the person you're discussing? Psychologically, according to the most impressive features of his or her personality? Emotionally, leading up to a climax or crisis in the subject's life, or to an intense peak of happiness? Or in some other way?

4. Will your attitude toward your subject (whether you admire or dislike him) determine the details you select, and omit? To what extent will your focus on the subject's personality, occupation, or experiences determine your selection and arrangement of details?

5. To what extent will your attitude toward your subject determine your choice of language in writing about the person? If you're writing about yourself, can you avoid the self-indulgence of being easier on yourself than you'd be on someone else ("I am firm; you are stubborn; she is a pig-headed fool.")? Must the tone of your writing match the mood of the subject during the experience(s) you're discussing? (Sometimes, but if the person is bored you'll still want to write about the boredom in an interesting manner.)

Additional Writing Topics

1. Write an account of a memorable experience in your childhood or high school years, such as meeting an influential person, taking an unusual vacation, living through a notable event in local or national history, experiencing an accident or other crisis. Allow its significance to emerge through carefully selected details rather than through an overt interpretation.

2. Have you ever felt like an alien in a new environment? (For instance, you might have been the new kid on the block, new to high school or

college, or a visitor to a foreign country.) Tell the story of your transformation from an outsider to an insider, if such occurred. If it didn't, explain why you remained an alien.

3. Have you ever been separated, physically or psychologically, from a relative or friend with whom you were once very close, as John Leonard was from his brother? Tell the story of your first—or another supposedly memorable—meeting after the absence.

4. Write an imaginary autobiographical portrait of yourself as you expect to be ten (or twenty) years from now. (Specify which age.) What major characteristics of your present personality or life style will you have retained? Which do you expect to have changed, and why?

5. Interview someone with an occupation you want to know more about, ordinary or extraordinary. What skills, training, and personal qualities does the job require? What are its most rewarding aspects? Its drawbacks? (See Terkel, "John Fuller, Mail Carrier," pp. 23–27.)

6. Initiations—into the mysteries of dating, drinking, cooking, team sports, dormitory (or other group) living, or other phenomena, are often meaningful for unexpected reasons. Tell the story of your initiation into a memorable group or activity, and let your chosen details and tone convey its significance. (This may be humorous; see "Learning to Drive," pp. 109–113.)

7. Discuss the impact of a particular person, book, or experience that has changed your life. Explain enough of what you were like beforehand so readers can recognize the effects of this encounter or longer-term association.

8. Write a pseudo-diary, an imaginary account of how you would lead a day in your life if all your wishes were fulfilled (or if all your worst fears were realized).

9. Have you ever worshipped someone as a hero, or modeled yourself after someone? Characterize the relationship, perhaps through narrating an incident or two. Has this relationship been beneficial or harmful to you? Show why, through the incidents you select and the mood your words create.

10. Through using your own experiences or those of someone you know well, write an essay showing the truth or falsity of an adage about human nature, such as:

a. Quitters never win. Or do they?

b. Try hard and you'll succeed. Or will you?

c. It doesn't matter whether you win or lose, it's how you play the game.

d. Absence makes the heart grow fonder—or, Out of sight out of mind.

PART II

Determining Ideas in a Sequence

▶━━━━━━━━━━━━━━━━━━━━━━━━━━━━━━◀

2 *Narration*

Narration, telling a story, is a particularly attractive mode of writing. Ours is a storytelling culture. It is as old as Indian legends, Br'er Rabbit, Grimm's fairy tales, and the stories of Edgar Allan Poe. It is as new as speakers' warm-up jokes ("A funny thing happened on my way to . . .") and anecdotal leads to otherwise impersonal news stories. Thus *Newsweek* begins its lead article for August 9, 1982, "Reagan's War on Drugs," with a dramatic vignette that starts:

> U.S. Customs Service officers in Miami spotted the "mule" the moment he stepped off Avianca Flight 6 from Bogota: Gabriel Antonio Pino, 27, was simply too nervous to be an ordinary tourist. An intense search of Pino's suitcase and clothing uncovered no drugs, but X-rays revealed. . . .

The characters, the conflict, the motives, the plot of the above incident or any vivid narrative are a particularly easy form of writing for readers to remember. Narratives can be whole novels, stories, essays, or segments of other types of writing.

They can be as long and complicated as Charles Dickens's novels or an account of the Watergate break-in, trial, and aftermath. Or they can be as short and to the point as the following narrative by student Myrna Greenfield, complete in a single paragraph:

> now every dream i'd ever dreamed about college roommates said they are your best friends and the two of you fall in love with two men who are best friends and you get married after college to the best friends and you move to minneapolis or new rochelle and live next door and you have kids who grow up to be best friends with your best friend's kids. but kim was coolish and i was warmish and kim loved beethoven and i loved beatles and kim was neat and i was sloppy and kim was quiet and i was noisy as all hell broke loose. so much for the dream.

Myrna, as an author writing in the first person, has efficiently (although with unconventional punctuation), narrated two stories. The first, structured by a unified chronological progression, relates the myth of a college woman's stereotyped life history. The second, emphasizing variations on the theme of incompatibility, tells the story of the actual relationship between the author and her roommate. There are two main characters in the first story: Myrna's idealized version of herself and Kim. The two characters in the second story are the actual roommates. Each story has a setting: college and the suburbs in the first; college in the second. Each story covers a period of time—the entire life span in the first; the recent past in the second. The second sentence negates the first and leads to the short, punchy emotional climax, "so much for the dream."

A narrative need not be fictional, as the above examples and the essays in this section indicate. When you're writing a narrative based on real people, actual incidents, you shape the material to emphasize the *point of view, sequence of action* (a chase, an exploration), *a theme* (greed, pleasure), *a particular relationship between characters* (love, antagonism), or the *personalities* of the *people involved* (vigorous, passive). This shaping—supplying information or other specific details where necessary, deleting trivial or irrelevant material—is essential in transforming skeletal diary entries (see Didion and Allen in the previous section) into three-dimensional configurations.

A narrative can *exist for its own sake*. As sixteenth-century poet and courtier Sir Philip Sidney observed, such writing can attract "children from play and old men from the chimney corner." Through a narrative you can also *illustrate or explore a personality or an idea*. In this section E. B. White's "Once More to the Lake" uses a rural environment as the setting in which to examine the continuity of generations in relationships between fathers and sons. Tim Payne's "On the Beach at Bar Harbor" focuses on an understanding of nature that leads to a new perspective on himself. Through a narrative you can *present a whole or partial biography or autobiography*. "Resurrection," from Frederick Douglass's *Life and Times*, recounts his defiance of a Simon Legree-type overseer. This was "the turning-point in my career as a slave . . . It recalled the departed self-confidence, and inspired me again with a determination to be free."

Through narration you can *impart information* or an *account of historical events*, either from an impartial or an eyewitness point of view. Natalie Crouter's "Release from Captivity," an excerpt from her World War II diary, details her first-hand account of being freed from a Japanese prision camp in 1945:

> . . . when the soldiers heard [our noise] they thought it was Nipponese inside and put their hands on their rifles all ready to mow [us] down. They called out, "We order you to surrender!" and our men cried out, "We can't. We are American prisoners of war in here." The answer from the outside was, "The Hell you are! Not now— we're here!"

Through a narration you can *present a powerful argument, overt or implicit*. George Orwell does this in "Shooting an Elephant," an unforgettable narrative of how and why, as a colonial officer, he allowed the Burmese natives to pressure him into committing an ethically and socially irresponsible act.

To write a narrative you can ask, What do I want to demonstrate? Through what characters, performing what actions or thinking what thoughts? In what setting and time frame? From what point of view do I want to tell the tale? Narratives have as many purposes, as many plots, as many characters as there are people to write them. You have but to examine your life, your thoughts, your experiences, to find an unwritten library of narratives yet to tell. Therein lie a thousand tales. Or a thousand and one. . . .

◄──►

E. B. WHITE

White, born in 1899 in Mount Vernon, New York, and educated at Cornell University (A.B., 1921), has frequently been
called "the finest essayist in the United States." His career as a
writer began as a reporter for the *Seattle Times* (1922–23), but
for nearly sixty years he has been an essayist and contributing
editor for *The New Yorker*. His column "One Man's Meat" appeared regularly in *Harper's* for five years (1938-43). Among
White's numerous awards are honorary degrees, a fellowship
in the American Academy of Arts and Sciences, membership in
the National Institute of Arts and Letters, a Presidential Medal
of Freedom (1963), and a National Medal for Literature (1971).
He has published several volumes of essays (including *Is Sex
Necessary?* (1929), with James Thurber), two volumes of poetry,
and three well-known children's books, *Stuart Little* (1945),
Charlotte's Web (1952), and *The Trumpet of the Swan* (1970). In
1959, White revised William Strunk's popular guidebook for
writing, *The Elements of Style*. His humane common sense, good
humor, and preference for eloquent plainspokenness are manifested in his classic advice on style. He suggests that readers,
for instance, compare the "eight short, easy words" of Thomas
Paine's "These are the times that try men's souls" with the un-
gainly "Soulwise, these are trying times." These same qualities
are apparent in "Once More to the Lake," a narrative of father
and son, timeless generations in the eternal Maine countryside.

Once More to the Lake

O ne summer, along about 1904, my father rented a camp   1
on a lake in Maine and took us all there for the month of
August. We all got ringworm from some kittens and had to rub
Pond's Extract on our arms and legs night and morning, and
my father rolled over in a canoe with all his clothes on; but
outside of that the vacation was a success and from then on
none of us ever thought there was any place in the world like
that lake in Maine. We returned summer after summer—always
on August 1st for one month. I have since become a salt-water

man, but sometimes in summer there are days when the rest-
lessness of the tides and the fearful cold of the sea water and
the incessant wind which blows across the afternoon and into
the evening make me wish for the placidity of a lake in the
woods. A few weeks ago this feeling got so strong I bought
myself a couple of bass hooks and a spinner and returned to
the lake where we used to go, for a week's fishing and to revisit
old haunts.

2   I took along my son, who had never had any fresh water
up his nose and who had seen lily pads only from train windows.
On the journey over to the lake I began to wonder what it would
be like. I wondered how time would have marred this unique,
this holy spot—the coves and streams, the hills that the sun set
behind, the camps and the paths behind the camps. I was sure
the tarred road would have found it out and I wondered in what
other ways it would be desolated. It is strange how much you
can remember about places like that once you allow your mind
to return into the grooves which lead back. You remember one
thing, and that suddenly reminds you of another thing. I guess
I remembered clearest of all the early mornings, when the lake
was cool and motionless, remembered how the bedroom smelled
of the lumber it was made of and of the wet woods whose scent
entered through the screen. The partitions in the camp were
thin and did not extend clear to the top of the rooms, and as I
was always the first up I would dress softly so as not to wake
the others, and sneak out into the sweet outdoors and start out
in the canoe, keeping close along the shore in the long shadows
of the pines. I remembered being very careful never to rub my
paddle against the gunwale for fear of disturbing the stillness
of the cathedral.

3   The lake had never been what you would call a wild lake.
There were cottages sprinkled around the shores, and it was in
farming country although the shores of the lake were quite heavily wooded. Some of the cottages were owned by nearby farmers,
and you would live at the shore and eat your meals at the farmhouse. That's what our family did. But although it wasn't wild,
it was a fairly large and undisturbed lake and there were places
in it which, to a child at least, seemed infinitely remote and
primeval.

I was right about the tar: it led to within half a mile of the   4
shore. But when I got back there, with my boy, and we settled
into a camp near a farmhouse and into the kind of summertime
I had known, I could tell that it was going to be pretty much
the same as it had been before—I knew it, lying in bed the first
morning, smelling the bedroom, and hearing the boy sneak quietly out and go off along the shore in a boat. I began to sustain
the illusion that he was I, and therefore by simple transposition,
that I was my father. This sensation persisted, kept cropping
up all the time we were there. It was not an entirely new feeling,
but in this setting it grew much stronger. I seemed to be living
a dual existence. I would be in the middle of some simple act,
I would be picking up a bait box or laying down a table fork, or
I would be saying something, and suddenly it would be not I
but my father who was saying the words or making the gesture.
It gave me a creepy sensation.

We went fishing the first morning. I felt the same damp   5
moss covering the worms in the bait can, and saw the dragonfly
alight on the tip of my rod as it hovered a few inches from the
surface of the water. It was the arrival of this fly that convinced
me beyond any doubt that everything was as it always had been,
that the years were a mirage and there had been no years. The
small waves were the same, chucking the rowboat under the
chin as we fished at anchor, and the boat was the same boat,
the same color green and the ribs broken in the same places,
and under the floor-boards the same fresh-water leavings and
debris—the dead helgramite, the wisps of moss, the rusty dis-
carded fishhook, the dried blood from yesterday's catch. We
stared silently at the tips of our rods, at the dragonflies that came
and went. I lowered the tip of mine into the water, tentatively,
pensively dislodging the fly, which darted two feet away, poised,
darted two feet back, and came to a rest again a little farther up
the rod. There had been no years between the ducking of this
dragonfly and the other one—the one that was part of memory.
I looked at the boy, who was silently watching his fly, and it
was my hands that held his rod, my eyes watching. I felt dizzy
and didn't know which rod I was at the end of.

We caught two bass, hauling them in briskly as though   6
they were mackerel, pulling them over the side of the boat in a

businesslike manner without any landing net, and stunning them with a blow on the back of the head. When we got back for a swim before lunch, the lake was exactly where we had left it, the same number of inches from the dock, and there was only the merest suggestion of a breeze. This seemed an utterly enchanted sea, this lake you could leave to its own devices for a few hours and come back to, and find that it had not stirred, this constant and trustworthy body of water. In the shallows, the dark, watersoaked sticks and twigs, smooth and old, were undulating in clusters on the bottom against the clean ribbed sand, and the track of the mussel was plain. A school of minnows swam by, each minnow with its small individual shadow, doubling the attendance, so clear and sharp in the sunlight. Some of the other campers were in swimming, along the shore, one of them with a cake of soap, and the water felt thin and clear and unsubstantial. Over the years there had been this person with the cake of soap, this cultist, and here he was. There had been no years.

7   Up to the farmhouse to dinner through the teeming, dusty field, the road under our sneakers was only a two-track road. The middle track was missing, the one with the marks of the hooves and the splotches of dried, flaky manure. There had always been three tracks to choose from in choosing which track to walk in; now the choice was narrowed down to two. For a moment I missed terribly the middle alternative. But the way led past the tennis court, and something about the way it lay there in the sun reassured me; the tape had loosened along the backline, the alleys were green with plantains and other weeds, and the net (installed in June and removed in September) sagged in the dry noon, and the whole place steamed with midday heat and hunger and emptiness. There was a choice of pie for dessert, and one was blueberry and one was apple, and the waitresses were the same country girls, there having been no passage of time, only the illusion of it as in a dropped curtain—the waitresses were still fifteen; their hair had been washed, that was the only difference—they had been to the movies and seen the pretty girls with the clean hair.

8   Summertime, oh summertime, pattern of life indelible, the fade-proof lake, the woods unshatterable, the pasture with the

sweetfern and the juniper forever and ever, summer without end; this was the background, and the life along the shore was the design, the cottages with their innocent and tranquil design, their tiny docks with the flagpole and the American flag floating against the white clouds in the blue sky, the little paths over the roots of the trees leading from camp to camp and the paths leading back to the outhouses and the can of lime for sprinkling, and at the souvenir counters at the store the miniature birch-bark canoes and the post cards that showed things looking a little better than they looked. This was the American family at play, escaping the city heat, wondering whether the newcomers in the camp at the head of the cove were "common" or "nice," wondering whether it was true that the people who drove up for Sunday dinner at the farmhouse were turned away because there wasn't enough chicken.

It seemed to me, as I kept remembering all this, that those times and those summers had been infinitely precious and worth saving. There had been jollity and peace and goodness. The arriving (at the beginning of August) had been so big a business in itself, at the railway station the farm wagon drawn up, the first smell of the pine-laden air, the first glimpse of the smiling farmer, and the great importance of the trunks and your father's enormous authority in such matters, and the feel of the wagon under you for the long ten-mile haul, and at the top of the last long hill catching the first view of the lake after eleven months of not seeing this cherished body of water. The shouts and cries of the other campers when they saw you, and the trunks to be unpacked, to give up their rich burden. (Arriving was less exciting nowadays, when you sneaked up in your car and parked it under a tree near the camp and took out the bags and in five minutes it was all over, no fuss, no loud wonderful fuss about trunks.)

Peace and goodness and jollity. The only thing that was wrong now, really, was the sound of the place, an unfamiliar nervous sound of the outboard motors. This was the note that jarred, the one thing that would sometimes break the illusion and set the years moving. In those other summertimes all motors were inboard; and when they were at a little distance, the noise they made was a sedative, an ingredient of summer sleep. They were one-cylinder and two-cylinder engines, and some were make-and-break and some were jump-spark, but they all made a sleepy sound across the lake. The one-lungers throbbed and fluttered, and the twin-cylinder ones purred and purred, and that was a quiet sound too. But now the campers all had outboards. In the daytime, in the hot mornings, these motors made a petulant, irritable sound; at night, in the still evening when the afterglow lit the water, they whined about one's ears like mosquitoes. My boy loved our rented outboard, and his great desire was to achieve singlehanded mastery over it, and authority, and he soon learned the trick of choking it a little (but not too much), and the adjustment of the needle valve. Watching him I would remember the things you could do with the old one-cylinder engine with the heavy flywheel, how you could have it eating out of your hand if you got really close to it spiritually. Motor boats in those days didn't have clutches, and you would make a landing by shutting off the motor at the proper time and coasting in with a dead rudder. But there was a way of reversing them, if you learned the trick, by cutting the switch and putting it on again exactly on the final dying revolution of the flywheel, so that it would kick back against compression and begin reversing. Approaching a dock in a strong following breeze, it was difficult to slow up sufficiently by the ordinary coasting method, and if a boy felt he had complete mastery over his motor, he was tempted to keep it running beyond its time and then reverse it a few feet from the dock. It took a cool nerve, because if you threw the switch a twentieth of a second too soon you would catch the flywheel when it still had speed enough to go up past center, and the boat would leap ahead, charging bull-fashion at the dock.

11   We had a good week at the camp. The bass were biting well and the sun shone endlessly, day after day. We would be tired at night and lie down in the accumulated heat of the little bedrooms after the long hot day and the breeze would stir almost imperceptibly outside and the smell of the swamp drift in through the rusty screens. Sleep would come easily and in the morning the red squirrel would be on the roof, tapping out his gay routine. I kept remembering everything, lying in bed in the mornings—the small steamboat that had a long rounded stern like

the lip of a Ubangi, and how quietly she ran on the moonlight sails, when the older boys played their mandolins and the girls sang and we ate doughnuts dipped in sugar, and how sweet the music was on the water in the shining night, and what it had felt like to think about girls then. After breakfast we would go up to the store and the things were in the same place—the minnows in a bottle, the plugs and spinners disarranged and pawed over by the youngsters from the boys' camp, the fig newtons and the Beeman's gum. Outside, the road was tarred and cars stood in front of the store. Inside, all was just as it had always been, except there was more Coca-Cola and not so much Moxie and root beer and birch beer and sarsaparilla. We would walk out with a bottle of pop apiece and sometimes the pop would backfire up our noses and hurt. We explored the streams, quietly, where the turtles slid off the sunny logs and dug their way into the soft bottom; and we lay on the town wharf and fed worms to the tame bass. Everywhere we went I had trouble making out which was I, the one walking at my side, the one walking in my pants.

One afternoon while we were there at that lake a thunderstorm came up. It was like the revival of an old melodrama that I had seen long ago with childish awe. The second-act climax of the drama of the electrical disturbance over a lake in America had not changed in any important respect. This was the big scene, still the big scene. The whole thing was so familiar, the first feeling of oppression and heat and a general air around camp of not wanting to go very far away. In midafternoon (it was all the same) a curious darkening of the sky, and a lull in everything that had made life tick; and then the way the boats suddenly swung the other way at their moorings with the coming of a breeze out of the new quarter, and the premonitory rumble. Then the kettle drum, then the snare, then the bass drum and cymbals, then crackling light against the dark, and the gods grinning and licking their chops in the hills. Afterward the calm, the rain steadily rustling in the calm lake, the return of light and hope and spirits, and the campers running out in joy and relief to go swimming in the rain, their bright cries perpetuating the deathless joke about how they were getting simply drenched, and the children screaming with delight at the new sensation of bathing in the rain, and the joke about getting drenched linking the generations in a strong indestructible chain. And the comedian who waded in carrying an umbrella.

13   When the others went swimming my son said he was going in too. He pulled his dripping trunks from the line where they had hung all through the shower, and wrung them out. Languidly, and with no thought of going in, I watched him, his hard little body, skinny and bare, saw him wince slightly as he pulled up around his vitals the small, soggy, icy garment. As he buckled the swollen belt suddenly my groin felt the chill of death.

Content

1. Characterize White's son. Why is he referred to as "my son" and "the boy" but never by name?

2. How do the ways in which the boy and his father relate to the lake environment emphasize their personal relationship? In which ways are these similar to the relationship between the narrator and his father, the boy's grandfather?

3. White emphasizes the "peace and goodness and jollity" of the summers at the lake. What incidents and details reinforce this emphasis?

4. In light of the good will, good humor, and tranquility on which this essay focuses, why does White end with "As he buckled the swollen belt suddenly my groin felt the chill of death" (¶ 13)? What relation has this to the preceding sentence? To the rest of the essay?

Strategies/Structures

1. Many narratives proceed chronologically from the beginning to the end of the time period they cover, relating the events of that period in the sequence in which they occurred. Instead, White organizes this narrative topically. What are the major topics? Why do they come in the order they do, concluding with the thunderstorm and its aftermath?

2. What are the effects of White's frequent repetition of phrases ("there had been no years") and words ("same")? What details or incidents does he use to illustrate the cycle of time?

3. What makes this lake, unnamed, a "holy spot" (¶ 2)? What is the "cathedral" to which White refers in the same paragraph?

Language

1. What language contributes to the relaxed mood of this essay? In what ways does the mood fit the subject?

2. Beginning writers are often advised when writing description to be sparing of adjectives and adverbs—to put the weight on nouns and verbs instead. Does White do this? Consistently? Pick a paragraph and analyze it to illustrate your answer.

For Writing

1. Tell the story of your experiences in a particular place—school building, restaurant, vacation spot, hometown, place visited—that emphasizes the influence of the place on your experiences and on your understanding of them. Identify what makes it memorable, but do not describe it in the picture-pretty manner of a travel brochure.

2. Write a narrative in which you focus on a significant relationship between yourself at a particular age and another member of your family of a different generation from yourself, either older or younger. If you emphasize its specific features you will probably capture some of its common or universal elements as well.

GEORGE ORWELL

Born in Bengal while his English father was in the Bengal civil service, Orwell (1903–1950)—the pseudonym for Eric Blair— was educated at Eton College but left before graduating to serve with the Indian imperial police in Burma from 1922 to 1927. Disillusioned with the service he decided to become a writer, and returned to Europe. His temporary employment as a dishwasher in Paris provided some of the material for his first book, *Down and Out in Paris and London* (1933); this was quickly followed by *Burmese Days* (1935). Ever active in the cause of political and personal freedom, Orwell fought in the Spanish Civil War, and was later a war correspondent for the B.B.C. and the *Observer* during World War II. His opposition to totalitarian government is most distinctly expressed in his last two novels, *Animal Farm* (1945) and *Nineteen Eighty-Four* (1949). The "tiny incident" in which Orwell, as an English police officer in Burma, shot an elephant to please a crowd of expectant Burmese, "gave me a better glimpse . . . of the real nature of imperialism—the real motives for which despotic governments act."

Shooting an Elephant

1   In Moulmein, in lower Burma, I was hated by large numbers of people—the only time in my life that I have been important enough for this to happen to me. I was sub-divisional police officer of the town, and in an aimless, petty kind of way anti-European feeling was very bitter. No one had the guts to raise a riot, but if a European woman went through the bazaars alone somebody would probably spit betel juice over her dress. As a police officer I was an obvious target and was baited whenever it seemed safe to do so. When a nimble Burman tripped me up on the football field and the referee (another Burman) looked the other way, the crowd yelled with hideous laughter. This happened more than once. In the end the sneering yellow faces of young men that met me everywhere, the insults hooted after me when I was at a safe distance, got badly on my nerves. The young Buddhist priests were the worst of all. There were several thousands of them in the town and none of them seemed to have anything to do except stand on street corners and jeer at Europeans.

2   All this was perplexing and upsetting. For at that time I had already made up my mind that imperialism was an evil thing and the sooner I chucked up my job and got out of it the better. Theoretically—and secretly, of course—I was all for the Burmese and all against their oppressors, the British. As for the job I was doing, I hated it more bitterly than I can perhaps make clear. In a job like that you see the dirty work of Empire at close quarters. The wretched prisoners huddling in the stinking cages of the lock-ups, the grey, cowed faces of the long-term convicts, the scarred buttocks of the men who had been flogged

with bamboos—all these oppressed me with an intolerable sense of guilt. But I could get nothing into perspective. I was young and ill-educated and I had had to think out my problems in the utter silence that is imposed on every Englishman in the East. I did not even know that the British Empire is dying, still less did I know that it is a great deal better than the younger empires that are going to supplant it. All I knew was that I was stuck between my hatred of the empire I served and my rage against the evil-spirited little beasts who tried to make my job impossible. With one part of my mind I thought of the British Raj as an unbreakable tyranny, as something clamped down, *in saecula saeculorum*, upon the will of prostrate peoples: with another part I thought that the greatest joy in the world would be to drive a bayonet into a Buddhist priest's guts. Feelings like these are the normal by-products of imperialism; ask any Anglo-Indian official, if you can catch him off duty.

One day something happened which in a roundabout way   3
was enlightening. It was a tiny incident in itself, but it gave me a better glimpse than I had had before of the real nature of imperialism—the real motives for which despotic governments act. Early one morning the sub-inspector at a police station the other end of the town rang me up on the 'phone and said that an elephant was ravaging the bazaar. Would I please come and do something about it? I did not know what I could do, but I wanted to see what was happening and I got on to a pony and started out. I took my rifle, an old .44 Winchester and much too small to kill an elephant, but I thought the noise might be useful *in terrorem*. Various Burmans stopped me on the way and told me about the elephant's doings. It was not, of course, a wild elephant, but a tame one which had gone "must." It had been chained up, as tame elephants always are when their attack of "must" is due, but on the previous night it had broken its chain and escaped. Its mahout, the only person who could manage it when it was in that state, had set out in pursuit, but had taken the wrong direction and was now twelve hours' journey away, and in the morning the elephant had suddenly reappeared in the town. The Burmese population had no weapons and were quite helpless against it. It had already destroyed somebody's bamboo hut, killed a cow and raided some fruit-stalls and de-

voured the stock; also it had met the municipal rubbish van and, when the driver jumped out and took to his heels, had turned the van over and inflicted violences upon it.

4   The Burmese sub-inspector and some Indian constables were waiting for me in the quarter where the elephant had been seen. It was a very poor quarter, a labyrinth of squalid bamboo huts, thatched with palm-leaf, winding all over a steep hillside. I remember that it was a cloudy, stuffy morning at the beginning of the rains. We began questioning the people as to where the elephant had gone and, as usual, failed to get any definite information. That is invariably the case in the East; a story always sounds clear enough at a distance, but the nearer you get to the scene of events the vaguer it becomes. Some of the people said that the elephant had gone in one direction, some said that he had gone in another, some professed not even to have heard of any elephant. I had almost made up my mind that the whole story was a pack of lies, when we heard yells a little distance away. There was a loud, scandalized cry of "Go away, child! Go away this instant!" and an old woman with a switch in her hand came round the corner of a hut, violently shooing away a crowd of naked children. Some more women followed, clicking their tongues and exclaiming; evidently there was something that the children ought not to have seen. I rounded the hut and saw a man's dead body sprawling in the mud. He was an Indian, a black Dravidian coolie, almost naked, and he could not have been dead many minutes. The people said that the elephant had come suddenly upon him round the corner of the hut, caught him with its trunk, put its foot on his back and ground him into the earth. This was the rainy season and the ground was soft, and his face had scored a trench a foot deep and a couple of yards long. He was lying on his belly with arms crucified and head sharply twisted to one side. His face was coated with mud, the eyes wide open, the teeth bared and grinning with an expression of unendurable agony. (Never tell me, by the way, that the dead look peaceful. Most of the corpses I have seen looked devilish.) The friction of the great beast's foot had stripped the skin from his back as neatly as one skins a rabbit. As soon as I saw the dead man I sent an orderly to a friend's house nearby to borrow an elephant rifle. I had already sent back the pony,

not wanting it to go mad with fright and throw me if it smelt the elephant.

The orderly came back in a few minutes with a rifle and five cartridges, and meanwhile some Burmans had arrived and told us that the elephant was in the paddy fields below, only a few hundred yards away. As I started forward practically the whole population of the quarter flocked out of the houses and followed me. They had seen the rifle and were all shouting excitedly that I was going to shoot the elephant. They had not shown much interest in the elephant when he was merely ravaging their homes, but it was different now that he was going to be shot. It was a bit of fun to them, as it would be to an English crowd; besides they wanted the meat. It made me vaguely uneasy. I had no intention of shooting the elephant—I had merely sent for the rifle to defend myself if necessary—and it is always unnerving to have a crowd following you. I marched down the hill, looking and feeling a fool, with the rifle over my shoulder and an ever-growing army of people jostling at my heels. At the bottom, when you got away from the huts, there was a metalled road and beyond that a miry waste of paddy fields a thousand yards across, not yet ploughed but soggy from the first rains and dotted with coarse grass. The elephant was standing eight yards from the road, his left side towards us. He took not the slightest notice of the crowd's approach. He was tearing up bunches of grass, beating them against his knees to clean them and stuffing them into his mouth.

I had halted on the road. As soon as I saw the elephant I knew with perfect certainty that I ought not to shoot him. It is a serious matter to shoot a working elephant—it is comparable to destroying a huge and costly piece of machinery—and obviously one ought not to do it if it can possibly be avoided. And at that distance, peacefully eating, the elephant looked no more dangerous than a cow. I thought then and I think now that his attack of "must" was already passing off; in which case he would merely wander harmlessly about until the mahout came back and caught him. Moreover, I did not in the least want to shoot him. I decided that I would watch him for a little while to make sure that he did not turn savage again, and then go home.

But at that moment I glanced round at the crowd that had

5

6

7

followed me. It was an immense crowd, two thousand at the least and growing every minute. It blocked the road for a long distance on either side. I looked at the sea of yellow faces above the garish clothes—faces all happy and excited over this bit of fun, all certain that the elephant was going to be shot. They were watching me as they would watch a conjurer about to perform a trick. They did not like me, but with the magical rifle in my hands I was momentarily worth watching. And suddenly I realized that I should have to shoot the elephant after all. The people expected it of me and I had got to do it; I could feel their two thousand wills pressing me forward, irresistibly. And it was at this moment, as I stood there with the rifle in my hands, that I first grasped the hollowness, the futility of the white man's dominion in the East. Here was I, the white man with his gun, standing in front of the unarmed native crowd—seemingly the leading actor of the piece; but in reality I was only an absurd puppet pushed to and fro by the will of those yellow faces behind. I perceived in this moment that when the white man turns tyrant it is his own freedom that he destroys. He becomes a sort of hollow, posing dummy, the conventionalized figure of a sahib. For it is the condition of his rule that he shall spend his life in trying to impress the "natives," and so in every crisis he has got to do what the "natives" expect of him. He wears a mask, and his face grows to fit it. I had got to shoot the elephant. I had committed myself to doing it when I sent for the rifle. A sahib has got to act like a sahib; he has got to appear resolute, to know his own mind and do definite things. To come all that way, rifle in hand, with two thousand people marching at my heels, and then to trail feebly away, having done nothing—no, that was impossible. The crowd would laugh at me. And my whole life, every white man's life in the East, was one long struggle not to be laughed at.

8   But I did not want to shoot the elephant. I watched him beating his bunch of grass against his knees, with that preoccupied grandmotherly air that elephants have. It seemed to me that it would be murder to shoot him. At that age I was not squeamish about killing animals, but I had never shot an elephant and never wanted to. (Somehow it always seems worse to kill a *large* animal.) Besides, there was the beast's owner to

be considered. Alive, the elephant was worth at least a hundred pounds; dead, he would only be worth the value of his tusks, five pounds, possibly. But I had got to act quickly. I turned to some experienced-looking Burmans who had been there when we arrived, and asked them how the elephant had been behaving. They all said the same thing: he took no notice of you if you left him alone, but he might charge if you went too close to him.

It was perfectly clear to me what I ought to do. I ought to 9 walk up to within, say, twenty-five yards of the elephant and test his behavior. If he charged, I could shoot; if he took no notice of me, it would be safe to leave him until the mahout came back. But also I knew that I was going to do no such thing. I was a poor shot with a rifle and the ground was soft mud into which one would sink at every step. If the elephant charged and I missed him, I should have about as much chance as a toad under a steam-roller. But even then I was not thinking particularly of my own skin, only of the watchful yellow faces behind. For at that moment, with the crowd watching me, I was not afraid in the ordinary sense, as I would have been if I had been alone. A white man mustn't be frightened in front of "natives"; and so, in general, he isn't frightened. The sole thought in my mind was that if anything went wrong those two thousand Burmans would see me pursued, caught, trampled on and reduced to a grinning corpse like that Indian up the hill. And if that happened it was quite probable that some of them would laugh. That would never do. There was only one alternative. I shoved the cartridges into the magazine and lay down on the road to get a better aim.

The crowd grew very still, and a deep, low, happy sigh, 10 as of people who see the theatre curtain go up at last, breathed from innumerable throats. They were going to have their bit of fun after all. The rifle was a beautiful German thing with crosshair sights. I did not then know that in shooting an elephant one would shoot to cut an imaginary bar running from ear-hole to ear-hole. I ought, therefore, as the elephant was sideways on, to have aimed straight at his ear-hole; actually I aimed several inches in front of this, thinking the brain would be further forward.

11   When I pulled the trigger I did not hear the bang or feel the kick—one never does when a shot goes home—but I heard the devilish roar of glee that went up from the crowd. In that instant, in too short a time, one would have thought, even for the bullet to get there, a mysterious, terrible change had come over the elephant. He neither stirred nor fell, but every line of his body had altered. He looked suddenly stricken, shrunken, immensely old, as though the frightful impact of the bullet had paralysed him without knocking him down. At last, after what seemed a long time—it might have been five seconds, I dare say—he sagged flabbily to his knees. His mouth slobbered. An enormous senility seemed to have settled upon him. One could have imagined him thousands of years old. I fired again into the same spot. At the second shot he did not collapse but climbed with desperate slowness to his feet and stood weakly upright, with legs sagging and head drooping. I fired a third time. That was the shot that did for him. You could see the agony of it jolt his whole body and knock the last remnant of strength from his legs. But in falling he seemed for a moment to rise, for as his hind legs collapsed beneath him he seemed to tower upward like a huge rock toppling, his trunk reaching skywards like a tree. He trumpeted, for the first and only time. And then down he came, his belly towards me, with a crash that seemed to shake the ground even where I lay.

12   I got up. The Burmans were already racing past me across the mud. It was obvious that the elephant would never rise again, but he was not dead. He was breathing very rhythmically with long rattling gasps, his great mound of a side painfully rising and falling. His mouth was wide open—I could see far down into caverns of pale pink throat. I waited a long time for him to die, but his breathing did not weaken. Finally I fired my two remaining shots into the spot where I thought his heart must be. The thick blood welled out of him like red velvet, but still he did not die. His body did not even jerk when the shots hit him, the tortured breathing continued without a pause. He was dying, very slowly and in great agony, but in some world remote from me where not even a bullet could damage him further. I felt that I had got to put an end to that dreadful noise. It seemed dreadful to see the great beast lying there, powerless

to move and yet powerless to die, and not even to be able to finish him. I sent back for my small rifle and poured shot after shot into his heart and down his throat. They seemed to make no impression. The tortured gasps continued as steadily as the ticking of a clock.

In the end I could not stand it any longer and went away. 13
I heard later that it took him half an hour to die. Burmans were bringing dahs and baskets even before I left, and I was told they had stripped his body almost to the bones by the afternoon.

Afterwards, of course, there were endless discussions about 14
the shooting of the elephant. The owner was furious, but he was only an Indian and could do nothing. Besides, legally I had done the right thing, for a mad elephant has to be killed, like a mad dog, if its owner fails to control it. Among the Europeans opinion was divided. The older men said I was right, the younger men said it was a damn shame to shoot an elephant for killing a coolie, because an elephant was worth more than any damn Coringhee coolie. And afterwards I was very glad that the coolie had been killed; it put me legally in the right and it gave me a sufficient pretext for shooting the elephant. I often wondered whether any of the others grasped that I had done it solely to avoid looking a fool.

Content

1. What is the thesis of Orwell's essay? Does it appear overtly in the essay? If so, where? If not, how much of the essay must one read before the thesis becomes apparent?

2. Is Orwell in his role as a police officer in Burma a sympathetic figure in the narrative? If so, why does he begin by telling his readers that he "was hated by large numbers of people" (¶ 1)? Is Orwell the narrator of the incident the same person—in age and opinions—as Orwell the police officer?

3. Why are the Burmese in this essay shown primarily in groups? Why is the elephant's owner never characterized or identified by name? Could the incident, or its equivalent, have taken place in any other colonial country?

4. What does Orwell say he should have done with regard to the elephant (¶ 9)? Why did he betray his own convictions (¶ 7)? What clues do your answers provide as to why Orwell wrote "Shooting an Ele-

phant"? Do you think he was as analytic during the actual experience as he became when interpreting it later, as he wrote the essay?

Strategies/Structures

1. The elephant itself may be understood literally. Orwell considers its economic function for the Burmese as equivalent to that of a "huge and costly piece of machinery". In what ways is this true? Does the elephant have any other symbolic meanings? If so, identify some and show how the symbolism is congruent with Orwell's actions and the point of the essay.

2. Why does Orwell describe the wounded elephant as looking "shrunken, immensely old" (¶ 11)? Is this simile compatible with the comparison, at the end of the same paragraph, of the elephant with a "huge rock toppling" and "a tree"?

3. Why does Orwell devote so much space to the preparations for shooting the elephant (¶s 7–9) and to the actual shooting (¶s 10–12)? Why is the conclusion (¶s 13–14) so short, in comparison with those sections?

Language

1. How does Orwell's fairly simple language throughout this essay relate to his attitude toward his subject?

2. Why does he use such vivid language in describing the corpse of the coolie (¶ 4) and the final agonies of the elephant (¶s 11–12)?

For Writing

1. Write an essay narrating an extended incident in which you (or someone you know well) acted contrary to better judgment. In the process of showing why you acted as you did, convey your current attitude toward your previous action—perhaps remorse or shame or pleasure. No matter what the action, you will want to try to present yourself as a sympathetic character.

2. Write an essay on one of the following quotations from "Shooting an Elephant." Although your discussion may include an analysis of Orwell's essay, it does not have to.

   a. "Somehow it always seems *worse* to kill a large animal." (¶ 8)
   b. "When the white man turns tyrant it is his own freedom that he destroys." (¶ 7)

   c. A person in authority "wears a mask and his face grows to fit
     it." (¶ 7)

3. Write an essay in which you argue that Orwell should or should
not have shot the elephant.

▶──◀

FREDERICK DOUGLASS

Douglass (1817–1895) was born a slave in Talbot County,
Maryland. Unlike many of his peers of the Eastern Shore, he
learned to read, and the power of this accomplishment coupled
with an iron physique and will to match, enabled him to escape to New York in 1838. He became a spokesman for the abolitionist movement, and for the next twenty-five years toured
the country on its behalf. He served as an advisor to Harriet
Beecher Stowe, author of *Uncle Tom's Cabin,* and to President
Lincoln, and after the war campaigned for civil rights for blacks
and women. His political significance was acknowledged by his
appointment as Minister to Haiti in 1890.

    Slave narratives, written or dictated by the hundreds in the
nineteenth century, provided memorable accounts of the physical, geographical, and psychological movement from captivity
to freedom, from dependence to independence. Douglass's autobiography is memorable for its forthright language and absence of stereotyping of either whites or blacks; his people are
multi-dimensional. This episode, taken from the first version of
The Narrative of the Life of Frederick Douglass, an American Slave
(1845), explains the incident that was "the turning point in my
career as a slave," for it enabled him to make the transformation from slave to human being.

Resurrection

I have already intimated that my condition was much worse,   1
during the first six months of my stay at Mr. Covey's, than
in the last six. The circumstances leading to the change in Mr.
Covey's course toward me form an epoch in my humble history.

You have seen how a man was made a slave; you shall see how a slave was made a man. On one of the hottest days of the month of August, 1833, Bill Smith, William Hughes, a slave named Eli, and myself, were engaged in fanning wheat. Hughes was clearing the fanned wheat from before the fan. Eli was turning, Smith was feeding, and I was carrying wheat to the fan. The work was simple, requiring strength rather than intellect; yet, to one entirely unused to such work, it came very hard. About three o'clock of that day, I broke down; my strength failed me; I was seized with a violent aching of the head, attended with extreme dizziness; I trembled in every limb. Finding what was coming, I nerved myself up, feeling it would never do to stop work. I stood as long as I could stagger to the hopper with grain. When I could stand no longer, I fell, and felt as if held down by an immense weight. The fan of course stopped; every one had his own work to do; and no one could do the work of the other, and have his own go on at the same time.

2   Mr. Covey was at the house, about one hundred yards from the treading-yard where we were fanning. On hearing the fan stop, he left immediately, and came to the spot where we were. He hastily inquired what the matter was. Bill answered that I was sick, and there was no one to bring wheat to the fan. I had by this time crawled away under the side of the post and rail-fence by which the yard was enclosed, hoping to find relief by getting out of the sun. He then asked where I was. He was told by one of the hands. He came to the spot, and, after looking at me awhile, asked me what was the matter. I told him as well as I could, for I scarce had strength to speak. He then gave me a savage kick in the side, and told me to get up. I tried to do so, but fell back in the attempt. He gave me another kick, and again told me to rise. I again tried, and succeeded in gaining my feet; but, stooping to get the tub with which I was feeding the fan, I again staggered and fell. While down in this situation, Mr. Covey took up the hickory slat with which Hughes had been striking off the half-bushel measure, and with it gave me a heavy blow upon the head, making a large wound, and the blood ran freely; and with this again told me to get up. I made no effort to comply, having now made up my mind to let him do his worst. In a short time after receiving this blow, my head

grew better. Mr. Covey had now left me to my fate. At this moment I resolved, for the first time, to go to my master, enter a complaint, and ask his protection. In order to do this, I must that afternoon walk seven miles; and this, under the circumstances, was truly a severe undertaking. I was exceedingly feeble; made so as much by the kicks and blows which I received, as by the severe fit of sickness to which I had been subjected. I, however, watched my chance, while Covey was looking in an opposite direction, and started for St. Michael's: I succeeded in getting a considerable distance on my way to the woods, when Covey discovered me, and called after me to come back, threatening what he would do if I did not come. I disregarded both his calls and his threats, and made my way to the woods as fast as my feeble state would allow; and thinking I might be overhauled by him if I kept the road, I walked through the woods, keeping far enough from the road to avoid detection, and near enough to prevent losing my way. I had not gone far before my little strength again failed me. I could go no farther. I fell down, and lay for a considerable time. The blood was yet oozing from the wound on my head. For a time I thought I should bleed to death; and think now that I should have done so, but that the blood so matted my hair as to stop the wound. After lying there about three quarters of an hour, I nerved myself up again, and started on my way, through bogs and briers, barefooted and bareheaded, tearing my feet sometimes at nearly every step; and after a journey of about seven miles, occupying some five hours to perform it, I arrived at master's store. I then presented an appearance enough to affect any but a heart of iron. From the crown of my head to my feet, I was covered with blood. My hair was all clotted with dust and blood; my shirt was stiff with blood. My legs and feet were torn in sundry places with briers and thorns, and were also covered with blood. I suppose I looked like a man who had escaped a den of wild beasts, and barely escaped them. In this state I appeared before my master, humbly entreating him to interpose his authority for my protection. I told him all the circumstances as well as I could, and it seemed, as I spoke, at times to affect him. He would then walk the floor, and seek to justify Covey by saying he expected I deserved it. He asked me what I wanted. I told him, to let me get a new home; that as sure as I lived with Mr. Covey again, I should live with but to die with him; that Covey would surely kill me; he was in a fair way for it. Master Thomas ridiculed the idea that there was any danger of Mr. Covey's killing me, and said that he knew Mr. Covey, that he was a good man, and that he could not think of taking me from him; that, should he do so, he would lose the whole year's wages; that I belonged to Mr. Covey for one year, and that I must go back to him, come what might; and that I must not trouble him with any more stories, or that he would himself *get hold of me*. After threatening me thus, he gave me a very large dose of salts, telling me that I might remain in St. Michael's that night, (it being quite late,) but that I must be off back to Mr. Covey's early in the morning; and that if I did not, he would *get hold of me*, which meant that he would whip me. I remained all night, and, according to his orders, I started off to Covey's in the morning, (Saturday morning,) wearied in body and broken in spirit. I got no supper that night, or breakfast that morning. I reached Covey's about nine o'clock; and just as I was getting over the fence that divided Mrs. Kemp's fields from ours, out ran Covey with his cowskin, to give me another whipping. Before he could reach me, I succeeded in getting to the cornfield; and as the corn was very high, it afforded me the means of hiding. He seemed very angry, and searched for me a long time. My behavior was altogether unaccountable. He finally gave up the chase, thinking, I suppose, that I must come home for something to eat; he would give himself no further trouble in looking for me. I spend that day mostly in the woods, having the alternative before me,—to go home and be whipped to death, or stay in the woods and be starved to death. That night, I fell in with Sandy Jenkins, a slave with whom I was somewhat acquainted. Sandy had a free wife who lived about four miles from Mr. Covey's; and it being Saturday, he was on his way to see her. I told him my circumstances, and he very kindly invited me to go home with him. I went home with him, and talked this whole matter over, and got his advice as to what course it was best for me to pursue. I found Sandy an old adviser. He told me, with great solemnity, I must go back to Covey; but that before I went, I must go with him into another part of the woods, where there was a certain *root*, which, if I would take some of it with me, carrying it *always on my right side,* would render it impossible for Mr. Covey, or any other white man, to whip me. He said he had carried it for years; and since he had done so, he had never received a blow, and never expected to while he carried it. I at first rejected the idea, that the simple carrying of a root in my pocket would have any such effect as he had said, and was not disposed to take it; but Sandy impressed the necessity with much earnestness, telling me it could do no harm, if it did no good. To please him, I at length took the root, and, according to his direction, carried it upon my right side. This was Sunday morning. I immediately started for home; and upon entering the yard gate, out came Mr. Covey on his way to meeting. He spoke to me very kindly, bade me drive the pigs from a lot near by, and passed on towards the church. Now, this singular conduct of Mr. Covey really made me begin to think that there was something in the *root* which Sandy had given me; and had it been on any other day than Sunday, I could have attributed the conduct to no other cause than the influence of that root; and as it was, I was half inclined to think the *root* to be something more than I at first had taken it to be. All went well till Monday morning. On this morning, the virtue of the *root* was fully tested. Long before daylight, I was called to go and rub, curry, and feed, the horses. I obeyed, and was glad to obey. But whilst thus engaged, whilst in the act of throwing down some blades from the loft, Mr. Covey entered the stable with a long rope; and just as I was half out of the loft, he caught hold of my legs, and was about tying me. As soon as I found what he was up to, I gave a sudden spring, and as I did so, he holding to my legs, I was brought sprawling on the stable floor. Mr. Covey seemed now to think he had me, and could do what he pleased; but at this moment—from whence came the spirit I don't know—I resolved to fight; and, suiting my action to the resolution, I seized Covey hard by the throat; and as I did so, I rose. He held on to me, and I to him. My resistance was so entirely unexpected, that Covey seemed taken all aback. He trembled like a leaf. This gave me assurance, and I held him uneasy, causing the blood to run where I touched him with the ends of my fingers. Mr. Covey soon called out to Hughes for help. Hughes came, and while Covey held me, attempted to tie my right hand. While he was in the act of doing so, I watched my chance, and gave him a heavy kick close under the ribs. This kick fairly sickened Hughes, so that he left me in the hands of Mr. Covey. This kick had the effect of not only weakening Hughes, but Covey also. When he saw Hughes bending over with pain, his courage quailed. He asked me if I meant to persist in my resistance. I told him I did, come what might; that he had used me like a brute for six months, and that I was determined to be used so no longer. With that, he strove to drag me to a stick that was lying just out of the stable door. He meant to knock me down. But just as he was leaning over to get the stick, I seized him with both hands by his collar, and brought him by a sudden snatch to the ground. By this time, Bill came. Covey called upon him for assistance. Bill wanted to know what he could do. Covey said, "Take hold of him, take hold of him!" Bill said his master hired him out to work, and not to help whip me; so he left Covey and myself to fight our own battle out. We were at it for nearly two hours. Covey at length let me go, puffing and blowing at a great rate, saying that if I had not resisted, he would not have whipped me half so much. The truth was, that he had not whipped me at all. I considered him as getting entirely the worst end of the bargin; for he had drawn no blood from me, but I had from him. The whole six months afterwards, that I spent with Mr. Covey, he never laid the weight of his finger upon me in anger. He would occasionally say, he didn't want to get hold of me again. "'No," thought I, "you need not; for you will come off worse than you did before."

3   This battle with Mr. Covey was the turning-point in my career as a slave. It rekindled the few expiring embers of freedom, and revived within me a sense of my own manhood. It recalled the departed self-confidence, and inspired me again with a determination to be free. The gratification afforded by the triumph was a full compensation for whatever else might follow, even death itself. He only can understand the deep satisfaction which I experienced, who has himself repelled by force the bloody arm of slavery. I felt as I never felt before. It was a glorious resurrection, from the tomb of slavery, to the heaven of freedom. My long-crushed spirit rose, cowardice departed,

bold defiance took its place; and I now resolved that, however long I might remain a slave in form, the day had passed forever when I could be a slave in fact. I did not hesitate to let it be known of me, that the white man who expected to succeed in whipping, must also succeed in killing me.

Content

1. Twelve years after he successfully defied Mr. Covey, Douglass identified this incident as "the turning point in my career as a slave" (¶ 3). Why? Would Douglass have been able to recognize its significance at the time or only in retrospect?

2. What, if anything, does Douglass expect his audience to do about slavery, as a consequence of having read his narrative?

3. If Douglass doesn't really believe that Sandy's magic root protected him from a Sunday beating by Mr. Covey (¶ 2), why does he discuss the root at all?

4. Why does Douglass explain his changed self image as a "resurrection, from the tomb of slavery, to the heaven of freedom"?

Strategies/Structures

1. Douglass's account begins with Friday afternoon and ends with Monday morning, but some events receive considerable emphasis while others are scarcely mentioned. Which ones does he focus on? Why?

2. Why is paragraph 2 so long? Should it have been divided into shorter units, or is the longer unit preferable? Justify your answer.

3. Douglass provides considerable details about his appearance after his first beating by the Covey (¶ 2), but scarcely any about the appearance of either Covey or Master Thomas. Why?

4. Would slave owners have been likely to read Douglass's autobiography? Why or why not? Would Douglass's emphasis have been likely to change for an audience of Northern post-Civil War blacks? Southern antebellum whites?

Language

1. How sophisticated is Douglass's level of diction? Is it appropriate for the narrative he tells?

2. Why does Douglass choose this level of verbal sophistication?

For Writing

1. Write a narrative in which you recount and explain the significance of an event in which you participated that was a turning point in your life or that provided you with an important change of self-image, or of status in the eyes of others. Provide enough specific details so readers unfamiliar with either you or the situation can experience it as you did. Be sure to depict the personalities of the central characters; their physical appearance may not be nearly as significant.

2. Write a narrative intended to inspire your readers in which you recount an incident expressing the difficulties of a minority or oppressed person or group. You can also try to move your readers to take action concerning the problem. Yet try to move them by example, rather than through preaching or an excess of emotion. Understatement is usually more appealing than overstatement.

NATALIE CROUTER

Boston born (1898) and bred, Natalie Crouter had been living for a decade in Baguio, the beautiful, mountain-ringed summer capital of the Philippines, with her husband Jerry, an American businessman, and two children, June and Fred ("Bedie"). Shortly after the bombing of Pearl Harbor, the Crouters, along with five hundred other American civilians, were taken prisoner by the Japanese; they were interned in a prison camp throughout World War II. Although they had their own self-government, school, and hospital, and were generally not mistreated, at the time Crouter wrote the diary entry below, near the war's end, they were in Bilibid Prison in Manila and on the verge of starving to death.

Like Frederick Douglass, Crouter had no formal training in writing, but like Douglass she had a fascinating story to tell, an exacting eye for detail, and a fiery spirit made tougher by oppression. Crouter kept a secret diary of her wartime experience, at the risk of being executed if it were discovered. This excerpt from January 31 to February 5, 1945 narrates the return of the U. S. Marines to Manila to free the captives who had been isolated from the outer world for four years.

Release from Captivity

January 31, 1945. Jerry traded a pound of sugar for four co-   1
conuts as we need the fat in them. We have had no meat in
over a month from the Japanese, since leaving Baguio. No fruit
for six or eight months except a small banana at Christmas.

At supper we opened a can of Spam and had two thin   2
slices each, saving a fourth for breakfast. We decided to eat all
of it, not save any, to celebrate our anniversary.

As we were finishing, Peg and Walter and Carl came with   3
a big pot of steaming tea. It revived and cheered us no end,
after the day of exhaustion. I said, "Two surprises—first the
sugar and second Peg's party. I wonder if there will be a third."
There was—the vanguard of the American Army!

There were shots outside the wall. I ran to the building   4
and was going to stop at the Board and read the evening news
bulletin when Bedie grabbed me. With a suppressed thrill in his
voice, he said, "Mummie, you must come. Don't stop to read.
There's a heavy humming noise getting nearer in the north and
people think it is tanks coming in." Filipinos were running up
the street, pecking cautiously out of doors and windows, all
looking in one direction. The view was limited so I suggested
we go to Betty's porch at the other end. As we passed a window,
Bedie looked out and came back nearly bursting. He insisted he
had seen a tank going by and that it was American. He acted
very nervous and said we ought to go downstairs. He begged
me so insistently that I turned back and we started down. Halfway down, all hell broke loose and there has been no peace
since.

Rifles, machine guns and bigger guns began ripping all   5
around us and we could hear the grind of more than one tank.
The Committee ordered everyone inside and people poured into
the building.

Kaito had returned from the hospital a little while before   6
and [said] that [when] the Americans reached Caloocan all our
Japanese staff would leave and we would be given our release.
While he was telling this, bedlam broke loose and Kaito went
out the door like a shot. He returned shortly, looking very sick

and sad, to say good-bye as he would probably not see us again. The whine of bullets, the ping and sing of shot of all kinds was in the air and we were ordered to *stay* in the building. Very soon all families on the second floor were ordered downstairs for the night. A trek of mattresses and nets began.

7   At dusk, we saw a silent line of Japanese in blue shirts creep from the gate to the front door. They went through the long hall, upstairs and out on the roof—of all places—with machine gun and bullets, grenades and gasoline. This made us extremely nervous, to put it mildly.

8   A flamethrower tore through the building next to the men's barracks just outside the [prison] wall and the building was a seething mass of flame immediately. It made me sick to see how quickly it happened and to wonder if any people might be inside. Fires began to rage in all directions. The sky was ablaze all night. The oil gray pall has hung over us ever since, some of it a greasy brown color. At sunset, the sun was a copper disk in the sky, as it is during forest-fire time at home [in New England].

9   Everyone went around talking about whether it was or wasn't the American Army. It wasn't very long before we were sure. Some of the usual nervy, hardy camp members went up on the roof to see what was going on and when the tank went by outside one of our walls it stopped and they heard a southern voice drawl, "Okay, Harvey, let's turn around and go back down this street again." Another pair of tanks was heard "God damning" each other in the dark. There was no mistake about this language—it was distinctly American soldiers! The Marines and Army were here! And they had caught the Japanese "with their pants down." There couldn't have been good communication or the Japanese would have had time to leave.

10   Yamato told the Committee members that he would go to get our release papers. He left poor Tanabe sitting in charge on the front steps for hours, half the night, with his sword in his lap. Miss McKim talked with him now and then.

11   A fire broke out just behind us to the north and the flames piled high and bamboo crackled and popped like pistols. I was so excited all night that I almost burst. I would doze off, waken with a jump at some enormous detonation. I was up most of the night, going from one end of the building to the other to

watch new fires that leapt into the sky. Jerry, who was tied to crutches [legs swollen with beriberi] and to his bed, scolded me—"You darn fool, go to bed. You'll be dead tomorrow if you don't stop running around." He was right but I didn't care and just answered. "I don't care if I am. This is the biggest night of my life and I'm not going to miss any of it."

Jo went out to do guard duty at 1 A.M. and I was dashing 12 back and forth to see fires and pillars of smoke and all the rest of the racket. Later Jo lit a candle and opened a can of Spam and a coconut and we sat on the floor and ate it on our corn crust which tasted heavenly with red glare shining in the windows on it and all the fiends of war making a din outside. Bedie was everywhere at once, missing nothing and reporting each new item like an old hand.

Miss McKim tried to persuade Ebiko to move his men off 13 the roof but he evaded and they stayed. Once in the night, they came down to roll an empty gasoline drum to the back gate near our door, where they put gasoline and fixed a fuse in order to blow up a tank if it tried to come in that way. The young Formosans were still guarding around the inside walls and corners, loaded down with equipment. Strands of wire were being switched around on the roof as though they were mining it.

When Yamato had had his sore hand fixed by Dr. Mather, 14 he had asked how soon it would be well and the doctor replied, "in about a week." Yesterday the hand was worse and Yamato asked the question again and the doctor said "two weeks." Poor Yamato looked sunk and said, "Oh you will have to give me some medicine to take with me in case we have to leave." The doctor told him he would.

February 4, 1945. The eight Japanese were still on the roof and 15 the Formosans were still guarding us when daylight came.

Carl took Yamato to the doctor to have his hand dressed 16 and he was given a package of sulfa to take with him. Later he said good-bye to a number of people and told them he was going "to meet my destiny." He had not returned during the evening, which left Tanabe sitting dumb and mournful with sword on his lap on the front steps. There were fires and flames as near as the fighting as the tanks went around and around outside our walls all day. A dead soldier lay in the square where roads crossed just beyond the corner wall. Filipinos looted his pockets, took off his belt, then his outer pants, kicking the body over and leaving it there clad only in underpants. It might even be Kaito or Sugano who helped us so much—but it is now only another symbol, this time representing Change, the dying New Order in East Asia.

17   About 10, we saw Carl go out the gate to join Major Wilson in receiving orders and release from Major Ebiko and Yamato, who at last satisfied his correct soul by turning us over with all the proper formality. About noon Carl came back and we were all called into the main corridor. We crowded about the small office space, then someone said, "Gangway." We all pressed over to one side as the clank of hobnails and sound of heavy feet came from the stairs. The eight soldiers had received their orders to come down from the roof. This was the most dramatic and exciting moment of all. It pictured our release more vividly than anything could. They had been persuaded to withdraw so that our danger would be less. They were giving in that much and were leaving Bilibid. They filed through the narrow lane we left, they and we silent, their faces looking sunk and trapped. The corporal's fat face was sullen and defeated. One short, beady-eyed pleasant fellow looked at us with a timid friendly grin—a good sport to the end. With machine-gun bullets and grenades in their hands, they trooped out the door, joining the still jaunty Formosans at the gate. They all went out without a backward look and the gate stood open behind them. We were alone—and turned toward Carl who read the Release. He emphasized the change of [release] dates on it and described the meeting in Ebiko's quarters. We cheered and then Carl took the hand-sewn Baguio American flag out of the drawer and held it up high. The crowd broke up and began to move away singing "The Star Spangled Banner" and "God Bless America." I went out the front door and around in our door at the side where June was trying to tell Jerry who had his face in his hands, his head bowed. I put my arm around his shoulders and the three of us sat there with tears running down our checks for quite a long while, not saying anything.

Ebiko, Oura, Yamato, Kaito, Tanabe, Sugano—all the good 18
and the bad went out the front gate and locked us in with double
barricade.

I began to feel horribly sick in my soul as I watched war 19
hour after hour—snipers picking off men; men cornering
snipers, creeping down alleys; hunting; cornering; killing.
There was plenty to watch, hour after hour, our own men and
the enemy.

This is the Release. 20

February 4, 1945

Message 21

Commandant Major Ebiko: 1. The Japanese Army is
now going to release all the prisoners of war and internees here on its own accord. 2. We are assigned to another duty and shall be here no more. 3. You are at
liberty to act and live as free persons, but you must be
aware of probable dangers if you go out. 4. We shall
leave here foodstuffs, medicines and other necessities of
which you may avail yourselves for the time being. 5.
We have arranged to put up signboard at the front gate,
bearing the following context:—Lawfully released Prisoners of War and Internees are quartered here. Please do
not molest them unless they make positive resistance."

February 5, 1945. I was awakened by feminine shrieks of delight 22
and men's cries of "Hooray!" Little Walter came rushing in calling to his mother, "Mummie, Come, Come! Do you want to see
a real live Marine? They are here!" I was too worn down to go
out and join the crowd, so I just rested there letting the tears
run down and listening to the American boys' voices—Southern,
Western, Eastern accents—with bursts of laughter from our internees—laughter free and joyous with a note in it not heard in
three years. I drifted into peaceful oblivion, wakening later amid
mosquitoes and perspiration to listen to the rat-a-tat-tats, booms,
clatter of shrapnel, explosions of ammunition dumps, seeing
scarlet glare in every direction. There is battle all around us right
up to the walls; two great armies locked in death grip. Today

we watched flames leap and roar over at the Far Eastern University building just two blocks away. It is the Japanese Intelligence and Military Police Headquarters. The building was peppered with bullet holes Sunday morning and a dead soldier is slumped out half across one windowsill of an open window.

23   Three groups were converging, all trying to get to Manila first, in terrific rivalry! They didn't expect to find us alive and were racing with time to catch us before anything happened. The officers knew that we internees and the American soldiers were in Bilibid but the enlisted men did not. They were just looking for a place to spend the night when they started breaking down the barricade at our front gate. Major Wilson and Carl and some others began to hack it down from inside and when the soldiers heard this they thought it was Nipponese inside and put their hands on their rifles all ready to mow down. They called out, "We order you to surrender!" and our men cried out, "We can't. We are American prisoners of war in here." The answer from the outside was, "The Hell you are! Not now— we're here!" And they broke the door barricade and came in laughing with relief at finding us alive and not having to shoot their way through a nest of Japanese. There were not many dry eyes among our men, who were laughing with relief too. Some of them said that Tokyo had said over the radio that they would take us out and shoot us and this started their rush to Manila for a quick rescue. It worked, for they came through ahead of expectation or communication.

24   Our old friend George was only the first—for we have seen thousands now; huge, husky men, almost overpowering in their health and energy. They have such an American look; above all, secure and well fed.

25   After hunger, saving, scrimping, worrying, no news, the only kindness shown us required to be hidden from those high up; to emerge into all kinds of news, boys heaping kindness and attention on us, food in every direction, new avenues of life opening every hour—the mental and spiritual chaos is beyond expression. Like a rush of waves, a mighty sea breaks in and we swallow huge gulps of efficiency and freedom which leave us breathless and gasping on a new shore.

Fire began to burn on Echague and we saw the Great East-   26
ern and Marco Polo hotels burst into flame, burn fiercely and
spread, spread, spread. Our forces, which by now were coming
in faster, began to dynamite buildings in an effort to stem the
conflagration. It kept coming nearer and nearer.

Gen. Fellers expressed his great admiration for the way in   27
which MacArthur has conducted operations. Three divisions
have landed in Lingayen, Zambales, and Batangas respectively.
They have all coverged on Manila, arriving within 18 hours of
each other. But for MacArthur's insistence, the present campaign in the Philippines would have been delayed for another
year. He expresses regret that he is three days behind schedule.

About 7 as dark closed over us, we groped about our ce-   28
ment space and got ready for bed, to rest after talking with anti-
tank gunners, machine-gunners and infantry boys, watching
sparks fly upwards all around us in the battle din and exploding
munition dumps. Word crept around for us to be packed and
ready to leave on a moment's notice with bedroll and handbag
only. Our weary minds staggered but we filled the zipper bag,
the duffle bag and two straw bags with change of clothes, some
food cans, several coconuts, the precious sugar bought with
topaz. In less than half an hour, we were told we were to be
moved outside the city at once. We piled our three airplane
luggage suitcases, two leather ones, two big straw sacks and the
typewriter into the middle of the space against the cement wall
(to keep the heat from reaching it!), left all the loose things
hanging on lines, hooks, and sitting on shelves as they were
and walked out into the dark lit by sparks and flames. I held
onto my bag with [diary] notes and three pieces of jewelry—
one thing always packed and portable—and we walked off without a qualm or backward look at ivories, silver, brocades and
other possessions we had saved for three years (worth about
four thousand dollars). Jerry hobbled out on crutches and the
children carried some things out with him, saying they would
come back for me who stayed with what remained to be carried.
It seemed ages that I waited and it was. Suddenly I realized it
was silent, that there was no hum of humanity. I went outside
calling June and Bedie and there was not a soul left in the prison

yard. It was the loneliest, most terrifying feeling I have ever known. A young American soldier who was left to guard heard me and came looking very anxious about my still being there. Just then the children arrived and loaded themselves down. The soldier took another bundle of bedding and we were led out through the grassy compound where we had driven in weeks ago, then through other long, walled-in compounds and buildings full of junk and cobwebs and dust, out to a street next to Rizal Avenue. We sat on our rolls and bags under the eaves of Filipino huts which had been evacuated, and the fire crept nearer and nearer, until it was only two blocks away. Army trucks and jeeps roared up, people and bags piled in and the vehicles roared off around a corner. We were all cheering and the Filipinos were calling good-bye. We were among the last as usual to pile into a light, fast ¼ ton truck and off down Rizal Avenue. The heat and glare and flame increased behind us, and we had a full view of the avenue of fire which was approaching. Nobody was nervous or upset or hysterical. The soldiers could not get over how calm we were, but it was just one more thing to most of us, and for the children it was adventure out in the wide world. All of the kids were very quiet or else cheering the soldier boys who simply adored them and lavished affection on each one. The children hung onto soldiers' hands and hero-worshipped day and night.

29   We went through dark streets during our flight from the wall of flame, in trucks and jeeps. Filipinos were grouped everywhere, cheering us and waving. Outside the city we went faster, leaving the black pillar of smoke behind us and only the red glow over us still. They said there were snipers everywhere but we did not think about it or even realize it so we were not afraid. All we could take in was that we were free. Along shell-torn and unrepaired streets, in and out we went, looking at buildings blown up in partial destruction, windows smashed everywhere, ruins in silhouette surrounding us. We finally pulled in at the model shoe factory [which] was Division Headquarters and going full tilt.

30   In the entrance hall, radio men and telephone operators were working every second. How could they hear or send any-

thing in that madhouse of noise! The stairs were crowded with men in olive drab going up and down, up and down.

As we leaned over the rail of the balcony, we could see 31 downstairs the 800 prisoners who lived on the other side of our wall. They had been taken out of Bilibid first and we had watched the never-ending line stream from their compound through ours to the back gate. First had come the stretcher cases, then those who could walk, many helping each other. It was a slow procession of sick, exhausted men, in ragged clothes, touseled hair, many unshaven faces with sores. I shall never forget that line of military prisoners wavering through the dark yard, with the glare in the sky pitilessly showing up their condition.

As we looked down from the balcony, we could see that 32 some were not so badly off and were walking around, but many were actually skin and bone. Collarbones stood out like shelves. Eyes were gaunt and hollow. Faces were drawn tight with nerves. Elbows were bony knobs. Arms and legs were literally pipe-stems. *There* was starvation and we felt that our troubles were nothing. Yet we were told that they had worried when our children cried, that they had loved the little rhythm band and the singing. There was one tall fellow who haunts my memory. He must have had a magnificent physique and handsome features once, but his ribs and all other bones stood out like a skeleton without flesh and he could not even sit up on his pallet. He just lay there with a slight smile on his face. I looked down at him many times, praying that they would bring him back to health.

Beyond, in another section, were emaciated, staring-eyed 33 mental cases, terror on their faces, unstrung nerves jangling openly. June said it made her really sick to look at them all— she couldn't bear it.

Bedie stayed up all night though we had spread our blan- 34 kets on the balcony floor. We only saw him once or twice and then he was off again. He says he made "fifteen friends"—one a Don Bell from Ohio. We let him run, for it is once in a lifetime. He was shown the inside of tanks, amphibian trucks known as Alligators or Water Buffalo or Ducks, and all sorts of new, compact marvels of American invention and efficiency in this war.

35   I watched the tanks and trucks roaring past Headquarters
on the road toward Manila, and looked at all the thousands of
trucks and jeeps and new kinds of equipment. In part of my
brain flickered two pieces from the past—a shadowy voice saying, "We had the best time of our lives in here—sorry to leave."
And again the sight of primitive carts at night flashing by on a
dark road, drawn by six men with Oriental faces straining in
fatigue, pulling these carts to meet—tanks flashing by— Where
am I? In the past? In the future? In the present? We are where
the past and future meet in combat and who will survive?

Content

1. Even though she is writing in the midst of the Battle of Manila,
Crouter concentrates on small, day-by-day details of the war rather
than on battle strategy. Why? What is the effect of this focus?
2. Crouter originally intended her diary to be a private record of her
wartime experiences and a place to express her hopes and fears. But,
as the war continued, she spent an hour or more per day on her notes,
writing on book margins, envelope backs, and other scraps of paper.
Crouter realized that the diary had become her most prized possession,
and that she was writing for an outside audience—her children and
grandchildren-to-be. How does this conception of an external audience
influence the nature and amount of information she provides? Can you,
a reader presumably unfamiliar with the situation, understand both the
situation and Natalie's attitude toward it? Why or why not?
3. Crouter's personality emerges in part through her reaction to the
soldiers, both Japanese and Americans, and to her fellow prisoners.
What kind of person is she? Is she patriotic? Does she love her family?
4. Why does she begin the January 31 entry with a discussion of food?

Strategies/Structures

1. What advantages are there in recording and interpreting events
day-by-day, as a diarist does? Are there disadvantages to this method
as well?

Language

1. At least twice in the essay Crouter uses very figurative language.
In paragraph 8 she calls the sun a "copper disk in the sky" and in

paragraph 25 she compares freedom to "a rush of waves." Do these passages add to or detract from the essay, which is generally more prosaic?

For Writing

1. Keep a diary for a week, focusing on eyewitness events memorable or simply typical of your age, occupation, area of the country, place of residence, or era.
2. Several weeks later, go back to your original diary and rewrite it so that a particular audience external to yourself will understand it. What changes have you had to make, and why?

▶───────────────────────────────────◀

TIM PAYNE

Payne was born in Hartford, Connecticut in 1959 and has lived in Annandale, Virginia since 1967. He earned a B.A. in English, Phi Beta Kappa, from the College of William and Mary in 1982, and, on a Mellon Fellowship, is currently a graduate student in English at the University of Virginia.

Payne's essay, like the other narratives in this section, uses a chronological framework to recount a sequence of events in which the narrator was a major participant. Apparently a simple action on the surface, the picking up of shells on the beach assumes a symbolic significance whose meaning Payne implies but leaves for the reader to ponder.

A year after writing the essay Payne said, "My feelings about Bar Harbor are still the same—complex, challenging, and positive. I have pried at and forced and squeezed the experience for widely scattered significance, and I have dressed it up in quickly decaying robes of nostalgia and rhetoric. But the hard fact of the place and of my time there remains, an austere but steadfast viewing point against which I can measure my changing perspective of myself."

Writers often use natural phenomena—the climate, natural settings, the weather—as "objective correlatives" of the psychological or emotional state of the characters in those settings, such as a heavy rainstorm to accompany sadness. So Payne uses the setting—and its changes—to reinforce his changing mood.

❖ *On the Beach at Bar Harbor*

1   **B**ar Harbor, Maine, arrived midway in the two week camping trip which had to serve as my summer vacation—the period for recuperation. It followed an exhausting, numbing freshman year and would precede three tedious months of summer work and a horrendously disconcerting sophomore year. Two weeks to recover from one entire year and to prepare for another call for a tight and intense schedule of rest and relaxation. Although three days into the trip I had written to myself with naive confidence and optimism, "Perhaps the experience is effecting its purpose," I was depending a lot upon the Bar Harbor experience to work some magic on me.

2   Dan and I drove into a camping area on the north side of one finger of the harbor early Thursday afternoon. Clouds immediately began to attack the sun, allowing winter to sweep in and overpower the tentative and unrooted spring warmth and the equally unrooted elation which I had stumbled into after a frightening and depressing Tuesday full of rain. After we set up camp, Dan went off to explore the beach and perhaps to seek some poetic inspiration for his next letter to Phyllis. I thought I would read to ward off the forces of depression which were hovering hungrily around my aloneness; but Holden Caulfield was himself depressed as hell, as I recall, and Mr. Thoreau was unsympathetically referring to his aloneness as solitude. So with my "intense rest" schedule's winged chariot perched heavily on my back, I decided I'd go force some uplifting significance out of the beach myself.

3   Getting *to* the beach was a little more work than I had expected, however. The beach dropped off from an untapered stretch of pine trees with the unsettling abruptness of a roller-coaster drop or of the editing in a home movie. As far as I could see, a teetering pile of rocks was the only way down to beach-level—certainly a far cry from the soliciting accessibility of the big-name beaches farther south.

I climbed down. There wasn't much sand; in its place was   4
a forbidding carpet of bruise-colored oyster shells that crackled
accusingly under my shoes. I went down closer to the water,
stepping around or between the shells when I could. The waves
in this secluded section of the harbor were uninspiring. No
pressing sense of the powerful forces of the sea greeted me or
flooded over and into me. But there *was* something unsettling
and even foreboding about the boulders scattered haphazardly
across the beach. They were left, I am told, by long-extinct glaciers which carved this land and have stood for centuries against
the tidal push and tug of the harbor, unmoved. And yet somehow, when I first saw them, they reminded me of a child's toys,
silent on the lawn, abandoned merely for the night.

It was growing cold again. The icy clouds had left, but now   5
the sun was descending and evening was blowing in. I crouched
down against my bare legs, and looked for shells. You always
have to bring home some shells from a beach, I remembered, if
there are any worth bringing. I picked up one or two small conch-
like shells and a few spiral gut pieces of other such shells—
perhaps because conch shells and even appreciable *pieces* of conch
shells are such a rare find on populous beaches, or perhaps
because these were all there were except for the mobs of oyster
shells. I carried these shells around for a while, but they soon
became heavy in my hand, like a fish which is too small. I threw
them back down on the beach, and I felt free of something but
also afraid of having gained nothing, as yet, from the beach.

Even so I was all right. The cold was not so oppressive   6
now, or perhaps I was up for it, feeling myself a bit pugnacious.
There was nothing inviting or accomodating about this beach,
and still I was all right. I was used to beaches and cities and
vacations that played for you. And you would play up to them,
and they would play some more, selling themselves. This beach
was unkempt and unpolished, colored by its stark boulders and
the clumps of green and yellow sea plants, varnished so heavily
with a lifeless brown as to look like vomit. It was indifferent,
but oddly so, almost transcendingly so, like a large animal interrupted at its bath. And this indifference whetted my com-
bative spirit, my desire to overcome and take something.

I walked along the beach and met Dan. We sat down on   7
some rocks at the water's edge. The tide was coming in, and as

it rose it reabsorbed and inspirited the vomited sea plants which, I could now see, were actually connected to what *had* been the beach and was *now* the harbor floor. And then I also spotted a *real* shell-find—whole sand dollars. No too-small fish this time. I quickly collected several of the sand dollars, but then I got selective and threw back all but the few most perfect ones. As we got up from the rocks, however, to escape being overtaken by the tide, even these felt too heavy in my hand to carry home, and I threw them back in as well. Again I felt free of something, and afraid.

8   The rising tide eventually took away all of the beach and covered the foreboding rocks, in pushing up to the foot of the steep climb that led back up to camp-level. There was a house perched on the upper level, overlooking the harbor and boldly pressing toward the edge. It too was stark, and there was a tension in its immobility, as if it were bracing itself against something, preparing for something. It seemed not to be inhabited, although it must have been, for it was well kept-up and well secured, looking out at nothing but the lapping harbor and the soft, darkening mountain on the other side. Staring out unflinchingly and intently, as the silent tide turned back out, and Dan and I turned in—I, like a certain heaviness in the hand of something.

Content

1. Why does Payne spend much of the first third of the essay explaining his depressed state upon arrival at Bar Harbor? What changes of mood does he experience on the beach?

2. Payne explains that he "was used to beaches and cities and vacations that played for you" (¶ 6). What, as a consequence, did he expect to gain from a vacation at the beach?

3. But Bar Harbor, in contrast to Payne's expectation, is "indifferent" (¶ 6). What effects does this unexpected, difficult setting have on Payne? What does he gain from the experience? Has he completely come to terms with it by the end of the essay?

4. Do you think Payne, in retrospect, considered his experience at Bar Harbor a "good" vacation? Does a vacation have to be enjoyable to be meaningful? Can a good vacation involve considerable effort, as Payne's did?

Strategies/Structures

1. In fulfillment of his belief that "You always have to bring home some shells from a beach . . . if there are any worth bringing" (¶ 5), Payne first collects pieces of conch shells (¶ 5), then whole sand dollars (¶ 7). Why does he throw them back?

2. Why does Payne present the image of the house, the only man-made structure in the entire essay, so near the end? How does he interpret it in the context of the natural setting (¶ 8)?

3. Why is Dan in the essay? If he is of some significance, why does Payne say so little about him?

4. Through what means does Payne convey his changes of attitude throughout the essay? What natural features are "objective correlatives" of his moods?

Language

1. Why at Bar Harbor does Payne think of Salinger's Holden Caulfield, depressed hero of *Catcher in the Rye*, and Henry David Thoreau's solitary stay at Walden Pond (¶ 2)?

2. Why does Payne refer to the oyster shells as "bruise colored" (¶ 4) and as occurring in "mobs" (¶ 5)? What is the effect of saying that the sea plants looked like "vomit" (¶ 6)?

3. The usual advice to writers is "Show, don't tell." Yet Payne tells the readers twice that he was "afraid" (¶s 5, 7). Does he ever *show*, through his actions or interpretation of the setting, that he is afraid? Of what is he afraid?

4. What is Payne's tone throughout the essay? Does he ever sound fearful? Is his image one of cowardice, strength, or something else?

For Writing

1. Write an essay in which you show how you encountered some unexpected aspects of a setting, natural or man-made, as Payne did at Bar Harbor, and indicate their significance or impact on you. Did they help you to mature or contribute to your self-understanding?

2. Select a symbol that has a powerful meaning for you, and write an essay in which you explain its significance, as Payne has done here with the Bar Harbor beach; and as Lai Man Lee does with her jade bracelet (pp. 295–97), and Angela Bowman does with Freddie the Fox and her black doll (pp. 470–73).

Strategies for Writing— Narration

1. You'll need to consider, "What is the purpose of my narrative?" Am I telling the tale for its own sake, or using it to make a larger point?

2. For what audience am I writing this? What will they have experienced or be able to understand, and what will I need to explain? How do I want my audience to react?

3. What is the focus, the conflict of my narrative? How will it begin? Gain momentum and develop to a climax? End? What emphasis will I give each part, or separate scenes or incidents within each part?

4. Will I write from first or third person point of view? Will I be a major character in my narrative? As a participant or as an observer? Or both, if my present self is observing my past self?

5. What is my attitude toward my material? What tone do I want to use? Will it be consistent throughout, or will it change during the course of events?

Additional Writing Topics

1. Write two versions of the earliest experience you can remember that involved some fright, danger, discovery, or excitement. Write the first version as the experience appeared to you at the time it happened. Then, write another version interpreting how the experience appears to you now.

2. Write a narrative of an experience you had that taught you a difficult lesson (see Orwell's "Shooting an Elephant," pp. 47–55). You can either make explicit the point of the lesson, or imply it through your reactions to the experience.

3. Sometimes a meaningful incident or significant relationship with someone can help us to mature, easily or painfully, as Frederick Douglass explains in "Resurrection," pp. 57–63. Tell the story of such an incident or relationship in your own life or in the life of someone you know well.

4. Have you ever witnessed an event important to history, sports, science, or some other field of endeavor? If so, tell the story either as an eyewitness, or from the point of view of someone looking back on it and more aware now of its true meaning. (See Natalie Crouter's "Release From Captivity," pp. 64–75.)

5. If you have ever been to a place that is particularly significant to you, narrate an incident, as Tim Payne does in "On the Beach at Bar Harbor," pp. 75–78, to show its significance through specific details.

6. Tell the story of a special relationship you have (or had) with another person—parent or grandparent, brother or sister, friend, spouse, teacher. ((See E.B. White, "Once More to the Lake," pp. 39–46.) You may wish to convey its essence through narrating one or two typical incidents.

7. Explain what it's like to be a typical student or employee (on an assembly line, in a restaurant or store, or elsewhere) through an account of "A Day in the Life of . . . ." If you find that life to be boring or demeaning, your narrative might be an implied protest or an argument for change.

8. Write a fairy tale or fable, a story with a moral. Make it suitable for children (but don't talk down to them) or for people of your own age.

9. Imagine you're an inanimate object (a teakettle, car, watch or other object of your choice), or an animal, bird, or plant. Tell its life history, either from its point of view or your own.

10. Imagine that you're telling a major news event of the day (or of your lifetime) to someone fifty years from now. What details will you have to include and explain to make sure your reader understands it?

3 Process Analysis

▶─────────────────────────────────◀

Analysis divides something into its component parts and explains what they are, on the assumption that it is easier to consider and to understand the subject in smaller segments than in a large, complicated whole (see Division and Classification, pp. 227–30). To analyze the human body, you could divide it into systems—skeletal, circulatory, respiratory, digestive—before identifying and defining the components of each. Of the digestive system, for instance, you would discuss the mouth, pharynx, esophagus, stomach, and large and small intestines.

You can analyze a process in the same way, focusing on *how* rather than *what*. A *directive process analysis* identifies the steps in how to make or do something: how to sail a catamaran; how to get to Kuala Lumpur; how to make pasta—as the quartet of good cooks provides varying directions for in the following selection. An *informative process analysis* can identify the stages by which something is created or formed. In the essays that follow, Rachel Carson offers an illuminating commentary on the formation of the earth in "The Grey Beginnings"; and Ann Upperco explains the comically painful process of "Learning to Drive." Or a process analysis can explain how something functions or works: Berton Roueché does this in "The Neutral Spirit: A Portrait of Alcohol."

Thus, to write an informative analysis of how the digestive system works, you could explain the process by which food is ingested, and broken down as it passes through the esophagus, stomach, and small and large intestines. The complexity of your analysis would depend on the sophistication of your audience. For general readers you might explain the peristaltic movement as "a strong, wave-like motion that forces food through the digestive tract." Medical students would require a far more detailed explanation of the same phenomenon—in far more technical language.

The following suggestions for writing an essay of process analysis are in themselves—you guessed it—a process analysis.

To write about a process, for whatever audience, you first have to *make sure you understand it yourself*. If it's a process you can perform, such as hitting a good tennis forehand or parallel parking, try it out before you begin to write, and note the steps and possible variations from start to finish.

Early on you'll need to *identify the purpose or function of the process and its likely outcome:* "How to lose twenty pounds in ten weeks." Then the steps or stages in the process occur in a given sequence; it's helpful to list them in their logical or natural order and to provide time markers so your readers will know what comes first, second, and thereafter. "First have a physical exam. Next: work out a sensible diet, under medical supervision. Then . . . ."

If the process involves many simultaneous operations, for clarity *you may need to classify all aspects of the process and discuss each one separately*. For instance, since playing the violin requires bowing with the right hand and fingering with the left, it makes sense to consider each by itself. After you've done this, however, be sure to *indicate how all of the separate elements of the process fit together*. To play the violin successfully the right hand has to know what the left hand is doing. If the process you're discussing is cyclic or circular—as in the life cycle of a plant, or the water cycle, involving evaporation, condensation, and precipitation—start with whatever seems to you most logical or most familiar to your readers.

If you're using specialized or technical language, *define your terms* unless you're writing for an audience of experts. You'll also need to *identify specialized equipment and be explicit about whatever techniques and measurements your readers need to know.* For instance, novice cooks couldn't follow Claudia Roden's directions for cooking pasta (throw freshly made pasta "into boiling salted water", see p. *86*) without knowing how much water and how much salt. Yet a complicated discussion of the differences among cheeses to add to the pasta (domestic or imported Parmesan? what brand? freshly grated or prepackaged?) might be more than inexperienced cooks could cope with, although more knowledgeable cooks might appreciate such refinements.

If sub-processes are involved in the larger process, you can either explain these where they would logically come in the sequence, or consider them in footnotes or an appendix. You don't want to sidetrack your reader from the main thrust. For instance, if you were to explain the process of Prank Day, an annual ritual at Cal Tech, you might begin with the time by which all seniors have to be out of their residence halls for the day, 8 A.M. You might then follow a typical prank through from beginning to end: the selection of a senior's parked car to disassemble; the transportation of its parts to the victim's dorm room; the reassembling of the vehicle; the victim's consternation when he encounters it in his room with the motor running. If the focus is on the process of playing the prank, you probably wouldn't want to give directions on how to disassemble and reassemble the car; to do so would require a hefty manual. But you might want to supplement your discussion with helpful hints on how to pay (or avoid paying) for the damage.

After you've finished your essay, if it explains how to perform a process, ask a friend, preferably one who's unfamiliar with the subject, to try it out. (Even people who know how to tie shoelaces can get all tangled up in murky directions.) She can tell you what's unclear, what needs to be explained more fully—and even point out where you're belaboring the obvious. If your paper is an informative analysis of a process ("How Pheromones Work"), ask your reader to tell you how well he understands what you've said. If, by the end, he's still asking you what a pheromone is, you'll know you've got to run the paper through your typewriter once again.

IRMA S. ROMBAUER AND MARION ROMBAUER BECKER,
CLAUDIA RODEN, ELIZABETH DAVID, AND MARCELLA
HAZAN

Each of these expert cooks is the author of a classic cookbook
renowned for the high quality of the food therein and the
thoughtful and imaginative instructions on how to prepare it. It
is interesting to compare the variations in the directions on the
relatively simple process of how to cook pasta, as provided by
Rombauer and Becker in *The Joy of Cooking*, Claudia Roden in
A Book of Middle Eastern Food, Elizabeth David in *A Book of
Mediterranean Food*, and Marcella Hazan in *The Classic Italian
Cookbook*.

How to Cook Pasta

IRMA S. ROMBAUER AND MARION ROMBAUER BECKER

Cooking Pastas

F reshly made pastas are an incomparable treat. Noodles are 1
those most frequently made in the home, as they do not
require the difficult-to-purchase high-gluten flours that other
pasta forms demand.

Because pasta shapes are so variable we give the weight 2
rather than the volume for amounts to be cooked. And at meals
where pasta is the predominant ingredient of the main dish, the
individual serving is more generous than the usual meat or vegetable serving, so we allow ¼ pound of dry pasta per serving.

All pastas should be added gradually to a large quantity 3
of rapidly boiling water so that the boiling is not disturbed. As
in the cooking of all cereals, it is essential that the outer surfaces
be penetrated as quickly as possible. This requires a kettle large
enough to accommodate about 7 quarts of rapidly boiling water

for a pound of pasta. Add 1 tablespoon salt and 1 tablespoon olive oil. The dry material softens as it is gradually lowered into continuously boiling water, until all the pasta floats free. No matter which pasta you are cooking, do not overcook. The timing can be gauged only by tasting—not once, but several times. If the noodles are very thin or freshly made, a few minutes suffice. The perfect state any Italian recognizes as *al dente* is reached when no taste of raw flour remains and the pasta still offers slight resistance to the bite. Thick forms of commercial pastas with uncertain shelf histories may need cooking as long as 15 or 20 minutes. When the *al dente* state is reached, remove the pasta from the water with a pasta scoop and let the pasta drip-dry momentarily over the pot before releasing it into a large warm buttered bowl or spooning it with a pasta server. When all the pasta is drained and tossed in butter, portion it into hot bowls; served thus without a sauce, it is called *al burro*. Pass the grated cheese.

CLAUDIA RODEN

Rishta/Fresh Noodles

> *Recipes for* rishta, *an Italian-type pasta, appeared in the early Arab manuscripts. The word itself means "thread" in Persian. Today pastas of all kinds are becoming increasingly popular all over the Middle East.*

1 F ive minutes before they [freshly made noodles] are to be served, throw them into boiling salted water and simmer for about 5 minutes, stirring occasionally to prevent them from sticking to the pan.

2   Drain and serve immediately with salt, pepper, and a generous amount of butter.

This pasta is similar to Italian tagliatelli, but commercial dried varieties will require longer cooking, usually at least 10
3 minutes.

ELIZABETH DAVID

To Cook Spaghetti

B uy imported Italian spaghetti.   1
Do not break it up unless you want it to turn to a pudding.   2
Allow approximately 3 ozs. of spaghetti per person; use a very
large saucepan, at least 8 pints capacity for a half pound. Have
the water well salted and boiling rapidly. The time of cooking
varies between 10 and 20 minutes according to the quality of the
spaghetti. Have a heated dish, preferably one which will bear a
flame underneath, to receive the cooked *pasta*, with a coating of
good olive oil on the bottom.

Put the drained spaghetti into this receptacle and stir it   3
round, much as you would toss a salad, for a minute or two,
so that the whole mass receives a coating of oil and assumes an
attractive shiny appearance instead of the porridgy mass too
often seen.

Lastly, if you are serving the classic spaghetti *Bolognese*,   4
that is, with a thick tomato and mushroom sauce, see that it is
highly flavored, of a suitable thickness, and *plentiful*, accompanied by a generous dish of grated cheese.

MARCELLA HAZAN

How to Cook Pasta

T here is probably no single cooking process in any of the   1
world's cuisines simpler than the boiling of pasta. This
very simplicity appears to have had an unsettling effect on some
writers, to judge from the curiously elaborate and often mis-
leading procedures described in many Italian cook books. One
book tells you to drop pasta into boiling water a little bit at a
time. Another counsels you to lift it painstakingly strand by
strand when draining it. A third suggests you can keep pasta
warm in a 200° oven until you are ready to sauce it. Ah, pasta,

what sins have been committed in thy name! Here is the way it is really done.

2   **Water**   It is important to cook pasta in abundant water, but it is not necessary to drown it. Italians calculate 1 liter of water per 100 grams of pasta. This works out to slightly more than 4 quarts for 1 pound of pasta. Stick to just 4 quarts of water for every pound of pasta. It will be quite sufficient.

3   **Salt**   When the water comes to a boil, add 1½ heaping table-spoons of salt for every 4 quarts of water. If the sauce you are going to be using is very bland, you may put in an additional ½ tablespoon of salt.

4   **When and how to put in the pasta**   Put in the pasta when the salted water has come to a rapid boil. Add all the pasta at once. When you put it in a little at a time, it cannot all cook evenly. If you are cooking long pasta, such as spaghetti or *perciatelli*, after dropping it in the pot you must bend it in the middle with a wooden spoon to force the strands entirely under water. Never, never break spaghetti in two. Stir the pasta with a wooden spoon to keep it from sticking together. Cover the pot after you put in the pasta to accelerate the water's return to a boil. Watch it, lest it boil over. When it returns to a boil, uncover, and cook at a lively but not too fierce a boil, until it is *al dente.*

5   **Al dente**   *Al dente* means "firm to the bite," and that is how Italians eat pasta. Unfortunately, they are the only ones who do. Of course, it is not easy to switch to firm pasta when one is used to having it soft and mushy, and it is very tempting to ingratiate oneself with one's readers by not pressing the issue. The whole point of pasta, however, is its texture and consistency, and overcooking destroys these. Soft pasta is no more fit to eat than a limp and soggy slice of bread.

6   In the course of civilization's long and erratic march, no other discovery has done more than, or possibly as much as, pasta has to promote man's happiness. It is therefore well worth learning how to turn it out at its best.

7   No foolproof cooking times can be given, but you can begin by ignoring those on the box. They are invariably excessive.

There are so many variables, such as the type and make of pasta, the hardness and quantity of water, the heat source, even the altitude (it is impossible to make good pasta at over 4,500 feet above sea level), that the only dependable procedure is to taste the pasta frequently while it boils. As soon as pasta begins to lose its stiffness and becomes just tender enough so that you can bite through without snapping it, it is done. You should try at first to stop the cooking when you think the pasta is still a little underdone. Do not be afraid to stop too early. It is probably already overcooked, and, in any case, it will continue to soften until it is served. Once you have learned to cook and eat pasta *al dente*, you'll accept it no other way.

Draining, saucing, and serving pasta   The instant pasta is done 8 you must stop its cooking and drain it. Adding a glass of cold water to the pot as you turn off the heat is helpful, but it is not necessary if you are very quick about emptying the pot into the pasta colander. Give the colander a few vigorous sideways and up-and-down jerks to drain the pasta of all its water. Transfer the pasta without delay to a warm serving bowl. If grated cheese is called for, add it at this point and mix it into the pasta. The pasta's heat will melt it partially so that it will blend creamily with the sauce. Add the sauce and toss the pasta rapidly with two forks or a fork and spoon, coating it thoroughly with sauce. Add a thick pat of butter, unless you are using a sauce dominated by olive oil, toss briefly, and bring to the table immediately, serving it in warm soup plates. *Note:* There are two important points to remember in this whole operation:

1. The instant pasta is done, drain it, sauce it, and serve it with the briefest interval possible, because pasta continues to soften at every stage from the colander to the table.

2. Sauce the pasta thoroughly, but avoid prolonged tossings and exaggerated liftings of strands into the air, because there is one thing worse than soft pasta and that is cold pasta.

Content

1. Each set of directions explains the process of how to cook pasta from start to finish, yet some directions are far more detailed than others. What are the essential steps in the process? What additional

information do these extra details present? For what purposes is it included?

2. Some of the explanations supplied are very precise, as in Rombauer and Becker's explanation of how to recognize when the pasta is *al dente* (¶ 3) and in Hazan's discussion of the same point (¶s 5, 7). Other directions are less precise. Can you tell what Roden means by "A *generous* amount of butter" (¶ 3), or David by spaghetti sauce that it "*highly* flavored, of a *suitable* thickness, and *plentiful* . . ." (¶ 4)?

3. Do all the instructions of these expert cooks agree on the essentials? If there are discrepancies, are these due to the absence of details, or to actual differences of opinion on the process of how to cook pasta?

Strategies/Structures

1. Could the process of how to cook pasta be organized in any way other than step-by-step? If so, in what other ways? If not, why not?

2. Which set of directions is intended for the most experienced cook? Which for the least experienced? How can you tell? How does your answer relate to your own experience in cooking pasta?

3. Which of these explanations of a process is most interesting to read? Why? Which is least interesting?

Language

1. Each author includes foreign terms in these recipes. What do each of the following mean: *al dente, al burro, Bolognese, rishta?*

2. Based on language choice, which recipe most clearly encourages the preparation of pasta in a truly Italian style? Give examples of language use that support your choice.

For Writing

1. Provide directions on how to do something you know how to do well, such as water ski, make pizza, or play a violin, for an audience unfamiliar with your subject. Identify the steps in the order in which they occur, and define unfamiliar terms, as necessary, when you come to them.

2. Provide directions on how to do something you know well for an audience that knows a great deal about the subject, such as how to write a particular computer program; how to make pie crust; how to make a jump shot, or hit a good tennis backhand.

BERTON ROUECHÉ

Roueché (b. 1911), a distinguished staff writer on *The New Yorker*, began his journalistic career in 1934 as a reporter for the *Kansas City Star*. He has received many awards for his medical writing, including honors from the Lasker Foundation, the American Medical Association, and the American Medical Writers Association. Many of his *New Yorker* articles and other writings have been collected in such books as *Eleven Blue Men, and Other Narratives of Medical Detection* (1953); *Curiosities of Medicine: An Assembly of Medical Diversions, 1552–1962* (1963), and *The Neutral Spirit: A Portrait of Alcohol* (1960), from which the following chapter is taken. In the course of explaining the process of alcohol absorption into the body, Roueché also conveys his attitude about excessive drinking.

The Neutral Spirit: A Portrait of Alcohol

M uch of the misbelief with which emotion has fantasied alcohol derives from a cloudy conception of its general metabolism. No aspect of its nature, however, is more nearly transparent, and none has been so well established for so many years. A rough but accurate description of the way the body disposes of alcohol has been on conspicuous record since the second quarter of the nineteenth century.

It was inscribed there in 1842 by the prodigious German chemist Justus von Liebig (whose other triumphs include the discovery of chloroform, the detection of the importance of protein substances, and, with Friedrich Wöhler, the creation of modern physiological chemistry). Prior to that time, as the American encyclopedist Ernest Hurst Cherrington has noted, it was universally assumed that "alcohol leaves the body unchanged through the lungs, skin, and kidneys, that within the organism it is neither transformed nor destroyed, [and] that it is ejected from the body in its original form and condition." Von Liebig demolished this traditional supposition with a series of definitive experiments, which he crisply summarized in *Die Tierchemie oder Organische Chemie in Ihrer Anwendung auf Physiologie und Pathologie*, the most monumental of his many monumental works. "According to all observations made," he reported, "there is no trace of alcohol in the breath, in the sweat, or in the urine after the consumption of alcoholic liquors." He then, just as crisply, proclaimed the truth of the matter. The process involved, he wrote, was the familiar physiological phenomenon known as oxidation. "There can be no doubt that alcohol's constituent elements have become fused with oxygen in the body, that its carbon and hydrogen leave the body as carbonic acid [carbon dioxide and water]." This being the case, he added, it was possible, if not desirable, to consider alcohol a food, for oxidation is invariably accompanied by the release of heat and energy. Subsequent investigators have found it necessary to correct von Liebig's elucidation in only one detail. It is not quite true that alcohol undergoes a total combustion in the body. A variable fraction (from two to possibly ten per cent) escapes through the lungs, the kidneys, and the skin as unaltered alcohol.

3   The susceptibility of ethyl (or beverage) alcohol to oxidation is probably its most distinctive trait. For one thing, it makes ethyl alcohol, alone among the many alcohols, a generally acceptable beverage. Contrary to common conviction, ethyl alcohol is not inherently the least toxic of alcohols. It is merely the least intractably toxic. The other alcohols, being all but incombustible, can, at best, be broken down and expelled from the body only after long and racking physiological exertion. They thus tend inevitably to accumulate in the blood stream, and when ingested in more than small amounts, they swiftly reach an unwieldy concentration. "A man who drinks, say, a pint of whisky in one day has no ethyl alcohol left in his body the next day," the late Howard W. Haggard, director of the Laboratory of Applied Physiology at Yale, noted, "but a man who drinks this amount of methyl [or wood] alcohol does not get rid of it completely for perhaps a week. He not only has a long period of intoxication, but if he drinks [again] within the week, he [places himself] in great danger." The danger includes blindness, for one of the oxidation products of methyl alcohol is formic acid (the protec-

tive venom of ants), which has the power to destroy the optic nerve. Ethyl alcohol's ready oxidation also distinguishes it from the majority of other foods, including all fats and proteins and most carbohydrates. Their molecular structure is too complex for immediate combustibility. They must first be radically re-modeled by prolonged (from one to several hours) immersion in the various digestive acids and enzyme catalysts that are secreted for that purpose in the mouth, the stomach, and the small intestine. Only then can their essential elements be assimilated into the body. Alcohol needs no such preparation. It is as naturally assimilable as water.

Most foods are absorbed into the body from the small in- 4 testine. So, it seems probable, are the many essential salts and minerals. Even water, though almost incomparably diffusible, is confined to a single entrance. It can be assimilated solely through the walls of the large intestine. Alcohol is more versatile. Although the small intestine constitutes its principal port of entry, it can also be absorbed directly from the stomach, through the rectum (by enema), and, most remarkably, through the lungs (by inhalation). The fact that alcohol can be absorbed from the stomach is sometimes assumed to explain its galvanic initial impact. This assumption, though superficially plausible, is just the reverse of the truth. The amount of alcohol that is assimilated into the body through the walls of the stomach is relatively small, being hardly twenty per cent of the total quantity ingested. Moreover, its passage, while metronomically regular, is lethargically slow, and the principles of diffusion that control the process are largely impervious to interference.

This ability of the stomach to circumspectly admit alcohol 5 directly into the body would thus appear to be a defensive mechanism. It has, at any rate, the effect of protecting the body from a paralyzing inundation. A further safeguard is the valvular link between the stomach and the small intestine known as the pyloric sphincter. The pyloric sphincter has as its primary purpose the retention of food in the stomach until the digestive action that takes place there is complete, but it also tends to trip and close at the repeated touch of any irritating substance. Alcohol can create such a spasm. The maximum movement of alcohol through the pylorus occurs with the first drink. With the second, the rate abruptly decreases. If that is soon followed by a third, the controlling mechanism comes fully into play, and the flow into the small intestine is practically halted; the alcohol thus trapped in the stomach is eventually released at a rate determined by a complexity of forces. Unlike the stomach, the small intestine is incapable of exercising any control over the absorption of alcohol. Absorption there is rapid, constant, and complete. It continues without remission until all alcohol has been eliminated from the gastrointestinal tract.

6   Among the various factors that variously influence the rate of alcohol absorption by the stomach and the small intestine, the speed with which it is drunk is of crucial importance. Although the absorption of alcohol directly from the stomach is almost flawlessly controlled, the effect on the body of a quick succession of highly alcoholic drinks (whiskey, gin, rum, brandy) is often swift and shattering. It can, as barroom athletes are occasionally inspired to demonstrate, be fatal. One conclusive demonstration occurred in Chicago in 1954. A commuter informed a group of friends in a tavern there that he could drink seventeen dry Martinis in something less than one hour. He did, but as he emptied the final glass, he toppled off his stool. He was dead when he hit the floor. (That he chose to prove his strength with dry Martinis is, of course, irrelevant. Despite the almost mystical awe in which the Martini is commonly held, it is not an intoxicating drink of unique powers. Alcohol, and alcohol alone, is what produces intoxication. The other elements that are present in, or added to, alcoholic drinks contribute only flavor, aroma, and color. A Martini is no more, and no less, intoxicating than any other drink that contains the same amount of alcohol. If the number and variety of spirits in a drink increased its power to intoxicate, the most potent drink in the bartender's manual would be, perhaps, a pousse-café. The supposed brute virility of the Martini lies not in the glass but in the conditioned mind of the drinker.) More recently, on Christmas Day, 1958, a seven-year-old New Jersey boy slipped back to the dining room after a family dinner, emptied a bottle containing about ten ounces of wine, went into convulsions, and died within an hour.

The chief deterrent to the prompt absorption of alcohol is   7
food. Eating while drinking perceptibly slows absorption, and
the effect of even several drinks can be substantially retarded if
they are soon followed by a meal. (In a recent monograph, *The
Neurology of Alcoholism,* J.M. Nielsen, clinical professor of neurology at the University of California at Los Angeles, describes
a drinking bout he witnessed in a neighboring bar between two
alcoholics. "The wager stated that he who first became unable
to stand would pay the bill," he reports. "One of the contestants
ordered the bartender to put a raw egg into each drink; the other
protested, but in vain, and took his 'straight.' The man who
took the eggs won and was able to walk home, while the other
became helpless.") In general, the larger the meal, the more
slowly absorption proceeds. Quantity is not, however, the only
factor involved. Some foods are much more effective than others
in hobbling both alcohol's absorption from the stomach and its
passage through the pylorus. Milk is perhaps the most widely
celebrated member of this group, but its inhibitory powers are
equaled by butter, cheese, meat, eggs—in fact, by all foods rich
in protein. For protein, being the most chemically complicated
of foods, lingers longest in the stomach, and alcohol caught in
its deliberate embrace is held there until the completion of the
digestive process.

Water is also capable of perceptibly delaying alcohol aborp-   8
tion. When taken with or just after a drink, it notably blunts its
thrust. As a rule—though one to which there are striking exceptions—it is the concentration of alcohol in a drink that determines the rate of absorption. An ounce or two of whiskey
well diluted with water, as in a conventional highball, is absorbed less rapidly than the same amount poured over ice. This
would seem to suggest (and did for many years to many investigators) that alcohol is absorbed most quickly in its least diluted
form. But such, paradoxically, is not the case. Absorption is most
rapid when the alcohol is diluted to a concentration of between
ten and thirty-five per cent. "Concentrations of alcohol of fifty
per cent (a hundred proof) or greater exert a depressant effect
on absorption," Harold E. Himwich, director of research at the
Galesburg State Research Hospital, in Illinois, has recently noted.

"[They produce] a sort of local narcosis. In addition, high concentrations are irritating to the mucosa and evoke the secretion of mucus, which also delays absorption."

9   Another factor that has a bearing on absorption is the nature of the dilutent. Milk (as in eggnog), tomato juice (as in the Bloody Mary cocktail), melted butter (as in hot buttered rum), and other liquids rich in food substances are firmer curbs than water. Soda water, on the other hand, quickens the absorption rate, because carbon dioxide, which forms the effervescent essence of all animated beverages, sweeps imperiously through the stomach, and alcohol caught up in its rush is flung directly into the small intestine. It is this vivacious element that gives champagne and sparkling burgundy the headiness that distinguishes them from sedentary wines.

Content

1. According to Roueché's essay, what are the biochemical causes of drunkenness?
2. What commonly-held opinions about drinking (¶s 2–4) does Roueché's essay dispute? Are his explanations convincing?
3. What is the nature of Roueché's illustrations and examples? Given the wealth of research and literature on the subject, why has Roueché chosen these particular ones?
4. Would this essay be appropriate for a person to read who was just beginning to drink alcoholic beverages? Why or why not? Would it be suitable for a more experienced drinker?

Strategies/Structures

1. Why does Roueché begin his essay with an older, inaccurate explanation of the impact of alcohol on the body before he provides the scientific evidence that "proclaimed the truth of the matter" (¶ 2)?
2. Roueché's essay begins with the more unfamiliar technical aspects of alcohol absorption (¶s 2–7); and concludes with a more familiar analysis of the nature and effects of diluting alcoholic beverages (¶s 8–9). Since writers are usually advised to begin with familiar matters before moving to the unfamiliar, what justifies the reversal of the more common pattern here?
3. Scientific writing is often presumed to be neutral, and value-free. Is this true of Roueché's essay? Does he believe alcohol is truly a "neu-

tral spirit," as his title states? If the title is ironic, what evidence from the essay leads to this interpretation?

Language

1. Roueché uses the metaphor "barroom athletes" (¶ 6). What does this connote? How do his illustrations reinforce the implication that much drinking is competitive? Do you agree with this interpretation?

2. If you need to, consult an up-to-date college or scientific dictionary for the meanings of metabolism (¶ 1), oxidation (2), combustion (2), ethyl alcohol (3), methyl alcohol (3), assimilate (3), inhibitory (7).

For Writing

1. Write an essay focusing on a particular experience someone you know well or you yourself have had with alcohol—either a single incident or several episodes over time. You yourself need not have been drinking.

2. Other aspects of living, including diet, cures for particular diseases, exercise, and sex, are also susceptible to various misconceptions. Select one aspect of one of these subjects, and after explaining the phenomenon, such as the drinking man's diet or laetrile as a cure for cancer, analyze one or more of its shortcomings: "the cancer diet is inadequate because. . . ." After that, provide an accurate interpretation of the phenomenon.

RACHEL CARSON

Rachel Carson (1907–1964) was the naturalist daughter of a mother who, she said, embodied Albert Schweitzer's " 'reverence for life' more than anyone I know." She earned a bachelor's degree in biology from the Pennsylvania College for Women in 1929, and a master's degree in biology from John Hopkins in 1932. Carson was a publications editor for the U.S. Fish and Wildlife Service from 1936 until her National Book Award-winning *The Sea Around Us* (1951) earned enough royalties to enable her to write full time.

Her first book, *Under the Sea Wind: A Naturalist's Picture of Ocean Life* (1941), launched her reputation "as a rigorous scientist who wrote with flair and beauty." This reputation was confirmed by her later works, including *The Edge of the Sea* (1955) and the controversial *Silent Spring* (1962), an indictment of the harmful use of chemical pesticides which "prompted the federal government to take action against water and air pollution, as well as against persistent pesticides." With keen poetic awareness, Carson's writings combine a thorough understanding of scientific literature with firsthand observations of the minutiae of natural life on sea and shore. Her evocative style of writing about scientific phenomena is apparent in "The Grey Beginnings" below. This portion of *The Sea Around Us* presents her interpretation of the process by which the world began, the seas were formed, and life evolved from a single-celled speck to fish to mammals to mankind, who despite high intelligence and domination of the land, can return to "mother sea only on her own terms."

The Grey Beginnings

And the earth was without form, and void; and darkness was upon the face of the deep.

GENESIS

1   Beginnings are apt to be shadowy, and so it is with the beginnings of that great mother of life, the sea. Many people have debated how and when the earth got its ocean, and it is not surprising that their explanations do not always agree. For the plain and inescapable truth is that no one was there to see, and in the absence of eyewitness accounts there is bound to be a certain amount of disagreement. So if I tell here the story of how the young planet Earth acquired an ocean, it must be a story pieced together from many sources and containing whole chapters the details of which we can only imagine. The story is founded on the testimony of the earth's most ancient rocks, which were young when the earth was young; on other evidence written on the face of the earth's satellite, the moon; and on

hints contained in the history of the sun and the whole universe
of star-filled space. For although no man was there to witness
this cosmic birth, the stars and the moon and the rocks were
there, and, indeed, had much to do with the fact that there is
an ocean.

The events of which I write must have occurred somewhat   2
more than 2 billion years ago. As nearly as science can tell that
is the approximate age of the earth, and the ocean must be very
nearly as old. It is possible now to discover the age of the rocks
that compose the crust of the earth by measuring the rate of
decay of the radioactive materials they contain. The oldest rocks
found anywhere on earth—in Manitoba—are about 2.3 billion
years old. Allowing 100 million years or so for the cooling of the
earth's materials to form a rocky crust, we arrive at the supposition that the tempestuous and violent events connected with
our planet's birth occurred nearly 2½ billion years ago. But this
is only a minimum estimate, for rocks indicating an even greater
age may be found at any time.

The new earth, freshly torn from its parent sun, was a ball   3
of whirling gases, intensely hot, rushing through the black spaces
of the universe on a path and at a speed controlled by immense
forces. Gradually the ball of flaming gases cooled. The gases
began to liquefy, and Earth became a molten mass. The materials
of this mass eventually became sorted out in a definite pattern:
the heaviest in the center, the less heavy surrounding them, and
the least heavy forming the outer rim. This is the pattern which
persists today—a central sphere of molten iron, very nearly as
hot as it was 2 billion years ago, an intermediate sphere of semi-
plastic basalt, and a hard outer shell, relatively quite thin and
composed of solid basalt and granite.

The outer shell of the young earth must have been a good   4
many millions of years changing from the liquid to the solid
state, and it is believed that, before this change was completed,
an event of the greatest importance took place—the formation
of the moon. The next time you stand on a beach at night,
watching the moon's bright path across the water, and conscious
of the moon-drawn tides, remember that the moon itself may
have been born of a great tidal wave of earthly substance, torn
off into space. And remember that if the moon was formed in

this fashion, the event may have had much to do with shaping the ocean basins and the continents as we know them.

5   There were tides in the new earth, long before there was an ocean. In response to the pull of the sun the molten liquids of the earth's whole surface rose in tides that rolled unhindered around the globe and only gradually slackened and diminished as the earthly shell cooled, congealed, and hardened. Those who believe that the moon is a child of earth say that during an early stage of the earth's development something happened that caused this rolling, viscid tide to gather speed and momentum and to rise to unimaginable heights. Apparently the force that created these greatest tides the earth has ever known was the force of resonance, for at this time the period of the solar tides had come to approach, then equal, the period of the free oscillation of the liquid earth. And so every sun tide was given increased momentum by the push of the earth's oscillation, and each of the twice-daily tides was larger than the one before it. Physicists have calculated that, after 500 years of such monstrous, steadily increasing tides, those on the side toward the sun became too high for stability, and a great wave was torn away and hurled into space. But immediately, of course, the newly created satellite became subject to physical laws that sent it spinning in an orbit of its own about the earth. This is what we call the moon.

6   There are reasons for believing that this event took place after the earth's crust had become slightly hardened, instead of during its partly liquid state. There is to this day a great scar on the surface of the globe. This scar or depression holds the Pacific Ocean. According to some geophysicists, the floor of the Pacific is composed of basalt, the substance of the earth's middle layer, while all other oceans are floored with a thin layer of granite, which makes up most of the earth's outer layer. We immediately wonder what became of the Pacific's granite covering and the most convenient assumption is that it was torn away when the moon was formed. There is supporting evidence. The mean density of the moon is much less than that of the earth (3.3 compared with 5.5), suggesting that the moon took away none of the earth's heavy iron core, but that it is composed only of the granite and some of the basalt of the outer layers.

The birth of the moon probably helped shape other regions 7
of the world ocean besides the Pacific. When part of the crust
was torn away, strains must have been set up in the remaining
granite envelope. Perhaps the granite mass cracked open on the
side opposite the moon scar. Perhaps, as the earth spun on its
axis and rushed on its orbit through space, the cracks widened
and the masses of granite began to drift apart, moving over a
tarry, slowly hardening layer of basalt. Gradually the outer portions of the basalt layer became solid and the wandering continents came to rest, frozen into place with oceans between them.
In spite of theories to the contrary, the weight of geologic evidence seems to be that the locations of the major ocean basins
and the major continental land masses are today much the same
as they have been since a very early period of the earth's history.

But this is to anticipate the story, for when the moon was 8
born there was no ocean. The gradually cooling earth was en-
veloped in heavy layers of cloud, which contained much of the
water of the new planet. For a long time its surface was so hot
that no moisture could fall without immediately being recon-
verted to steam. This dense, perpetually renewed cloud covering
must have been thick enough that no rays of sunlight could
penetrate it. And so the rough outlines of the continents and
the empty ocean basins were sculptured out of the surface of
the earth in darkness, in a Stygian world of heated rock and
swirling clouds and gloom.

As soon as the earth's crust cooled enough, the rains began 9
to fall. Never have there been such rains since that time. They
fell continuously, day and night, days passing into months, into
years, into centuries. They poured into the waiting ocean basins,
or, falling upon the continental masses, drained away to become
sea.

That primeval ocean, growing in bulk as the rains slowly 10
filled its basins, must have been only faintly salt. But the falling
rains were the symbol of the dissolution of the continents. From
the moment the rains began to fall, the lands began to be worn
away and carried to the sea. It is an endless, inexorable process
that has never stopped—the dissolving of the rocks, the leaching
out of their contained minerals, the carrying of the rock frag-

ments and dissolved minerals to the ocean. And over the eons of time, the sea has grown ever more bitter with the salt of the continents.

11   In what manner the sea produced the mysterious and wonderful stuff called protoplasm we cannot say. In its warm, dimly lit waters the unknown conditions of temperature and pressure and saltiness must have been the critical ones for the creation of life from nonlife. At any rate they produced the result that neither the alchemists with their crucibles nor modern scientists in their laboratories have been able to achieve.

12   Before the first living cell was created, there may have been many trials and failures. It seems probable that, within the warm saltiness of the primeval sea, certain organic substances were fashioned from carbon dioxide, sulphur, nitrogen, phosphorus, potassium, and calcium. Perhaps these were transition steps from which the complex molecules of protoplasm arose—molecules that somehow acquired the ability to reproduce themselves and begin the endless stream of life. But at present no one is wise enough to be sure.

13   Those first living things may have been simple microorganisms rather like some of the bacteria we know today—mysterious borderline forms that were not quite plants, not quite animals, barely over the intangible line that separates the nonliving from the living. It is doubtful that this first life possessed the substance chlorophyll, with which plants in sunlight transform lifeless chemicals into the living stuff of their tissues. Little sunshine could enter their dim world, penetrating the cloud banks from which fell the endless rains. Probably the sea's first children lived on the organic substances then present in the ocean waters, or, like the iron and sulphur bacteria that exist today, lived directly on inorganic food.

14   All the while the cloud cover was thinning, the darkness of the nights alternated with palely illumined days, and finally the sun for the first time shone through upon the sea. By this time some of the living things that floated in the sea must have developed the magic of chlorophyll. Now they were able to take the carbon dioxide of the air and the water of the sea and of these elements, in sunlight, build the organic substances they needed. So the first true plants came into being.

Another group of organisms, lacking the chlorophyll but   15
needing organic food, found they could make a way of life for
themselves by devouring the plants. So the first animals arose,
and from that day to this, every animal in the world has followed
the habit it learned in the ancient seas and depends, directly or
through complex food chains, on the plants for food and life.

As the years passed, and the centuries, and the millions   16
of years, the stream of life grew more and more complex. From
simple, one-celled creatures, others that were aggregations of
specialized cells arose, and then creatures with organs for feeding, digesting, breathing, reproducing. Sponges grew on the
rocky bottom of the sea's edge and coral animals built their
habitations in warm, clear waters. Jellyfish swam and drifted in
the sea. Worms evolved, and starfish, and hard-shelled creatures
with many-jointed legs, the arthropods. The plants, too, progressed, from the microscopic algae to branched and curiously
fruiting seaweeds that swayed with the tides and were plucked
from the coastal rocks by the surf and cast adrift.

During all this time the continents had no life. There was   17
little to induce living things to come ashore, forsaking their all-
providing, all-embracing mother sea. The lands must have been
bleak and hostile beyond the power of words to describe. Imagine a whole continent of naked rock, across which no covering
mantle of green had been drawn—a continent without soil, for
there were no land plants to aid in its formation and bind it to
the rocks with their roots. Imagine a land of stone, a silent land,
except for the sound of the rains and winds that swept across
it. For there was no living voice, and no living thing moved over
the surface of the rocks.

Meanwhile, the gradual cooling of the planet, which had   18
first given the earth its hard granite crust, was progressing into
its deeper layers; and as the interior slowly cooled and contracted, it drew away from the outer shell. This shell, accom-
modating itself to the shrinking sphere within it, fell into folds
and wrinkles—the earth's first mountain ranges.

Geologists tell us that there must have been at least two   19
periods of mountain building (often called "revolutions") in that
dim period, so long ago that the rocks have no record of it, so
long ago that the mountains themselves have long since been

worn away. Then there came a third great period of upheaval and readjustment of the earth's crust, about a billion years ago, but of all its majestic mountains the only reminders today are the Laurentian hills of eastern Canada, and a great shield of granite over the flat country around Hudson Bay.

20   The epochs of mountain building only served to speed up the processes of erosion by which the continents were worn down and their crumbling rock and contained minerals returned to the sea. The uplifted masses of the mountains were prey to the bitter cold of the upper atmosphere and under the attacks of frost and snow and ice the rocks cracked and crumbled away. The rains beat with greater violence upon the slopes of the hills and carried away the substance of the mountains in torrential streams. There was still no plant covering to modify and resist the power of the rains.

21   And in the sea, life continued to evolve. The earliest forms have left no fossils by which we can identify them. Probably they were soft-bodied, with no hard parts that could be preserved. Then, too, the rock layers formed in those early days have since been so altered by enormous heat and pressure, under the foldings of the earth's crust, than any fossil they might have contained would have been destroyed.

22   For the past 500 million years, however, the rocks have preserved the fossil record. By the dawn of the Cambrian period, when the history of living things was first inscribed on rock pages, life in the sea had progressed so far that all the main groups of backboneless or invertebrate animals had been developed. But there were no animals with backbones, no insects or spiders, and still no plant or animal had been evolved that was capable of venturing onto the forbidding land. So for more than three-fourths of geologic time the continents were desolate and uninhabited, while the sea prepared the life that was later to invade them and make them habitable. Meanwhile, with violent tremblings of the earth and with the fire and smoke of roaring volcanoes, mountains rose and wore away, glaciers moved to and fro over the earth, and the sea crept over the continents and again receded.

23   It was not until Silurian time, some 350 million years ago, that the first pioneer of land life crept out on the shore. It was an arthropod, one of the great tribe that later produced crabs

and lobsters and insects. It must have been something like a modern scorpion, but, unlike some of its descendants, it never wholly severed the ties that united it to the sea. It lived a strange life, half-terrestrial, half-aquatic, something like that of the ghost crabs that speed along the beaches today, now and then dashing into the surf to moisten their gills.

Fish, tapered of body and stream-molded by the press of running waters, were evolving in Silurian rivers. In times of drought, in the drying pools and lagoons, the shortage of oxygen forced them to develop swim bladders for the storage of air. One form that possessed an air-breathing lung was able to survive the dry period by burying itself in mud, leaving a passage to the surface through which it breathed. 24

It is very doubtful that the animals alone would have succeeded in colonizing the land, for only the plants had the power to bring about the first amelioration of its harsh conditions. They helped make soil of the crumbling rocks, they held back the soil from the rains that would have swept it away, and little by little they softened and subdued the bare rock, the lifeless desert. We know very little about the first land plants, but they must have been closely related to some of the larger seaweeds that had learned to live in the coastal shallows, developing strengthened stems and grasping, rootlike holdfasts to resist the drag and pull of the waves. Perhaps it was in some coastal lowlands, periodically drained and flooded, that some such plants found it possible to survive, though separated from the sea. This also seems to have taken place in the Silurian period. 25

The mountains that had been thrown up by the Laurentian revolution gradually wore away, and as the sediments were washed from their summits and deposited on the lowlands, great areas of the continents sank under the load. The seas crept out of their basins and spread over the lands. Life fared well and was exceedingly abundant in those shallow, sunlit seas. But with the later retreat of the ocean water into the deeper basins, many creatures must have been left stranded in shallow, landlocked bays. Some of these animals found means to survive on land. The lakes, the shores of the rivers, and the coastal swamps of those days were the testing grounds in which plants and animals either became adapted to the new conditions or perished. 26

As the lands rose and the seas receded, a strange fishlike 27 creature emerged on the land, and over the thousands of years its fins became legs, and instead of gills it developed lungs. In the Devonian sandstone this first amphibian left its footprint.

28   On land and sea the stream of life poured on. New forms evolved; some old ones declined and disappeared. On land the mosses and the ferns and the seed plants developed. The reptiles for a time dominated the earth, gigantic, grotesque, and terrifying. Birds learned to live and move in the ocean of air. The first small mammals lurked inconspicuously in hidden crannies of the earth as though in fear of the reptiles.

29   When they went ashore the animals that took up a land life carried with them a part of the sea in their bodies, a heritage which they passed on to their children and which even today links each land animal with its origin in the ancient sea. Fish, amphibian, and reptile, warm-blooded bird and mammal—each of us carries in our veins a salty stream in which the elements sodium, potassium, and calcium are combined in almost the same proportions as in sea water. This is our inheritance from the day untold millions of years ago, when a remote ancestor, having progressed from the one-celled to the many-celled stage, first developed a circulatory system in which the fluid was merely the water of the sea. In the same way, our lime-hardened skeletons are a heritage from the calcium-rich ocean of Cambrian time. Even the protoplasm that streams within each cell of our bodies has the chemical structure impressed upon all living matter when the first simple creatures were brought forth in the ancient sea. And as life itself began in the sea, so each of us begins his individual life in a miniature ocean within his mother's womb, and in the stages of his embryonic development repeats the steps by which his race evolved, from gill-breathing inhabitants of a water world to creatures able to live on land.

30   Some of the land animals later returned to the ocean. After perhaps 50 million years of land life, a number of reptiles entered the sea about 170 million years ago, in the Triassic period. They were huge and formidable creatures. Some had oarlike limbs by which they rowed through the water; some were web-footed, with long, serpentine necks. These grotesque monsters disappeared millions of years ago, but we remember them when we come upon a large sea turtle swimming many miles at sea, its

barnacle-encrusted shell eloquent of its marine life. Much later, perhaps no more than 50 million years ago, some of the mammals, too, abandoned a land life for the ocean. Their descendants are the sea lions, seals, sea elephants, and whales of today.

Among the land mammals there was a race of creatures 31 that took to an arboreal existence. Their hands underwent remarkable development, becoming skilled in manipulating and examining objects, and along with this skill came a superior brain power that compensated for what these comparatively small mammals lacked in strength. At last, perhaps somewhere in the vast interior of Asia, they descended from the trees and became again terrestrial. The past million years have seen their transformation into beings with the body and brain of man.

Eventually man, too, found his way back to the sea. Standing on its shores, he must have looked out upon it with wonder and curiosity, compounded with an unconscious recognition of his lineage. He could not physically re-enter the ocean as the seals and whales had done. But over the centuries, with all the skill and ingenuity and reasoning powers of his mind, he has sought to explore and investigate even its most remote parts, so that he might re-enter it mentally and imaginatively.

He built boats to venture out on its surface. Later he found 33 ways to descend to the shallow parts of its floor, carrying with him the air that, as a land mammal long unaccustomed to aquatic life, he needed to breathe. Moving in fascination over the deep sea he could not enter, he found ways to probe its depths, he let down nets to capture its life, he invented mechanical eyes and ears that could re-create for his senses a world long lost, but a world that, in the deepest part of his subconscious mind, he had never wholly forgotten.

And yet he has returned to his mother sea only on her 34 own terms. He cannot control or change the ocean as, in his brief tenancy of earth, he has subdued and plundered the continents. In the artificial world of his cities and towns, he often forgets the true nature of his planet and the long vistas of its history, in which the existence of the race of men has occupied a mere moment of time. The sense of all these things comes to him most clearly in the course of a long ocean voyage, when he watches day after day the receding rim of the horizon, ridged and furrowed by waves; when at night he becomes aware of the earth's rotation as the stars pass overhead; or when, alone in this world of water and sky, he feels the loneliness of his earth in space. And then, as never on land, he knows the truth that his world is a water world, a planet dominated by its covering mantle of ocean, in which the continents are but transient intrusions of land above the surface of the all-encircling sea.

Content

1. Given the fact that Carson must use considerable speculation to explain evolution from the "shadowy" beginnings to man's domination of land (¶ 1), what are the most convincing sorts of evidence she presents throughout the essay to make her case? Would such evidence convince a creationist (one who believes that God created the Earth all at once)? Why or why not?

2. How much scientific background do Carson's readers need to be able to understand her explanation? Since 1951, when Carson wrote *The Sea Around Us*, new evidence has been discovered that suggests that the continents and oceans moved considerably during their formative periods. Does this undermine or otherwise affect the status of Carson's explanation?

Strategies/Structures

1. Why is it appropriate for Carson to organize her subject chronologically, although in paragraphs 4–18 some of the events she describes occur simultaneously. What words, phrases, and information does she provide to help readers keep the time sequences clearly in mind?

2. What would Carson's essay have lost had she proceeded in reverse chronological order, from contemporary times to most ancient, from the most complex forms of life to the simplest to the shadowy beginnings?

3. Carson's vivid descriptions enable her readers to visualize what she says. Identify some of these descriptions. How can Carson, or any writer, be so precise about phenomena she has never seen?

Language

1. On which of the following terms would a dictionary help? Which are defined in Carson's text: congealed (¶ 5), viscid (5), resonance (5), oscillation (5), Stygian from Styx (8), leaching (10), chlorophyll (14), organic (14), food chains (15), terrestrial (23), protoplasm (29)?

2. Although scientists are encouraged to write objectively, the fac
Carson is not objective toward her subject is one of her most conspicuous assets. In paragraph 34, for instance, she discusses human reverence for the sea, and it is clear there and throughout that she shares
this reverence. Identify some of Carson's interpretive language and
figures of speech that convey her attitude toward her subject.

3. Carson's verbs, active and varied, contribute to the impression of
dynamic, unceasing activity in the evolutionary process. Locate some
of these verbs and explain why they are effective.

For Writing

1. In paragraph 29 Carson explains our marine heritage in terms of
an analogy, "as life itself began in the sea, so each of us begins his
individual life in a miniature ocean within his mother's womb. . . ."
Write an essay in which you use an extended metaphor or analogy to
explain some phenomenon of science or human society. (Examples:
"The heart is like a pump. . . ."; "Students are like cattle, branded
with ID numbers. . . .")

Or analyze the controlling metaphor in a play, film, or work of
literature to show how it symbolizes and parallels the condition of, or
relationships among, the characters to which it pertains. (Examples:
The boxing ring in the "Rocky" movies as analogous to life's hardships;
The Doll's House as a title for Ibsen's play about a woman captive to her
husband's wishes.)

2. Write an essay in which you analyze the process of something with
which you are familiar to provide information for readers who are not.
For instance, you could analyze a child's typical development and maturation during one significant segment of his or her life, perhaps the
first month, or the first year, of elementary school or high school. Or
you could explain the life cycle of a particular species of plant or animal—ferns, bees, your pet dog.

ANN UPPERCO

Ann Upperco (b. 1960) grew up in Arlington, Virginia, and
majored in religion at the College of William and Mary (B.A.,
1982). There she worked on the college yearbook and was
inducted into the Society for Collegiate Journalists. Cur-

)yed in the Chicago office of a Mennonite agency,
:es to "a life of travel and adventure."
had been a highly anxious writer, procrastinating
ods of time and then spending miserable, long
; to grind out a paper in time to meet a deadline.
n writing "Learning to Drive," she explains, "I
wrote i. ̣ one sitting, then revised it. I think this method of
sitting down and writing something and then going back to revise is what enabled me to get over my fear of writing." She
says of the genesis of the essay, "I had originally intended to
write a series of vignettes on the individual driving styles of
each member of my family, which would have been amusing.
But the more I thought about it, the more comfortable I felt
with the idea of poking fun at myself rather than my family.
. . . Writing this essay was almost fun."

In writing specifically about her own process of learning
to drive, Upperco has captured a universal set of experiences
participated in by a set of universal figures, comical to contemplate from the safe distance of time, however painful the trau-
mas of a new driver may have been when they occurred. The
tense, skittish novice driver is counterpointed against the patient teacher, her reassuring father, with the nervous figure of
her mother hovering uneasily in the background.

❖ *Learning to Drive*

1   G reater love hath no man for his children than to teach them
how to drive. As soon as I turned 15 years and 8 months—
the requisite age for obtaining a learner's permit—my father took
me around our neighborhood to let me get a feel for the huge
Chevrolet we own. The quiet, tree-shaded, narrow streets of the
neighborhood witnessed the blunders of yet another new driver:
too-wide (or too-narrow) turns; sudden screeching halts (those
power brakes take some getting used to); defoliation of low-
hanging trees by the radio antenna or the car too close to the
curb; driving on the wrong side of the street to avoid the parked
cars on the right side.

2   Through it all my father murmured words of advice and
encouragement, drawing on a seemingly bottomless well of pa-

tience which I never before knew he possessed. One day while driving on the highway, I drifted dangerously close to a car in the lane to my right, almost scraping the shiny chrome strip right off its side. Dad looked nonchalantly into the terrified face of the other driver—a mere six inches away—then turned back to me and said, "You might want to steer to the left a bit; you're just a little close on this side." A mile further down the road, Dad chuckled and said, "I think you gave that poor lady a scare—her eyes were as big as golfballs!" Here was he, not only unperturbed, but actually amused by the whole incident while I watched my whole life pass before my eyes.

Not long after this incident I had another near miss, this time while intentionally changing lanes. I still was not accustomed to using the rearview mirror, so Dad had told me to glance over my shoulder to make sure all was clear. Being right-handed, I automatically looked over my right shoulder, and not seeing anything, proceeded to veer left. Not until I almost plowed into another car did I realize that when turning left, I needed to glance over my left shoulder to avoid causing a wreck. Despite the danger, Dad stuck it out, continuing to give me tips to improve my driving.

Confident now of my driving prowess, I cajoled my parents into letting me drive every chance I got. Dad usually sat up front with me, to the relief of Mom, an uneasy driver herself whose nerves were still recovering from my brother's driving apprenticeship two years earlier. This arrangement suited me perfectly; Mom's behavior in the front seat tended to make me a trifle nervous. Gripping the dashboard as if it would fall off if she let go, and frequently pressing to the floor the non-existent brake on her side of the car, Mom would periodically utter spine-chilling gasps at the slightest provocation—none of which increased my newly-won confidence behind the wheel. Whether Dad never suffered from such a case of jitters or whether he merely hid it better, I'm not sure. But whatever the reasons, he managed to remain calm, at least outwardly, when riding with me.

When I had mastered (in a manner of speaking) the skill of driving our full-size, power-steering, power-brake tank, Dad proceeded to show me the secrets of operating the small, standard-shift rattle-trap-of-a-Pinto which adorned the curb in front of our house. Had I known at the time the humiliation and tribulation I'd have to endure at the wheel of that car, I'm not sure I would have embarked as willingly on the adventure. But Dad, glutton for punishment that he is, knew what was in store; as he buckled his seat belt he braced both feet against the floor and said, "Okay, let's give it a try." For at least an hour, I lurched up and down our driveway, trying to get a feel for "slipping the clutch." (Poor Dad didn't realize I hardly even knew which was the clutch, much less what "slipping" it entailed.) After one particularly violent jolt that almost sent us through the garage door, Dad decided to let me try taking the car around the block. Ostensibly, he wanted me to practice driving in all four gears, though I really think he was more concerned about the fate of the garage door than anything else.

6   Once out on the street (after a bristly encounter with the forsythia bush which unfortunately stood at the end of the driveway), I embarrassed myself completely. To keep from stalling, I'd rev the engine while I tried to slip the clutch. I couldn't even pretend to be a racing driver; the car didn't have the decency to sound like a high-powered race car, it just roared like an outraged lion with a thorn in its paw. Feeling conspicuous about making all this noise, I let the clutch out too soon, which either stalled the car, or, worse still, made it jerk down the street like a bucking bronco. The poor car looked like a see-saw with the front end first taking a nose-dive while the rear-end flew up, then leaping into the air as the rear end came back down. Jolting around the block with tires screeching and rubber burning, I provided my neighbors with the best free entertainment they'd seen in a long time, since the days when my brother was learning how to drive that beastly little car.

7   With this display of ineptitude, I tumbled from the pedestal of special privilege which a driver's permit had given me; once again the kids too young to drive regarded me as simply the klutz I was. Good ol' Dad stuck by me through the ignominy of it all, assuring me that everybody who learned to drive a stick-shift underwent the same ordeal. It still amazes me that with all that lurching around, he was willing to go with me again.

8   Now that I have several years' experience behind me, I actually enjoy driving—especially driving a stick-shift. I'll often

take to the road to relax, emptying my mind by concentrating on the mechanics of driving. Had it not been for Dad's patient, calm perseverance, I might still be the public menace today that I was three years ago. As for Dad, he lucked out—I'm the last kid in the family.

Content

1. Could one learn how to drive—or how not to drive—from reading this essay? If not, what is its point?
2. What is the point of the last paragraph? What impact does the fact that not only did Upperco learn to drive but to enjoy it have on the rest of the essay?
3. Why is this essay funny? Does Upperco expect her readers to laugh at her attempts to learn to drive? Why should close escapes from accidents provoke laughter instead of terrified relief?

Strategies/Structures

1. What determines the organization of this essay?
2. How can you tell that Upperco is writing from the perspective of someone who has mastered the skill of driving, rather than from the viewpoint of a learner? What effect has this on the tone of the essay?
3. Much of Upperco's humor is visual. What comic scenes does she create and how does she help readers to see them?

Language

1. What does Upperco's terminology reveal about her intended readers? Are they experienced drivers? Novices? Unable to drive at all?
2. At what point in the essay do you know that it's humorous? Are readers supposed to laugh *with* the new driver, or *at* her?
3. Find some instances where Upperco uses overstated language, understated language, and slang to enhance the humor. What is the effect of the occasional direct quotation of Mr. Upperco's comments (¶s 2, 5)?
4. What is the effect of mixing fairly formal language—for instance, "requisite age," "witnessed," "defoliation," (¶ 1)—with informal language—"get a feel for" (¶ 1), "klutz," "good ol' Dad," (¶ 7)?

For Writing

1. Write an essay in which you explain the process by which you learned or are still learning to do something fairly complicated. You can write it either (1) to explain to your readers how to do the same thing or (2) to entertain your readers by showing, as Upperco does, the amusing pitfalls of the learning process.

2. Write a narrative essay in which you at your present age and level of maturity are narrating an incident in which you at a younger age and a different level of maturity are one of the principal characters. You may use this dual characterization and split point of view as the basis for humor, if you wish.

Strategies for Writing—
Process Analysis

1. Is the purpose of your essay to provide directions—a step-by-step explanation of how to do or make something? Or is the essay's purpose informative, to explain how something happens or works? Do you known your subject well enough to explain it clearly and accurately?

2. If you're providing directions, how much does your audience already know about how to perform the process? Should you start with definitions of basic terms ("sauté," dado") and explanations of sub-processes, or can you focus on the main process at hand? Should you simplify the process for a naive audience, or are your readers sophisticated enough to understand its complexities? Likewise, if you're providing an informative explanation, where will you start? How complicated will your explanation become? The assumed expertise of your audience will help determine your answers.

3. Have you presented the process in logical or chronological sequence (first, second, third. . .)? Have you furnished an overview so that your readers will have the outcome (or desired results) and major aspects of the process in mind before they immerse themselves in the particulars of the individual steps?

4. Does your language fit both the subject, however general or technical, and the audience? Do you use technical terms when necessary? Which of these do you need to define or explain for your intended readers?

5. What tone will you use in your essay? A serious or matter-of-fact tone will indicate that you're treating your subject "straight." An ironic, exaggerated, or understated tone will indicate that you're treating it humorously.

Additional Writing Topics

1. Write an essay in which you provide directions on how to perform a process—how to do or make something at which you are particularly skilled. In addition to the essential steps, you may wish to explain your own special technique or strategy that makes your method unique or better. Some possible subjects (which may be narrowed or adapted as you and your instructor wish) are:

   a. How to play a particular computer game
   b. How to play chess or bridge
   c. How to scuba dive, hang glide, rappel

d. How to make a good first impression (on a propective employer, on a date, on your date's parents)
e. How to study for a test
f. How to be happy
g. How to build a basic library of books, tapes, or records
h. How to lose (or gain) weight
i. How to shop at a garage sale or secondhand store
j. How to repair your own car
k. How to live cheaply (but enjoyably)
l. How to rope a calf, drive a tractor, ride a horse
m. How to administer first aid for choking, drowning, burns, or some other medical emergency
n. How to get rich
o. Anything else you know that others might want to learn

2. Write an informative essay in which you explain how one of the following occurs or works. Although you should pick a subject you know something about, you may need to supplement your information by consulting outside sources.

a. How I made a major decision (to be—or not to be—a member of a particular profession, to practice a particular religion or lifestyle. . .)
b. How a computer (or amplifier, piano, microwave oven, or other machine) works
c. How a solar heating system works
d. How a professional develops skill in his or her chosen field; i.e., how one becomes a skilled electrical engineer, geologist, chef, tennis coach, surgeon . . . ; pick a field you're interested in
e. How birds fly (or learn to fly), or some other process in the natural world
f. How a system of the body (circulatory, digestive, respiratory, skeletal, neurological) works
g. How the earth (or the solar system) was formed
h. How the scientific method (or a particular variation of it) functions
i. How a well-run business (pick one of your choice—manufacturing, restaurant, clothing or hardware store, television repair service . . .) functions
j. How advertisers appeal to prospective customers
k. How our federal government (or your particular local or state government) came into existence, or has changed over time
l. How a particular drug or other medicine was developed
m. How a great idea (on the nature of love, justice, truth, beauty. . .) found acceptance

n. How a particular culture (ethnic, regional, tribal) or sub-culture (preppies, pacifists, punk rockers, motorcycle gangs . . .) developed

3. Write a humorous paper explaining a process of the kind identified below. You will need to provide a serious analysis of the method you propose, even though the subject itself is intended to be amusing. (You can treat any of the above topics humorously if you're so inclined.)

a. How to get good grades without actually studying
b. How to be popular
c. How to survive in college
d. How to withstand an unhappy love affair
e. How to be a model babysitter/son/daughter/student/employee/ lover/spouse/parent
f. How to become a celebrity

4 Cause and Effect

Writers concerned with cause and effect relationships ask *"Why did something happen?,"* or *"What* are its consequences?," or both. Why did the United States develop as a democracy, rather than as some other form of government? What have the effects of this form of government been on its population? Or you, as a writer, may choose to examine a chain reaction in which, like a Rube Goldberg cartoon device, Cause *A* produces Effect *B* which in turn causes *C* which produces Effect *D:* Peer pressure (Cause *A*) causes young men to drink to excess (Effect *B*), which causes them to drive unsafely (Cause *C*, a corollary of Effect *B*) and results in high accident rates in unmarried males under 25 (Effect *D*).

Although process analysis also deals with events or phenomena in sequence, that's concerned with the *how* rather than the *why.* To focus on the process of drinking and driving would be to explain, as an accident report might, how Al C. O'Hall became intoxicated (he drank seventeen beers and a bourbon chaser in two hours at the Dun Inn); how he then roared off at ninety miles an hour, lost control of his lightweight sportscar on a curve, and plowed into an oncoming sedan.

Two conditions have to be met to prove a given cause:

> *B* cannot occur without *A.*
> Whenever *A* occurs, *B* must also occur.

Thus a biologist who observed, repeatedly, that photosynthesis occurred in green plants (*B*) whenever a light source was present (*A*), and that it only occurred under this condition could infer that light causes photosynthesis. This would be the immediate cause. The more *remote* or *ultimate cause* might be the source of the light if it were natural (the sun). Artificial light (electricity) would have a yet more remote cause, such as water or nuclear power.

But don't be misled by a coincidental time sequence. Just because *A* preceded *B* in time doesn't necessarily mean that *A* caused *B*. Although it may appear to rain every time you wash your car, the carwash doesn't cause the rain. To blame the carwash would be an example of the *post hoc, ergo propter hoc* fallacy (Latin for "after this, therefore because of this").

Indeed, in cause and effect papers ultimate causes may be of greater significance than immediate ones, especially when you're considering social, political, or psychological causes rather than exclusively physical phenomena. Looking for possible causes from multiple perspectives is a good way to develop ideas to write on. It's also a sure way to avoid oversimplification, attributing a single cause to an effect that results from several. Thus if you wanted to probe the causes of Al C. O'Hall's excessive drinking, looking at the phenomenon from the following perspectives would give you considerable breadth for discussion:

Perspective	*Reason (Attributed cause)*
Al, a 20-year-old, unmarried male:	"Because I like the taste."
Al's best friend:	"Because he thinks drinking is cool."
Al's mother:	"Because Al wants to defy me."
Al's father:	"Because Al wants to be my pal."
Physician:	"Because Al is addicted to alcohol. There's a strong probability that this is hereditary."
Sociologist:	"Because 79.2% of American males 21 and under drink at least once a week. It's a social

Perspective	Reason (Attributed Cause)
	trend encouraged by peer pressure."
Criminologist:	"Because Al derives anti-social pleasure from breaking the law."
Brewer or distiller:	"Because of my heavy advertising campaign."

All of these explanations may be partly right; none—not even the genetic explanation—is in itself sufficient. (Even if Al were genetically predisposed to alcoholism as the child of an alcoholic parent, he'd have to drink to become an alcoholic.) Taken together they, and perhaps still other explanations, can be considered the complex cause of Al's behavior. To write a paper on the subject, using Al as a case in point, you might decide to discuss all the causes. Or you might concentrate on the most important causes and weed out those that seem irrelevant or less significant. Or, to handle a large, complex subject in a short paper you could limit your discussion to a particular cause or type of causes, say, the social or the psychological. You have the same options for selectivity in discussing multiple effects.

The essays that follow treat cause and effect in a variety of ways. In "Who's Afraid of Math, and Why?" Sheila Tobias painstakingly examines a great many possible causes of the fact that girls are far more fearful of math and math-related activities than boys are. Tobias rules out some causes (notably, genetic) and offers a possible solution to overcoming the social and psychological pressures that cause the problem. In "On Magic in Medicine," Lewis Thomas provides a brilliant analysis of the *post hoc* fallacy to demonstrate flaws in the argument that most illnesses today are attributable to "two great arrays of causative mechanisms: (1) the influence of things in the environment, and (2) one's personal life-style." At times, he claims, the effects are confused with the causes; and he shows the consequences of the erroneous notion that "you can live on and on if only you will eat breakfast and play tennis." Robert Jastrow's "Man of Wisdom" explores the significant cause and effect sequence that culminated in the development of human intelligence. And Jennifer McBride's "The Rock Fantasy" emphasizes the effects of rock stars on their teenage audience.

A paper of cause and effect analysis requires you, as a thoughtful and careful writer, to know your subject well enough to avoid oversimplification, and to shore up your analysis with specific, convincing details. You won't be expected to explain all the causes or effects of a particular phenomenon: that might be impossible for most humans, even the experts. But you can do a sufficiently thorough job with your chosen segment of the subject to satisfy yourself and convince your readers. Why? Because. . . .

◀──▶

SHEILA TOBIAS

> Tobias was born in 1935 in Brooklyn, educated at Radcliffe
> College (A.B., 1957) and Columbia University (A.M., 1962; M.
> Phil. History, 1974), is a member of Phi Beta Kappa, a former
> Woodrow Wilson Fellow, and a founding member of the Na-
> tional Organization for Women. She worked as a journalist for
> ABC, CBS, and National Educational Television in New York
> from 1963 to 1967. Switching to academia, she became an ad-
> ministrative assistant at Cornell from 1967 to 1970, and was
> Associate Provost at Wesleyan University from 1970 to 1978,
> where she currently serves as an educational advisor. Tobias is
> well known for her work in women's studies and efforts in
> achieving educational and occupational equality for women and
> minorities. Her research on the occupations of women led her
> to realize that few women were in scientific and technical fields
> because they lacked the necessary training in mathematics, and
> led to her book on *Overcoming Math Anxiety* (1978). As the se-
> lection from that book reveals below, there are many reasons
> why people fear math, and why women are more likely than
> men to have these anxieties.

Who's Afraid of Math, and Why?

1   The first thing people remember about failing at math is that it felt like sudden death. Whether the incident occurred while learning "word problems" in sixth grade, coping with equations in high school, or first confronting calculus and statistics in college, failure came suddenly and in a very frightening way. An idea or a new operation was not just difficult, it was impossible! And, instead of asking questions or taking the lesson slowly, most people remember having had the feeling that they would never go any further in mathematics. If we assume that the curriculum was reasonable, and that the new idea was but the next in a series of learnable concepts, the feeling of utter

defeat was simply not rational; yet "math anxious" college students and adults have revealed that no matter how much the teacher reassured them, they could not overcome that feeling.

A common myth about the nature of mathematical ability 2 holds that one either has or does not have a mathematical mind. Mathematical imagination and an intuitive grasp of mathematical principles may well be needed to do advanced research, but why should people who can do college-level work in other subjects not be able to do college-level math as well? Rates of learning may vary. Competency under time pressure may differ. Certainly low self-esteem will get in the way. But where is the evidence that a student needs a "mathematical mind" in order to succeed at learning math?

Consider the effects of this mythology. Since only a few 3 people are supposed to have this mathematical mind, part of what makes us so passive in the face of our difficulties in learning mathematics is that we suspect all the while we may not be one of "them," and we spend our time waiting to find out when our nonmathematical minds will be exposed. Since our limit will eventually be reached, we see no point in being methodical or in attending to detail. We are grateful when we survive fractions, word problems, or geometry. If that certain moment of failure hasn't struck yet, it is only temporarily postponed.

Parents, especially parents of girls, often expect their chil- 4 dren to be nonmathematical. Parents are either poor at math and had their own sudden-death experiences, or, if math came easily for them, they do not know how it feels to be slow. In either case, they unwittingly foster the idea that a mathematical mind is something one either has or does not have.

Although fear of math is not a purely female phenomenon, 5 girls tend to drop out of math sooner than boys, and adult women experience an aversion to math and math-related activities that is akin to anxiety. A 1972 survey of the amount of high school mathematics taken by incoming freshmen at Berkeley revealed that while 57 percent of the boys had taken four years of high school math, only 8 percent of the girls had had the same amount of preparation. Without four years of high school math, students at Berkeley, and at most other colleges and universities, are ineligible for the calculus sequence, unlikely to attempt chemistry or physics, and inadequately prepared for statistics and economics.

6   Unable to elect these entry-level courses, the remaining 92 percent of the girls will be limited, presumably, to the career choises that are considered feminine: the humanities, guidance and counseling, elementary school teaching, foreign languages, and the fine arts.

7   Boys and girls may be born alike with respect to math, but certain sex differences in performance emerge early according to several respected studies, and these differences remain through adulthood. They are:

1. Girls compute better than boys (elementary school and on).
2. Boys solve word problems better than girls (from age thirteen on).
3. Boys take more math than girls (from age sixteen on).
4. Girls learn to hate math sooner and possibly for different reasons.

8   Why the differences in performance? One reason is the amount of math learned and used at play. Another may be the difference in male-female maturation. If girls do better than boys at all elementary school tasks, then they may compute better for no other reason that that arithmetic is part of the elementary school curriculum. As boys and girls grow older, girls become, under pressure, academically less competitive. Thus, the falling off of girls' math performance between ages ten and fifteen may be because:

1. Math gets harder in each successive year and requires more work and commitment.
2. Both boys and girls are pressured, beginning at age ten, not to excel in areas designated by society to be outside their sex-role domains.
3. Thus girls have a good excuse to avoid the painful struggle with math; boys don't.

9   Such a model may explain girls' lower achievement in math overall, but why should girls even younger than ten have difficulty in problem-solving? In her review of the research on sex differences, psychologist Eleanor Maccoby noted that girls are

generally more conforming, more suggestible, and more dependent upon the opinion of others than boys (all learned, not innate, behaviors). Being so, they may not be as willing to take risks or to think for themselves, two behaviors that are necessary in solving problems. Indeed, in one test of third-graders, girls were found to be not nearly as willing to estimate, to make judgments about "possible right answers," or to work with systems they had never seen before. Their very success at doing what is expected of them up to that time seems to get in the way of their doing something new.

If readiness to do word problems, to take one example, is 10 as much a function of readiness to take risks as it is of "reasoning ability," then mathematics performance certainly requires more than memory, computation, and reasoning. The differences in math performance between boys and girls—no matter how consistently those differences show up—cannot be attributed simply to differences in innate ability.

Still, if one were to ask the victims themselves, they would 11 probably disagree: they would say their problems with math have to do with the way they are "wired." They feel they are somehow missing something—one ability or several—that other people have. Although women want to believe they are not mentally inferior to men, many fear that, where math is concerned, they really are. Thus, we have to consider seriously whether mathematical ability has a biological basis, not only because a number of researchers believe this to be so, but because a number of victims agree with them.

The search for some biological basis for math ability or 12 disability is fraught with logical and experimental difficulties. Since not all math underachievers are women, and not all women are mathematics-avoidant, poor performance in math is unlikely to be due to some genetic or hormonal difference between the sexes. Moreover, no amount of research so far has unearthed a "mathematical competency" in some tangible, measurable substance within the body. Since "masculinity" cannot be injected into women to test whether or not it improves their mathematics, the theories that attribute such ability to genes or hormones must depend for their proof on circumstantial evidence. So long as about 7 percent of the Ph.D.'s in mathematics are earned by women, we have to conclude either that these women have genes, hormones, and brain organization different from those of the rest of us, or that certain positive experiences in their lives have largely undone the negative fact that they are female, or both.

13   Genetically, the only difference between males and females (albeit a significant and pervasive one) is the presence of two chromosomes designated X in every female cell. Normal males exhibit an X-Y combination. Because some kinds of mental retardation are associated with sex-chromosomal anomalies, a number of researchers have sought a converse linkage between specific abilities and the presence or absence of the second X. But the linkage between genetics and mathematics is not supported by conclusive evidence.

14   Since intensified hormonal activity commences at adolescence, a time during which girls seem to lose interest in mathematics, much more has been made of the unequal amounts in females and males of the sex-linked hormones androgen and estrogen. Biological researchers have linked estrogen—the female hormone—with "simple repetitive tasks" and androgen—the male hormone—with "complex restructuring tasks." The assumption here is not only that such specific talents are biologically based (probably undemonstrable) but also that one cannot be good at *both* repetitive and restructuring kinds of assignments.

15   The fact that many girls tend to lose interest in math at the age they reach puberty (junior high school) suggests that puberty might in some sense cause girls to fall behind in math. Several explanations come to mind: the influence of hormones, more intensified sex-role socialization, or some extracurricular learning experience exclusive to boys of that age.

16   One group of seventh-graders in a private school in New England gave a clue as to what children themselves think about all of this. When asked why girls do as well as boys in math until the sixth grade, while sixth-grade boys do better from that point on, the girls responded: "Oh, that's easy. After sixth grade, we have to do real math." The answer to why "real math" should be considered to be "for boys" and not "for girls" can be found not in the realm of biology but only in the realm of ideology of sex differences.

Parents, peers, and teachers forgive a girl when she does 17 badly in math at school, encouraging her to do well in other subjects instead. " 'There, there,' my mother used to say when I failed at math," one woman says. "But I got a talking-to when I did badly in French." Lynn Fox, who directs a program for mathematically gifted junior high boys and girls on the campus of Johns Hopkins University, has trouble recruiting girls and keeping them in her program. Some parents prevent their daughters from participating altogether for fear that excellence in math will make them too different. The girls themselves are often reluctant to continue with mathematics, Fox reports, because they fear social ostracism.

Where do these associations come from? 18

The association of masculinity with mathematics some- 19 times extends from the discipline to those who practice it. Students, asked on a questionnaire what characteristics they associate with a mathematician (as contrasted with a "writer"), selected terms such as rational, cautious, wise, and responsible. The writer, on the other hand, in addition to being seen as individualistic and independent, was also described as warm, interested in people, and altogether more compatible with a feminine ideal.

As a result of this psychological conditioning, a young 20 woman may consider math and math-related fields to be inimical to femininity. In an interesting study of West German teenagers, Erika Schildkamp-Kuendiger found that girls who identified themselves with the feminine ideal underachieved in mathematics, that is, did less well than would have been expected of them based on general intelligence and performance in other subjects.

Not all the skills that are necessary for learning mathe- 21 matics are learned in school. Measuring, computing, and manipulating objects that have dimensions and dynamic properties of their own are part of the everyday life of children. Children who miss out on these experiences may not be well primed for math in school.

Feminists have complained for a long time that playing 22 with dolls is one way of convincing impressionable little girls that they may only be mothers or housewives—or, as in the case of the Barbie doll, "pinup girls"—when they grow up. But doll-playing may have even more serious consequences for little girls than that. Do girls find out about gravity and distance and shapes and sizes playing with dolls? Probably not.

23   A curious boy, if his parents are tolerant, will have taken apart a number of household and play objects by the time he is ten, and, if his parents are lucky, he may even have put them back together again. In all of this he is learning things that will be useful in physics and math. Taking parts out that have to go back in requires some examination of form. Building something that stays up or at least stays put for some time involves working with structure.

24   Sports is another source of math-related concepts for children which tends to favor boys. Getting to first base on a not very well hit grounder is a lesson in time, speed, and distance. Intercepting a football thrown through the air requires some rapid intuitive eye calculations based on the ball's direction, speed, and trajectory. Since physics is partly concerned with velocities, trajectories, and collisions of objects, much of the math taught to prepare a student for physics deals with relationships and formulas that can be used to express motion and acceleration.

25   What, then, can we conclude about mathematics and sex? If math anxiety is in part the result of math avoidance, why not require girls to take as much math as they can possibly master? If being the only girl in "trig" is the reason so many women drop math at the end of high school, why not provide psychological counseling and support for those young women who wish to go on? Since ability in mathematics is considered by many to be unfeminine, perhaps fear of success, more than any bodily or mental dysfunction, may interfere with girls' ability to learn math.

Content

1. Does Tobias convincingly dispel what she calls "a common myth about the nature of mathematical ability" (¶ 2)—"that one either does or does not have a mathematical mind"? Have you or others whom you know ever been the victims of this myth?

2. What, according to Tobias, are the causes of the myth identified in paragraph 2? What are the effects?

3. In support of her claim in paragraph 10 that "the differences in math performance between boys and girls . . . cannot be attributed simply to differences in innate ability," Tobias offers evidence from research in biology (¶ 12–14), psychology (¶ 17–20), and the typical life experiences of boys and girls (¶ 21–25). Are some elements of the evidence more convincing than others? Why or why not?

Strategies/Structures

1. Does one have to know math to understand this essay? Is Tobias addressing primarily readers who are afraid of math? What, if anything, does she do to put such readers at ease?
2. Has Tobias successfully overcome the resistance anxious or indifferent readers might have to the subject of math anxiety? If so, through what means? If not, why not?

Language

1. What is a myth? Does Tobias's definition of the "myth about the nature of mathematical ability" (¶ 2) illustrate the general characteristics of the term?
2. How does Tobias define the concept of an underachiever in math (¶ 9)? Feminists (¶ 22)? Is either a value-free definition? Should it be?

For Writing

1. As Tobias demonstrates, when parents expect their children, especially girls, to be non-mathematical, the children often turn out to live up (or down) to such an expectation. This is an example of a self-fulfilling prophecy. Identify, describe, and explain another self-fulfilling prophecy that you have observed in your own life or elsewhere in society, and identify drawbacks. For example, to what extent do children become high or low achievers because they are expected to? With what consequences?
2. Present a portrait of a typical victim of math anxiety, yourself or someone you know well. Explain two or three of the causes and effects of this problem, noting where your analysis corroborates or differs from Tobias's explanation.
3. (or combine with above) Write an essay showing steps parents and/or teachers can take to give children the confidence and competence to do math. Should such adults treat girls any differently than boys?

▶───◀

LEWIS THOMAS

> Thomas (b. 1913), a physician and medical researcher, lives in
> his native New York, where he is currently president of the
> Memorial Sloan-Kettering Cancer Center. An alumnus of
> Princeton (1933) and the Harvard Medical School (1937), he
> taught at the University of Minnesota Medical School and at
> the New York University Bellevue Medical Center, and was a
> dean of the Yale University Medical School. Essays from Thom-
> as's monthly column in the *New England Journal of Medicine*
> have been collected in two volumes, *The Lives of a Cell: Notes of a
> Biology Watcher* (winner of the 1975 National Book Award) and
> *The Medusa and the Snail: More Notes of a Biology Watcher* (1979).
> *The Youngest Science: Notes of a Medicine Watcher* (1983) is "an
> autobiographical survey of 20th-century medicine."
>
> In "On Magic in Medicine," Thomas gently pokes fun at
> some modern prescriptions for good living, noting the public's
> historic inclination to follow the magical medicine man rather
> than common sense and proven fact. For a general audience,
> Thomas characteristically uses simple terminology and humor
> to discuss scientific phenomena.

On Magic in Medicine

1   Medicine has always been under pressure to provide public
explanations for the diseases with which it deals, and
the formulation of comprehensive, unifying theories has been
the most ancient and willing preoccupation of the profession.
In the earliest days, hostile spirits needing exorcism were the
principal pathogens, and the shaman's duty was simply the
development of improved techniques for incantation. Later on,
especially in the Western world, the idea that the distribution
of body fluids among various organs determined the course of
all illnesses took hold, and we were in for centuries of bleeding,
cupping, sweating, and purging in efforts to intervene. Early in
this century the theory of autointoxication evolved, and a large
part of therapy was directed at emptying the large intestine and

keeping it empty. Then the global concept of focal infection became popular, accompanied by the linked notion of allergy to the presumed microbial pathogens, and no one knows the resulting toll of extracted teeth, tonsils, gallbladders, and appendixes: the idea of psychosomatic influences on disease emerged in the 1930s and, for a while, seemed to sweep the field.

Gradually, one by one, some of our worst diseases have   2
been edited out of such systems by having their causes indisputably identified and dealt with. Tuberculosis was the paradigm. This was the most chronic and inexorably progressive of common human maladies, capable of affecting virtually every organ in the body and obviously influenced by crowding, nutrition, housing and poverty; theories involving the climate in general, and night air and insufficient sunlight in particular, gave rise to the spa as a therapeutic institution. It was not until the development of today's effective chemotherapy that it became clear to everyone that the disease had a single, dominant, central cause. If you got rid of the tubercle bacillus you were rid of the disease.

But that was some time ago, and today the idea that com-   3
plicated diseases can have single causes is again out of fashion. The microbial infections that can be neatly coped with by antibiotics are regarded as lucky anomalies. The new theory is that most of today's human illnesses, the infections aside, are multifactorial in nature, caused by two great arrays of causative mechanisms: 1) the influence of things in the environment and 2) one's personal life-style. For medicine to become effective in dealing with such diseases, it has become common belief that the environment will have to be changed, and personal ways of living will also have to be transformed, and radically.

These things may turn out to be true, for all I know, but   4
it will take a long time to get the necessary proofs. Meanwhile, the field is wide open for magic.

One great difficulty in getting straightforward answers is   5
that so many of the diseases in question have unpredictable courses, and some of them have a substantial tendency toward spontaneous remission. In rheumatoid arthritis, for instance, when such widely disparate therapeutic measures as copper bracelets, a move to Arizona, diets low in sugar or salt or meat

or whatever, and even an inspirational book have been accepted by patients as useful, the trouble in evaluation is that approximately 35 percent of patients with this diagnosis are bound to recover no matter what they do. But if you actually have rheumatoid arthritis or, for that matter, schizophrenia, and then get over it, or if you are a doctor and observe this to happen, it is hard to be persuaded that it wasn't *something* you did that was responsible. Hence you need very large numbers of patients and lots of time, and a cool head.

6   Magic is back again, and in full force. Laetrile cures cancer, acupuncture is useful for deafness and low-back pain, vitamins are good for anything, and meditation, yoga, dancing, biofeedback, and shouting one another down in crowded rooms over weekends are specifics for the human condition. Running, a good thing to be doing for its own sake, has acquired the medicinal value formerly attributed to rare herbs from Indonesia.

7   There is a recurring advertisement, placed by Blue Cross on the op-ed page of *The New York Times*, which urges you to take advantage of science by changing your life habits, with the suggestion that if you do so, by adopting seven easy-to-follow items of life-style, you can achieve eleven added years beyond what you'll get if you don't. Since today's average figure is around seventy-two for all parties in both sexes, this might mean going on until at least the age of eighty-three. You can do this formidable thing, it is claimed, by simply eating breakfast, exercising regularly, maintaining normal weight, not smoking cigarettes, not drinking excessively, sleeping eight hours each night, and not eating between meals.

8   The science which produced this illumination was a careful study by California epidemiologists, based on a questionnaire given to about seven thousand people. Five years after the questionnaire, a body count was made by sorting through the county death certificates, and the 371 people who had died were matched up with their answers to the questions. To be sure, there were more deaths among the heavy smokers and drinkers, as you might expect from the known incidence of lung cancer in smokers and cirrhosis and auto accidents among drinkers. But there was also a higher mortality among those who said they didn't eat breakfast, and even higher in those who took no exercise,

no exercise at all, not even going off in the family car for weekend picnics. Being up to 20 percent overweight was not so bad, surprisingly, but being *underweight* was clearly associated with a higher death rate.

The paper describing these observations has been widely 9 quoted, and not just by Blue Cross. References to the Seven Healthy Life Habits keep turning up in popular magazines and in the health columns of newspapers, always with that promise of eleven more years.

The findings fit nicely with what is becoming folk doctrine 10 about disease. You become ill because of not living right. If you get cancer it is, somehow or other, your own fault. If you didn't cause it by smoking or drinking or eating the wrong things, it came from allowing yourself to persist with the wrong kind of personality, in the wrong environment. If you have a coronary occlusion, you didn't run enough. Or you were too tense, or you *wished* too much, and didn't get a good enough sleep. Or you got fat. Your fault.

But eating breakfast? It is a kind of enchantment, pure 11 magic.

You have to read the report carefully to discover that there 12 is another, more banal way of explaining the findings. Leave aside the higher deaths in heavy smokers and drinkers, for there is no puzzle in either case; these are dangerous things to do. But it is hard to imagine any good reason for dying within five years from not eating a good breakfast, or any sort of breakfast.

The other explanation turns cause and effect around. Among 13 the people in that group of seven thousand who answered that they don't eat breakfast, don't go off on picnics, are underweight, and can't sleep properly, there were surely some who were already ill when the questionnaire arrived. They didn't eat breakfast because they couldn't stand the sight of food. They had lost their appetites, were losing weight, didn't feel up to moving around much, and had trouble sleeping. They didn't play tennis or go off on family picnics because they didn't *feel* good. Some of these people probably had an undetected cancer, perhaps of the pancreas; others may have had hypertension or early kidney failure or some other organic disease which the questionnaire had no way of picking up. The study did not

ascertain the causes of death in the 371, but just a few deaths
from such indiscerned disorders would have made a significant
statistical impact. The author of the paper was careful to note
these possible interpretations, although the point was not made
strongly, and the general sense you have in reading it is that
you can live on and on if only you will eat breakfast and
play tennis.

14   The popular acceptance of the notion of Seven Healthy Life
Habits, as a way of staying alive, says something important
about today's public attitudes, or at least the attitudes in the
public mind, about disease and dying. People have always wanted
causes that are simple and easy to comprehend, and about which
the individual can *do* something. If you believe that you can
ward off the common causes of premature death—cancer, heart
disease, and stroke, diseases whose pathogenesis we really do
not understand—by jogging, hoping, and eating and sleeping
regularly, these are good things to believe even if not necessarily
true. Medicine has survived other periods of unifying theory,
constructed to explain all of human disease, not always as benign
in their effects as this one is likely to be. After all, if people can
be induced to give up smoking, stop overdrinking and overeating, and take some sort of regular exercise, most of them are
bound to feel the better for leading more orderly, regular lives,
and many of them are surely going to look better.

15   Nobody can say an unfriendly word against the sheer goodness of keeping fit, but we should go carefully with the promises.

16   There is also a bifurcated ideological appeal contained in
the seven-life-habits doctrine, quite apart from the subliminal
notion of good luck in the numbers involved (7 come 11). Both
ends of the political spectrum can find congenial items. At the
further right, it is attractive to hear that the individual, the good
old freestanding, free-enterprising American citizen, is responsible for his own health and when things go wrong it is his own
damn fault for smoking and drinking and living wrong (and he
can jolly well pay for it). On the other hand, at the left, it is nice
to be told that all our health problems, including dying, are
caused by failure of the community to bring up its members to
live properly, and if you really want to improve the health of
the people, research is not the answer; you should upheave the

present society and invent a better one. At either end, you can't lose.

In between, the skeptics in medicine have a hard time of 17 it. It is much more difficult to be convincing about ignorance concerning disease mechanisms than it is to make claims for full comprehension, especially when the comprehension leads, logically or not, to some sort of action. When it comes to serious illness, the public tends, understandably, to be more skeptical about the skeptics, more willing to believe the true believers. It is medicine's oldest dilemma, not to be settled by candor or by any kind of rhetoric; what it needs is a lot of time and patience, waiting for science to come in, as it has in the past, with the solid facts.

Content

1. What is "magic in medicine"? Why does Thomas claim that "the field is wide open for magic" (¶ 4)?

2. For which kinds of medical problems does Thomas say the explanation of a single cause is sufficient (¶ 3)? Which kinds of medical problems does Thomas attribute to multiple causes (¶ 3)?

3. Why is Thomas skeptical about the alleged effectiveness of the "Seven Healthy Life Habits"?

4. Why does Thomas claim that the research which led to the claims for the advantages of the "Seven Healthy Life Habits" "turns cause and effect around" (¶ 13)?

5. What does Thomas mean by his conclusion that "it is much more difficult to be convincing about ignorance concerning disease mechanisms than it is to make claims for full comprehension" (¶ 17)?

Strategies/Structures

1. Why does Thomas begin his essay with a historical explanation? Why is paragraph 2, the discussion of tuberculosis, arranged historically?

2. Identify some paragraphs in which Thomas presents effects before causes? What justifies this organization?

3. Is Thomas writing this essay for believers in magic as it relates to medicine? For skeptics? For others? Or for some combination of these readers?

Language

1. How does Thomas use the word *paradigm* in paragraph 2? Why does he choose *edited out* in paragraph 2, sentence 1, rather than *eliminated* or *removed*? What are *lucky anomalies* (¶ 3)? What does Thomas mean by *multifactorial in nature* (¶ 3)? *spontaneous remission* (¶ 5)?

2. Comment on the appropriateness and connotations of the italicized words in the following sentence from paragraph 16: There is also a *bifurcated ideological appeal* contained in the *seven-life-habits doctrine*, quite apart from the *subliminal notion of good luck* in the numbers involved *(7 come 11)*.

For Writing

1. Identify the multiple causes of a phenomenon which is commonly believed to have a single cause, such as the Civil War, World War I, the Civil Rights movement, grade inflation.

2. Describe another circumstance/phenomenon for which people have sought a "magical cure" or single cause explanation and show why it is really more complicated than that. Possible topics include cancer, inflation, warts, love.

3. Explain several of the most significant common effects of a particular technical or social phenomenon, such as computers, automobiles, the printing press, television, shopping centers, superhighways.

▶ ─────────────────────────────────────── ◀

ROBERT JASTROW

Born in 1925, Jastrow is best known for his research on nuclear forces and in planetary science, and for his writings on astronomy. His professional duties currently include the Directorship of the Goddard Institute for Space Studies of NASA, a position held since 1961, and two adjunct professorships, one in geophysics at Columbia University (since 1961) and one at Dartmouth College (since 1973). Jastrow has written *Origin of the Solar System* (1963), *Red Giants and White Dwarfs: The Evolution of Stars, Planets and Life* (1967), and *Until the Sun Dies* (1977) and has co-edited several books. The "Man of Wisdom" essay printed below explains the evolution of the human brain.

Drawing on Darwin's theory of natural selection, Jastrow portrays this gradual process as part of the broad spectrum of creation.

Man of Wisdom

S tarting about one million years ago, the fossil record shows   1
an accelerating growth of the human brain. It expanded at first at the rate of one cubic inch[1] of additional gray matter every hundred thousand years; then the growth rate doubled; it doubled again; and finally it doubled once more. Five hundred thousand years ago the rate of growth hit its peak. At that time the brain was expanding at a phenomenal rate of ten cubic inches every hundred thousand years. No other organ in the history of life is known to have grown as fast at this.[2]

What pressures generated the explosive growth of the hu-   2
man brain? A change of climate that set in about two million years ago may supply that part of the answer. At that time the world began its descent into a great Ice Age, the first to afflict the planet in hundreds of millions of years. The trend toward colder weather set in slowly at first, but after a million years patches of ice began to form in the north. The ice patches thickened into glaciers as more snow fell, and then the glaciers merged into great sheets of ice, as much as two miles thick. When the ice sheets reached their maximum extent, they covered two-thirds of the North American continent, all of Britain and a large part of Europe. Many mountain ranges were buried entirely. So much water was locked up on the land in the form of ice that the level of the earth's oceans dropped by three hundred feet.

---

[1] One cubic inch is a heaping tablespoonful. [Author's footnote.]

[2] If the brain had continued to expand at the same rate, men would be far brainier today than they actually are. But after several hundred thousand years of very rapid growth the expansion of the brain slowed down and in the last one hundred thousand years it has not changed in size at all. [Author's footnote.]

3   These events coincided precisely with the period of most rapid expansion of the human brain. Is the coincidence significant, or is it happenstance?

4   The story of human migrations in the last million years provides a clue to the answer. At the beginning of the Ice Age Homo [man] lived near the equator, where the climate was mild and pleasant. Later he moved northward. From his birthplace in Africa[3] he migrated up across the Arabian peninsula and then turned to the north and west into Europe, as well as eastward into Asia.

5   When these early migrations took place, the ice was still confined to the lands in the far north; but eight hundred thousand years ago, when man was already established in the temperate latitudes, the ice moved southward until it covered large parts of Europe and Asia. Now, for the first time, men encountered the bone-chilling blasts of freezing winds that blew off the cakes of ice to the north. The climate in southern Europe had a Siberian harshness then, and summers were nearly as cold as European winters are today.

6   In those difficult times, the traits of resourcefulness and ingenuity must have been of premium value. Which individual first thought of stripping the pelt from the slaughtered beast to wrap around his shivering limbs? Only by such inventive flights of the imagination could the naked animal survive a harsh climate. In every generation, the individual endowed with the attributes of strength, courage, and improvisation were the ones more likely to survive the rigors of the Ice Age; those who were less resourceful, and lacked the vision of their fellows, fell victims to the climate and their numbers were reduced.

7   The Ice Age winter was the most devastating challenge that Homo had ever faced. He was naked and defenseless against the cold, as the little mammals had been defenseless against the dinosaurs one hundred million years ago. Vulnerable to the pressures of a hostile world, both animals were forced to live

---

[3] Until recently, the consensus among anthropologists placed the origin of man in Africa. However, some recent evidence suggests that Asia may have been his birthplace. [Author's footnote.]

by their wits; and both became, in their time, the brainiest animals of the day.

The tool-making industry of early man also stimulated the 8 growth of the brain. The possession of a good brain had been one of the factors that enabled Homo to make tools at the start. But the use of tools became, in turn, a driving force toward the evolution of an even better brain. The characteristics of good memory, foresight, and innovativeness that were needed for tool-making varied in strength from one individual to another. Those who possessed them in the greatest degree were the practical heroes of their day; they were likely to survive and prosper, while the individuals who lacked them were more likely to succumb to the pressures of the environment. Again these circumstances pruned the human stock, expanding the centers of the brain in which past experiences were recorded, future actions were contemplated, and new ideas were conceived. As a result, from generation to generation the brain grew larger.

The evolution of speech may have been the most important 9 factor of all. When early man mastered the loom of language, his progress accelerated dramatically. Through the spoken word a new invention in tool-making, for example, could be communicated to everyone; in this way the innovativeness of the individual enhanced the survival prospects of his fellows, and the creative strength of one became the strength of all. More important, through language the ideas of one generation could be passed on to the next, so that each generation inherited not only the genes of its ancestors but also their collective wisdom, transmitted through the magic of speech.

A million years ago, when this magic was not yet perfected, 10 and language was a cruder art, those bands of men who possessed the new gift in the highest degree were strongly favored in the struggle for existence. But the fabric of speech is woven out of many threads. The physical attributes of a voice box, lips, and tongue were among the necessary traits; but a good brain was also essential, to frame an abstract thought or represent an object by a word.

Now the law of the survival of the fittest began to work 11 on the population of early men. Steadily, the physical apparatus for speech improved. At the same time, the centers of the brain devoted to speech grew in size and complexity, and in the course of many generations the whole brain grew with them. Once more, as with the use of tools, reciprocal forces came into play in which speech stimulated better brains, and brains improved the art of speech, and the curve of brain growth spiraled upward.

12 Which factor played the most important role in the evolution of human intelligence? Was it the pressure of the Ice-Age climate? Or tools? Or language? No one can tell; all worked together, through Darwin's law of natural selection, to produce the dramatic increase in the size of the brain that has been recorded in the fossil record in the last million years. The brain reached its present size about one hundred thousand years ago, and its growth ceased. Man's body had been shaped into its modern form several hundred thousand years before that. Now brain and body were complete. Together they made a new and marvelous creature, charged with power, intelligence, and creative energy. His wits had been honed by the fight against hunger, cold, and the natural enemy; his form had been molded in the crucible of adversity. In the annals of anthropology his arrival is celebrated by a change in name, from Homo erectus—the Man who stands erect—to Homo sapiens—the Man of wisdom.

13 The story of man's creation nears an end. In the beginning there was light; then a dark cloud appeared, and made the sun and earth. The earth grew warmer; its body exhaled moisture and gases; water collected on the surface; soon the first molecules struggled across the threshold of life. Some survived; other perished; and the law of Darwin began its work. The pressures of the environment acted ceaselessly, and the forms of life improved.

14 The changes were imperceptible from one generation to the next. No creature was aware of its role in the larger drama; all felt only the pleasure and pain of existence; and life and death were devoid of a greater meaning.

15 But to the human observer, looking back on the history of life from the perspective of many eons, a meaning becomes evident. He sees that through the struggle against the forces of adversity, each generation molds the shapes of its descendants. Adversity and struggle lie at the root of evolutionary progress. Without adversity there is no pressure; without pressure there is no change.

These circumstances, so painful to the individual, create 16 the great currents that carry life forward from the simple to the complex. Finally, man stands on the earth, more perfect than any other. Intelligent, self-aware, he alone among all creatures has the curiosity to ask: How did I come into being? What forces have created me? And, guided by his scientific knowledge, he comes to the realization that he was created by all who came before him, through their struggle against adversity.

Content

1. Jastrow argues that modern-day man "was created by all who came before him, through their struggle against adversity" (¶ 16). Is the order in which he presents his evidence for this claim—chronological, paralleling the sequence of human evolution and development—the most appropriate sequence in which to make his argument?

2. Does Jastrow cite evidence for each claim he makes about the stages of human evolution? At what points does he resort to speculation rather than fact? Does speculation weaken his argument?

3. Does Jastrow think that there is a causal connection between the changes in climate that occurred before the first Ice Age (¶ 2) and the "explosive growth of the human brain," or are these phenomena merely coincidental? How convincing is the evidence he marshals to support his argument of "the survival of the fittest" (¶s 6–12)?

Strategies/Structures

1. How elaborate an understanding of principles of "natural selection" and the law of "the survival of the fittest" does Jastrow expect his readers to have?

2. Would Jastrow's argument be convincing to people who hold the "creationist" theory of the universe, or only to believers in the theory of evolution?

3. Although Jastrow's assertions about the history of human development are based on observations about people as they are today, he presents the causes of mankind's current state in the chronological order in which they allegedly occurred. Is this the most convincing order? How compelling would such an argument be that began with recent phenomena and moved backward, step-by-step?

Language

1. What do the labels for prehistoric peoples at different stages reveal about them: Ice Age Homo (¶ 4), Homo erectus (¶ 12), Homo sapiens (¶ 12)? Since the first eleven paragraphs of the essay focus on Ice Age Homo, and only the last five paragraphs focus on Homo sapiens (¶s 12–16), why is the essay titled "Man of Wisdom"?

2. For most of the essay, Jastrow's writing is very straightforward, as if he were recording history. Then, in paragraph 13, the writing turns "mythic," almost Biblical: "In the beginning there was light. . . ." What effect does Jastrow create by doing this?

For Writing

1. Write an essay in which you elaborate on or take issue with Jastrow's claim that "without adversity there is no pressure; without pressure there is no change."

2. Write an essay in which, as Jastrow does, you deduce the cause or causes of a phenomenon by observing its effect(s).

3. Write an essay in which you demonstrate, in a biological or social sense, the Darwinian principle of "the survival of the fittest."

JENNIFER McBRIDE

McBride was born in Roanoke, Virginia in 1958 and grew up there. As an undergraduate English major at the College of William and Mary (B.A., 1980) she won state and national awards for a student newspaper article of investigative reporting, detailing CIA activities on campus in the late 1960s. She is currently a reporter on the *Henderson* (N.C.) *Daily Dispatch*, working on political, governmental, police, and feature assignments. Of "The Rock Fantasy," she observed in 1982, "It seems that teenagers don't idolize rock musicians as much as they once did—but maybe it's just me and I'm getting older!"

McBride's analysis of the appeal of rock stars and rock concerts deals extensively with the causes and effects of the behaviors of rock stars and their audiences, and the influence each has on the other. In the process, she presents an implied criticism of their collective behavior—an implied argument that rock stars are cynical manipulators and that their gullible audiences foolishly endow them with divine characteristics they don't deserve.

❖ *The Rock Fantasy*

If a Mecca exists for today's youth, it must take the form of a rock concert. Such a colossal event draws people from surprisingly distant places and from oddly diverging lifestyles. The sophisticated college student may be seated next to the wide-eyed junior high cheerleader, the latter showing fright at the approach of a wild-eyed freak. How do these incompatible character types find a mutual appeal in rock concerts? What induces young people to exchange the few dollars earned through babysitting or car washing for a concert ticket?

To many, the answer is immediately obvious—the music is the source of appeal at a concert. The quality of the sound produced, however, frequently casts doubt on this explanation. Unquestionably, rock concerts are loud; the decibel level at some reportedly exceeds that attained by a jet plane on take-off. In addition, this aural assault is often intensified by an out-of-tune guitar, by the faltering voice of the performer, or by the bad acoustics in the concert hall. Rock groups generally correct these problems in a studio; their recordings may even boast pleasing harmonies with intelligible lyrics. So why do we battle crowds to secure choice seating at a concert? Why endure the stench of beer spilled in our lap? Somehow an evening spent at home listening to a $100 speaker system and staring wistfully at the rock star's poster on the wall constitutes an inadequate substitute for the real thing. The atmosphere is just not the same.

A concert creates a magical, otherworldly atmosphere, reminiscent of a childhood never-never land. An eerie darkness shrouds the hall, and then, just as in our favorite fairy tale, the supernatural being (otherwise identified by the vulgar term, "rock star") appears in a burst of light. In another context he would have been known as a "god out of the machine." Bizarre lighting schemes and gimmicks such as mock hangings or fire-breathing contribute to the atmosphere of otherworldliness in some acts. The fans are permitted only a brief glimpse of the star before he vanishes once more in the darkness, only to materialize the following evening in a concert hall hundreds of miles away. The stage becomes the rock star's only natural habitat; for us, he can have no existence apart from it. We can scarcely conceive of our idols performing such mundane activities as going to the dentist, shopping for tuna fish, or changing the baby. Perhaps we have a need to believe in an illusory creature of the night, somehow different from ourselves. Who fits this description better than a rock star?

4   Many rock musicians consciously work to maintain the aura of mystery surrounding themselves. Typically, they walk on stage and proceed to sneer at or completely ignore the audience. If a star is especially articulate, he may yell, "A-a-all ri-i-ight! Gonna rock to-o- ni-i-ight!" He cannot use the vocabulary of the common man, for fear of being mistakenly identified as such. Besides, a few well-timed thrusts of the hips communicate the message just as well. The audience responds wildly to this invitation, and the concert is off to a good start. The performer has successfully gauged the mood of the spectators; now his task is to manipulate it, through his choice of material and through such actions as dancing, prancing, foot-stomping, and unearthly screaming. His movements, gestures, and often, his bizarre clothing, high heels, and make-up deliberately violate accepted standards of conduct and appearance. He can afford to take chances and to risk offending people; after all, as every good student of mythology knows, deities are not bound by the same restrictions as mere mortals. The Dionysus figure on the stage tempts us to follow him into the never-never land where inhibitions are nonexistent.

5   Initially, the audience may be content to allow the performer alone to defy civilized constraints. We rebel vicariously; the smashing of instruments onstage perhaps serves as a catharsis for our own destructive impulses. As the intensity and excitement of the concert mount, however, the audience is drawn ino the act. People begin to sing along, clap, yell, dance, or shake their fists. This is a particularly favorable setting for the

release of tensions by the timid. No one can hear their screams (the music is too loud) and no one can see the peculiar movements of their bodies (the hall is dark, and the strange smoke reduces visibility—everyone's eyes are glued to the stage anyhow). The rock god has successfully asserted his power over our bodies, and now all that remains is for him to master our minds and our imaginations.

Since inhibitions have been jarred loose by the pulsating, rhythm, our thoughts can at last run free. Like children, we return to the world of fantasy (with a few adult modifications). The bright young star in front of us flashes overt sexuality and personifies D. H. Lawrence's Phallic Force. The spectators begin to wonder about his sex life, which must be infinitely more fulfilling than their own. The college girl concludes that the rock star would be a much more exciting lover than that bespectacled "preppie" in biology lab. Her younger sister can safely dream of a tender first experience with the rock star. Objectively, she knows that it will never really happen and thus, she need not even have guilt feelings about this fantasy. The males in the audience recognize the star's appeal and fancy themselves enjoying the most interesting fringe benefit of his job—obliging the "groupies." 6

Obviously, young people project their fantasies onto the rock star, endowing him with the powers, attractions, and beliefs that they wish to see in themselves or in those close to them. They can create his personality at will because in one sense, he is just a figment of their imaginations. Thus some may choose to regard him as a sex symbol; for others, he may represent nonconformity and the youthful search for individuality. Unquestionably, in the past, a major appeal of rock music was the shock effect it produced on parents. This attraction may diminish now that the early rock and roll "rebels" are parents themselves and the age of the young devotees is steadily decreasing. At present, however, many young teens still attend rock concerts, believing that they are asserting independence and maturity. Ironically, they conform perfectly—to the expectations and pressures of their peer group. 7

For young people, familiarity with rock music is a status symbol, a sign of sophistication. Everyone eagerly awaits the 8 great rite of passage—driving the car (unescorted by adults) to a concert; such a feat elevates the teenager to the rank of home-room hero for a day. A concert gives the teen a chance to brag about how many albums he owns or about his knowledge of the star's personal life. In this manner, he may join the ranks of the enlightened, sophisticated crowd at school. He finds security in identifying with this group, and profiteers at concerts successfully capitalize on this need to fit in. How else do we explain the fact that teenagers (and even older people) spend ten dollars for a rock star t-shirt which invariably shrinks four sizes the first time that it is washed?

9   The idealistic, socially conscious members of the audience may see the rock star as a messiah or guru, a proponent of truth, love, and peace. They project their own attitudes regarding justice, materialism, and other social issues onto the performer. Apparently, they see no inconsistency in the rock star lamenting greed in our culture; maybe they forget that he escapes from the stage into a limousine which whisks him quickly to the airport and his waiting jet.

10   This idealistic group has become smaller in recent years, with the absence of a burning social issue uniting youthful con-sciousnesses and with the tendency toward introspection and self-absorption. The new breed of concert-goer seeks no message or hidden meanings in the lyrics as a way of justifying his musical preferences. Rock music is thus no great social force; what is of importance is his specific personal reaction to it. Perhaps this idea is best expressed in a popular song from a few years ago in which the singer simply asserts that although the music is "only" rock and roll, he likes it simply because he likes it. For such a person, this whole analysis of the reasons why he likes it would be beside the point.

Content

1. McBride assumes throughout that the characteristic rock audience is young—primarily high school and college student age. What effects does she say rock stars have on this audience? Does McBride imply, or do you think, that rock stars would have the same effects on an older audience, say the parents or grandparents of the rock fans? Why or why not?

2. In McBride's opinion, to what extent is the rock star his own creation, and to what extent is he "a figment of [the audience's] imaginations" (¶ 7)? Do you agree with her interpretation?

3. Why is it to the star's advantage to be "mysterious"? What are the causes of this mystery? What are its effects?

4. What effect does McBride intend to have on her readers by pointing out the rock star's manipulative (¶ 4) and contradictory (¶ 9) behavior?

Strategies/Structures

1. Is McBride writing for an audience of rock fans? How does her attitude toward the subject influence your answer? At what point in the essay are you aware of her attitude?

2. McBride asks a number of rhetorical questions (¶s 1, 2, 3, 9). Why? Does she provide answers to her own questions? Does she expect readers to answer them?

Language

1. What is the significance of the title of this essay, "The Rock Fantasy"? In how many senses can you interpret "fantasy"?

2. McBride uses many sensory details—of sound, appearance, and smell—to convey the atmosphere of rock concerts. Identify the precise language in which she does so.

3. McBride refers to the star as "the rock god" (¶ 5). Through what figures of speech does she reinforce this image?

4. If you need to, look up the meanings of Dionysus (¶ 4), vicarious (¶ 5), catharsis (¶ 5), and a more elaborate reference to D.H. Lawrence's Phallic Force (¶ 6) than the footnote supplies. (You could probably find the latter in an encyclopedia article on Lawrence.)

For Writing

1. As McBride does, analyze a social or cultural phenomenon (dirt biking, symphony concerts, a wine-and-cheese party, a political rally, a wedding or funeral) with which you yourself are familiar, to show its causes, and its effects on the participants.

2. Choose a sports star or entertainer (actor or actress, comedian, musician) that you either admire or dislike a great deal, describe his or her typical performance, and explain its effects on the audience. Does the audience characteristically project any qualities onto the star?

Strategies for Writing— Cause and Effect

1. What is the purpose of your cause and effect paper? Will you be focusing on the cause(s) of something, or its effect(s), short or long term? Will you be using cause and effect to explain a process? Analyze a situation? Present a prediction or an argument?

2. How much does your audience know about your subject? Will you have to explain some portions of the cause and effect relationship in more detail than others to compensate for their lack of knowledge? Or do they have sufficient background so you can focus primarily on new information or interpretations?

3. Is the cause and effect relationship you're writing about valid? Or might there be other possible causes (or effects) that you're overlooking? If you're emphasizing causes, how far back do you want to go? If you're focusing on effects, how many do you wish to discuss, and with how many examples?

4. Will you be using narration, description, definition, process analysis, argument or other strategies in your explanation or analysis of cause(s) and effect(s)?

5. How technical or non-technical will your language be? Will you need to qualify any of your claims or conclusions with "probably," or "in most cases," or other admissions that what you're saying is not absolutely certain? What will your tone be—explanatory, persuasive, argumentative, humorous?

Additional Writing Topics

Write an essay explaining either the causes or the effects of one of the following:

1. National unemployment (or teenage unemployment)
2. Teenage pregnancy
3. The rise or fall of a particular city, state, nation, or empire
4. The popularity of a given television show, movie or rock star, film, book, or type of book (such as romance, Gothic, Western)
5. Current taste in clothing, food, or cars
6. The Civil War, the Depression, World War II, or other historical event
7. The popularity of spectator or active sports
8. Your personality or temperament

9. The American Dream, that "if you work hard you're bound to succeed"
10. Success in college or in business
11. Being "born again," or losing one's religious faith
12. Racial, sexual, or religious discrimination
13. An increasingly higher proportion of working women (or working mothers of young children)
14. The "baby boom" generation currently flooding the job market
15. A sudden change in personal status (from being a high school student to being a college freshman; from living at home to living away from home; from being dependent to being self-supporting; from being single to being married; from being childless to being a parent; from being married to being divorced . . .)

PART III

Clarifying Ideas

▶━━━━━━━━━━━━━━━━━━━━━━━━━━━━━━◀

5 *Description*

When you describe a person, place, thing, or phenomenon, you want your readers to see it as you do, experience its sounds, tastes, smells, or textures. You may or may not wish to interpret it for them as well.

If you don't, you can describe something *objectively*, impartially, sticking to the facts without evaluating them and letting your readers infer what they wish. Technical and scientific descriptions usually aim for objectivity, as would the author of a manual describing the components of a home computer, or an astronaut explaining the size, appearance, and composition of a newly-discovered crater on the moon. So do atlases and some travel guides when describing places, for the authors cannot afford to let their personal preferences influence their presentations of Altoona and Oshkosh, which (bigosh!) must be described as impartially as San Francisco and New Orleans.

Thus the anonymous author (the acme of impartiality) of *The Random House Encyclopedia* (New York, 1977) describes Nevada by citing the major facts about its land and economy, population, education, and history. Its opening paragraph includes such information as:

> At an average altitude of 5,500 ft (1.676m) Nevada is a semi-desert region of nearly 100 basins separated by

short mountain ranges. . . . Grazing and mining are important to the economy, but tourism is the state's major source of income. Visitors are drawn by the legalized gambling and the lenient divorce laws. . . . The city of Las Vegas offers a wide range of entertainment. . . .

Although including some details and excluding others is a form of interpretation, the *Random House Encyclopedia* makes no value judgments; prospective travelers can decide for themselves whether or not they will find the "semi-desert" climate or the "legalized gambling" attractive.

In contrast, Joan Didion's "Marrying Absurd" (pp. 268–71), an indictment of Las Vegas weddings, condemns the place and its venal inhabitants as well as the practice mentioned in her judgmental title. The desert setting is a "moonscape of rattlesnakes and mesquite"—neither mentioned by Random House. Las Vegas, Didion says,

is the most extreme and allegorical of American settlements, bizarre and beautiful in its venality and in its devotion to immediate gratification, a place the tone of which is set by mobsters and call girls and ladies' room attendants with amyl nitrite poppers in their uniform pockets. . . . There is no "time" in Las Vegas, no night and no day and no past and no future. . . .

Its values, she says, are hedonistic and money-oriented, as reflected by the only people she identifies, "mobsters," "call girls," and "ladies' room attendants." It is a place so "extreme," so weird, that even the ordinary measurements of time do not function. It is horrible, she implies.

The descriptions in this section are, for the most part, interpretive. Kris King's Ontonagon is closer to Didion than to the *Random House Encyclopedia*. She provides an impressionistic overview of its appearance ("an ugly, weatherbeaten town") before focusing on its people, denizens of Macey's diner where they "choke" the food in ketchup, and of the Laundromat, with "dead flies on the windowsill." Conversely, Mark Twain wants us to relish the joys of his Uncle John's farm. Thus, he shows us how "inviting" a "prize watermelon" looks "when it is cooling itself in a tub of water under the bed, waiting." He lets us hear its "crackling sound" on being cut open, and offers a taste of the illicit succulence of a watermelon "acquired by art," as opposed to one that "has been honestly come by."

N. Scott Momaday wants us to appreciate his Kiowa grand-mother, not only as she looked when she prayed, "standing by the side of her bed at night, naked to the waist, the light of a kerosene lamp moving upon her dark skin . . . long black hair . . . [lying] against her breasts like a shawl." But also he wants us to see her as a representative of the Kiowa culture, people "made of lean and leather," with an "ancient awe of the sun," a vitality infused by its warmth, at peace with the prairies in the shadow of Rainy Mountain. From an equally appreciative point of view Annie Dillard meticulously describes the behavior of insects, particularly moths, not as biological specimens but as living creatures in a sacred universe:

> And then this moth-essence, this spectacular skeleton, began to act as a wick. She kept burning. The wax rose in the moth's body . . . and widened into flame, a saf-fron-yellow flame that robed her to the ground like an immolating monk.

All of these essays exhibit subtle but systematic patterns of organization. Even when they describe chaos, such as the assemblage of machines and equipment in Fred Brown's front yard in "The Pine Barrens," the organization itself is not chaotic. John McPhee views Brown's yard as he proceeds from "an un-paved road that curves along the edge of a wide cranberry bog" toward the house. He goes from far to near, outside to inside. He conveys his dominant impression of the scene, attracted first by "the pump that stands in his yard" but observes:

> It was something of a wonder that I noticed the pump, because there were, among other things, eight automo-biles in the yard, two of them on their sides and one of them upside down, all ten years old or older. Around the cars were old refrigerators, vacuum cleaners, partly dismantled radios . . . mandolins, engine heads, and maybe a thousand other things.

As he moves from the front of the yard to the back, McPhee reaches the house, "two stories high . . . covered with tarpaper," its vigorous clutter matching its occupant, Fred Brown, seventy-nine going on sixty. The sight images change to sound as Brown calls out, "Come in. Come in. Come on the hell in," and then they change to smell, for Brown is eating large slices of raw onion.

Yet none of these essays is purely descriptive. All involve narration, as the writers tell of their personal involvement with the subject, through conversation, scene setting, and actions of people and animals. McPhee, Momaday, and Twain use a great deal of exposition (explanations of their subject). McPhee begins with an extensive comparison of the Pine Barrens with Yosemite, the Grand Canyon, and "most of the national parks in the United States," not only to convey its vast size, but its natural beauty, significance, and potential fragility as an endangered area.

Rarely do any literary techniques occur in isolation. Although the organization of *The Essay Connection* is intended to highlight many of the major techniques of nonfiction writing, it would be unrealistic to present pure types, for they rarely exist. Even when you are writing an essay to experiment with a particular technique, such as description or narration, you're bound to employ others as well.

MARK TWAIN

"Mark Twain" is the river boatmen's term Samuel Langhorne Clemens (1835–1910) adopted as his pen name. Born and reared in Florida, Missouri, Twain is best known for his two novels immortalizing life on the Mississippi River in the mid-nineteenth century—*The Adventures of Tom Sawyer* (1876) and *Huckleberry Finn* (1885). Beloved American classics, they defy Twain's definition of a *classic* as "a book which people praise and don't read." Twain began writing burlesques as an apprentice printer on his brother's newspaper, but soon embarked on the travels that led to his other well-known works: *Innocents Abroad* (1869), *Roughing It* (1872), *A Tramp Abroad* (1880), and, returning to the region of his idyllic boyhood, *Life on the Mississippi* (1883). He also wrote many other novels, collections of short stories, burlesques, and satires. He was embittered in later life by a business failure and by the death of his wife and one of his daughters; to repay his enormous business debts he lectured and wrote extensively, a popular figure beloved for his wit. He retired to his extravagant home, "Stormfield," in Redding, Connecticut, to pass humorous judgment on "the damned human race" in his final, vitriolic writings. His *Autobiography*, published posthumously in 1924, presents an idyllic but comically realistic picture of a country childhood, specific in time (pre-Civil War) and place (Missouri), yet timeless.

Uncle John's Farm

For many years I believed that I remembered helping my grandfather drink his whisky toddy when I was six weeks old, but I do not tell about that any more, now; I am grown old and my memory is not as active as it used to be. When I was younger I could remember anything, whether it had happened or not; but my faculties are decaying now, and soon I shall be so I cannot remember any but the things that never happened. It is sad to go to pieces like this, but we all have to do it.

2   My uncle, John A. Quarles, was a farmer, and his place was in the country four miles from Florida. He had eight children and fifteen or twenty negroes, and was also fortunate in other ways, particularly in his character. I have not come across a better man than he was. I was his guest for two or three months every year, from the fourth year after we removed to Hannibal till I was eleven or twelve years old. I have never consciously used him or his wife in a book, but his farm has come very handy to me in literature once or twice. In *Huck Finn* and in *Tom Sawyer, Detective* I moved it down to Arkansas. It was all of six hundred miles, but it was no trouble; it was not a very large farm—five hundred acres, perhaps—but I could have done it if it had been twice as large. And as for the morality of it, I cared nothing for that; I would move a state if the exigencies of literature required it.

3   It was a heavenly place for a boy, that farm of my uncle John's. The house was a double log one, with a spacious floor (roofed in) connecting it with the kitchen. In the summer the table was set in the middle of that shady and breezy floor, and the sumptuous meals—well, it makes me cry to think of them. Fried chicken, roast pig; wild and tame turkeys, ducks, and geese; venison just killed; squirrels, rabbits, pheasants, partridges, prairie-chickens; biscuits, hot batter cakes, hot buckwheat cakes, hot "wheat bread," hot rolls, hot corn pone; fresh corn boiled on the ear, succotash, butter-beans, stringbeans, tomatoes, peas, Irish potatoes, sweet potatoes; butter-milk, sweet milk, "clabber"; watermelons, muskmelons, cantaloupes—all fresh from the garden; apple pie, peach pie, pumpkin pie, apple dumplings, peach cobbler—I can't remember the rest. . . .

4   The farmhouse stood in the middle of a very large yard, and the yard was fenced on three sides with rails and on the rear side with high palings; against these stood the smoke-house; beyond the palings was the orchard; beyond the orchard were the negro quarters and the tobacco fields. The front yard was entered over a stile made of sawed-off logs of graduated heights; I do not remember any gate. In a corner of the front yard were a dozen lofty hickory trees and a dozen black walnuts, and in the nutting season riches were to be gathered there.

5   Down a piece, abreast the house, stood a little log cabin against the rail fence; and there the woody hill fell sharply away,

past the barns, the corncrib, the stables, and the tobacco-curing house, to a limpid brook which sang along over its gravelly bed and curved and frisked in and out and here and there and yonder in the deep shade of overhanging foliage and vines—a divine place for wading, and it had swimming pools, too, which were forbidden to us and therefore much frequented by us. For we were little Christian children and had early been taught the value of forbidden fruit. . . .

I can see the farm yet, with perfect clearness. I can see all 6 its belongings, all its details; the family room of the house, with a "trundle" bed in one corner and a spinning-wheel in another— a wheel whose rising and falling wail, heard from a distance, was the mournfulest of all sounds to me, and made me homesick and low spirited, and filled my atmosphere with the wandering spirits of the dead; the vast fireplace, piled high, on winter nights, with flaming hickory logs from whose ends a sugary sap bubbled out, but did not go to waste, for we scraped it off and ate it; the lazy cat spread out on the rough hearthstones; the drowsy dogs braced against the jambs and blinking; my aunt in one chimney corner, knitting; my uncle in the other, smoking his corn-cob pipe; the slick and carpetless oak floor faintly mirroring the dancing flame tongues and freckled with black indentations where fire coals had popped out and died a leisurely death; half a dozen children romping in the background twilight; "split"-bottomed chairs here and there, some with rockers; a cradle—out of service, but waiting, with confidence; in the early cold mornings a snuggle of children, in shirts and chemises, occupying the hearthstone and procrastinating—they could not bear to leave that comfortable place and go out on the wind-swept floor space between the house and kitchen where the general tin basin stood, and wash.

Along outside of the front fence ran the country road, dusty 7 in the summertime, and a good place for snakes—they liked to lie in it and sun themselves; when they were rattlesnakes or puff adders, we killed them; when they were black snakes, or racers, or belonged to the fabled "hoop" breed, we fled, without shame; when they were "house snakes," or "garters," we carried them home and put them in Aunt Patsy's work basket for a surprise; for she was prejudiced against snakes, and always when she took the basket in her lap and they began to climb out of it it disordered her mind. She never could seem to get used to them; her opportunities went for nothing. And she was always cold toward bats, too, and could not bear them; and yet I think a bat is as friendly a bird as there is. My mother was Aunt Patsy's sister and had the same wild superstitions. A bat is beautifully soft and silky; I do not know any creature that is pleasanter to the touch or is more grateful for caressings, if offered in the right spirit. I know all about these coleoptera, because our great cave, three miles below Hannibal, was multitudinously stocked with them, and often I brought them home to amuse my mother with. It was easy to manage if it was a school day, because then I had ostensibly been to school and hadn't any bats. She was not a suspicious person, but full of trust and confidence; and when I said, "There's something in my coat pocket for you," she would put her hand in. But she always took it out again, herself; I didn't have to tell her. It was remarkable, the way she couldn't learn to like private bats. The more experience she had, the more she could not change her views. . . .

8   Beyond the road where the snakes sunned themselves was a dense young thicket, and through it a dim-lighted path led a quarter of a mile; then out of the dimness one emerged abruptly upon a level great prairie which was covered with wild strawberry plants, vividly starred with prairie pinks, and walled in on all sides by forests. The strawberries were fragrant and fine, and in the season we were generally there in the crisp freshness of the early morning, while the dew beads still sparkled upon the grass and the woods were ringing with the first songs of the birds.

9   Down the forest slopes to the left were the swings. They were made of bark stripped from hickory saplings. When they became dry they were dangerous. They usually broke when a child was forty feet in the air, and this was why so many bones had to be mended every year. I had no ill luck myself, but none of my cousins escaped. There were eight of them, and at one time and another they broke fourteen arms among them. But it cost next to nothing, for the doctor worked by the year—twenty-five dollars for the whole family. I remember two of the Florida doctors, Chowning and Meredith. They not only tended

an entire family for twenty-five dollars a year, but furnished
the medicine themselves. Good measure, too. Only the largest persons could hold a whole dose. Castor oil was the
principal beverage. . . .

The country schoolhouse was three miles from my uncle's   10
farm. It stood in a clearing in the woods and would hold about
twenty-five boys and girls. We attended the school with more
or less regularity once or twice a week, in summer, walking to
it in the cool of the morning by the forest paths, and back in
the gloaming at the end of the day. All the pupils brought their
dinners in baskets—corn dodger, buttermilk, and other good
things—and sat in the shade of the trees at noon and ate them.
It is the part of my education which I look back upon with the
most satisfaction. My first visit to the school was when I was
seven. A strapping girl of fifteen, in the customary sunbonnet
and calico dress, asked me if I "used tobacco"—meaning did I
chew it. I said no. It roused her scorn. She reported me to all
the crowd, and said:

"Here is a boy seven years old who can't chew tobacco."   11

By the looks and comments which this produced I realized   12
that I was a degraded object, and was cruelly ashamed of myself.
I determined to reform. But I only made myself sick; I was not
able to learn to chew tobacco. I learned to smoke fairly well, but
that did not conciliate anybody and I remained a poor thing,
and characterless. I longed to be respected, but I never was able
to rise. Children have but little charity for one another's defects.

As I have said, I spent some part of every year at the farm   13
until I was twelve or thirteen years old. The life which I led
there with my cousins was full of charm, and so is the memory
of it yet. I can call back the solemn twilight and mystery of the
deep woods, the earthy smells, the faint odors of the wild flowers, the sheen of rain-washed foliage, the rattling clatter of drops
when the wind shook the trees, the far-off hammering of wood-
peckers and the muffled drumming of wood pheasants in the
remoteness of the forest, the snapshot glimpses of disturbed
wild creatures scurrying through the grass—I can call it all back
and make it as real as it ever was, and as blessed. I can call back
the prairie, and its loneliness and peace, and a vast hawk hanging motionless in the sky, with his wings spread wide and the

blue of the vault showing through the fringe of their end feathers. I can see the woods in their autumn dress, the oaks purple,
the hickories washed with gold, the maples and the sumachs
luminous with crimson fires, and I can hear the rustle made by
the fallen leaves as we plowed through them. I can see the blue
clusters of wild grapes hanging among the foliage of the saplings, and I remember the taste of them and the smell. I know
how the wild blackberries looked, and how they tasted, and the
same with the pawpaws, the hazelnuts, and the persimmons;
and I can feel the thumping rain, upon my head, of hickory nuts
and walnuts when we were out in the frosty dawn to scramble
for them with the pigs, and the gusts of wind loosed them and
sent them down. I know the stain of blackberries, and how pretty
it is, and I know the stain of walnut hulls, and how little it minds
soap and water, also what grudged experience it had of either
of them. I know the taste of maple sap, and when to gather it,
and how to arrange the troughs and the delivery tubes, and how
to boil down the juice, and how to hook the sugar after it is
made, also how much better hooked sugar tastes than any that
is honestly come by, let bigots say what they will. I know how
a prize watermelon looks when it is sunning its fat rotundity
among pumpkin vines and "simblins"; I know how to tell when
it is ripe without "plugging" it; I know how inviting it looks
when it is cooling itself in a tub of water under the bed, waiting;
I know how it looks when it lies on the table in the sheltered
great floor space between house and kitchen, and the children
gathered for the sacrifice and their mouths watering; I know the
crackling sound it makes when the carving knife enters its end,
and I can see the split fly along in front of the blade as the knife
cleaves its way to the other end; I can see its halves fall apart
and display the rich red meat and the black seeds, and the heart
standing up, a luxury fit for the elect; I know how a boy looks
behind a yard-long slice of that melon, and I know how he feels;
for I have been there. I know the taste of the watermelon which
has been honestly come by, and I know the taste of the watermelon which has been acquired by art. Both taste good, but the
experienced know which tastes best. I know the look of green
apples and peaches and pears on the trees, and I know how
entertaining they are when they are inside of a person. I know

how ripe ones look when they are piled in pyramids under the trees, and how pretty they are and how vivid their colors. I know how a frozen apple looks, in a barrel down cellar in the wintertime, and how hard it is to bite, and how the frost makes the teeth ache, and yet how good it is, notwithstanding. I know the disposition of elderly people to select the specked apples for the children, and I once knew ways to beat the game. I know the look of an apple that is roasting and sizzling on a hearth on a winter's evening, and I know the comfort that comes of eating it hot, along with some sugar and a drench of cream. I know the delicate art and mystery of so cracking hickory nuts and walnuts on a flatiron with a hammer that the kernels will be delivered whole, and I know how the nuts, taken in conjunction with winter apples, cider, and doughnuts, make old people's old tales and old jokes sound fresh and crisp and enchanting, and juggle an evening away before you know what went with the time. I know the look of Uncle Dan'l's kitchen as it was on the privileged nights, when I was a child, and I can see the white and black children grouped on the hearth, with the firelight playing on their faces and the shadows flickering upon the walls, clear back toward the cavernous gloom of the rear, and I can hear Uncle Dan'l telling the immortal tales which Uncle Remus Harris was to gather into his book and charm the world with, by and by; and I can feel again the creepy joy which quivered through me when the time for the ghost story was reached— and the sense of regret, too, which came over me, for it was always the last story of the evening and there was nothing between it and the unwelcome bed. . . .

Content

1. Even though Twain's opening two paragraphs warn that he is quite capable of remembering anything, "whether it had happened or not," including moving his uncle's farm "six hundred miles . . . if the exigencies of literature required it," what he says throughout this essay appears true and convincing. Why? Is there anything that seems too good to be true?

2. Twain recalls how the farm was "a heavenly place for a boy." What made it so? Do his memories of children's broken bones (¶ 9) and his

childhood shame at being unable to chew tobacco (¶ 11) diminish his pleasant recollections?

Strategies/Structures

1. Twain's description depends on details appealing to the sense of sight, sound, taste, touch, and smell. In places, this description also involves long lists or catalogues—of foods (¶ 3), of the sights and sounds and activities of farm life (¶ 13). How does he vary the itemization to keep the lists and details appealing and not monotonous?

2. Why does Twain pack so many details into such a long paragraph (13)? If he had broken it up, where could he have done so? With what effects?

3. Twain also employs some very long sentences. Paragraph 6 consists of two sentences, one of 9 words, the other of 234 words. What devices does he use in long sentences to provide unity? Variety?

4. In this largely descriptive account, Twain also provides characterizations of the local doctors (¶ 9), and many interpretations ("The life was . . . full of charm," [¶ 13]), and narration of incidents: for instance, of Aunt Patsy and the snakes (¶ 7). Explain how these techniques which are not in themselves strictly descriptive contribute to the overall picture of life on the farm.

Language

1. Twain manages the difficult feat of using the language of an adult to recall events from his childhood. Find a typical passage in which he enables us to see the experience as a child would but to imply or offer an adult's interpretation.

2. In the last paragraphs (13–15) Twain's reminiscences are identified by many sentences beginning with parallel constructions, "I can call back," "I know," "I remember." What is the effect of this much repetition?

For Writing

1. Identify a place that had considerable significance—pleasant or unpleasant—for you as a child, and describe it to emphasize your attitude toward it. Use sensory details, where appropriate, to help your readers to recreate your experiences.

2. Pick an aspect of your childhood relationship with a parent or other

relative, or a critical experience in your elementary schooling, and describe it so the reader shares your experience.

▶───◀

JOHN McPHEE

McPhee (b. 1931) lives and writes in his hometown of Princeton, New Jersey. He is a graduate of Princeton University. There, since 1975, he has taught a writing seminar in "The Literature of Fact" which focuses on "the application of creative writing techniques to journalism and other forms of non-fiction." From 1957–1964 he was a staff reporter for *Time* magazine, and then became a staff writer for *The New Yorker*, where he has remained ever since. His writings cover a wide variety of subjects, often involving travel to out-of-the-way niches of forgotten America and a close, thoughtful, precise, and often loving analysis of what he has found. Among his many books are *A Sense of Where You Are* (1965), *Oranges* (1967), *The Survival of the Bark Canoe* (1975), and *Coming into the Country* (1978). *The Pine Barrens* (1967), from which the following selection is taken, describes a legendary terrain that has been characterized as "both an archetype and another country," its unspoiled naturalness and independent natives threatened by the encroachments of superhighways and land developments.

The Pine Barrens

F rom the fire tower on Bear Swamp Hill, in Washington Township, Burlington County, New Jersey, the view usually extends about twelve miles. To the north, forest land reaches to the horizon. The trees are mainly oaks and pines, and the pines predominate. Occasionally, there are long, dark, serrated stands of Atlantic white cedars, so tall and so closely set that they seem to be spread against the sky on the ridges of hills, when in fact they grow along streams that flow through the forest. To the east, the view is similar, and few people who are not native to the region can discern essential differences from the high cabin of the fire tower, even though one difference is that huge areas out in this direction are covered with dwarf forests, where a man can stand among the trees and see for miles over their uppermost branches. To the south, the view is twice broken slightly—by a lake and by a cranberry bog—but otherwise it, too, goes to the horizon in forest. To the west, pines, oaks, and cedars continue all the way, and the western horizon includes the summit of another hill—Apple Pie Hill—and the outline of another fire tower, from which the view three hundred and sixty degrees around is virtually the same as the view from Bear Swamp Hill, where, in a moment's sweeping glance, a person can see hundreds of square miles of wilderness. The picture of New Jersey that most people hold in their minds is so different from this one that, considered beside it, the Pine Barrens, as they are called, become as incongruous as they are beautiful. West and north of the Pine Barrens is New Jersey's central transportation corridor, where traffic of freight and people is more concentrated than it is anywhere else in the world. The corridor is one great compression of industrial shapes, industrial sounds, industrial air, and thousands and thousands of houses webbing over the spaces between the factories. Railroads and magnificent highways traverse this crowded scene, and by 1985 New Jersey hopes to have added so many additional high-speed roads that the present New Jersey Turnpike will be quite closely neighbored by the equivalent of at least six other turnpikes, all going in the same direction. In and around the New Jersey corridor, towns indistinguishably abut one another. Of the great unbroken city that will one day reach at least from Boston to Richmond, this section is already built. New Jersey has nearly a thousand people per square mile—the greatest population density of any state in the Union. In parts of northern New Jersey, there are as many as forty thousand people per square mile. In the central area of the Pine Barrens—the forest land that is still so undeveloped that it can be called wilderness—there are only fifteen people per square mile. This area, which includes about six hundred and fifty thousand acres, is nearly as large as Yosemite National Park. It is almost identical in size with Grand Canyon National Park, and it is much larger than Sequoia National Park, Great Smoky Mountains National Park, or, for that matter, most of the national parks in the United States. The people who live in the Pine Barrens are concentrated mainly in small forest towns, so the region's uninhabited sections are quite large—twenty thousand acres here, thirty thousand acres there—and in one section of well over a hundred thousand acres there are only twenty-one people. The Pine Barrens are so close to New York that on a very clear night a bright light in the pines would be visible from the Empire State Building. A line ruled on a map from Boston to Richmond goes straight through the middle of the Pine Barrens. The halfway point between Boston and Richmond—the geographical epicenter of the developing megalopolis—is in the northern part of the woods, about twenty miles from Bear Swamp Hill.

Technically, the Pine Barrens are much larger than the thousand or so square miles of them that remain wild, and their original outline is formed by the boundaries of a thick layer of sand soils that covers much of central and southern New Jersey—down the coast from the outskirts of Asbury Park to the Cape May Peninsula, and inland more than halfway across the state. Settlers in the seventeenth and eighteenth centuries found these soils unpromising for farms, left the land uncleared, and began to refer to the region as the Pine Barrens. People in New Jersey still use the term, with variants such as "the pine belt," "the pinelands," and, most frequently, "the pines." Gradually, development of one kind or another has moved in over the edges of the forest, reducing the circumference of the wild land and creating a man-made boundary in place of the natural one. This transition line is often so abrupt that in many places on the periphery of the pines it is possible to be at one moment in farmland, or even in a residential development or an industrial zone, and in the next moment to be in the silence of a bewildering green country, where a journey of forty or fifty miles is necessary to get to the farms and factories on the other side. I don't know where the exact center of the pines may be, but in recent years I have spent considerable time there and have made outlines of the integral woodland on topographic maps and road maps, and from them I would judge that the heart of the pine country is in or near a place called Hog Wallow. There are twenty-five people in Hog Wallow. Some of them describe it, without any apparent intention to be clever, as a suburb of Jenkins, a town three miles away, which has forty-five people. One resident of Hog Wallow is Frederick Chambers Brown. I met him one summer morning when I stopped at his house to ask for water.

3   Fred Brown's house is on an unpaved road that curves along the edge of a wide cranberry bog. What attracted me to it was the pump that stands in his yard. It was something of a wonder that I noticed the pump, because there were, among other things, eight automobiles in the yard, two of them on their sides and one of them upside down, all ten years old or older. Around the cars were old refrigerators, vacuum cleaners, partly dismantled radios, cathode-ray tubes, a short wooden ski, a large wooden mallet, dozens of cranberry pickers' boxes, many tires, an orange crate dated 1946, a cord or so of firewood, mandolins, engine heads, and maybe a thousand other things. The house itself, two stories high, was covered with tarpaper that was peeling away in some places, revealing its original shingles, made of Atlantic white cedar from the stream courses of the surrounding forest. I called out to ask if anyone was home, and a voice called back, "Come in. Come in. Come on the hell in."

4   I walked through a vestibule that had a dirt floor, stepped up into a kitchen, and went on into another room that had several overstuffed chairs in it and a porcelain-topped table, where Fred Brown was seated, eating a pork chop. He was dressed in a white sleeveless shirt, ankle-top shoes, and undershorts. He gave me a cheerful greeting and, without asking why I had come or what I wanted, picked up a pair of khaki trousers that had been tossed onto one of the overstuffed chairs and asked me to sit down. He set the trousers on another chair, and he apologized for being in the middle of his breakfast, explaining that he seldom drank much but the night before he had had a few drinks and this had caused his day to start slowly. "I don't know what's the matter with me, but there's got to be something the matter with me, because drink don't agree with me anymore," he said. He had a raw onion in one hand, and while he talked he shaved slices from the onion and ate them between bites of the chop. He was a muscular and well-built

man, with short, bristly white hair, and he had bright, fast-moving eyes in a wide-open face. His legs were trim and strong, with large muscles in the calves. I guessed that he was about sixty, and for a man of sixty he seemed to be in remarkably good shape. He was actually seventy-nine. "My rule is: Never eat except when you're hungry," he said, and he ate another slice of the onion.

In a straight-backed chair near the doorway to the kitchen sat a young man with long black hair, who wore a visored red leather cap that had darkened with age. His shirt was coarse-woven and had eyelets down a V neck that was laced with a thong. His trousers were made of canvas, and he was wearing gum boots. His arms were folded, his legs were stretched out, he had one ankle over the other, and as he sat there he appeared to be sighting carefully past his feet, as if his toes were the outer frame of a gunsight and he could see some sort of target in the floor. When I had entered, I had said hello to him, and he had nodded without looking up. He had a long, straight nose and high cheekbones, in a deeply tanned face that was, somehow, gaunt. I had no idea whether he was shy or hostile. Eventually, when I came to know him, I found him to be as shy a person as I have ever had a chance to know. His name is Bill Wasovwich, and he lives alone in a cabin about half a mile from Fred. First his father, then his mother left him when he was a young boy, and he grew up depending on the help of various people in the pines. One of them, a cranberry grower, employs him and has given him some acreage, in which Bill is building a small cranberry bog of his own, "turfing it out" by hand. When he is not working in the bogs, he goes roaming, as he puts it, setting out cross-country on long, looping journeys, hiking about thirty miles in a typical day, in search of what he calls "events"—surprising a buck, or a gray fox, or perhaps a poacher or a man with a still. Almost no one who is not native to the pines could do this, for the woods have an undulating sameness, and the understory— huckleberries, sheep laurel, sweet fern, high-bush blueberry— is often so dense that a wanderer can walk in a fairly tight circle and think that he is moving in a straight line. State forest rangers spend a good part of their time finding hikers and hunters, some of whom have vanished for days. In his long, pathless journeys,

Bill always emerges from the woods near his cabin—and about when he plans to. In the fall, when thousands of hunters come into the pines, he sometimes works as a guide. In the evenings, or in the daytime when he is not working or roaming, he goes to Fred Brown's house and sits there for hours. The old man is a widower whose seven children are long since gone from Hog Wallow, and he is as expansively talkative and worldly as the young one is withdrawn and wild. Although there are fifty-three years between their ages, it is obviously fortunate for each of them to be the other's neighbor.

6   That first morning, while Bill went on looking at his out-stretched toes, Fred got up from the table, put on his pants, and said he was going to cook me a pork chop, because I looked hungry and ought to eat something. It was about noon, and I was even hungrier than I may have looked, so I gratefully accepted his offer, which was a considerable one. There are two or three small general stores in the pines, but for anything as fragile as a fresh pork chop it is necessary to make a round trip from Fred's place of about fifty miles. Fred went into the kitchen and dropped a chop into a frying pan that was crackling with hot grease. He has a fairly new four-burner stove that uses bottled gas. He keeps water in a large bowl on a table in the kitchen and ladles some when he wants it. While he cooked the meat, he looked out a window through a stand of pitch pines and into the cranberry bog. "I saw a big buck out here last night with velvet on his horns," he said. "Them horns is soft when they're in velvet." On a nail high on one wall of the room that Bill and I were sitting in was a large meat cleaver. Next to it was a billy club. The wall itself was papered in a flower pattern, and the wallpaper continued out across the ceiling and down the three other walls, lending the room something of the appearance of the inside of a gift box. In some parts of the ceiling, the paper had come loose. "I didn't paper this year." Fred said. "For the last couple months, I've had sinus." The floor was covered with old rugs. They had been put down in random pieces, and in some places as many as six layers were stacked up. In winter, when the temperature approaches zero, the worst cold comes through the floor. The only source of heat in the house is a wood-burning stove in the main room. There were seven calendars on the walls, all current and none with pictures of nudes.

Fading into pastel on one wall was a rotogravure photograph of President and Mrs. Eisenhower. A framed poem read:

> God hath not promised
> Sun without rain
> Joy without sorrow
> Peace without pain.

Noticing my interest in all this, Fred reached into a drawer and showed me what appeared to be a postcard. On it was a photograph of a woman, and Fred said with a straight face that she was his present girl, adding that he meets her regularly under a juniper tree on a road farther south in the pines. The woman, whose appearance suggested strongly that she had never been within a great many miles of the Pine Barrens, was wearing nothing at all.   7

I asked Fred what all those cars were doing in his yard, and he said that one of them was in running condition and the rest were its predecessors. The working vehicle was a 1956 Mercury. Each of the seven others had at one time or another been his best car, and each, in turn, had lain down like a sick animal and had died right there in the yard, unless it had been towed home after a mishap elsewhere in the pines. Fred recited, with affection, the history of each car. Of one old Ford, for example, he said, "I upset that up to Speedwell in the creek." And of an even older car, a station wagon, he said, "I busted that one up in the snow. I met a car on a little hill, and hit the brake, and hit a tree." One of the cars had met its end at a narrow bridge about four miles from Hog Wallow, where Fred had hit a state trooper, head on.   8

The pork was delicious and almost crisp. Fred gave me a potato with it, and a pitcher of melted grease from the frying pan to pour over the potato. He also handed me a loaf of bread and a dish of margarine, saying, "Here's your bread. You can have one piece or two. Whatever you want."   9

Fred apologized for not having a phone, after I asked where I would have to go to make a call, later on. He said, "I don't have no phone because I don't have no electric. If I had electric, I would have had a phone in here a long time ago." He uses a kerosene lamp, a propane lamp, and two flashlights.   10

He asked where I was going, and I said that I had no particular destination, explaining that I was in the pines because   11

I found it hard to believe that so much unbroken forest could still exist so near the big Eastern cities, and I wanted to see it while it was still there. "Is that so?" he said, three times. Like many people in the pines, he often says things three times. "Is that so? Is *that* so?"

12   I asked him what he thought of a plan that has been developed by Burlington and Ocean counties to create a supersonic jetport in the pines, connected by a spur of the Garden State Parkway to a new city of two hundred and fifty thousand people, also in the pines.

13   "They've been talking about that for three years, and they've never give up," Fred said.

14   "It'd be the end of these woods," Bill said. This was the first time I heard Bill speak. I had been there for an hour, and he had not said a word. Without looking up, he said again, "It'd be the end of these woods, I can tell you that."

15   Fred said, "They could build ten jetports around me. I wouldn't give a damn."

16   "You ain't going to be around very long," Bill said to him. "It would be the end of these woods."

17   Fred took that as a fact, and not as an insult. "Yes, it would be the end of these woods," he said. "But there'd be people here you could do business with."

18   Bill said, "There ain't no place like this left in the country, I don't believe—and I travelled around a little bit, too."

19   Eventually, I made the request I had intended to make when I walked in the door. "Could I have some water?" I said to Fred. "I have a jerry can and I'd like to fill it at the pump."

20   "Hell, yes," he said. "That isn't my water. That's God's water. That's God's water. That right, Bill?"

21   "I *guess* so," Bill said, without looking up. "It's good water, I can tell you that."

22   "That's God's water," Fred said again. "Take all you want."

Content

1. What is McPhee's attitude toward the Pine Barrens as a place? What is his attitude toward its inhabitants, as represented by Fred Brown and Bill Wasovvwich? Does his attitude toward the people reinforce his

attitude toward the place? How does McPhee want his readers to feel about the Pine Barrens?

2. Why does McPhee compare the Pine Barrens with various national parks (¶ 1)?

3. What does the description of Fred Brown, a presumably typical resident of the Pine Barrens, tell readers about the territory itself?

4. What does the description of Bill Wasovwich, Brown's guest, add to our knowledge of the Pine Barrens?

Strategies/Structures

1. McPhee's description begins by looking at the Pine Barrens from a fire tower—the vista extends as far as the eye can see, "about twelve miles." How broad does this view become by the middle of paragraph 1? What is the perspective by the end of the paragraph?

2. In paragraph 2 McPhee narrows his focus from the vast extent of the Pine Barrens to its center. Yet this is also a transition paragraph. What does it lead to?

3. What governs the organization of McPhee's description of Fred Brown's yard and house (¶s 3,4)? What governs the organization of details in his description of Brown's kitchen (¶ 6)?

4. Argue for or against including the descriptions of the photograph of the woman "wearing nothing at all" (¶ 7) and of the old cars in Brown's yard (¶ 8). Why does McPhee recount Brown's explanation of the history of each car in such detail?

Language

1. McPhee's description of the Pine Barrens moves from silence to sound, from conversation to phrases repeated three times. What is the effect of concluding with the triple repetition of "That's God's water"?

2. McPhee occasionally includes short quotations from the Pine Barrens residents, among them: " 'Come on the hell in' " (¶ 3); " 'Turfing it out' " (¶ 5); " 'Them horns is soft when they're velvet' " (¶ 6). What is the effect of this language in juxtaposition with McPhee's own style?

For Writing

1. Describe a place of natural or historic significance, or perhaps simply an attractive small town, that is in danger of having its ecology or character altered by some developments of modern civilization. Convey

its character and your attitude toward it, as McPhee does, in part through your selection and organization of details.

2. Describe a person and a place to show either how they are in harmony or at odds with each other.

N. SCOTT MOMADAY

Momaday (b. 1934) is a Kiowa Indian from Oklahoma, though he never learned the Kiowa language. He was educated at the University of New Mexico (A.B., 1958) and Stanford (M.A., 1960; Ph.D., 1963), where he received a fellowship in creative writing. Also a former Guggenheim Fellow (1966–67), Momaday has taught English and comparative literature at the University of California at Santa Barbara (1963–69), at Berkeley (1969–73), and at his alma mater Stanford (1973–present). He is a prominent, articulate spokesman for Native American rights and culture in person and in his writings, including *House Made of Dawn,* which won a Pulitzer Prize in 1968, and *The Way to Rainy Mountain,* the collection of Kiowa folk tales from which the introductory autobiographical essay below is taken.

A Kiowa Grandmother

1   A single knoll rises out of the plain in Oklahoma, north and west of the Wichita Range. For my people, the Kiowas, it is an old landmark, and they gave it the name Rainy Mountain. The hardest weather in the world is there. Winter brings blizzards, hot tornadic winds arise in the spring, and in summer the prairie is an anvil's edge. The grass turns brittle and brown, and it cracks beneath your feet. There are green belts along the rivers and creeks, linear groves of hickory and pecan, willow and witch hazel. At a distance in July or August the steaming foliage seems almost to writhe in fire. Great green and yellow grasshoppers are everywhere in the tall grass, popping up like

corn to sting the flesh, and tortoises crawl about on the red earth, going nowhere in the plenty of time. Loneliness is an aspect of the land. All things in the plain are isolate; there is no confusion of objects in the eye, but *one* hill or *one* tree or *one* man. To look upon that landscape in the early morning, with the sun at your back, is to lose the sense of proportion. Your imagination comes to life, and this, you think, is where Creation was begun.

I returned to Rainy Mountain in July. My grandmother had 2 died in the spring, and I wanted to be at her grave. She had lived to be very old and at last infirm. Her only living daughter was with her when she died, and I was told that in death her face was that of a child.

I like to think of her as a child. When she was born, the 3 Kiowas were living the last great moment of their history. For more than a hundred years they had controlled the open range from the Smoky Hill River to the Red, from the headwaters of the Canadian to the fork of the Arkansas and Cimarron. In alliance with the Comanches, they had ruled the whole of the southern Plains. War was their sacred business, and they were among the finest horsemen the world has ever known. But warfare for the Kiowas was preeminently a matter of disposition rather than of survival, and they never understood the grim, unrelenting advance of the U.S. Cavalry. When at last, divided and ill-provisioned, they were driven onto the Staked Plains in the cold rains of autumn, they fell into panic. In Palo Duro Canyon they abandoned their crucial stores to pillage and had nothing then but their lives. In order to save themselves, they surrendered to the soldiers at Fort Sill and were imprisoned in the old stone corral that now stands as a military museum. My grandmother was spared the humiliation of those high gray walls by eight or ten years, but she must have known from birth the affliction of defeat, the dark brooding of old warriors.

Her name was Aho, and she belonged to the last culture 4 to evolve in North America. Her forebears came down from the high country in western Montana nearly three centuries ago. They were a mountain people, a mysterious tribe of hunters whose language has never been positively classified in any major group. In the late seventeenth century they began a long migration to the south and east. It was a journey toward the dawn, and it led to a golden age. Along the way the Kiowas were befriended by the Crows, who gave them the culture and religion of the Plains. They acquired horses, and their ancient nomadic spirit was suddenly free of the ground. They acquired Tai-me, the sacred Sun Dance doll, from that moment the object and symbol of their worship, and so shared in the divinity of the sun. Not least, they acquired the sense of destiny, therefore courage and pride. When they entered upon the southern Plains they had been transformed. No longer were they slaves to the simple necessity of survival; they were a lordly and dangerous society of fighters and thieves, hunters and priests of the sun. According to their origin myth, they entered the world through a hollow log. From one point of view, their migration was the fruit of an old prophecy, for indeed they emerged from a sunless world.

5   Although my grandmother lived out her long life in the shadow of Rainy Mountain, the immense landscape of the continental interior lay like memory in her blood. She could tell of the Crows, whom she had never seen, and of the Black Hills, where she had never been. I wanted to see in reality what she had seen more perfectly in the mind's eye, and traveled fifteen hundred miles to begin my pilgrimage.

6   Yellowstone, it seemed to me, was the top of the world, a region of deep lakes and dark timber, canyons and waterfalls. But, beautiful as it is, one might have the sense of confinement there. The skyline in all directions is close at hand, the high wall of the woods and deep cleavages of shade. There is a perfect freedom in the mountains, but it belongs to the eagle and the elk, the badger and the bear. The Kiowas reckoned their stature by the distance they could see, and they were bent and blind in the wilderness.

7   Descending eastward, the highland meadows are a stairway to the plain. In July the inland slope of the Rockies is luxuriant with flax and buckwheat, stonecrop and larkspur. The earth unfolds and the limit of the land recedes. Clusters of trees, and animals grazing far in the distance, cause the vision to reach away and wonder to build upon the mind. The sun follows a longer course in the day, and the sky is immense beyond all

comparison. The great billowing clouds that sail upon it are shadows that move upon the grain like water, dividing light. Farther down, in the land of the Crows and Blackfeet, the plain is yellow. Sweet clover takes hold of the hills and bends upon itself to cover and seal the soil. There the Kiowas paused on their way; they had come to the place where they must change their lives. The sun is at home on the plains. Precisely there does it have the certain character of a god. When the Kiowas came to the land of the Crows, they could see the dark lees of the hills at dawn across the Bighorn River, the profusion of light on the grain shelves, the oldest deity ranging after the solstices. Not yet would they veer southward to the caldron of the land that lay below; they must wean their blood from the northern winter and hold the mountains a while longer in their view. They bore Tai-me in procession to the east.

A dark mist lay over the Black Hills, and the land was like iron. At the top of a ridge I caught sight of Devil's Tower upthrust against the gray sky as if in the birth of time the core of the earth had broken through its crust and the motion of the world was begun. There are things in nature that engender an awful quiet in the heart of man; Devil's Tower is one of them. Two centuries ago, because they could not do otherwise, the Kiowas made a legend at the base of the rock. My grandmother said: [8]

> Eight children were there at play, seven sisters and their brother. Suddenly the boy was struck dumb; he trembled and began to run upon his hands and feet. His fingers became claws, and his body was covered with fur. Directly there was a bear where the boy had been. The sisters were terrified; they ran, and the bear after them. They came to the stump of a great tree, and the tree spoke to them. It bade them climb upon it, and as they did so it began to rise into the air. The bear came to kill them, but they were just beyond its reach. It reared against the tree and scored the bark all around with its claws. The seven sisters were borne into the sky, and they became the stars of the Big Dipper.

From that moment, and so long as the legend lives, the Kiowas have kinsmen in the night sky. Whatever they were in the mountains, they could be no more. However tenuous their well-being, however much they had suffered and would suffer again, they had found a way out of the wilderness.

9   My grandmother had a reverence for the sun, a holy regard that now is all but gone out of mankind. There was a wariness in her, and an ancient awe. She was a Christian in her later years, but she had come a long way about, and she never forgot her birthright. As a child she had been to the Sun Dances; she had taken part in those annual rites, and by then she had learned the restoration of her people in the presence of Tai-me. She was about seven when the last Kiowa Sun Dance was held in 1887 on the Washita River above Rainy Mountain Creek. The buffalo were gone. In order to consummate the ancient sacrifice—to impale the head of a buffalo bull upon the medicine tree—a delegation of old men journeyed into Texas, there to beg and barter for an animal from the Goodnight herd. She was ten when the Kiowas came together for the last time as a living Sun Dance culture. They could find no buffalo; they had to hang an old hide from the sacred tree. Before the dance could begin, a company of soldiers rode out from Fort Sill under orders to disperse the tribe. Forbidden without cause the essential act of their faith, having seen the wild herds slaughtered and left to rot upon the ground, the Kiowas backed away forever from the medicine tree. That was July 20, 1890, at the great bend of the Washita. My grandmother was there. Without bitterness, and for as long as she lived, she bore a vision of deicide.

10   Now that I can have her only in memory, I see my grand-mother in the several postures that were peculiar to her: standing at the wood stove on a winter morning and turning meat in a great iron skillet; sitting at the south window, bent above her beadwork, and afterwards, when her vision failed, looking down for a long time into the fold of her hands; going out upon a cane, very slowly as she did when the weight of age came upon her; praying. I remember her most often at prayer. She made long, rambling prayers out of suffering and hope, having seen many things. I was never sure that I had the right to hear, so exclusive were they of all mere custom and company. The last time I saw her she prayed standing by the side of her bed at night, naked to the waist, the light of a kerosene lamp moving upon her dark skin. Her long, black hair, always drawn and

braided in the day, lay upon her shoulders and against her breasts like a shawl. I do not speak Kiowa, and I never understood her prayers, but there was something inherently sad in the sound, some merest hesitation upon the syllables of sorrow. She began in a high and descending pitch, exhausting her breath to silence; then again and again—and always the same intensity of effort, of something that is, and is not, like urgency in the human voice. Transported so in the dancing light among the shadows of her room, she seemed beyond the reach of time. But that was illusion; I think I knew then that I should not see her again.

Houses are like sentinels in the plain, old keepers of the   11
weather watch. There, in a very little while, wood takes on the appearance of great age. All colors wear soon away in the wind and rain, and then the wood is burned gray and the grain appears and the nails turn red with rust. The windowpanes are black and opaque; you imagine there is nothing within, and indeed there are many ghosts, bones given up to the land. They stand here and there against the sky, and you approach them for a longer time than you expect. They belong in the distance; it is their domain.

Once there was a lot of sound in my grandmother's house,   12
a lot of coming and going, feasting and talk. The summers there were full of excitement and reunion. The Kiowas are a summer people; they abide the cold and keep to themselves, but when the season turns and the land becomes warm and vital they cannot hold still; an old love of going returns upon them. The aged visitors who came to my grandmother's house when I was a child were made of lean and leather, and they bore themselves upright. They wore great black hats and bright ample shirts that shook in the wind. They rubbed fat upon their hair and wound their braids with strips of colored cloth. Some of them painted their faces and carried the scars of old and cherished enmities. They were an old council of warlords, come to remind and be reminded of who they were. Their wives and daughters served them well. The women might indulge themselves; gossip was at once the mark and compensation of their servitude. They made loud and elaborate talk among themselves, full of jest and gesture, fright and false alarm. They went abroad in fringed and

flowered shawls, bright beadwork and German silver. They were at home in the kitchen, and they prepared meals that were banquets.

13   There were frequent prayer meetings, and great nocturnal feasts. When I was a child I played with my cousins outside, where the lamplight fell upon the ground and the singing of the old people rose up around us and carried away into the darkness. There were a lot of good things to eat, a lot of laughter and surprise. And afterwards, when the quiet returned, I lay down with my grandmother and could hear the frogs away by the river and feel the motion of the air.

14   Now there is a funeral silence in the rooms, the endless wake of some final word. The walls have closed in upon my grandmother's house. When I returned to it in mourning, I saw for the first time in my life how small it was. It was late at night, and there was a white moon, nearly full. I sat for a long time on the stone steps by the kitchen door. From there I could see out across the land; I could see the long row of trees by the creek, the low light upon the rolling plains, and the stars of the Big Dipper. Once I looked at the moon and caught sight of a strange thing. A cricket had perched upon the handrail, only a few inches away from me. My line of vision was such that the creature filled the moon like a fossil. It had gone there, I thought, to live and die, for there, of all places, was its small definition made whole and eternal. A warm wind rose up and purled like the longing within me.

15   The next morning I awoke at dawn and went out on the dirt road to Rainy Mountain. It was already hot, and the grasshoppers began to fill the air. Still, it was early in the morning, and the birds sang out of the shadows. The long yellow grass on the mountain shone in the bright light, and a scissortail hied above the land. There, where it ought to be, at the end of a long and legendary way, was my grandmother's grave. Here and there on the dark stones were ancestral names. Looking back once, I saw the mountain and came away.

Content

1. Momaday has three subjects—the land, the people, and their culture. How does he interrelate them? Does he have an explicit central thesis? If so, what is it? If not, can you frame one?

2. Is Momaday writing for a Kiowa audience? What audience would need to know the historical information he presents?

3. Although it is fitting to include a legend (¶ 8) in the introduction to a book of tales and legends, why else might Momaday have included the legend of Devil's Tower? What does he follow the tale of the Kiowa "kinsmen in the night sky" with a historical account of the white man's abolition of the Sun Dance (¶ 9)?

4. In describing his grandmother's life Momaday describes the life of the Kiowa tribe. How does he convey the essence of the group through the individual?

5. What is Rainy Mountain literally? Symbolically? What is the way to Rainy Mountain? Is there only one way?

Strategies/Structures

1. Momaday begins and ends his essay with descriptions of the landscape, placing small creatures (grasshoppers in paragraphs 1 and 15, and a cricket in paragraph 14) against a vista. Why does he choose these particular details? Why does he use the same imagery at the beginning and ending of the essay?

2. What effects does Momaday gain from juxtaposing the close-up and the distant vista, not only at the beginning and the end, but in his descriptions of single individuals against the background of their tribal history and culture?

3. Momaday punctuates his visual descriptions with sounds—his grandmother praying (¶ 10), the Kiowa summer gatherings (¶ 12), the feasting (¶ 13). Show how these sights and sounds work together to create a richer context than either sort would by itself. Does Momaday also use images of touch, taste, and smell?

Language

1. How can Momaday identify with the Kiowas if he doesn't speak their language? How does he relate to his grandmother, since he can't talk to her?

2. Consult a good dictionary for definitions of the following words in this essay: tornadic (¶ 1), solstices (7), deicide (9), sentinels (11), purled (14).

For Writing

1. Present an episode in your family history that is related to the territory—the land or the town—from which your family comes. For

instance, you might tell how they celebrated a particular holiday or performed their favorite outdoor activity.

2. Describe a member of your family in terms of actions, beliefs, ways of dressing or behaving, that are typical of other members of your extended family or other residents of your hometown.

◄──────────────────────────────────►

ANNIE DILLARD

Dillard was born in 1945 and grew up in Pittsburgh; she attended Hollins College and lived for a decade in the Roanoke Valley of Virginia, where she began the close observations of nature that won her a Pulitzer Prize for nonfiction in 1974 with *Pilgrim at Tinker Creek*. She has also published essays in major magazines, poetry, *Tickets for a Prayer Wheel* (1973), and other philosophical commentaries on nature, *Holy the Firm* (1977) from which "Transfiguration" (Professor Thomas Cooley's title) is reprinted below. This essay is typical of what one critic has called Dillard's "intense, almost religious meditations on the beauty and suffering in nature."

Transfiguration

1   I live on northern Puget Sound, in Washington State, alone. I have a gold cat, who sleeps on my legs, named Small. In the morning I joke to her blank face, Do you remember last night? Do you remember? I throw her out before breakfast, so I can eat.

2   There is a spider, too, in the bathroom, with whom I keep a sort of company. Her little outfit always reminds me of a certain moth I helped to kill. The spider herself is of uncertain lineage, bulbous at the abdomen and drab. Her six-inch mess of a web works, works somehow, works miraculously, to keep her alive and me amazed. The web itself is in a corner behind the toilet, connecting tile wall to tile wall and floor, in a place where there

is, I would have thought, scant traffic. Yet under the web are sixteen or so corpses she has tossed to the floor.

The corpses appear to be mostly sow bugs, those little 3 armadillo creatures who live to travel flat out in houses, and die round. There is also a new shred of earwig, three old spider skins crinkled and clenched, and two moth bodies, wingless and huge and empty, moth bodies I drop to my knees to see.

Today the earwig shines darkly and gleams, what there is 4 of him: a dorsal curve of thorax and abdomen, and a smooth pair of cerci[1] by which I knew his name. Next week, if the other bodies are any indication, he will be shrunken and gray, webbed to the floor with dust. The sow bugs beside him are hollow and empty of color, fragile, a breath away from brittle fluff. The spider skins lie on their sides, translucent and ragged, their legs drying in knots. And the moths, the empty moths, stagger against each other, headless, in a confusion of arching strips of chitin like peeling varnish, like a jumble of buttresses for cathedral domes, like nothing resembling moths, so that I should hesitate to call them moths, except that I have had some experience with the figure Moth reduced to a nub.

Two summers ago I was camping alone in the Blue Ridge 5 Mountains in Virginia. I had hauled myself and gear up there to read, among other things, James Ramsey Ullman's *The Day on Fire*, a novel about Rimbaud[2] that had made me want to be a writer when I was sixteen; I was hoping it would do it again. So I read, lost, every day sitting under a tree by my tent, while warblers swung in the leaves overhead and bristle worms trailed their inches over the twiggy dirt at my feet; and I read every night by candlelight, while barred owls called in the forest and pale moths massed round my head in the clearing, where my light made a ring.

Moths kept flying into the candle. They would hiss and 6 recoil, lost upside down in the shadows among my cooking

---

[1] An insect's posterior feelers.
[2] Arthur Rimbaud (1854–91), a French poet, began writing at 16 and composed his major works before he was 20.

pans. Or they would singe their wings and fall, and their hot wings, as if melted, would stick to the first thing they touched—a pan, a lid, a spoon—so that the snagged moths could flutter only in tiny arcs, unable to struggle free. These I could release by a quick flip with a stick; in the morning I would find my cooking stuff gilded with torn flecks of moth wings, triangles of shiny dust here and there on the aluminum. So I read, and boiled water, and replenished candles, and read on.

7   [One night a moth flew into the candle, was caught, burnt dry, and held. I must have been staring at the candle, or maybe I looked up when a shadow crossed my page; at any rate, I saw it all. A golden female moth, a biggish one with a two-inch wingspan, flapped into the fire, dropped her abdomen into the wet wax, stuck, flamed, frazzled and fried in a second. Her moving wings ignited like tissue paper, enlarging the circle of light in the clearing and creating out of the darkness the sudden blue sleeves of my sweater, the green leaves of jewelweed by my side, the ragged red trunk of a pine. At once the light contracted again and the moth's wings vanished in a fine, foul smoke. At the same time her six legs clawed, curled, blackened, and ceased, disappearing utterly. And her head jerked in spasms, making a spattering noise; her antennae crisped and burned away and her heaving mouth parts crackled like pistol fire. When it was all over, her head was, so far as I could determine, gone, gone the long way of her wings and legs. Had she been new, or old? Had she mated and laid her eggs, had she done her work? All that was left was the glowing horn shell of her abdomen and thorax—a fraying, partially collapsed gold tube jammed upright in the candle's round pool.

8   And then this moth-essence, this spectacular skeleton, began to act as a wick. She kept burning. The wax rose in the moth's body from her soaking abdomen to her thorax to the jagged hole where her head should be, and widened into flame, a saffron-yellow flame that robed her to the ground like any immolating monk. That candle had two wicks, two flames of identical height, side by side. The moth's head was fire. She burned for two hours, until I blew her out.

She burned for two hours without changing, without bend- 9
ing or leaning—only glowing within, like a building fire glimpsed
through silhouetted walls, like a hollow saint, like a flame-faced
virgin gone to God, while I read by her light, kindled, while
Rimbaud in Paris burnt out his brains in a thousand poems,
while night pooled wetly at my feet.

And that is why I believe those hollow crisps on the bath- 10
room floor are moths. I think I know moths, and fragments of
moths, and chips and tatters of utterly empty moths, in any
state. How many of you, I asked the people in my class, which
of you want to give your lives and be writers? I was trembling
from coffee, or cigarettes, or the closeness of faces all around
me. (Is this what we live for? I thought; is this the only final
beauty: the color of any skin in any light, and living, human
eyes?) All hands rose to the question. (You, Nick? Will you?
Margaret? Randy? Why do I want them to mean it?) And then
I tried to tell them what the choice must mean: you can't be
anything else. You must go at your life with a broadax. . . . They
had no idea what I was saying. (I have two hands, don't I? And
all this energy, for as long as I can remember. I'll do it in the
evenings, after skiing, or on the way home from the bank, or
after the children are asleep. . . .) They thought I was raving
again. It's just as well.

I have three candles here on the table which I disentangle 11
from the plants and light when visitors come. Small usually
avoids them, although once she came too close and her tail
caught fire; I rubbed it out before she noticed. The flames move
light over everyone's skin, draw light to the surface of the faces
of my friends. When the people leave I never blow the candles
out, and after I'm asleep they flame and burn.

Content

1. What continuity—of lifestyle, of values—exists between Dillard's
life in her house and her life in the wilderness? Why does she choose
descriptions of dead moths (¶s 4, 10) to link the two locations?

2. Much descriptive writing centers around a subject but, like this
essay, does not have an explicit thesis. Frame one for the essay.

3. What is Dillard saying in paragraph 10 about the values writers hold and the way they work? What has this to do with the burning moth of paragraphs 7–9? With the flaming candles of paragraph 11?

Strategies/Structures

1. Is Dillard writing for an audience that observes natural phenomena as carefully as she does?

2. Dillard includes a number of unusual specific details in her descriptions of the spider and moths. Identify some of these and show why they are more precise than the average casual observer would notice.

3. In paragraphs 8 and 9 Dillard uses extended religious imagery to describe the burning moth. What connotations does this convey? How appropriate are these to her subject and her attitude toward it?

4. Not until near the end of the essay (¶ 10) does Dillard introduce her views about writing. Why does she wait until then?

Language

1. Dillard never refers to any living creatures by the indefinite "it," but always by specific gender; the spider, moth, and cat are female. What does this use of specific personal pronouns indicate about Dillard's attitude toward these creatures? Does this influence your reaction to them? If so, in what ways?

2. Identify the strong, active verbs in paragraph 7, describing the death of the moth. How do these verbs contribute to the description?

For Writing

1. Observe very carefully the activities of an insect or two, or plant life in a limited area. Write a description of what you have seen that implies, but does not directly state, your attitude toward it. Avoid sentimentality; don't pour too much emotion, positive or negative, into your description. Let your choice of details speak for you.

2. Following the above instructions, write about the appearance and activities of one or two much larger animals, such as a dog, horse, or zoo inhabitant, that you have observed carefully. Does the animals' size affect the sorts of details you select and the language you use to write about them?

KRISTIN KING

Kris King (b. 1958) grew up in the Philadelphia area, received an associate degree in nursing in 1978, and has worked at intervals as a nurse while pursuing an education in English with an emphasis on creative writing. She earned a B.A. and membership in Phi Beta Kappa from the College of William and Mary in 1980, and attended Cambridge University the following year, where she received a Draper's Scholarship, and was on the Christ's College rowing and tennis teams. After a year's employment as a nurse in Boston, she is now a graduate student in English at Boston University.

"Ontonagon" describes a small town in northern Michigan that King knew only as an outsider from vacationing in the woods nearby. Like many temporary residents in an unfamiliar place, she found it curious. But as she implicitly compared it with her ideal of a small town, she judged it deficient. Like many descriptions, this one shows some ways in which Ontonagon is a typical small town, other ways in which it is unusual. Although the writing is understated, King's negative attitude is unmistakable.

❖ *Ontonagon*

I ndustry blasted the ore out of the earth and Ontonagon developed under the settling dirt. The ore held out for ten years, then the blasting stopped. Production closed and big industry moved on, leaving behind a loading platform and four empty Northern Iron freight cars. The townspeople stayed on; they had nowhere to go or couldn't summon up the interest to leave. They opened five-and-dime stores, hardware, and live bait shops. Some worked in the paper mill by the tracks, others joined the logging crews.

Ontonagon was an ugly, weather-beaten town. It pushed into the southern tip of Lake Superior and suffered for having hacked away all the trees. In winter the wind blew snow off the ice-chunked lake into the sealed-up town. In summer it blew smut from the pulp factory into the screen doors of the diners.

3   There were two diners in town. People recommended Cliff's for Tuesday Fish Special, but Macey's for everything else. We stopped in at Macey's once for pizza. A girl with an apron over sweatshirt and jeans took our order, then bent over a chest freezer, pulled out a pizza, and slapped it in the oven. She opened our warm Cokes behind the counter and carried them over to us with straws in them. We took the straws out and drank from the bottles and looked at the drab oils crowded on the wall. While we waited, the screen door slammed shut on a pair of thick-soled boots. A man in a red plaid lumber jacket and stubbled chin clumped in. He eased himself onto a stool,

4   "Got any homefries 'n ham, Peg?"

5   "Comin up. . . . Do you want onions 'long side?"

6   "Not today. Heard about the washed out timber line north of sixty-one?"

7   "Caught it on the news this mornin'. Tom's workin that area. . . . Some big order down Chicago way."

8   "Well with the rain 'n all, it'll set 'em back some fer sure." The girl handed him his ham and potatoes. He mixed them together, choked them in ketchup, and started shoveling. He didn't look up until he'd gulped the last from his thick coffee mug. Then he left some change on the counter and nodded at Peg on the way out.

9   The people in town never gave much more than a nod. They'd pass each other on the street and look up when there was just enough time to nod and nothing more. There really wasn't much to say and conversations ended awkwardly so people didn't bother. The town had one theater, a Christian Science reading center, a clothing and hardware store, two diners, and five bars. All the stores had wood floors and last year's stock on the shelves. We never came into town except to buy food or do laundry.

10   The Laundromat was at the end of the town where sand and grass had started to take over between the sidewalk slabs. We came here twice during the week to do wash. After I'd pulled every one of the ten-cent laundry soap knobs, checked the pay

phone for money, and read the labels of all twelve brands of cigarettes, there was nothing left to do. I'd sit and watch the women in their tight knit pants and sleeveless blouses folding loads of diapers and more knit pants and more sleeveless blouses. They'd move slowly washer to dryer to folding table, counting out dimes and adjusting temperatures. Between loads they would sit and smoke and stare at the dead flies on the windowsill.

In the winter they would be there still.   11

Content

1. Why did Ontonagon come into being? What does it look like now?
2. King appears as a character in her own essay. Why? How does she continually indicate that she is an outsider? What would the essay gain—or lose—without her?
3. Why has King included the vignette in Macey's diner (¶s 3–8)?
4. How does the town reflect the character of its people?

Strategies/Structures

1. What visual details does King supply? What details of taste? Touch? Smell? Sound?
2. King moves from a large, outdoor vista of the whole town "pushing" into Lake Superior to inside Macey's diner, outside to the main street, to inside the Laundromat. What is the effect of this organization? Would another pattern have been more or less appropriate in relation to her point?
3. What does the last line (¶ 11) mean? Does it appropriately belong in a single sentence paragraph, or should it be incorporated into the preceding paragraph?

Language

1. King refers to the people in her essay as "we" and "they" (¶s 9, 10). What is the effect of these references? Why does she never identify the others whom she calls "we"?
2. What is the tone of King's essay? Is it consistent throughout? How does her language reveal her attitude toward the town?

For Writing

1. Write a description of a place you have visited that you either liked or disliked a great deal and have seen essentially as an outsider. You may include yourself as a character if you wish, but keep the focus on the place rather than on yourself. Identify some of its unusual features, and some characteristics that are typical, using appropriate details of sight, sound, smell, and touch. Don't make your description picture-postcard pretty, even if you like the place. Be realistic—you'll be more convincing.

2. Describe a place or characterize a person or a relationship through a series of several vignettes that reveal different facets of your subject, as King does with the scenes inside the diner and the Laundromat. Use typical people in typical, revealing encounters.

Strategies for Writing— Description

1. What is your main purpose in writing this descriptive essay? To present and interpret factual information about the subject? To recreate its essence as you experienced it? What mixture of objective information and subjective impressions will best fit your purpose?

2. If your audience is completely unfamiliar with your subject, how much and what kinds of basic information will you have to provide so they can understand what you're talking about? (Can you assume that they've seen lakes, but not necessarily Lake Tahoe, the subject of your paper?) If your readers are familiar with the subject, in what ways can you describe it so they'll discover new aspects of it?

3. What particular characteristics of your subject do you wish to emphasize? Will you use in this description details revealed by your senses—sight, sound, taste, smell, touch? Any other sort of information? Non-sensory details will be particularly necessary if you're trying to describe an abstraction, such as somebody's temperament or state of mind.

4. How will you organize your description? From the most dominant to the least dominant details? From the most to the least familiar aspects (or vice versa)? According to what an observer is likely to notice first, second . . . last? Or according to some other pattern?

5. Will you use much general language, or will your description be highly specific throughout? Do you want to evoke a clear, distinct image of the subject? Or a mood—nostalgic, thoughtful, happy, sad, or otherwise?

Additional Writing Topics

1. Places

    a. Your dream house (or room)

    b. Your favorite spot on earth

    c. A ghost town, or a dying or decaying neighborhood

    d. A foreign city or country you have visited

    e. A shopping mall

    f. A factory, farm, store, or other place where you've worked

    g. The waiting room of a bus station, airport, hospital, or dentist's office

    h. A mountain, beach, lake, forest, desert, field, or other natural setting you know well

2. People

See Chapter 1, Discovering Yourself and Others, pp. 1–34.

3. Situations or events

   a. A holiday, birthday, or community celebration
   b. A high school or college party
   c. A farmer's market, flea market, garage sale, swap meet, or auction
   d. An athletic event
   e. A performance of a play or concert
   f. A ceremony—a graduation, wedding, christening, bar mitzvah, an initiation, the swearing-in of a public official
   g. A family or school reunion
   h. A confrontation—between team members and referees or the coach, strikers and scabs, protesters and police

4. Experiences or feelings

   a. Love—romantic, familial, patriotic, or religious
   b. Isolation or rejection
   c. Fear
   d. Aspiration
   e. Success
   f. Anger
   g. Peace, contentment, or happiness
   h. An encounter with birth or death

6   Definition

The easiest way to define something is to identify it as a member of a class and then to specify the characteristics that make it distinctive from all the other members of that class. You could define yourself as a "student," but that wouldn't be sufficient to discriminate between you as a college undergraduate, and pupils in kindergarten, elementary, junior high, or high school; graduate students; or, for that matter, a person independently studying aardvarks, gourmet cooking, or the nature of the universe.

As you make any kind of writing more specific, you lower the level of abstraction, usually a good idea in definition. So you could identify—and thereby define—yourself by specifying "college student," or more specifically yet, your class status, "college freshman." That might be sufficient for some contexts, such as in filling out an application blank. Or you might need to indicate where you go to school, "at Cuyahoga Community College" or "Michigan State University." (Initials won't always work—readers might think you mean Memphis State, or Mississippi, or Montana.)

But if you're writing an entire essay devoted to defining exactly what kind of student you are, a phrase or a sentence will be insufficient, even if expanded to include "a computer science major" or "a business major with an accounting specialty, and a varsity diver." Although the details of that definition would separate and thereby distinguish you from, certainly, most other members of your class, they wouldn't convey the essence of what you as a person are like in your student role.

You could consider that sentence your core definition, and expand each key word into a separate paragraph to create an essay-length definition that could include "college student," "accounting major," and "varsity diver." But that still might not cover it. You could approach the subject through considering *cause-and-effect*. Why did you decide to go to college? Because you love to learn? Because you need to get specialized training for your chosen career? To get away from home? What have been the short-term effects of your decision to attend college? What are the long-term effects likely to be—on yourself, on your chosen field, perhaps on the world?

Or you might define yourself as a college student by *comparing and contrasting* your current life with that of a friend still in high school; or with someone who hasn't gone to college; or with a person you admire who has already graduated. If you work part or full-time while attending college, you could write an *analysis* of its effect on your studying; or an *argument*, using yourself as an *extended example*, of why it's desirable (or undesirable) for college students to work. Or among many other possibilities, you could write a *narrative* of a typical week or semester at college. Each of these modes of writing could be an essay of definition. Each would be only partial, unless you wrote a book, for every definition is, by definition, selective. But each would serve your intended purpose.

The essays in this section represent different types of definition, approached from diverse perspectives. In "Hidden Name and Complex Fate" Ralph Ellison, himself named after Ralph Waldo Emerson, explores various dimensions of the impact that a person's name has on the way others define him, and on his own self-definition. The essay by former New York Knick Bill Bradley (now a U.S. Senator) on "Fame and Self-Identity" defines each of those terms as a reciprocal of the other. By means of illustrations, others' definitions, synonyms, and analysis, he explores various ways people treat popular athletes, and comes to a critical conclusion.

Judy Syfers's "I Want a Wife" defines what she considers the essential nature of a wife according to the wife's functions.

An ideal wife will serve as a wage-earner, secretary, house-keeper, "nurturant attendant" of the children, hostess, entertainer, and sexual companion, among other roles. Syfers defines by both negative and positive examples: "I want a wife who will not bother me with rambling complaints about a wife's duties. But I want a wife who will listen to me when I feel the need to explain a rather difficult point I have come across in my course of studies." Because Syfers is writing satirically, however, it is possible to interpret the positive examples as negative and vice-versa, and still to agree with the emphatic conclusion of her definition, "My God, who *wouldn't* want a wife?"

Hans von Baeyer's extended definition of gravity in "The Wonder of Gravity" succeeds in making an abstraction concrete. He provides brief examples of the effects of gravity: "Because of gravity, the lower parts of animals differ from the upper parts." These precede an extended, eloquent explanatory analogy of a stone drifting in outer space moving through a river of time.

Student Laird Bloom's review of *The House on Henry Street* is, like other reviews attempting to convey the essence of the book at hand, both a definition of the book and an analysis of it. Through an overview of the book's contents, presentation of selected incidents, and commentary on the book's substance and style, Bloom provides a partial definition sufficient to enable his readers to decide whether or not to read the book.

Even these few examples reveal that definitions, short or extended, are extremely varied. When you write your own, you'll probably want to consider some of the following questions: What is the purpose or fundamental nature of whatever I'm defining? What is it made of? How does it work? What does it do, or not do? With what effects? In what ways is it unusual or unique? How can I make my definition, particularly of an abstraction, sufficiently specific so people will understand it? The answers are varied as the questions, as varied as the subject of definition.

RALPH ELLISON

Ellison, born in 1914 in Oklahoma, was named by his father after the noted 19th-century American poet and essayist Ralph Waldo Emerson, whose works as a schoolchild he consequently "avoided like the plague." Ellison studied music and sculpture at Tuskegee Institute. During the Depression he worked as a researcher in New York for the Federal Writer's Project. His only novel, *The Invisible Man* (1952), won instant critical acclaim and established Ellison's reputation as one of America's foremost authors. It tells of the maturation of a black youth from innocence and self-identity to sad experience and a painful social invisibility. This essay explores other aspects of the phenomenon of identity—the identity provided by the bestowal of names with historical or cultural significance on the recipients, innocent or otherwise.

Hidden Name and Complex Fate

1   Let Tar Baby, that enigmatic figure from Negro folklore, stand for the world. He leans, black and gleaming, against the wall of life utterly noncommittal under our scrutiny, our questioning, starkly unmoving before our naïve attempts at intimidation. Then we touch him playfully and before we can say *Sonny Liston!*[1] we find ourselves stuck. Our playful investigations become a labor, a fearful struggle, an *agon*. Slowly we perceive that our task is to learn the proper way of freeing ourselves to develop, in other words, technique.

2   Sensing this, we give him our sharpest attention, we question him carefully, we struggle with more subtlety; while he, in his silent way, holds on, demanding that we perceive the necessity of calling him by his true name as the price of our freedom. It is unfortunate that he has so many, many "true names"—

---

[1]A world heavyweight boxing champion in the 1960s.

all spelling chaos; and in order to discover even one of these we must first come into the possession of our own names. For it is through our names that we first place ourselves in the world. Our names, being the gift of others, must be made our own.

Once while listening to the play of a two-year-old girl who did not know she was under observation, I heard her saying over and over again, at first with questioning and then with sounds of growing satisfaction, "I am Mimi Livisay? . . . *I* am Mimi Livisay. I *am* Mimi Livisay . . . I am *Mimi* Li-vi-say! I am Mimi . . ."

And in deed and in fact she was—or became so soon thereafter, by working playfully to establish the unity between herself and her name.

For many of us this is far from easy. We must learn to wear our names within all the noise and confusion of the environment in which we find ourselves; make them the center of all of our associations with the world, with man and with nature. We must charge them with all our emotions, our hopes, hates, loves, aspirations. They must become our masks and our shields and the containers of all those values and traditions which we learn and/or imagine as being the meaning of our familial past.

And when we are reminded so constantly that we bear, as Negroes, names originally possessed by those who owned our enslaved grandparents, we are apt, especially if we are potential writers, to be more than ordinarily concerned with the veiled and mysterious events, the fusions of blood, the furtive couplings, the business transactions, the violations of faith and loyalty, the assaults; yes, and the unrecognized and unrecognizable loves through which our names were handed down unto us.

So charged with emotion does this concern become for some of us, that we have, earlier, the example of the followers of Father Divine and, now, the Black Muslims, discarding their original names in rejection of the bloodstained, the brutal, the sinful images of the past. Thus they would declare new identities, would clarify a new program of intention and destroy the verbal evidence of a willed and ritualized discontinuity of blood and human intercourse.

Not all of us, actually only a few, seek to deal with our names in this manner. We take what we have and make of them what we can. And there are even those who know where the old broken connections lie, who recognize their relatives across the chasm of historical denial and the artificial barriers of society, and who see themselves as bearers of many of the qualities which were admirable in the original sources of their common line (Faulkner has made much of this); and I speak here not of mere forgiveness, nor of obsequious insensitivity to the outrages symbolized by the denial and the division, but of the conscious acceptance of the harsh realities of the human condition, of the ambiguities and hypocrisies of human history as they have played themselves out in the United States.

9   Perhaps, taken in aggregate, these European names which (sometimes with irony, sometimes with pride, but always with personal investment) represent a certain triumph of the spirit, speaking to us of those who rallied, reassembled and transformed themselves and who under dismembering pressures refused to die. "Brothers and sisters," I once heard a Negro preacher exhort, "let us make up our faces before the world, and our names shall sound throughout the land with honor! For we ourselves are our *true* names, not their epithets! So let us, I say, Make Up Our Faces and Our Minds!"

10   Perhaps my preacher had read T. S. Eliot, although I doubt it. And in actuality, it was unnecessary that he do so, for a concern with names and naming was very much a part of that special area of American culture from which I come, and it is precisely for this reason that this example should come to mind in a discussion of my own experience as a writer.

11   Undoubtedly, writers begin their *conditioning* as manipulators of words long before they become aware of literature— certain Freudians would say at the breast. Perhaps. But if so, that is far too early to be of use at this moment. Of this, though, I am certain: that despite the misconceptions of those educators who trace the reading difficulties experienced by large numbers of Negro children in Northern schools to their Southern background, these children are, in *their* familiar South, facile manipulators of words. I know, too, that the Negro community is deadly in its ability to create nicknames and to spot all that is ludicrous in an unlikely name or that which is incongruous in conduct. Names are not qualities; nor are words, in this particular sense, actions. To assume that they are could cost one his

life many times a day. Language skills depend to a large extent upon a knowledge of the details, the manners, the objects, the folkways, the psychological patterns, of a given environment. Humor and wit depend upon much the same awareness, and so does the suggestive power of names.

"A small brown bowlegged Negro with the name 'Franklin   12
D. Roosevelt Jones' might sound like a clown to someone who looks at him from the outside," said my friend Albert Murray, "but on the other hand he just might turn out to be a hell of a fireside operator. He might just lie back in all of that comic juxtaposition of names and manipulate you deaf, dumb and blind—and you not even suspecting it, because you're thrown out of stance by his name! There you are, so dazzled by the F.D.R. image—which you *know* you can't see—and so delighted with your own superior position that you don't realize that it's *Jones* who must be confronted."

Well, as you must suspect, all of this speculation on the.   13
matter of names has a purpose, and now, because it is tied up so ironically with my own experience as a writer, I must turn to my own name.

For in the dim beginnings, before I ever thought con-   14
sciously of writing, there was my own name, and there was, doubtless, a certain magic in it. From the start I was uncomfortable with it, and in my earliest years it caused me much puzzlement. Neither could I understand what a poet was, nor why, exactly, my father had chosen to name me after one. Perhaps I could have understood it perfectly well had he named me after his own father, but that name had been given to an older brother who died and thus was out of the question. But why hadn't he named me after a hero, such as Jack Johnson, or a soldier like Colonel Charles Young, or a great seaman like Admiral Dewey, or an educator like Booker T. Washington, or a great orator and abolitionist like Frederick Douglass? Or again, why hadn't he named me (as so many Negro parents had done) after President Teddy Roosevelt?

Instead, he named me after someone called Ralph Waldo   15
Emerson, and then, when I was three, he died. It was too early for me to have understood his choice, although I'm sure he must have explained it many times, and it was also too soon for me

to have made the connection between my name and my father's love for reading. Much later, after I began to write and work with words, I came to suspect that he was aware of the suggestive powers of names and of the magic involved in naming.

16   I recall an odd conversation with my mother during my early teens in which she mentioned their interest in, of all things, prenatal culture! But for a long time I actually knew only that my father read a lot, and that he admired this remote Mr. Emerson, who was something called a "poet and philosopher"—so much so that he named his second son after him.

17   I knew, also, that whatever his motives, the combination of names he'd given me caused me no end of trouble from the moment when I could talk well enough to respond to the ritualized question which grownups put to very young children. Emerson's name was quite familiar to Negroes in Oklahoma during those days when World War I was brewing, and adults, eager to show off their knowledge of literary figures, and obviously amused by the joke implicit in such a small brown nubbin of a boy carrying around such a heavy moniker, would invariably repeat my first two names and then to my great annoyance, they'd add "Emerson."

18   And I, in my confusion, would reply, "No, *no, I'm* not Emerson; he's the little boy who lives next door." Which only made them laugh all the louder. "Oh no," they'd say, *you're* Ralph Waldo Emerson," while I had fantasies of blue murder.

19   For a while the presence next door of my little friend, Emerson, made it unnecessary for me to puzzle too often over this peculiar adult confusion. And since there were other Negro boys named Ralph in the city, I came to suspect that there was something about the combination of names which produced their laughter. Even today I know of only one other Ralph who had as much comedy made out of his name, a campus politician and deep-voiced orator whom I knew at Tuskegee, who was called in friendly ribbing, *Ralph Waldo Emerson Edgar Allan Poe,* spelled Powe. This must have been quite a trial for him, but I had been initiated much earlier.

20   During my early school years the name continued to puzzle me, for it constantly evoked in the faces of others

some secret. It was as though I possessed some treasure or some defect, which was invisible to my own eyes and ears; something which I had but did not *possess*, like a piece of property in South Carolina, which was mine but which I could not have until some future time. I recall finding, about this time, while seeking adventure in back alleys—which possess for boys a superiority over playgrounds like that which kitchen utensils possess over toys designed for infants—a large photographic lens. I remember nothing of its optical qualities, of its speed or color correction, but it gleamed with crystal mystery and it was beautiful.

Mounted handsomely in a tube of shiny brass, it spoke to me of distant worlds of possibility. I played with it, looking through it with squinted eyes, holding it in shafts of sunlight, and tried to use it for a magic lantern. But most of this was as unrewarding as my attempts to make the music come from a phonograph record by holding the needle in my fingers. 21

I could burn holes through newspapers with it, or I could pretend that it was a telescope, the barrel of a cannon, or the third eye of a monster—*I* being the monster—but I could do nothing at all about its proper function of making images; nothing to make it yield its secret. But I could not discard it. 22

Older boys sought to get it away from me by offering knives or tops, agate marbles or whole zoos of grass snakes and horned toads in trade, but I held on to it. No one, not even the white boys I knew, had such a lens, and it was my own good luck to have found it. Thus I would hold on to it until such time as I could acquire the parts needed to make it function. Finally I put it aside and it remained buried in my box of treasures, dusty and dull, to be lost and forgotten as I grew older and became interested in music. 23

I had reached by now the grades where it was necessary to learn something about Mr. Emerson and what he had written, such as the "Concord Hymn" and the essay "Self-Reliance," and in following his advice, I reduced the "Waldo" to a simple and, I hoped, mysterious "W," and in my own reading I avoided his works like the plague. I could no more deal with my name— I shall never really master it—than I could find a creative use 24 for my lens. Fortunately there were other problems to occupy my mind. Not that I forgot my fascination with names, but more about that later. . . .

Content

1. Most of Ellison's examples of the effects of names on one's identity are of blacks, from Tar Baby (¶ 1) to Frederick Douglass (¶ 14). Does his analysis apply equally well to whites? To other racial or ethnic groups?
2. What is Ellison's thesis? How should we make our names our own? Why has this been particularly difficult for blacks?
3. Based on evidence in this essay, what are some of the reasons people change their names?
4. What are some possible effects of naming a child after a famous person? After his father or her mother or other relative?

Strategies/Structures

1. Ellison's essay is neatly balanced between a general discussion of the subject and its application to himself. What connections are there between the two halves? What is the transition paragraph?
2. In this discussion of names, why does Ellison devote so much space to his finding of a photographic lens as a child? (¶s 20–24). Of what relevance is this to his main subject?

Language

1. The vocabulary in the first half of Ellison's essay seems more formal than the language in the second half of this essay. Note *agon* (¶ 1); "Fusions of blood, furtive couplings" (¶ 6); "ritualized discontinuity of blood and human intercourse" (¶ 7). Why should this be so?
2. Ellison wrote this esay in 1964, when "Negro" was the conventional, acceptable polite name for his race. Now the conventional, acceptable name is "black." What is the significance of each of these names? Of the name shift?

For Writing

1. Write an essay in which you explore the significance of your own name to yourself and to others. If you were named "for" anyone, why were you given this name? Does the meaning of your name bestow

upon you any special characteristics? Obligations? Social prestige, or political or cultural identification? Do you like or dislike your name? Why? Do you ever feel obliged to defend or explain it to others?

2. Under what circumstances is a change of name (or the use of an alias) desirable or appropriate? In marriage? To identify with a racial, religious, or ethnic group? Or to deny one's heritage? Or is it preferable to live with the names we were given at birth, whatever they may be?

BILL BRADLEY

Bradley (b. 1943) was born in Crystal City, Missouri, graduated in 1965 from Princeton University, where he was a basketball All-American, and studied for two years at Oxford University as a Rhodes Scholar, receiving his M.A. *cum laude* in 1968. Bradley played forward with the New York Knickerbockers from 1967 to 1977. His autobiography, *Life on the Run* (1976), philosophically interprets the nomadic life of a professional basketball player on and off the court, subject to constant pressure to hurry, to win, under the constant scrutiny of coaches, other players, and fans. Bradley's public exposure, quick intelligence, and coolness under pressure with the Knicks have proved enormously beneficial to his more recent career in politics; in 1978 he was elected Democratic Senator from New Jersey. Bradley's definition of the relationship between fame and self-identity is applicable to celebrities in a variety of fields.

Fame and Self-Identity

I n the middle of dinner a woman walks up and asks for my autograph. I tell her I'd be glad to do it later, after dinner. She walks away. Two minutes later, a man about 5'11" with husky shoulders and a flat nose walks up to me at the table. "Hey, Bradley, you Bradley," he says. He's had too much to drink. I smile, thinking of the time a drunk reporter walked with his coat to the front of a plane on a transcontinental flight and told everyone he was getting off. We were over Kansas.

2   "What's the matter, think you're too good?" the drunk blurts. "The lady just asked for an autograph. I was pro fighter. I ought to knock you out, you son-of-a-bitch. You're all alike. Lady has a kid. . . ." He can't stand still. He sways back and forth as he talks. I take a piece of paper without even nodding at him, scribble my name on it, and thrust it in his pocket.

3   "Okay, champ, you have it now," I say with a wink.

4   "Who knows," one of my friends says as our visitor staggers around tables heading for the reassuring darkness of the bar, "if he was a boxer maybe you got off easy."

5   When we leave the restaurant a man on the street recognizes me. He approaches and says simply as if he were an ordered antidote to the boxer, "Thank you for all the wonderful evenings you have given me. I think the Knicks are class." I say thanks for the words and we walk our separate ways.

6   There is no question about it. Being a member of a successful New York basketball team is a mixed blessing. The notoriety forces one to look at the world differently from other people. It provides money and access. At the same time, it sets one apart from the rest of society and denies one the privilege of being an equal member of a crowd. There is little chance, for example, for a public figure to fail without people knowing it, and no one grows without failing. Many avoid the embarrassment of public failure by never placing themselves in positions where they might fail. Therefore, they never grow. My constant problem is to find places where I am allowed to fail in private. Everyone does not thirst for fame. For me, fame holds as much danger as it does benefit.

7   If you are famous you get special service at banks, passport offices, and airline ticket counters, and come to expect that service while not respecting yourself for wanting it. Fame is being paid a lot of money for what people think about you as well as for what you do . . . having strange women approach you and say they want to meet you, know you in every way, right now . . . misassessing the amount of interest other people have in you . . . trying to find yourself while under the scrutiny of thousands of eyes . . . reacting instead of acting, being passive in-

stead of active . . . having people tell you what they want you to do with your life . . . learning to understand what others want from you . . . sensing people in a restaurant whispering and pointing toward your party . . . forgetting how hot the subways are in August . . . having someone write that if you visit this kid who is dying in a hospital he will get better . . . having strangers constantly test you and probe for the dimension of your "real" personality . . . coming into contact with ten times more people in a year than most people do in a lifetime . . . remaining unable to escape those few minutes or several years when what you did made you famous. . . .

The American historian Daniel Boorstin in his book *The* 8 *Image* has observed:

> The very agency which first makes the celebrity in the long run inevitably destroys him. . . . The newspapers make him and they unmake him—not by murder but by suffocation or starvation. . . . There is not even any tragedy in the celebrity's fall, for he is a man returned to his proper anonymous station. The tragic hero, in Aristotle's familiar definition, was man fallen from great estate, a great man with a tragic flaw. He had somehow become the victim of his own greatness. Yesterday's celebrity, however, is a commonplace man who has been fitted back into his proper commonplaceness not by any fault of his own, but by time itself.
>
> The hero was born of time: his gestation required at least a generation. As the saying went, he had "stood the test of time." He grew over generations. . . . Receding into the misty past, he became more and not less heroic. . . . Men of the last century were more heroic than those of today; men of antiquity were still more heroic. . . .
>
> The celebrity, on the contrary, is always contemporary. The hero is made by folk-lore, sacred texts and history books, and the celebrity is the creature of gossip, of public opinion, of newspapers, magazines and the ephemeral images of movie and television screens. The passage of time which creates and establishes the hero, destroys the celebrity. One is made, the other unmade,

by repetition. The celebrity is born in the daily papers, and never loses the mark of his fleeting origin.

9   The other Knicks and I got to our present positions of celebrity through similar routes. There are many encouragements for a boy to be an athlete while in high school. The good athlete is popular among his classmates, but the star athlete develops a reputation outside high school. Townspeople, adults, single him out for attention and interest. Teachers might favor him even if unconsciously. Growing up, when most young people struggle to define their tastes and develop their own sense of right and wrong, the star athlete lies protected in his momentary nest of fame. The community tells him that he is a basketball star. For the townspeople his future is as clearly outlined as his record-book past. They expect him to become an even greater athlete and to do those things which will bring about the fulfillment of what is wholly their fantasy. The adolescent who receives such attention rarely develops personal doubts. There is a smug cockiness about achievements, or a sincere determination to continue along a course that has brought success and praise. The athlete continues to devote his energies to sport. Compared with the natural fears and insecurities of his classmates, he has it easy. His self-assurance is constantly reinforced by public approval.

10   The athletes who succeed in making college teams have the high school experience duplicated on a grander scale. The few who excel on university teams find that admiration comes then, not from high school friends and adult family friends, but from the national press and from adults they have never met. They begin to see that they can make a good living simply by playing the sport. Self-definition again comes from external sources, not from within. While their physical skill lasts, professional athletes are celebrities—fondled and excused, praised and believed. Only toward the end of their careers do the stars realize that their sense of identity is insufficient.

Content

1. Bradley observes that "For me, fame holds as much danger as it does benefit" (¶ 6). What are some of the dangers that might accompany fame?

2. Explain and expand on the definitions of a celebrity and a hero that Bradley quotes from Daniel Boorstin (¶ 8).

3. Bradley seems to object to "self-definition" that "comes from external sources, not from within" (¶ 10). What is self-definition? If you agree with Bradley that it might better come from within than without, explain why. What aspects of one's self-definition must perforce come from external sources?

Strategies/Structures

1. Why does Bradley begin his discussion with the anecdote of his experiences inside and outside the restaurant?

2. Most of paragraph 7 is a single long sentence. What does Bradley gain by joining these separate elements of the definition? Why does he use ellipses, conventionally the symbols of omission, as connecting devices here? With what effect?

3. The advice generally given to writers who quote extensively from another source—as Bradley does from Boorstin (¶ 8) on the distinction between a hero and a celebrity—is to analyze or otherwise interpret the quotation. Yet Bradley does not do this explicitly. What does he do to integrate the quotation into his own text?

4. Is Bradley writing primarily for people likely to worship athletes as heroes? Or for a more general or skeptical audience? How can you tell? What is his own attitude toward his celebrity status?

Language

1. Explain the meaning of notoriety (¶ 6), "reacting instead of acting" (¶ 7), "forgetting how hot the subways are in August" (¶ 7), "having someone write you that if you visit this kid in a hospital he will get better." (¶ 7).

2. Bradley says notoriety provides "money and access"; how does he define "access" in paragraphs 6 and 7?

For Writing

1. Write an extended definition of "fame." If you have ever attained celebrity status, however briefly, as the result of a particular accomplishment (star performance in sports, music, or drama for instance) or association with a famous person (perhaps you have recently seen a particular sports or entertainment star, or even a famous politician), use your own experiences to illustrate the definition.

Comment in the course of your definition on the probable duration of the kind of fame you're discussing, whether it is likely to last or not, and why.

2. Write an extended definition of a quality that can be used to describe people—"attractive," "a go-getter," "assertive," "domineering," "generous," "selfish," or some other term that interests you. Illustrate it with examples of one or two people you know well, preferably in interaction with others. You may supplement this with fragmentary illustrations of the term, as Bradley does in paragraph 7.

◄──────────────────────────────────►

JUDY SYFERS

Syfers (b. 1937) earned a bachelor's degree in painting at the University of Iowa in 1962. She has lived for some time in San Francisco with two daughters, and describes herself as "not a 'writer' but a disenfranchised and fired [Syfers is divorced] housewife, now secretary." Syfers has published articles on such topics as abortion and union organizing.

Her definition of a wife, in the essay below, was first published in December 1971 in the inaugural issue of *Ms.*, a popular feminist magazine. The fact that it has been widely reprinted ever since testifies to its appeal to a much wider audience than originally intended.

I Want a Wife

1   I belong to that classification of people known as wives. I am A Wife. And, not altogether incidentally, I am a mother.

2   Not too long ago a male friend of mine appeared on the scene fresh from a recent divorce. He had one child, who is, of course, with his ex-wife. He is obviously looking for another wife. As I thought about him while I was ironing one evening, it suddenly occurred to me that I, too, would like to have a wife. Why do I want a wife?

3   I would like to go back to school so that I can become

economically independent, support myself, and, if need be, support those dependent upon me. I want a wife who will work and send me to school. And while I am going to school I want a wife to take care of my children. I want a wife to keep track of the children's doctor and dentist appointments. And to keep track of mine, too. I want a wife to make sure my children eat properly and are kept clean. I want a wife who will wash the children's clothes and keep them mended. I want a wife who is a good nurturant attendant to my children, who arranges for their schooling, makes sure that they have an adequate social life with their peers, takes them to the park, the zoo, etc. I want a wife who takes care of the children when they are sick, a wife who arranges to be around when the children need special care, because, of course, I cannot miss classes at school. My wife must arrange to lose time at work and not lose the job. It may mean a small cut in my wife's income from time to time, but I guess I can tolerate that. Needless to say, my wife will arrange and pay for the care of the children while my wife is working.

I want a wife who will take care of *my* physical needs. I   4
want a wife who will keep my house clean. A wife who will pick up after me. I want a wife who will keep my clothes clean, ironed, mended, replaced when need be, and who will see to it that my personal things are kept in their proper place so that I can find what I need the minute I need it. I want a wife who cooks the meals, a wife who is a *good* cook. I want a wife who will plan the menus, do the necessary grocery shopping, prepare the meals, serve them pleasantly, and then do the cleaning up while I do my studying. I want a wife who will care for me when I am sick and sympathize with my pain and loss of time from school. I want a wife to go along when our family takes a vacation so that someone can continue to care for me and my children when I need a rest and change of scene.

I want a wife who will not bother me with rambling com-   5
plaints about a wife's duties. But I want a wife who will listen to me when I feel the need to explain a rather difficult point I have come across in my course of studies. And I want a wife who will type my papers for me when I have written them.

I want a wife who will take care of the details of my social   6
life. When my wife and I are invited out by my friends, I want a wife who will take care of the babysitting arrangements. When

I meet people at school that I like and want to entertain, I want a wife who will have the house clean, will prepare a special meal, serve it to me and my friends, and not interrupt when I talk about the things that interest me and my friends. I want a wife who will have arranged that the children are fed and ready for bed before my guests arrive so that the children do not bother us. I want a wife who takes care of the needs of my guests so that they feel comfortable, who makes sure that they have an ashtray, that they are passed the hors d'oeuvres, that they are offered a second helping of the food, that their wine glasses are replenished when necessary, that their coffee is served to them as they like it. And I want a wife who knows that sometimes I need a night out by myself.

7   I want a wife who is sensitive to my sexual needs, a wife who makes love passionately and eagerly when I feel like it, a wife who makes sure that I am satisfied. And, of course, I want a wife who will not demand sexual attention when I am not in the mood for it. I want a wife who assumes the complete responsibility for birth control, because I do not want more children. I want a wife who will remain sexually faithful to me so that I do not have to clutter up my intellectual life with jealousies. And I want a wife who understands that *my* sexual needs may entail more than strict adherence to monogamy. I must, after all, be able to relate to people as fully as possible.

8   If, by chance, I find another person more suitable as a wife than the wife I already have, I want the liberty to replace my present wife with another one. Naturally, I will expect a fresh, new life; my wife will take the children and be solely responsible for them so that I am left free.

9   When I am through with school and have a job, I want my wife to quit working and remain at home so that my wife can more fully and completely take care of a wife's duties.

10   My God, who *wouldn't* want a wife?

Content

1. Syfers defines *wife* in terms of the purpose(s), activities, and personality traits of a person functioning in a wife's many roles. What are some of these?

2. What is the purpose of Syfers's definition of *wife*? How could she expect her intended audience of feminist women to react to this definition? How would more traditional women be expected to respond to this definition? Would men be expected to react in ways similar to their female counterparts?

3. Does Syfers mean what she says? For instance, does she really favor the sexual double standard identified in paragraphs 7 and 8? How can you tell?

Strategies/Structures

1. What determines the order in which the wife's expected services are identified?

2. Why does Syfers end her essay with a question (¶ 10)? Does the expletive "My God" enhance or detract from the effect?

3. Both Syfers and Ellison (pp. 194–200) use definitions to argue a point, yet the nature of their language and the manner of their appeals are quite different. Explain.

Language

1. Syfers always calls a *wife* by that label and never uses the pronouns *he* or *she*. Why not?

2. Why does Syfers use the short, simple (almost simplistic) phrase "I want a wife," and why does she repeat it so often?

For Writing

1. In response to Syfers's essay, write your own version of "I want a wife" or "I want a husband." Identify, in your definition, as Syfers does, some of the wife's or husband's most important roles, activities, and personality traits.

2. Write an essay in which you define the ideal relationship between husband and wife. How likely is this ideal to be realized? Or, after defining the ideal relationship between husband and wife, compare and contrast it with the ideal relationship between roommates or apartment mates. What are some conspicuous similarities and differences?

HANS C. von BAEYER

Born in Berlin in 1938 and raised in Germany, Switzerland, and Canada, von Baeyer was educated at Columbia and Vanderbilt Universities. He taught at McGill University before coming to The College of William and Mary in 1968 as a physics professor. In addition to teaching and research on elementary particle physics, von Baeyer directs the Virginia Associated Research Campus, and provides science education for the public through his writings and movies. "The Wonder of Gravity," reprinted below, received the 1979 Science Writing Award of the American Institute of Physics and the U.S. Steel Foundation. It illustrates von Baeyer's skill at explaining complex scientific concepts and phenomena for non-scientific audiences.

The Wonder of Gravity

1   On the 14th of March [1880], 100 years ago, Albert Einstein was born. The centenary of his birth provides the occasion for a celebration of his achievements and an affirmation of his universal fame. It is a jubilee of pure reason and a memorial to human kindness, humility and decency. . . .

2   The three deep mysteries which occupied Einstein throughout his life can be summed up in three questions: What is space? What is time? What is gravity? He did not answer them, of course. No mortal will. But he did discover relationships among them that had never been suspected, and he provided mathematical formulations which are radical and beautiful and, as far as we know, correct. His theory of gravity, worked out between 1910 and 1916, remains Einstein's greatest monument and probably the most profound feat of pure reasoning in the history of natural philosophy.

3   Gravity, like space, is ubiquitous and, like time, it cannot be turned off. Electricity, another familiar force, can be switched off, magnetism can be shielded, even the strong force which holds atomic nuclei together can be counteracted by antimatter,

but gravity passes through all materials, affects all matter equally and has no opposing force, no shield, no anti-gravity. Only God can turn it on and off, and He is proud of this prowess. "Can you bind the cluster of the Pleiades?" he rhetorically asks Job who replies humbly: ". . . I have spoken of great things which I have not understood, things too wonderful for me to know." Very few humans, like Isaac Newton and Albert Einstein, were allowed to lift the veil a little.

Because it is always there, and because one cannot affect 4 it, one is rarely conscious of gravity. And yet it dominates life. What triumph when the newborn infant first lifts his wobbly head from the mattress to peer around—the first victory over gravity. From that moment on, life is a constant battle. We win decisively when we first stand up, learn to ride a bicycle, climb a mountain, scramble up a rope, hit a homerun, erect a wall, fly a plane, tie up a tomato plant, build a dam, hang a painting, lift a dumbbell, clear a hurdle, ascend by elevator, hoist a flag or pull ourselves aboard a departing bus. Gravity, on the other hand, wins every time a pin drops, a plane crashes, a tower topples, an avalanche strikes and a baby rolls off the bed.

More significant than these major encounters are the never 5 ending little skirmishes that wear us down. Each day begins with a confrontation. We must rise from bed by lifting our bodies against the seductive powerful pull of gravity. Sometimes this little conflict escalates into a battle and ends in defeat. Gravity has captured another prisoner. At other times, proud of our early success, we taunt gravity by challenging it to a duel of pushups, kneebends or chinups. The outcome is inevitable: In the end gravity always wins. After the morning trauma we spend a day climbing stairs, rising from chairs, lifting food to our mouths (and occasionally dropping it), moving pots or books around (and occasionally dropping them); in short, either lowering things that are up or raising things that are down. Meanwhile, the heart is pumping blood against gravity and the muscles are guying bones against collapse. The battle ends only when our bodies are finally abandoned to gravity in the grave.

The world is shaped by gravity and the operations of nature 6 depend on it. After gathering the materials of the earth into a ball, it holds them together. Opposing the titanic convulsions of the young planet, it formed the mountains. It propels the rivers and streams. Gravity pulls the rain from the clouds and flattens the surface of the sea. It gives direction to the trunks of trees and the stems of flowers. Because of gravity, the lower parts of animals differ from the upper parts. Gravity acts as a restraining, organizing, direction-giving principle in nature. Inexorably it draws form out of chaos. It determines the shapes of stars and galaxies, the orbits of planets and the expansion of the universe. It binds the cluster of the Pleiades and keeps our feet firmly planted on the earth.

7   The organizing role of gravity in the scheme of nature was engrained in Greek philosophy. Aristotle taught that the natural motion of heavy things is down toward the center of the earth. This is a most reassuring state of affairs. The mystery of gravity has dissolved. Why does a stone fall? Well, why shouldn't it, replies the Philosopher, down is its natural tendency, and it just follows that innate inclination. Much rather you should ask, why does it come to rest on the floor? And the answer is that its natural tendency is checked there by the intervention of an artifice in the form of the opposing force of the floor.

8   To say that a thing is natural removes it from further speculation. Natural means normal, healthy, ordinary, rather than anomalous, pathological, in need of analysis and interpretation. The word "naturally" serves to end conversations, rather than to start them.

9   For almost 2000 years, Aristotle's answer satisfied most philosophers. It was in the seventeenth century that Isaac Newton made gravity into something extraordinary, something to be aware of, something in need of explanation. To him, as it was earlier to Galileo, the natural state of an apple, detached from its tree, is at rest. Only under the influence of this special effect, called gravity, does the apple abandon its natural state and begin to fall. To us, who are earthbound, it seems strange that motionlessness should be called natural. An astronaut in mid-flight would find this idea more plausible because he is used to the sight of a hammer calmly remaining in place after he has released it.

10   Newton, by formalizing and generalizing the concept of gravity, deepened its mystery. He showed that gravity is not

only a property of the earth but resides as well in the moon, the
sun and the planets. In fact, all material objects in the universe
attract each other. The manner in which they do follows certain
simple mathematical laws which Newton ingeniously unrav-
elled. But where does this force come from? What makes things
attract each other?

The technical name for Newton's description is action-at-   11
a-distance. It means that two objects, far apart, exert a pull on
each other without need for an intervening medium or mechanism. It is most strange. To influence another person we must
use touch, or sound carried through the air, or we can send a
letter, or at least let light reflect from our bodies to reveal us,
but the earth influences us, pulls on us, without any such me-
diation. It pulls on the moon over a distance of thousands of
miles. Action-at-a-distance is an idea far from common daily
experience. . . .

More than 60 years have passed since Einstein submitted   12
a better description for Newton's action-at-a-distance. Because
it is difficult to understand, we rarely hear about it. The old
words are so much easier to repeat, and General Relativity can
be left to the experts. To be sure, many popularizers, including
Einstein himself, have tried to explain it, but the Newtonian
view still overwhelmingly predominates.

Mathematics, the language of Einstein's theory, is difficult   13
for most people who have no trouble with words. A translation
is therefore necessary. Unfortunately, just as it is impossible to
capture a poem in prose, it is almost impossible to describe in
words the contents of any but the simplest equations. Nevertheless, the attempt must be made. The primary tool of the
translator is analogy, a powerful technique in human understanding. Analogies present pictures to symbolize the mathematics, but the images are of necessity imperfect. Perhaps we
can find solace in Robert Graves' poem:

> He is quick, thinking in
>   clear images,
> I am slow, thinking in
>   broken images.
> He becomes dull, trusting

to his clear images:
I become sharp, mistrust-
ing my broken images.

14   The most famous prediction of general relativity, and one
which is easily amenable to analogy, concerns the deflection of
starlight due to the curvature of space. Normally starlight reaches
the earth in a straight line. Einstein's theory predicted that a ray
of starlight grazing the sun should be bent a little bit, giving the
earth-bound observer the illusion that the star's position has
shifted. Because the sun is so brilliant, stars which are almost
behind it, so that their rays graze it on their way to the earth,
cannot normally be seen at all. The only opportunity is afforded
by a total solar eclipse when the sun is blocked out. Astronomers
looked for the effect as soon as possible after Einstein's prediction and confirmed it. The bending comes about because in the
vicinity of the sun, space is curved.

15   Einstein himself, in his book "The Evolution of Physics,"
written with Leopold Infeld, made an analogy to explain what
is meant by curved space: "Imagine an idealized American town
consisting of parallel streets with parallel avenues running per-
pendicular to them. The distance between the streets and also
between the avenues is always the same. With these assumptions fulfilled, the blocks are of exactly the same size. In this
way I can easily characterize the position of any block." This
image represents ordinary or Euclidian space. Cars follow straight
lines defined by streets and avenues. But imagine now that some
subterranean upheaval causes a hill to bulge up in the middle
of town, taking streets, avenues and houses with it. Then the
space represented by the grid of streets is curved or non-Euclid-
ian. A car would still follow the streets and avenues, but if it
happened to be on a road that grazes the hill, its path would be
bent a little bit along a curve near the hill. In the same way the
sun causes curvature of space and a deflection of starlight. . . .

16   [But the curvature of space] does not touch upon the true
cause of gravity. To come to gravity, it is necessary to dig deeper
and to invent other analogies. As they become more profound,
the images become increasingly more broken. The following
word-picture is offered with some trepidation and in the hope
that it will encourage others to improve it.

Consider a stone in outer space. The size of a fist, hard 17
and cold, it drifts in space. . . . The earth, the moon, the sun,
the stars and galaxies are far away, so prodigiously far that their
gravitational forces on the stone are too weak to be registered
by even the finest instruments. Only the light from the distant
stars, puncturing the translucent blackness, provides a link
between the stone and the rest of the universe. The stars form
a patterned background, like a vast cage, for the stone. This
stellar cage is necessary. It cannot be imagined away, because
the stone is real and is placed in the real universe. A universe
consisting of a stone, and nothing else besides, is unimaginable.

There is no motion. The stars are so far away that they 18
seem to stand still, like a ship in the distance, which, though
under full steam, seems to be at rest on the horizon. There is
no sound. The vast clouds of gas and dust which surge around
the stars and fill the spiral arms of galaxies are far away. The
stars don't twinkle because no air breaks or bends their steady
beams of light. There is no change.

The stone is very still. Needing neither support nor anchor, 19
it does not tremble, roll or pitch. The images of the stars, reflected on its polished surface, never vary in position by a hair's
breadth. (The stars provide the necessary framework. Without
them, stillness could not be defined. Trembling, rolling and
pitching would be meaningless words in a universe without
stars.)

Whether the stone is at rest, or moving steadily in a straight 20
line, is impossible to distinguish. There are no objects nearby
to be used as milestones for measuring the progress of the stone:
The stars are too distant to serve as markers. . . . Motion can
truly only be thought of in relation to "sensible objects" and
without them becomes meaningless. To illustrate this commonplace, Einstein, in the beginning of his first scientific paper on
relativity, takes us to a homely railway station where a conductor
is timing the arrival of a train by comparing the position of its
engine with the position of the hands of his watch. Motion, to
Einstein, is common, apparent and relative, rather than mathematical, true and absolute.

The stone is so far removed from sensible objects that its 21
state of motion cannot be defined. (The persistent objector now
invents a way of using an astronomical version of a radar speed

trap to gauge the stone's motion from the vantage point of some distant planet. The attempt is valiant. However, such a measurement would require untold millennia for its execution, and we must insist on a *real* stone, in the *real* universe, with *real* measurements made by *real* people. Real people cannot wait millennia for a radar signal to return. In the real common world of Einstein, this objection is sufficient to rule out the radar device and thereby to reestablish the point: Whether the stone is moving in a straight line at constant speed, or not, is a question without an answer.)

22   Consider the stone, then, in the bleak stillness of outer space. Nothing happens, nothing changes, nothing moves.

23   To end the monotony, add something to the image. Close by, say 10,000 miles away, let the earth appear, materialized by the power of thought. Round, smooth, white wispy veils of cloud over a bluish mottled surface, cool, silent, familiar and inviting, the space age vision of our home. In relation to this new neighbor, the true motion of the stone can be ascertained. The center of the earth provides a benchmark which now fixes the position of the stone, 10,000 miles away and motionless in outer space.

24   But the motionlessness is only momentary. Imperceptibly at first, then gathering speed, the stone begins to move toward the earth. More precisely, it falls toward the center of the earth. Gravity is at work. The general theory of relativity provides a picture of how this comes about.

25   In Einstein's theory, gravity is related to another concept, hitherto unmentioned and apparently quite different in nature: the idea of time. . . . The union is called space-time and takes the place of Newton's Absolute Space as the stage for physical phenomena, including the fall of the stone in the void. *Space-time* is much further removed from our everyday intuition than is *Absolute Space* or even *curved space*. We are reduced to broken images.

26   Begin once more. Consider the stone without the earth. Nothing seems to be changing—but silently in the background there is now a gentle unfolding: Time is elapsing. Unlike space, which reaches up and down, right and left, forward and back, time flows relentlessly in one direction. Time, like space, must

be measured by a common, sensible, real object like a clock. Let a watch appear on the stone therefore. The word time will be given meaning by the reading of the watch chained to the stone.

The complete union of space and time is unimaginable. 27 The best we can do is to imagine time as a fictitious sort of space. The stone's history can then be thought of in borrowed words: The stone is moving through time. This phrase, almost trite from overuse in science fiction, requires a little amplification. For the sake of concreteness, a graph can be constructed of space and time. Position (in one dimension) is measured along one axis and time along the other. If a point on the graph represents a real object, like the stone in outer space, then it will move along the graph as time progresses. Successive moments and positions are represented by successive points on the graph. Thus, by translating time into a position along an axis, as is done every day in the graphs on the financial pages of the newspaper, motion in time can be translated into ordinary motion in space.

The flow of time is represented by a flow of an imaginary 28 medium. Time becomes a river. In the bleakness of the void, a stone (carrying its watch) floats in a vast and silent current of clear and subtle liquid which pervades every pore of the universe and bears everything within it inexorably forward. The current is time. Its motion cannot be stopped, its depth cannot be plumbed, its substance cannot be detected—because it is not real. Unlike a real river in real space, this current exists in the four dimensional space-time.

The stone, like a stick of wood on the water, has no motion 29 of its own, but drifts wherever it is carried by the imaginary river of time.

Finally, in our imagination, the earth appears again, 10,000 30 miles away. On the river of time, both stone and earth are carried along. At first they seem to travel in parallel lines, keeping their distance. But soon it becomes apparent that the streamlines are bent gently toward the earth. The current, its flow modified by the presence of the huge mass of the earth, carries the stone closer and closer to its neighbor. The bending of the streamlines is barely perceptible at a great distance, but close in it becomes more pronounced. At the earth's surface, finally, the flow is wildly distorted from its original direction.

31   This is an image of curved space-time which is the crux of Einstein's theory of gravity. It is different, more profound and more subtle than the idea of curved space. The stone, when released, does not find itself in the mysterious grip of the earth, acting at a distance of 10,000 miles. Instead, it abandons itself to the soft embrace of the river of time which envelops it and inexorably carries it along.

32   Thus we return to the harmonious Greek conception of falling as a natural motion. In Newtonian physics, the earth does violence to the stone's natural inclination, which is to remain where it started. A force is needed to overcome its inertia. In Einstein's universe, the stone simply does what is most natural. It drifts along the curves of space-time toward the earth. With respect to the imaginary water of the river of time, it simply remains where it started.

33   Gravity, instead of pulling directly on objects far away, is mediated by space-time. The earth affects the streamlines, and the streamlines in turn guide the stone. Cause and effect are proximate: each point affects only the surrounding points, and they in turn pass the effect along the stream.

34   Einstein, who wrote equations rather than words, coaxed from them a number of definite experimental predictions. The most compelling one provided his motivation from the beginning. Galileo had observed that different masses fall at the same rate. . . . Since the pull of gravity is obviously stronger on larger masses (i.e. they are heavier) this observation is difficult to understand. Why shouldn't heavier things fall faster . . .? Newton's explanation was that nature has devised a cunning conspiracy: Although a heavy stone experiences a stronger pull of gravity than a light one, it has just precisely so much more inertia, it is just precisely so much harder to budge, that the two stones end up falling at equal rates. This theory explains the facts, but it is contrived to give the right answer. How much simpler, in comparison, is curved space-time. Place into the stream of time a second stone, 10 times heavier than the first, and right next to it. The two will drift on and down toward the earth at precisely the same rate, because the current carries both together. A feather will do the same thing. And so will a piano or a grain of sand. The proposition that all objects fall at the

same rate fits so effortlessly into the context of the curvature of space-time that the incomprehensible becomes obvious, and the abstruse compelling. . . .

Curved space and curved space-time are difficult ideas— 35 but they are better than action-at-a-distance. We could offer Albert Einstein no greater gift on his hundredth birthday than to move away from the rigid, cold, mystical view of Newton and toward his gentler and more homely way of thinking. Try it: Close your eyes and think of a stone in your hand. Imagine letting go. Now picture it carried silently, swiftly, along the river of time which happens to have a little bend in it right here, directed toward the floor. The stone follows the streamline of space-time just as a twig follows a stream. What could be more natural?

Content

1. Throughout, von Baeyer makes comparisons and contrasts between Newton's and Einstein's theories of gravity. Identify some of these instances.
2. What is gravity? What are some of its effects? Explain von Baeyer's definition, "Gravity acts as a restraining, organizing, direction-giving principle in nature" (¶ 6).
3. How does von Baeyer illustrate Einstein's concept of motion as "common, apparent, and relative" (¶ 20)? Of what relevance is the illustration of the train conductor and the oncoming train to the stone moving in outer space (¶ 20 and elsewhere)?

Strategies/Structures

1. Why does von Baeyer identify his role in this article as that of a translator (¶ 13)? What is he translating? For whom?
2. Why does von Baeyer quote Robert Graves's poem on clear and broken images? What has this to do with his discussion of analogies? With his explanation of how gravity works?
3. Would von Baeyer, a physicist himself, be likely to use analogies in explaining gravity to an audience of professional physicists? Physics students? General readers? Justify your answer in each case.
4. Is it easy to visualize the analogy of the stone in outer space (¶s 17–34)? Does this clarify the concept of gravity for you? This is an

unusually long analogy; does von Baeyer extract sufficient meaning and clarity from it to justify its protracted use?

Language

1. How does von Baeyer define "natural" in paragraph 8? With what does he contrast this concept? Why?
2. Von Baeyer has deliberately avoided using highly complicated scientific terminology in this essay. Why? Whether or not you are a scientist, can you understand him? Why or why not?

For Writing

1. Write a definition of an abstract term—something intangible that can be identified in terms of its effects, causes, manifestations, or other nonphysical properties, such as love, truth, justice, greed, stubbornness, or pride. Illustrate your definition with one or two specific examples with which you are familiar; use the examples as a basis for making generalizations that apply to other aspects of the term.
2. Write an essay to define a process (scientific, technical, or other), object, or phenomenon by explaining how it works. Be sure to write on something you yourself understand well. If possible, use an analogy to clarify your explanation, as von Baeyer uses the stone in space to explain gravity.

LAIRD BLOOM

Laird Bloom (b. 1964) attended high school in Clayton, Missouri and Williamsburg, Virginia, where he edited the student newspaper and wrote a weekly sports column for the *Virginia Gazette*. Winner of a National Merit Scholarship and various awards for high school journalism, Bloom is majoring in cellular and molecular biology at the University of Michigan.

"The Progressive's Pilgrim" is a good example of a book review that identifies a book's main points for readers unfamiliar with the book. The reviewer makes no claims to be an expert on the subject. He does, however, provide sufficient information about health and social conditions in New York's Lower East Side before World War I, as well as about Wald's reforming activities, to make the review self-explanatory and self-contained. His interpretive comments, though few, precisely convey the book's tone, spirit, and emphasis. *In toto*, this review is an extended definition of *The House on Henry Street*, answering the journalist's questions who, what, where, when, why, how, and under what circumstances, and thereby explaining its essence.

The Progressives' Pilgrim: A Review of Lillian D. Wald's "The House on Henry Street"

R eformers, through the years, have had a hard time making 1
themselves heard. There were, for instance, Jesus Christ, Martin Luther, Karl Marx. The image of the crusader for social justice has long been one of an outspoken idealist who is ignored or killed for his troubles. Lillian D. Wald's *The House on Henry Street* (1915; rpt. New York: Dover, 1971), though, shows the modern reformer in a different perspective. Writing from first-hand experience, she tells of the neighbors' love for the Henry Street Settlement workers and the needed reforms she was able to accomplish. She changes the reformer from an ethereal idealist to a practical friend to the man in the street—or gutter.

Wald begins during the Depression of 1893–94 when the 2
Henry Street Settlement is no more than a top-floor tenement room. She describes some of the shocking scenes in New York's impoverished Lower East Side which compelled her, as a visiting nurse, to begin relief work: new mothers hemorrhaging alone in filthy rooms because they cannot afford medical care, poor women carefully tending covered kettles of water to make their equally-poor friends believe that they have food for the table, quack doctors prescribing medicine and pocketing the money which friends have collected to pay for it, and children being

prohibited from attending school because their parents cannot afford to buy even a small amount of medicine to treat contagious diseases. She gives graphic descriptions of individual cases, often saddening or horrifying in the telling, but which close with Wald's characteristic happy endings of successful treatment and relief of the victims.

3 Her history of the reform movement she participated in covers many important aspects of the progressivism that was gaining strength nationwide as hers obtained support on the Lower East Side. Much of her early work dealt with reform for the poor and the laboring classes. She provided inexpensive but high-quality neighborhood nursing care and information and supplies for home treatment of minor illnesses. Her results in this area were particularly encouraging, as the mortality rate of children under her home care program was one-fourth that of children suffering from the same diseases in hospitals. Wald eventually grew familiar with city officials and was able to greatly improve public health, including providing midwife training courses, milk stations for infant nutrition, and nurses and medicines for public schools.

4 The Henry Street Settlement became almost a neighborhood "Y" as well, sponsoring clubs, classes, art courses, and a reading room which proved popular with youngsters. For future homemakers, the Settlement offered a course in cooking and hygiene.

5 Wald and her Settlement also managed to achieve progressive labor reform. The National Child Labor Committee, of which Wald and colleague Florence Kelley were members 1904-14, promoted the enactment of numerous laws regarding enforcement of minimum-age requirements and prohibiting "tenement industries," in which unregulated home businesses often had parents overworking their children. For older laborers, the Settlement sponsored a meeting hall for labor meetings. Wald lent her support whenever she could, especially when the issue was women's labor. Municipal and national laws regulating hours, pay, and working conditions can be credited to her.

6 *The House on Henry Street* reads like a Horatio Alger novel or a B-movie serial. The chapters could almost be retitled "Lillian Conquers the Whooping Cough" or "Lillian Protects Youth

against Decadence," for she seems to meet with success at every turn. However implausible this may seem, her consistent success on all fronts is what makes the book engaging. Wald shows herself, without being smug, as beloved by the neighborhood of Henry Street and respected by the lobbyists and government officials. To the poor tenement dwellers, she is a benevolent saint who brings entertainment, education, comfort—life—to a hitherto lifeless community. Wald's willingness to help anyone, young or old, sick or healthy, immigrant or native, conveys the author's warmth and compassion.

Toward the end of the book, there is a shift in tone in which much of the warmth is lost. In the loftier, more idealistic prose of Jane Addams, Wald writes of the Settlement's support for the Bolshevik Revolution in Russia and of its policies of acculturation for immigrants, a disappointing reversal from her narrative of anecdotes. The personality she has built up in her dealings with the Lower East Side neighborhood is diminished when she tries to go beyond it. This disconcerting attempt at transcendence is perhaps due to the fact that the book was first written in serial form for the *Atlantic Monthly* and may not have been written with unity in mind. Overall, though, the end of the book contains enough anecdotes to retain some of its enjoyable personal flavor. 7

The effect of Wald's book is to bring reform movements into perspective. Her personal experiences illustrate that there were real problems, that there were real people behind these problems, and that effective reforms were really possible. Wald, pilgrim of progress, has made the ideal a reality. 8

Content

1. Why should a book review for a general audience unfamiliar with the book be self-explanatory? What information does Bloom provide about the author? About New York's Lower East Side?

2. Has he omitted any information necessary to understand what the book is about?

3. Why is it important for the time period in which Wald was working in New York to be identified?

4. Bloom says the book is anecdotal in technique, yet he doesn't quote any anecdotes. Should he have done so?

Strategies/Structures

1. To what extent should a book reviewer make his opinion of the book apparent to readers? By what point in the review do you know Bloom's opinion of the book?

2. In paragraph 6 Bloom compares *The House on Henry Street* to "a Horatio Alger novel or a B-movie serial"? What is the effect of this comparison? If readers don't understand these allusions, are there explanatory details to supplement them?

3. Reviews usually provide some overall assessment of the book in question, often near the end. Does Bloom's review do this?

Language

1. In what senses does Bloom use *progressive* and *progressivism*? Does he ever define the term explicitly? Should he have done so?

2. What details or evaluative words provide clues about Bloom's opinion of the book?

For Writing

1. Write a review of a book, play, or a movie with which your readers are unfamiliar. Be sure to tell them enough about the main points of the content or plot so they can decide whether or not they want to read or see it. Will you have space to discuss other aspects of the work in detail, such as its style, accuracy, quality of writing, symbolism, or recurrent motifs?

2. Write a review of a play or movie you can be certain your readers are familiar with, and concentrate instead on the quality of the performance. Consider such aspects as how well the principals and supporting cast played their parts, and what was notable (either positive or negative) about such aspects as the sets, costumes, lighting and sound effects, timing and pace of the performance. How little or how much of your own values, taste, or personality will you make apparent in the reviews; i.e., Will you tell your readers what you liked best— and least—about the production, and why?

Strategies for Writing—Definition

1. What is the purpose of the definition (or definitions) I'm writing about? Do I want to explain the subject's particular characteristics? Identify its nature? Persuade readers of my interpretation of its meaning? Entertain readers with a novel, bizarre, or highly personal meaning? How long will my essay be? (A short essay will require a restricted subject that you can cover in the limited space.)

2. For whom am I providing the definition? Why are they reading it? Do they know enough about the background of the subject to enable me to deal with it in a fairly technical way? Or must I stick to the basics—or at least begin there? If I wish to persuade or entertain my readers, can I count on them to have a pre-existing definition in mind against which I can match my own?

3. Will my entire essay be a definition, or will I incorporate definition(s) as part of a different type of essay? What proportion of my essay will be devoted to definition? Where will I include definitions? As I introduce new terms or concepts? Where else, if at all?

4. What techniques of definition will I use: naming; providing examples, brief or extended; comparing and contrasting; considering cause and effect; analysis; argument; narrative; analogy; or a mixture? Will I employ primarily positive or negative means (i.e., *X* is, or *X* is not)?

5. How much denotative (objective) definition will I use in my essay? How much connotative (subjective) definition? Will my tone be serious? Authoritative? Entertaining? Sarcastic? Or otherwise?

Additional Writing Topics

Write an extended definition of one or more of the following trends, concepts, abstractions, phenomena, or institutions:

1. Women's liberation
2. Male chauvinism
3. Enthusiasm
4. Depression (economic or psychological)
5. Friendship
6. Marriage
7. Self-reliance
8. Democracy, Communism, Socialism, or some other political theory or form of government
9. Protestantism, Catholicism, Judaism, Buddhism, or some other religion

10. Personality
11. Character
12. Blues (musical or psychological)
13. A good job or profession
14. Country, Western, or soul (as in music or culture)
15. Comedy, tragedy, romance, or satire
16. A sport, game, hobby, or recreational activity
17. A Northerner, Southerner, Middle-Westerner, Texan, Californian, or person from some other state or region
18. A scientific or technical phenomenon of your choice (an eclipse, the "big bang" theory of creation, genetic engineering, DNA, the MX missile)

7 *Division and Classification*

To divide something is to separate it into its component parts. As a writer you can divide a large, complex subject into smaller segments, easier for you and your readers to deal with individually than to consider in a large, complicated whole. As the section on process analysis indicates (see pp. 82–117), writers usually employ division to explain the individual stages of a process—how the earth was formed; how a professional jockey (or potter or surgeon performs his or her job); how a Rubik's cube works. Process analysis also underlies explanations of how to make or do something, how to train your dog, or make a cake, or cut gems.

You could also divide your subject in other ways—according to types of dogs, cakes, or gems. And there would be still different ways to divide a discussion of dogs—by their size (miniature, small, medium, large); by the length of their hair (short or long); or according to their suitability as working dogs, pets, or show dogs.

As you start to divide your subject, you almost naturally begin to *classify* it as well, to sort it into categories of groups or families. You'll probably determine the subcategories according to some logical principle, or according to characteristics common to members of particular subgroups. Don't stretch to create esoteric groupings (dogs by hair color, for example) if your com-

227

mon sense suggests a more natural way. Some categories simply make more sense than others. A discussion of dogs by species could be logically arranged in alphabetical order—afghan, borzoi, bulldog, collie, Weimaraner. But a discussion that grouped dogs by species and subspecies would be easier to understand and more economical to write. For instance, you could consider all the common features of spaniels first, before dividing them into subspecies—cocker, springer, water—and discussing the differences.

Again, how minutely you refine the subcategories of your classification system depends on the length of your writing, your focus, and your emphasis. You could use a *binary* (two-part) *classification*. This is a favorite technique of classifiers who wish to sort things into two categories, those with a particular characteristic and those without it (drinkers and non-drinkers, swimmers and non-swimmers). Thus in an essay discussing the components of a large structure or organization—a farm, a corporation, a university—a binary classification might lead you to focus on management and labor, or the university's academic and non-academic functions. If you wanted to concentrate on the academic aspects of your own university, you might categorize them according to academic divisions—arts and sciences, business, education, music, public health. A smaller classification would examine the academic disciplines within a division— biology, English, history, mathematics. Or smaller yet, depending on your purpose—English literature, American literature, creative writing, linguistics. *Ad infinitum*, as the anonymous jingle observes:

> Big fleas have little fleas, and these
> Have littler fleas to bite 'em,
> And these have fleas, and these have fleas,
> And so on *ad infinitum*.

Of the essays in this section, James Thurber's "University Days" represents the most casual division of his larger subject, the general incompetence of himself, his fellow students, and his professors when he was an undergraduate at Ohio State. His series of narrative examples, equally funny and of roughly equal length, is arranged according to incompetence in the classroom (biology, economics, and gym) and incompetence outside the classroom, on the student newspaper, and in military drill, with "one hundred and nine men marching in one direction" and Thurber marching in the other.

The other essays in this section represent more obvious examples of classification. In "Writing for an Audience," Linda Flower explains how writers must consider their readers' knowledge of the subject at hand, their attitudes toward it, and their needs. This classification is subject to further refinement, as Flower indicates that writers have different attitudes toward the first two categories than toward the third; they are trying to change the readers' knowledge and attitudes, but to adapt to the readers' needs. Lewis Thomas, in "The Technology of Medicine," classifies his subject as "nontechnology," "halfway technology," and the "genuinely decisive technology of modern medicine." Each of these has specific functions, causes, and effects. As he classifies, Thomas also analyzes his subject through comparing the first two categories, which deal with medical problems after they have occurred and are very costly and difficult to deliver. He contrasts these with the last category; decisive technology, he demonstrates, is preventive, "relatively inexpensive, and relatively easy to deliver." In "Reflections on Horror Movies," Robert Brustein analyzes, defines, and illustrates three categories of horror movies: "Mad Doctor, Atomic Beast, and Interplanetary Monster." In all three of these essays the classification system provides the basis for the overall organization; but here, as in most essays, the authors use many other techniques of writing in addition—narration, definition, description, analysis, illustration, and comparison and contrast.

In writing essays based on division, you might ask the following questions to help organize your materials: What are the parts of the total unit? How can these be subdivided to make the subject more understandable to my readers? In essays of classification, where you're sorting or grouping two or more things, you can ask: Into what categories can I sort these items? According to what principles—of logic, common characteristics, "fitness"? Do I want my classification to emphasize the similarities among groups, or their differences? Once I've determined the groupings, am I organizing my discussion of each category in the same way, considering the same features in the same order? In many instances divisions and classifications are in the mind of the beholder. Is the glass half full or half empty? Your job as a writer is to help your readers recognize and accept the order of your universe.

JAMES THURBER

> Thurber (1894–1961) made his international reputation as a hu-
> morist at *The New Yorker*, where he worked half a century as
> editor, cartoonist, and writer, and which he described in *The
> Years with Ross* (1957). Among his numerous books, including
> collections of essays, short stories, and drawings (which Doro-
> thy Parker called "unbaked cookies"), are *Is Sex Necessary?*
> (1929, with E. B. White), *The Owl in the Attic and Other Perplexi-
> ties* (1931), *The Seal in the Bedroom and Other Predicaments* (1932),
> *My Life and Hard Times* (1933), *The Male Animal* (1940), and *Men,
> Women, and Dogs* (1943). Born in Columbus, Ohio, Thurber at-
> tended Ohio State University from 1913 to 1918, but left with-
> out earning a degree. "University Days" is a wry interpretation
> of his experiences at Ohio State. It is written with characteristic
> Thurber humor, which—in a parody of Wordsworth's "emo-
> tion recollected in tranquility"—he called "a kind of emotional
> chaos told about calmly and quietly in retrospect."

University Days

I passed all the other courses that I took at my University, but   1
I could never pass botany. This was because all botany students had to spend several hours a week in a laboratory looking
through a microscope at plant cells, and I could never see through
a microscope. I never once saw a cell through a microscope. This
used to enrage my instructor. He would wander around the
laboratory pleased with the progress all the students were making in drawing the involved and, so I am told, interesting structure of flower cells, until he came to me. I would just be standing
there. "I can't see anything," I would say. He would begin
patiently enough, explaining how anybody can see through a
microscope, but he would always end up in a fury; claiming that
I could *too* see through a microscope but just pretended that I
couldn't. "It takes away from the beauty of flowers anyway," I
used to tell him. "We are not concerned with beauty in this
course," he would say. "We are concerned solely with what I

may call the *mechanics* of flars." "Well," I'd say. "I can't see anything." "Try it just once again," he'd say, and I would put my eye to the microscope and see nothing at all, except now and again a nebulous milky substance—a phenomenon of maladjustment. You were supposed to see a vivid, restless clockwork of sharply defined plant cells. "I see what looks like a lot of milk," I would tell him. This, he claimed, was the result of my not having adjusted the microscope properly, so he would readjust it for me, or rather, for himself. And I would look again and see milk.

2   I finally took a deferred pass, as they called it, and waited a year and tried again. (You had to pass one of the biological sciences or you couldn't graduate.) The professor had come back from vacation brown as a berry, bright-eyed, and eager to explain cell-structure again to his classes. "Well," he said to me, cheerily, when we met in the first laboratory hour of the semester, "we're going to see cells this time, aren't we?" "Yes, sir," I said. Students to the right of me and left of me and in front of me were seeing cells; what's more, they were quietly drawing pictures of them in their notebooks. Of course, I didn't see anything.

3   "We'll try it," the professor said to me, grimly, "with every adjustment of the microscope known to man. As God is my witness, I'll arrange this glass so that you see cells through it or I'll give up teaching. In twenty-two years of botany, I—" He cut off abruptly for he was beginning to quiver all over, like Lionel Barrymore,[1] and he genuinely wished to hold onto his temper; his scenes with me had taken a great deal out of him.

4   So we tried it with every adjustment of the microscope known to man. With only one of them did I see anything but blackness or the familiar lacteal opacity, and that time I saw, to my pleasure and amazement, a variegated constellation of flecks, specks, and dots. These I hastily drew. The instructor, noting my activity, came from an adjoining desk, a smile on his lips and his eyebrows high in hope. He looked at my cell drawing. "What's that?" he demanded, with a hint of squeal in his voice.

---

[1] American actor, (1878–1954).

"That's what I saw," I said. "You didn't, you didn't, you *didn't!"* he screamed, losing control of his temper instantly, and he bent over and squinted into the microscope. His head snapped up. "That's your eye!" he shouted. "You've fixed the lens so that it reflects! You've drawn your eye!"

Another course that I didn't like, but somehow managed to pass, was economics. I went to that class straight from the botany class, which didn't help me any in understanding either subject. I used to get them mixed up. But not as mixed up as another student in my economics class who came there direct from a physics laboratory. He was a tackle on the football team, named Bolenciecwcz. At that time Ohio State University had one of the best football teams in the country, and Bolenciecwcz was one of its outstanding stars. In order to be eligible to play it was necessary for him to keep up in his studies, a very difficult matter, for while he was not dumber than an ox he was not any smarter. Most of his professors were lenient and helped him along. None gave him more hints, in answering questions, or asked him simpler ones than the economics professor, a thin, timid man named Bassum. One day when we were on the subject of transportation and distribution, it came Bolenciecwcz's turn to answer a question. "Name one means of transportation," the professor said to him. No light came into the big tackle's eyes. "Just any means of transportation," said the professor. Bolenciecwcz sat staring at him. "That is," pursued the professor, "any medium, agency, or method of going from one place to another." Bolenciecwcz had the look of a man who is being led into a trap. "You may choose among steam, horse-drawn, or electrically propelled vehicles," said the instructor. "I might suggest the one which we commonly take in making long journeys across land." There was a profound silence in which everybody stirred uneasily, including Bolenciecwcz and Mr. Bassum. Mr. Bassum abruptly broke this silence in an amazing manner. "Choo-choo-choo," he said, in a low voice, and turned instantly scarlet. He glanced appealingly around the room. All of us, of course, shared Mr. Bassum's desire that Bolenciecwcz should stay abreast of the class in economics, for the Illinois game, one of the hardest and most important of the season, was only a week off. "Toot, toot, too-tooooooot!" some student with a deep voice moaned, and we all looked encouragingly at Bol-enciecwcz. Somebody else gave a fine imitation of a locomotive letting off steam. Mr. Bassum himself rounded off the little show. "Ding, dong, ding, dong," he said, hopefully. Bolenciecwcz was staring at the floor now, trying to think, his great brow furrowed, hig huge hands rubbing together, his face red.

6   "How did you come to college this year, Mr. Bolen-ciecwcz?" asked the professor. "*Chuffa* chuffa, *chuffa* chuffa."

7   "M'father sent me," said the football player.

8   "What on?" asked Bassum.

9   "I git an 'lowance," said the tackle, in a low, husky voice, obviously embarrassed.

10   "No, no," said Bassum. "Name a means of transportation. What did you *ride* here on?"

11   "Train," said Bolenciecwcz.

12   "Quite right," said the professor. "Now, Mr. Nugent, will you tell us—"

13   If I went through anguish in botany and economics—for different reasons—gymnasium work was even worse. I don't even like to think about it. They wouldn't let you play games or join in the exercises with your glasses on and I couldn't see with mine off. I bumped into professors, horizontal bars, agricultural students, and swinging iron rings. Not being able to see, I could take it but I couldn't dish it out. Also, in order to pass gymnasium (and you had to pass it to graduate) you had to learn to swim if you didn't know how. I didn't like the swimming pool, I didn't like swimming, and I didn't like the swimming instructor, and after all these years I still don't. I never swam but I passed my gym work anyway, by having another student give my gymnasium number (978) and swim across the pool in my place. He was a quiet, amiable blonde youth, number 473, and he would have seen through a microscope for me if we could have got away with it, but we couldn't get away with it. Another thing I didn't like about gymnasium work was that they made you strip the day you registered. It is impossible for me to be happy when I am stripped and being asked a lot of questions. Still, I did better than a lanky agricultural student who was cross-examined just before I was. They asked each student what college he was in—that is, whether Arts, Engi-

neering, Commerce, or Agriculture. "What college are you in?" the instructor snapped at the youth in front of me. "Ohio State University," he said promptly.

It wasn't that agricultural student but it was another a 14 whole lot like him who decided to take up journalism, possibly on the ground that when farming went to hell he could fall back on newspaper work. He didn't realize, of course, that that would be very much like falling back full-length on a kit of carpenter's tools. Haskins didn't seem cut out for journalism, being too embarassed to talk to anybody and unable to use a typewriter, but the editor of the college paper assigned him to the cow barns, the sheep house, the horse pavilion, and the animal husbandry department generally. This was a genuinely big "beat," for it took up five times as much ground and got ten times as great a legislative appropriation as the College of Liberal Arts. The agricultural student knew animals, but nevertheless his stories were dull and colorlessly written. He took all afternoon on each one of them, on account of having to hunt for each letter on the typewriter. Once in a while he had to ask somebody to help him hunt. "C" and "L," in particular, were hard letters for him to find. His editor finally got pretty much annoyed at the farmer-journalist because his pieces were so uninteresting. "See here, Haskins," he snapped at him one day, "why is it we never have anything hot from you on the horse pavilion? Here we have two hundred head of horses on this campus—more than any other university in the Western Conference except Purdue—and yet you never get any real low down on them. Now shoot over to the horse barns and dig up something lively." Haskins shambled out and came back in about an hour; he said he had something. "Well, start it off snappily," said the editor. "Something people will read." Haskins set to work and in a couple of hours brought a sheet of typewritten paper to the desk; it was a two-hundred word story about some disease that had broken out among the horses. Its opening sentence was simple but arresting. It read: "Who has noticed the sores on the tops of the horses in the animal husbandry building?"

Ohio State was a land grant university and therefore two 15 years of military drill was compulsory. We drilled with old Springfield rifles and studied the tactics of the Civil War even though the World War was going on at the time.[2] At 11 o'clock each morning thousands of freshmen and sophomores used to deploy over the campus, moodily creeping up on the old chemistry building. It was good training for the kind of warfare that was waged at Shiloh but it had no connection with what was going on in Europe. Some people used to think there was German money behind it, but they didn't dare say so or they would have been thrown in jail as German spies. It was a period of muddy thought and marked, I believe, the decline of higher education in the Middle West.

16   As a soldier I was never any good at all. Most of the cadets were glumly indifferent soldiers, but I was no good at all. Once General Littlefield, who was commandant of the cadet corps, popped up in front of me during regimental drill and snapped, "You are the main trouble with this university!" I think he meant that my type was the main trouble with the university but he may have meant me individually. I was mediocre at drill, certainly—that is, until my senior year. By that time I had drilled longer than anybody else in the Western Conference, having failed at military at the end of each preceding year so that I had to do it all over again. I was the only senior still in uniform. The uniform which, when new, had made me look like an interurban railway conductor, now that it had become faded and too tight made me look like Bert Williams in his bellboy act. This had a definitely bad effect on my morale. Even so, I had become by sheer practice little short of wonderful at squad manoeuvres.

17   One day General Littlefield picked our company out of the whole regiment and tried to get it mixed up by putting it through one movement after another as fast as we could execute them: squads right, squads left, squads on right into line, squads right about, squads left front into line etc. In about three minutes one hundred and nine men were marching in one direction and I was marching away from them at an angle of forty degrees, all alone. "Company, halt!" shouted General Littlefield, "That man

---

[2] Two days after the World War I armistice was signed (on November 11, 1916), Thurber arrived in Paris to work for the state department as a code clerk.

is the only man who has it right!" I was made a corporal for my achievement.

The next day General Littlefield summoned me to his office. [18] He was swatting flies when I went in. I was silent and he was silent too, for a long time. I don't think he remembered me or why he had sent for me, but he didn't want to admit it. He swatted some more flies, keeping his eyes on them narrowly before he let go with the swatter. "Button up your coat!" he snapped. Looking back on it now I can see that he meant me although he was looking at a fly, but I just stood there. Another fly came to rest on a paper in front of the general and began rubbing its hind legs together. The general lifted the swatter cautiously. I moved restlessly and the fly flew away. "You startled him!" barked General Littlefield, looking at me severely. I said I was sorry. "That won't help the situation!" snapped the General, with cold military logic. I didn't see what I could do except offer to chase some more flies toward his desk, but I didn't say anything. He stared out the window at the faraway figures of co-eds crossing the campus toward the library. Finally, he told me I could go. So I went. He either didn't know which cadet I was or else he forgot what he wanted to see me about. It may have been that he wished to apologize for having called me the main trouble with the university; or maybe he had decided to compliment me on my brilliant drilling of the day before and then at the last minute decided not to. I don't know. I don't think about it much anymore.

Content

1. Thurber's essay discusses several of his experiences as a college student between 1913 and 1918. What details reveal this time period? What in this classic essay transcends the period in which it was written? Are students significantly different now from those in Thurber's day? Why or why not?

2. What kind of character does Thurber portray himself as when he was a student? Are Bolenciecwcz and Haskins similar to each other or to Thurber? Have the three any conspicuous differences? Why are these characters funny?

3. What are Thurber's professors like? In what ways is their behavior stereotypical of college professors? What characteristics are exaggerated? For what purposes does Thurber use such exaggerated features?

Strategies/Structures

1. What determines the basis for Thurber's categories?
2. In retrospect Thurber as author can laugh at some of his experiences as an undergraduate at Ohio State which were not funny at the time. Why? Does he expect his readers to laugh, too? Why or why not?
3. Thurber presents several incidents in the form of dramatic vignettes. Identify these incidents.
4. What is the thesis of Thurber's essay? Is it explicit or implicit? Why might an essay composed of distinct categories be likely to have an implicit rather than an explicit thesis?

Language

1. Why, in an essay of fairly simple language, does Thurber use "the familiar lacteal opacity" in paragraph 4?
2. Does he use any other complicated language? If so, where? For what purposes?

For Writing

1. Present a significant aspect of your college days through narration of an incident or two in which you are the main character. If you wish, you may use dialogue and describe other students or professors. And if you want to write humorously, you may exaggerate actions, gestures, speech mannerisms, or other features.
2. Write a straightforward essay about your college days in which you classify one or more major aspects of your experience—your courses, professors, fellow students, extracurricular activities, successes or failures. Use the classification as the basis for organizing your essay.

▶───────────────────────────────────◀

LINDA FLOWER

Flower (b. 1944) earned her Ph.D. in 1972 from Rutgers, and taught English at the University of Pittsburgh (1972–73) before directing the Business Communication program at Carnegie-Mellon University (1974–80). Since 1980, she has been an Associate Professor of English there. Her research on the composing process, including extensive study in cognitive psychology with Carnegie-Mellon colleague John R. Hayes, has been very influential in helping teachers and other researchers understand how people write. Flower's research has also resulted in a number of practical suggestions for writers, presented in her textbook *Problem-Solving Strategies for Writing* (1981), from which "Writing for an Audience" is excerpted. Gertrude Stein once said, "I write for myself and strangers." Be thinking as you read this of the likely audience for your writing.

Writing for an Audience

T he goal of the writer is to create a momentary common 1 ground between the reader and the writer. You want the reader to share your knowledge and your attitude toward that knowledge. Even if the reader eventually disagrees, you want him or her to be able for the moment to *see things as you see them.* A good piece of writing closes the gap between you and the reader.

Analyze your audience

The first step in closing that gap is to gauge the distance between 2 the two of you. Imagine, for example, that you are a student writing your parents, who have always lived in New York City, about a wilderness survival expedition you want to go on over spring break. Sometimes obvious differences such as age or background will be important, but the critical differences for writers usually fall into three areas: the reader's *knowledge* about the topic; his or her *attitude* toward it, and his or her personal or professional *needs.* Because these differences often exist, good writers do more than simply express their meaning; they pinpoint the critical differences between themselves and their reader and design their writing to reduce those differences. Let us look at these three areas in more detail.

Knowledge / This is usually the easiest difference to han- 3 dle. What does your reader need to know? What are the main

ideas you hope to teach? Does your reader have enough background knowledge to really understand you? If not, what would
he or she have to learn?

4   *Attitudes /* When we say a person has knowledge, we
usually refer to his conscious awareness of explicit facts and
clearly defined concepts. This kind of knowledge can be easily
written down or told to someone else. However, much of what
we "know" is not held in this formal, explicit way. Instead it is
held as an attitude or image—as a loose cluster of associations.
For instance, my image of lakes includes associations many people would have, including fishing, water skiing, stalled outboards, and lots of kids catching night crawlers with flashlights.
However, the most salient or powerful parts of my image, which
strongly color my whole attitude toward lakes, are thoughts of
cloudy skies, long rainy days, and feeling generally cold and
damp. By contrast, one of my best friends has a very different
cluster of associations: to him a lake means sun, swimming,
sailing, and happily sitting on the end of a dock. Needless to
say, our differing images cause us to react quite differently to a
proposal that we visit a lake. Likewise, one reason people often
find it difficult to discuss religion and politics is that terms such
as "capitalism" conjure up radically different images.

5   As you can see, a reader's image of a subject is often the
source of attitudes and feelings that are unexpected and, at times,
impervious to mere facts. A simple statement that seems quite
persuasive to you, such as "Lake Wampago would be a great
place to locate the new music camp," could have little impact
on your reader if he or she simply doesn't visualize a lake as a
"great place." In fact, many people accept uncritically any statement that fits in with their own attitudes—and reject, just as
uncritically, anything that does not.

6   Whether your purpose is to persuade or simply to present
your perspective, it helps to know the image and attitudes that
your reader already holds. The more these differ from your own,
the more you will have to do to make him or her *see* what you
mean.

7   *Needs /* When writers discover a large gap between their
own knowledge and attitudes and those of the reader, they

usually try to change the reader in some way. Needs, however, are different. When you analyze a reader's needs, it is so that you, the writer, can adapt to him. If you ask a friend majoring in biology how to keep your fish tank from clouding, you don't want to hear a textbook recitation on the life processes of algae. You expect the friend to adapt his or her knowledge and tell you exactly how to solve your problem.

The ability to adapt your knowledge to the needs of the   8
reader is often crucial to your success as a writer. This is especially true in writing done on a job. For example, as producer of a public affairs program for a television station, eighty percent of your time may be taken up planning the details of new shows, contacting guests, and scheduling the taping sessions. But when you write a program proposal to the station director, your job is to show how the program will fit into the cost guidelines, the FCC requirements for relevance, and the overall programming plan for the station. When you write that report your role in the organization changes from producer to proposal writer. Why? Because your reader needs that information in order to make a decision. He may be *interested* in your scheduling problems and the specific content of the shows, but he *reads* your report because of his own needs as station director of that organization. He has to act.

In college, where the reader is also a teacher, the reader's   9
needs are a little less concrete but just as important. Most papers are assigned as a way to teach something. So the real purpose of a paper may be for you to make connections between two historical periods, to discover for yourself the principle behind a laboratory experiment, or to develop and support your own interpretation of a novel. A good college paper doesn't just rehash the facts; it demonstrates what your reader, as a teacher, needs to know—that you are learning the thinking skills his or her course is trying to teach.

Effective writers are not simply expressing what they know,   10
like a student madly filling up an examination bluebook. Instead they are *using* their knowledge: reorganizing, maybe even rethinking their ideas to meet the demands of an assignment or the needs of their reader.

Sometimes it is also necessary to decide who is your pri-   11
mary audience as opposed to your secondary audience. Both

Audience chart for primary audience: The New Store Manager

Critical Features of the Reader

Knowledge	Attitude	Needs
Has general knowledge of bookstore operations but not a detailed understanding of how things work here. Doesn't know what tasks I've added to my job description.	Sees it as a student job—no responsibility. Assumes I'm a temporary.	General list of tasks. Time they take. Background or experience required. Needs info to give new trainees.

---

may read your paper, but the primary audience is the reader you most want to teach, influence, or convince. When this is the case, you will want to design the paper so the primary reader can easily find what he or she needs.

Content

1. How can you as a writer determine what your reader needs to know to understand your writing?

2. If you hold a strong attitude toward a subject, is it possible for you to understand a reader's contradictory view of the same issue? How can you be sure you are treating differing views fairly?

3. In what ways can a writer assess the reader's needs and adapt to them? What are some needs that the readers of your paper might have?

4. Explain and interpret the "audience chart for primary audience."

Strategies/Structures

1. How much does Flower assume her student audience knows about her subject. How does she accommodate their presumed level of knowledge in her writing?

2. What is Flower's attitude toward writing? How can you tell what attitude she assumes her student readers have toward writing? Does your attitude toward writing resemble this?

3. Flower's explanation of an audience's principal characteristics is divided into three parts. Why does she spend the least amount of space on knowledge and the most on needs? Why does she arrange the parts in the order she does?

Language

1. Does Flower define knowledge (¶ 3), attitudes (4–6), needs (7–10), implicitly? Explicitly? What does she mean by these terms?
2. What does Flower mean (¶ 11) by primary audience? Secondary audience?
3. What is Flower's primary audience for this selection from her textbook? What is her secondary audience?

For Writing

1. Write an essay identifying and interpreting the main characteristics of the primary audience for your customary writing. Your audience might be your boss, your classmates, your family, or a good friend. Include, if relevant, such characteristics as nationality, gender, race, age range, minimum level of education, special interests, religious or political affiliation, significant values and biases that may pertain to your subject.
2. If your actual audience is determined by necessity rather than desire, write a paper identifying the major characteristics of the ideal audience for your writing, describing the same characteristics as identified in #1 above.

◄

LEWIS THOMAS

"The Technology of Medicine," from *The Lives of a Cell*, categorizes three levels of medical technology (supportive, "halfway", and preventive) and demonstrates Thomas's talent for explaining medical phenomena in non-scientific terms. (A biographical sketch of Thomas appears on page 130.)

The Technology of Medicine

1   Technology assessment has become a routine exercise for the scientific enterprises on which the country is obliged to spend vast sums for its needs. Brainy committees are continually evaluating the effectiveness and cost of doing various things in space, defense, energy, transportation, and the like, to give advice about prudent investments for the future.

2   Somehow medicine, for all the $80-odd billion that it is said to cost the nation, has not yet come in for much of this analytical treatment. It seems taken for granted that the technology of medicine simply exists, take it or leave it, and the only major technologic problem which policy-makers are interested in is how to deliver today's kind of health care, with equity, to all the people.

3   When, as is bound to happen sooner or later, the analysts get around to the technology of medicine itself, they will have to face the problem of measuring the relative cost and effectiveness of all the things that are done in the management of disease. They make their living at this kind of thing, and I wish them well, but I imagine they will have a bewildering time. For one thing, our methods of managing disease are constantly changing—partly under the influence of new bits of information brought in from all corners of biologic science. At the same time, a great many things are done that are not so closely related to science, some not related at all.

4   In fact, there are three quite different levels of technology in medicine, so unlike each other as to seem altogether different undertakings. Practitioners of medicine and the analysts will be in trouble if they are not kept separate.

5   1. First of all, there is a large body of what might be termed "nontechnology," impossible to measure in terms of its capacity to alter either the natural course of disease or its eventual outcome. A great deal of money is spent on this. It is valued highly by the professionals as well as the patients. It consists of what is sometimes call "supportive therapy." It tides patients over through diseases that are not, by and large, understood. It is what is meant by the phrases "caring for" and "standing by." It is indispensable. It is not, however, a technology in any real

sense, since it does not involve measures directed at the underlying mechanism of disease.

It includes the large part of any good doctor's time that is 6 taken up with simply providing reassurance, explaining to patients who fear that they have contracted one or another lethal disease that they are, in fact, quite healthy.

It is what physicians used to be engaged in at the bedside 7 of patients with diphtheria, meningitis, poliomyelitis, lobar pneumonia, and all the rest of the infectious diseases that have since come under control.

It is what physicians must now do for patients with in- 8 tractable cancer, severe rheumatoid arthritis, multiple sclerosis, stroke, and advanced cirrhosis. One can think of at least twenty major diseases that require this kind of supportive medical care because of the absence of an effective technology. I would include a large amount of what is called mental disease, and most varieties of cancer, in this category.

The cost of this nontechnology is very high, and getting 9 higher all the time. It requires not only a great deal of time but also very hard effort and skill on the part of physicians; only the very best of doctors are good at coping with this kind of defeat. It also involves long periods of hospitalization, lots of nursing, lots of involvement of nonmedical professionals in and out of the hospital. It represents, in short, a substantial segment of today's expenditures for health.

2. At the next level up is a kind of technology best termed 10 "halfway technology." This represents the kinds of things that must be done after the fact, in efforts to compensate for the incapacitating effects of certain diseases whose course one is unable to do very much about. It is a technology designed to make up for disease, or to postpone death.

The outstanding examples in recent years are the trans- 11 plantations of hearts, kidneys, livers, and other organs, and the equally spectacular inventions of artificial organs. In the public mind, this kind of technology has come to seem like the equivalent of the high technologies of the physical sciences. The media tend to present each new procedure as though it represented a breakthrough and therapeutic triumph, instead of the makeshift that it really is.

In fact, this level of technology is, by its nature, at the same 12 time highly sophisticated and profoundly primitive. It is the kind of thing that one must continue to do until there is a genuine understanding of the mechanisms involved in disease. In chronic glomerulonephritis, for example, a much clearer insight will be needed into the events leading to the destruction of glomeruli by the immunologic reactants that now appear to govern this disease, before one will know how to intervene intelligently to prevent the process, or turn it around. But when this level of understanding has been reached, the technology of kidney replacement will not be much needed and should no longer pose the huge problem of logistics, cost, and ethics that it poses today.

13   An extremely complex and costly technology for the management of coronary heart disease has evolved—involving specialized ambulances and hospital units, all kinds of electronic gadgetry, and whole platoons of new professional personnel—to deal with the end results of coronary thrombosis. Almost everything offered today for the treatment of heart disease is at this level of technology, with the transplanted and artificial hearts as ultimate examples. When enough has been learned to know what really goes wrong in heart disease, one ought to be in a position to figure out ways to prevent or reverse the process, and when this happens the current elaborate technology will probably be set to one side.

14   Much of what is done in the treatment of cancer, by surgery, irradiation, and chemotherapy, represents halfway technology, in the sense that these measures are directed at the existence of already established cancer cells, but not at the mechanisms by which cells become neoplastic.

15   It is a characteristic of this kind of technology that it costs an enormous amount of money and requires a continuing expansion of hospital facilities. There is no end to the need for new, highly trained people to run the enterprise. And there is really no way out of this, at the present state of knowledge. If the installation of specialized coronary-care units can result in the extension of life for only a few patients with coronary disease (and there is no question that this technology is effective in a few cases), it seems to me an inevitable fact of life that as many of these as can be will be put together, and as much money as can be found will be spent. I do not see that anyone has much

choice in this. The only thing that can move medicine away from this level of technology is new information, and the only imaginable source of this information is research.

3. The third type of technology is the kind that is so effective that it seems to attract the least public notice; it has come to be taken for granted. This is the genuinely decisive technology of modern medicine, exemplified best by modern methods for immunization against diphtheria, pertussis, and the childhood virus diseases, and the contemporary use of antibiotics and chemotherapy for bacterial infections. The capacity to deal effectively with syphilis and tuberculosis represents a milestone in human endeavor, even though full use of this potential has not yet been made. And there are, of course, other examples: the treatment of endocrinologic disorders with appropriate hormones, the prevention of hemolytic disease of the newborn, the treatment and prevention of various nutritional disorders, and perhaps just around the corner the management of Parkinsonism and sickle-cell anemia. There are other examples, and everyone will have his favorite candidates for the list, but the truth is that there are nothing like as many as the public has been led to believe.

The point to be made about this kind of technology—the real high technology of medicine—is that it comes as the result of a genuine understanding of disease mechanisms, and when it becomes available, it is relatively inexpensive, and relatively easy to deliver.

Offhand, I cannot think of any important human disease for which medicine possesses the outright capacity to prevent or cure where the cost of the technology is itself a major problem. The price is never as high as the cost of managing the same diseases during the earlier stages of no-technology or halfway technology. If a case of typhoid fever had to be managed today by the best methods of 1935, it would run to a staggering expense. At, say, around fifty days of hospitalization, requiring the most demanding kind of nursing care, with the obsessive concern for details of diet that characterized the therapy of that time, with daily laboratory monitoring, and, on occasion, surgical intervention for abdominal catastrophe, I should think $10,000 would be a conservative estimate for the illness, as contrasted with today's cost of a bottle of chloramphenicol and a day or two of fever. The halfway technology that was evolving for poliomyelitis in the early 1950s, just before the emergence of the basic research that made the vaccine possible, provides another illustration of the point. Do you remember Sister Kenny, and the cost of those institutes for rehabilitation, with all those ceremonially applied hot fomentations, and the debates about whether the affected limbs should be totally immobilized or kept in passive motion as frequently as possible, and the masses of statistically tormented data mobilized to support one view or the other? It is the cost of that kind of technology, and its relative effectiveness, that must be compared with the cost and effectiveness of the vaccine.

19   Pulmonary tuberculosis had similar episodes in its history. There was a sudden enthusiasm for the surgical removal of infected lung tissue in the early 1950s, and elaborate plans were being made for new and expensive installations for major pulmonary surgery in tuberculosis hospitals, and then INH and streptomycin came along and the hospitals themselves were closed up.

20   It is when physicians are bogged down by their incomplete technologies, by the innumerable things they are obliged to do in medicine when they lack a clear understanding of disease mechanisms, that the deficiencies of the health-care system are most conspicuous. If I were a policy-maker, interested in saving money for health care over the long haul, I would regard it as an act of high prudence to give high priority to a lot more basic research in biologic science. This is the only way to get the full mileage that biology owes to the science of medicine, even though it seems, as used to be said in the days when the phrase still had some meaning, like asking for the moon.

Content

1. What is "supportive therapy" (¶ 5)? Why isn't it a technology?
2. Why does Thomas term the second level of technology "halfway technology" (¶ 10)? Why does this technology "make up for disease, or postpone death" (¶ 10)? Why is it "profoundly primitive" (¶ 12)?
3. Why does Thomas most strongly favor the third type of technology,

the "genuinely decisive technology of modern medicine" (¶ 16)? Why does he say that preventive technology is unobtrusive, taken for granted?

4. What does Thomas mean by "basic research in biologic science" (¶ 20)? Why does he believe that basic research will ultimately save money for health care "over the long haul"? What evidence does he provide to demonstrate this?

Strategies/Structures

1. What is the basis for Thomas's three-part classification?

2. Show how Thomas uses the three categories of technology (or nontechnology) in medicine as the three stages of an argument that he builds as the essay progresses. Could these have been arranged in any other order?

3. Thomas's thesis takes issue with the conventional views about health care delivery that he states in the first two paragraphs. Where does he state his thesis? Why does he wait until so late in the essay to present it?

Language

1. What does Thomas mean by the "technology" of medicine? Why does he continually use the term "technology" rather than "science" except in the last sentence of the essay?

2. Would a general audience understand the examples Thomas provides to illustrate each category? How does the simplicity or technicality of his language affect that understanding?

3. Consult your dictionary, if necessary, for definitions of the following: intractible (¶ 8), therapeutic (11), immunologic (12), intervene (12), neoplastic (14), pertussis (16), chemotherapy (16), hemolytic (16), Sister Kenny (18).

For Writing

1. Write an argument in which you defend or dispute Thomas's assertion that basic research in biologic science should be more heavily supported than applied technologic research.

2. Thomas refers briefly to past ("halfway technology") treatments of tuberculosis and polio and compares them to current ("high technology") treatments of the same disease. Pick a disease whose treatment and cure has changed dramatically over the years and analyze its history

to illustrate the truth of Thomas's assertion about "The Technology of Medicine."

3. Write an essay explaining and advocating the benefits of prevention (of alcoholism, drug abuse, unwanted pregnancies, obesity) over prolonged treatment or cure.

▶───◀

ROBERT BRUSTEIN

Brustein, born in 1927 in New York City, received his B.A. from Amherst College (1948), where he was a member of Phi Beta Kappa, and his M.A. and Ph.D. from Columbia University (1950, 1957). He has taught at Cornell, Vassar, and Columbia, and, since 1966, has been Dean of the Yale University School of Drama. An editor of *New York Review of Books,* Brustein has also written theatre criticism for *The New Republic* since 1959. He has won numerous awards, including Fulbright and Guggenheim fellowships, and is the author of *The Theatre of Revolt* (1964), *Seasons of Discontent* (1965), *The Third Theatre* (1969), and *Revolution as Theatre* (1971). In the following essay, Brustein categorizes horror movies as "Mad Doctor," "Atomic Bomb," and "Interplanetary Monster" and describes and interprets the major characteristics of each, with particular focus on the differences in their treatments of the Scientist and the Monster.

Reflections on Horror Movies

1   Although horror movies have recently been enjoying a vogue, they have always been perennial supporting features among Grade B and C fare. The popularity of the form is no doubt partly explained by its ability to engage the spectator's feelings without making any serious demand on his mind. In addition, however, horror movies covertly embody certain underground assumptions about science which reflect popular opinions.

The horror movies I am mainly concerned with I have di- 2
vided into three major categories: Mad Doctor, Atomic Beast
and Interplanetary Monster. They do not exhaust all the types
but they each contain two essential characters, the Scientist and
the Monster, towards whom the attitudes of the movies are in
a revealing state of change.

The Mad Doctor series is by far the most long lived of the 3
three. These films find their roots in certain European folk myths.
Dracula was inspired by an ancient Balkan superstition about
vampires, the Werewolf is a Middle European folk myth recorded, among other places, in the Breton *lais* of Marie de France,
and even Frankenstein, though out of Mary Shelley by the Gothic
tradition, has a medieval prototype in the Golem, a monster the
Jews fashioned from clay and earth to free them from oppression. The spirit of these films is still medieval, combining a vulgar
religiosity with folk superstitions. Superstition now, however,
has been crudely transferred from magic and alchemy to creative
science, itself a form of magic to the untutored mind. The devil
of the Vampire and Werewolf myths, who turned human beings
into baser animals, today has become a scientist, and the meta-
morphosis is given a technical name—it is a "regression" into
an earlier state of evolution. The alchemist and devil-conjuring
scholar, Dr. Faustus, gives way to Dr. Frankenstein, the research
physician, while the magic circle, the tetragrammaton, and the
full moon are replaced by test tubes, complicated electrical apparatus, and Bunsen burners.

Frankenstein, like Faustus, defies God by exploring areas 4
where humans are not meant to trespass. In Mary Shelley's book
(it is subtitled *A Modern Prometheus*), Frankenstein is a latter-day
Faustus, a superhuman creature whose aspiration embodies the
expansiveness of his age. In the movies, however, Frankenstein
loses his heroic quality and becomes a lunatic monomaniac, so
obsessed with the value of his work that he no longer cares
whether his discovery proves a boon or a curse to mankind.
When the mad doctor, his eyes wild and inflamed, bends over
his intricate equipment, pouring in a little of this and a little of
that, the spectator is confronted with an immoral being whose
mental superiority is only a measure of his madness. Like the
popular image of the theoretical scientist engaged in basic re-

search ("Basic research," says Charles Wilson, "is science's attempt to prove that grass is green"), he succeeds only in creating something badly which nature has already made well. The Frankenstein monster is a parody of man. Ghastly in appearance, clumsy in movement, criminal in behavior, imbecilic of mind, it is superior only in physical strength and resistance to destruction. The scientist has fashioned it in the face of divine disapproval (the heavens disgorge at its birth)—not to mention the disapproval of friends and frightened townspeople—and it can lead only to trouble.

5   For Dr. Frankenstein, however, the monster symbolizes the triumph of his intellect over the blind morality of his enemies and it confirms him in the ultimate soundness of his thought ("They thought I was mad, but this proves who is the superior being"). When it becomes clear that his countrymen are unimpressed by his achievement and regard him as a menace to society, the monster becomes the agent of his revenge. As it ravages the countryside and terrorizes the inhabitants, it embodies and expresses the scientist's own lust and violence. It is an extension of his own mad soul, come to life not in a weak and ineffectual body but in a body of formidable power. (In a movie like *Dr. Jekyll and Mr. Hyde,* the identity of monster and doctor is even clearer; Mr. Hyde, the monster, is the aggressive and libidinous element in the benevolent Dr. Jekyll's personality.) The rampage of the monster is the rampage of mad, unrestrained science which inevitably turns on the scientist, destroying him too. As the lava bubbles over the sinking head of the monster, the crude moral of the film frees itself from the horror and is asserted. Experimental science (and by extension knowledge itself) is superfluous, dangerous, and unlawful, for in exploring the unknown, it leads man to usurp God's creative power. Each of these films is a victory for obscurantism, flattering the spectator into believing that his intellectual inferiority is a sign that he is loved by God.

6   The Teen-age Monster films, a very recent phenomenon, amend the assumptions of these horror movies in a startling manner. Their titles—*I Was a Teenage Werewolf, I Was a Teenage Frankenstein, Blood of Dracula,* and *Teenage Monster*—(some wit awaits one called *I Had a Teenage Monkey on My Back)*—suggest

a Hollywood prank, but they are deadly serious, mixing the conventions of early horror movies with the ingredients of adolescent culture. The doctor, significantly enough, is no longer a fringe character whose madness can be inferred from the rings around his eyes and his wild hair but a respected member of society, a high-school chemistry teacher (*Blood of Dracula*) or a psychoanalyst (*Teenage Werewolf*) or a visiting lecturer from Britain (*Teenage Frankenstein*). Although he gives the appearance of benevolence—he pretends to help teen-agers with their problems—behind this facade he hides evil experimental designs. The monster, on the other hand, takes on a more fully developed personality. He is a victim who begins inauspiciously as an average, though emotionally troubled, adolescent and ends, through the influence of the doctor, as a voracious animal. The monster as teen-ager becomes the central character in the film and the teen-age audience is expected to identify and sympathize with him.

In *I Was a Teenage Werewolf,* the hero is characterized as 7 brilliant but erratic in his studies and something of a delinquent. At the suggestion of his principal, he agrees to accept therapy from an analyst helping maladjusted students. The analyst gets the boy under his control and, after injecting him with a secret drug, turns him into a werewolf. Against his will he murders a number of his contemporaries. When the doctor refuses to free him from this curse, he kills him and is himself killed by the police. In death, his features relax into the harmless countenance of an adolescent.

The crimes of the adolescent are invariably committed 8 against other youths (the doctor has it in for teen-agers) and are always connected with those staples of juvenile culture, sex and violence. The advertising displays show the male monsters, dressed in leather jackets and blue jeans, bending ambiguously over the diaphanously draped body of a luscious young girl while the female teen-age vampire of *Blood of Dracula,* her nails long and her fangs dripping, is herself half-dressed and lying on top of a struggling male (whether to rape or murder him is not clear). The identification of sex and violence is further underlined by the promotion blurbs: "In her eyes DESIRE! in her veins—the blood of a MONSTER!" (*Blood of Dracula*); "A Teenage

Titan on a Lustful Binge that Paralyzed a Town with Fear" (*Teenage Monster*). It is probable that these crimes are performed less reluctantly than is suggested and that the adolescent spectator is more thrilled than appalled by this "lustful binge" which captures the attention of the adult community. The acquistion of power and prestige through delinquent sexual and aggresive activity is a familiar juvenile fantasy . . ., one which we can see frequently acted out by delinquents in our city schools. In the Teenage Monster films, however, the hero is absolved of his aggressive and libidinous impulses. Although he both feels and acts on them, he can attribute the responsibility to the mad scientist who controls his behavior. What these films seem to be saying, in their underground manner, is that behind the harmless face of the high-school chemistry teacher and the intellectual countenance of the psychoanalyst lies the warped authority responsible for teen-age violence. The adolescent feels victimized by society—turned into a monster by society—and if he behaves in a delinquent manner, society and not he is to blame. Thus, we can see one direction in which the hostility for experimental research, explicit in the Mad Doctor films, can go— it can be transmuted into hatred of adult authority itself.

9   Or it can go underground, as in the Atomic Beast movies. The Mad Doctor movies, in exploiting the supernatural, usually locate their action in Europe (often a remote Bavarian village) where wild fens, spectral castles, and ominous graveyards provide the proper eerie background. The Atomic Beast movies depend for their effect on the contemporary and familiar and there is a corresponding change in locale. The monster (or "thing" as it is more often called) appears now in a busy American city— usually Los Angeles to save the producer money—where average men walk about in business suits. The thing terrorizes not only the hero, the heroine, and a few anonymous (and expendable) characters in Tyrolean costumes, but the entire world. Furthermore, it has lost all resemblance to anything human. It appears as a giant ant (*Them!*), a prehistoric animal (*Beast from Twenty Thousand Fathoms*), an outsized grasshopper (*Beginning of the End*) or a monstrous spider (*Tarantula*). Although these films, in their deference to science fiction, seem to smile more benignly on scientific endeavor, they are unconsciously closer

to the anti-theoretical biases of the Mad Doctor series than would first appear.

All these films are similarly plotted, so the plot of *The Beginning of the End* will serve as an example of the whole genre. The scene opens on a pair of adolescents necking in their car off a desert road. Their attention is caught by a weird clicking sound, the boy looks up in horror, the girl screams, the music stings and the scene fades. In the next scene, we learn that the car has been completely demolished and its occupants have disappeared. The police, totally baffled, are conducting fruitless investigations when word comes that a small town nearby has been destroyed in the same mysterious way. Enter the young scientist hero. Examining the wreckage of the town, he discovers a strange fluid which when analyzed proves to have been manufactured by a giant grasshopper. The police ridicule his conclusions and are instantly attacked by a fleet of these grasshoppers, each fifteen feet high, which wipe out the entire local force and a few state troopers. Interrupting a perfunctory romance with the heroine, the scientist flies to Washington to alert the nation. He describes the potential danger to a group of bored politicians and yawning big brass, but they remain skeptical until word comes that the things have reached Chicago and are crushing buildings and eating the occupants. The scientist is then put in charge of the army and air force. Although the military men want to evacuate the city and drop an atomic bomb on it, the scientist devises a safer method of destroying the creatures and proceeds to do so through exemplary physical courage and superior knowledge of their behavior. The movie ends on a note of foreboding: have the things been completely exterminated?

Externally, there seem to be very significant changes indeed, especially in the character of the scientist. No longer fang-toothed, long-haired, and subject to delirious ravings (Bela Lugosi, John Carradine, Basil Rathbone), the doctor is now a highly admired member of society, muscular, handsome, and heroic (John Agar). He is invariably wiser, more reasonable, and more humane than the bone-headed bureaucrats and trigger-happy brass that compose the members of his "team," and he even has sexual appeal, a quality which Hollywood's eggheads have never enjoyed before. The scientist-hero, however, is not a very convincing intellectual. Although he may use technical, polysyllabic language when discussing his findings, he always yields gracefully to the admonition to "tell us in our own words, Doc" and proves that he can speak as simply as you or I; in the crisis, in fact, he is almost monosyllabic. When the chips are down, he loses his glasses (a symbol of his intellectualism) and begins to look like everyone else. The hero's intellect is part of his costume and makeup, easily shed when heroic action is demanded. That he is always called upon not only to outwit the thing but to wrestle with it as well (in order to save the heroine) indicates that he is in constant danger of tripping over the thin boundary between specialist and average Joe.

12   The fact remains that there is a new separation between the scientist and the monster. Rather than being an extension of the doctor's evil will, the monster functions completely on its own, creating havoc through its predatory nature. We learn through charts, biological film, and the scientist's patient explanations that ants and grasshoppers are not the harmless little beasties they appear but actually voracious insects who need only the excuse of size to prey upon humanity. The doctor, rather than allying himself with the monster in its rampage against our cities, is in strong opposition to it, and reverses the pattern of the Mad Doctor films by destroying it.

13   And yet, if the individual scientist is absolved of all responsibility for the "thing," science somehow is not. These films suggest an uneasiness about science which, though subtle and unpremeditated, reflects unconscious American attitudes. These attitudes are sharpened when we examine the genesis of the thing for, though it seems to rise out of nowhere, it is invariably caused by a scientific blunder. The giant ants of *Them!*, for example, result from a nuclear explosion which caused a mutation in the species; another fission test has awakened, in *Beast from Twenty Thousand Fathoms*, a dinosaur encrusted in polar icecaps; the spider of *Tarantula* grows in size after having been injected with radioactive isotopes, and escapes during a fight in the lab between two scientists; the grasshoppers of *Beginning of the End* enlarge after crawling into some radioactive dust carelessly left about by a researcher. We are left with a puzzling substatement:

science destroys the thing but scientific experimentation has created it.

I think we can explain this equivocal attitude when we acknowledge that the thing "which is too horrible to name," which owes its birth to an atomic or nuclear explosion, which begins in a desert or frozen waste and moves from there to cities, and which promises ultimately to destroy the world, is probably a crude symbol for the bomb itself. The scientists we see represented in these films are unlike the Mad Doctors in another more fundamental respect: they are never engaged in basic research. The scientist uses his knowledge in a purely defensive manner, like a specialist working on rocket interception or a physician trying to cure a disease. The isolated theoretician who tinkers curiously in his lab (and who invented the atomic bomb) is never shown, only the practical working scientist who labors to undo the harm. The thing's destructive rampage against cities, like the rampage of the Frankenstein monster, is the result of too much cleverness, and the consequences for all the world are only too apparent.

These consequences are driven home more powerfully in movies like *The Incredible Shrinking Man* and *The Amazing Colossal Man* where the audience gets the opportunity to identify closely with the victims of science's reckless experimentation. The hero of the first movie is an average man who, through contact with fallout while on his honeymoon, begins to shrink away to nothing. As he proceeds to grow smaller, he finds himself in much the same dilemma as the other heroes of the *Atomic Beast* series: he must do battle with (now) gigantic insects in order to survive. Scientists can do nothing to save him—after a while they can't even find him—so as he dwindles into an atomic particle he finally turns to God for whom "there is no zero." The inevitable sequel, *The Amazing Colossal Man*, reverses the dilemma. The hero grows to enormous size through the premature explosion of a plutonium bomb. Size carries with it the luxury of power but the hero cannot enjoy his new stature. He feels like a freak and his body is proceeding to outgrow his brain and heart. Although the scientists labor to help him and even succeed in reducing an elephant to the size of a cat, it is too late; the hero has gone mad, demolished Las Vegas and fallen over Boulder

Dam. The victimization of man by theoretical science has become, in these two movies, less of a suggestion and more of a fact.

16   In the Interplanetary Monster movies, Hollywood handles the public's ambivalence towards science in a more obvious way, by splitting the scientist in two. Most of these movies feature both a practical scientist who wishes to destroy the invader and a theoretical scientist who wants to communicate with it. . . . In *Forbidden Planet* (a sophisticated thriller inspired in part by Shakespeare's *Tempest*), the good and evil elements in science are represented, as in *Dr. Jekyll and Mr. Hyde,* by the split personality of the scientist. He is urbane and benevolent (Walter Pidgeon plays the role) and is trying to realize an ideal community on the far-off planet he has discovered. Although he has invented a robot (Ariel) who cheerfully performs man's baser tasks, we learn that he is also responsible, though unwittingly, for a terrible invisible force (Caliban) overwhelming in its destructiveness. While he sleeps, the aggressive forces in his libido activate a dynamo he has been tinkering with which gives them enormous power to kill those the doctor unconsciously resents. Thus, Freudian psychology is evoked to endow the scientist with guilt. At the end, he accepts his guilt and sacrifices his life in order to combat the being he has created.

17   The Interplanetary Monster series sometimes reverses the central situation of most horror films. We often find the monster controlling the scientist and forcing him to do its evil will. . . . In *The Brain from Planet Arous*, a hideous brain inhabits the mind of a nuclear physicist with the intention of controlling the universe. As the physical incarnation of the monster, the scientist is at the mercy of its will until he can free himself of its influence. The monster's intellect, like the intellect of the Mad Doctor, is invariably superior, signified graphically by its large head and small body (in the last film named it is nothing but Brain). Like the Mad Doctor, its superior intelligence is always accompanied by moral depravity and an unconscionable lust for power. If the monster is to be destroyed at all, this will not be done by matching wits with it but by finding some chink in its armor. The chink quite often is a physical imperfection: in *War of the Worlds,* the invading Martians are stopped, at the height of their victory,

by their vulnerability to the disease germs of earth. Before this Achilles heel is discovered, however, the scientist is controlled to do evil, and with the monster and the doctor in collaboration again, even in this qualified sense, the wheel has come full circle.

The terror of most of these films, then, stems from the 18 matching of knowledge with power, always a source of fear for Americans—when Nietzsche's Superman enters comic book culture he loses his intellectual and spiritual qualities and becomes a muscle man. The muscle man, even with X-ray vision, poses no threat to the will, but muscle in collaboration with mind is generally thought to have a profound effect on individual destinies. The tendency to attribute everything that happens in the heavens, from flying saucers to Florida's cold wave, to science and the bomb . . . accounts for the extreme ways in which the scientist is regarded in our culture: either as a protective savior or as a destructive blunderer. It is little wonder that America exalts the physician (and the football player) and ignores the physicist. These issues, the issues of the great debate over scientific education and basic research, assert themselves crudely through the unwieldy monster and the Mad Doctor. The films suggest that the academic scientist, in exploring new areas, has laid the human race open to devastation either by human or interplanetary enemies—the doctor's madness, then, is merely a suitable way of expressing a conviction that the scientist's idle curiosity has shaken itself loose from prudence or principle. There is obviously a sensitive moral problem involved here, one which needs more articulate treatment than the covert and superstitious way it is handled in horror movies. That the problem is touched there at all is evidence of how profoundly it has stirred the American psyche.

Content

1. What differences among horror movies does Brustein's division of the subject into categories enable him to identify and explain?

2. Why is the relationship in horror movies between the Scientist and the Monster so important? How do the categories Brustein has established allow him to emphasize the changing relationships?

3. What is the underlying "sensitive moral problem" that Brustein

identifies in paragraph 18? Can an entertainment medium, such as horror movies, be expected to deal with moral issues? Why or why not?

4. What does Brustein mean by his statement that "the terror of most of these films stems from the matching of knowledge with power" (¶ 18)? Is he right in asserting that this is "always a source of fear for Americans"?

Strategies/Structures

1. Is Brustein writing primarily for horror movie fans? How much do the readers need to know about horror movies in order to understand Brustein's analysis?

2. What subcategories of his subject does Brustein establish within each of the major categories? How does his discussion of the subcategories reinforce the categorization he has established?

3. Why has Brustein arranged the three categories in the order in which they appear in this essay, beginning with Mad Doctor and ending with Interplanetary Monster? Does a thesis emerge as a consequence of this arrangement?

Language

1. Are Brustein's labels (Mad Doctor, Atomic Beast, Interplanetary Monster) appropriate for the categories he establishes? Are they descriptive? Restrictive? Or both? Explain your answer.

2. Consult your dictionary, if necessary, to learn the following words: alchemist (¶ 3), monomaniac (4), boon (4), ineffective (5), superfluous (6), voracious (6), diaphanous (8), exemplary (10), genesis (13), equivocal (14)

For Writing

1. Brustein claims that movies "embody the underground assumptions" of their viewers. If you agree, write an essay explaining the assumptions that movies of another type (such as musicals, romances, or Westerns) make. Or, instead, apply this generalization to an essay about a distinctive type of fiction, such as science fiction, gothics, Harlequin romances, detective stories, or Westerns.

2. Write an essay in which you explain your attitude toward scientists or science, and indicate the extent to which you think your views are typical of the attitudes of Americans in general. Do you or others regard

scientists in a particular field as "protective saviors" or "destructive blunderers," as Brustein claims? Or do you have entirely different views?

In developing your ideas for this essay, you might use answers to the following questions to help you. Have you studied science, or avoided the subject? Do you plan on a career in science? Do you know any scientists well? Do they resemble any of the stereotypes Brustein discusses?

Strategies for Writing—Division and Classification

1. Am I going to explain an existing system of classification, or am I going to invent a new one? Do I want to define a system by categorizing its components? Explain a process by dividing it into stages? Argue in favor of one category or another? Entertain through an amusing classification?

2. Do my readers know my subject but not my classification system? Know both subject and system? Or are they unacquainted with either? How will their knowledge (or lack of knowledge) of the subject or system influence how much I say about either? Will this influence the simplicity or complexity of my classification system?

3. According to what principle am I classifying or dividing my subject? Is it sensible? Significant? Does it emphasize the similarities or the differences among groups? Have I applied the prnciple consistently with respect to each category? How have I integrated my paper (to keep it from being just a long list), through providing interconnections among the parts and transitions between the divisions?

4. Have I organized my discussion of each category in the same way, considering the same features in the same order? Have I illustrated each category? Are the discussions of each category the same length? Should they be? Why or why not?

5. Have I used language similar in vocabulary level (equally technical, or equally informal) in each category? Have I defined any needed terms?

Additional Writing Topics

1. Write an essay in which you use division to analyze one of the subjects below. Explain or illustrate each of the component parts, showing how each part functions or relates to the functioning or structure of the whole.

   a. The organization of the college or university you attend
   b. An organization of which you are a member—team, band or orchestra, fraternity or sorority, social or political action group
   c. A typical (or atypical) weekday or weekend in your life
   d. Your budget, or the federal budget
   e. Your family
   f. A farm, kibbutz, or factory
   g. Geologic periods
   h. A poem

i. A short story, novel, play, or television or film drama
j. A hospital, city hall, bank, restaurant, supermarket, shopping mall

2. Write an essay in which you classify members of one of the following subjects. Make the basis of your classification apparent, consistent, and logical. You may want to identify each group or subgroup by a name or relevant term.

a. Types of cars (or sports cars), boats, or bicycles
b. People's temperaments or personality types
c. Vacations or holidays
d. Styles of music, or types of a particular kind of music (classical, country and western, folk, rock)
e. People's styles of spending money
f. Types of restaurants, or subcategories (such as types of fast-food restaurants)
g. Individual or family lifestyles
h. Types of post-high school educational institutions, or types of courses a given school offers
i. Clothing styles for your age group
j. Tennis players, skiers, golfers, runners, or other sports stars; or television or movie stars
k. Computer games

8   *Illustration and Example*

▶ ─────────────────────────── ◀

If generalizations are an essay's superstructure, illustrations are its building blocks, reinforcing and filling in the skeletal outline. Writers use examples or illustrations to clarify a general point, to make abstractions concrete. You could support the general assertion, "Women have been a powerful force in twentieth-century politics" by adding, "among them are Eleanor Roosevelt, Golda Meir, Indira Gandhi, and Margaret Thatcher." Each of these references is an example.

But is a simple allusion sufficient? An illustration is meaningful to the extent that your readers understand it. Can you count on them to understand your reference to Eleanor Roosevelt? If not, you'll have to provide enough details so they'll recognize why you've included her—perhaps because she was the first American ambassador to the United Nations. How much space you spend on the explanation depends on how important the example is to the point you're illustrating. It might warrant a sentence or two, or in an expanded version become the focus of the whole essay.

How many examples do you need to illustrate a point? Enough to make it clear, without becoming redundant or boring. In "Shooting an Elephant" (pp. 47–55), to demonstrate his thesis that "When the white man turns tyrant it is his own freedom

that he destroys," George Orwell spends the entire essay elab-
orating on a single incident, how and why he shot an elephant
he believed to be harmless. James Thurber uses three examples
in "University Days" (pp. 231–37) to illustrate his incompetence
as a student—his inability to see cells through a microscope, his
failure to learn to swim, and his utter ineptitude for military
drill. Although readers could probably generalize from a single
point, in this case three examples are funnier than one. The
authors of the Declaration of Independence (pp. 340–44) use a
great many examples, whose importance as well as number justifies their dramatic self-assertion.

The essays in this section themselves illustrate the variety
of types of examples writers can use, and the varied techniques
for using them. Joan Didion begins her indictment of Las Vegas
weddings, the subject of "Marrying Absurd," with a pungently
absurd anecdote that focuses on the 171 weddings performed
there in three hours, 67 by one justice of the peace who "got it
down from five to three minutes." After thirteen brief illustrations of wedding chapel advertising slogans, Didion concludes
the essay with two other equally revealing vignettes. She provides a brief glimpse of a drunken "bride in an orange minidress
and masses of flame-colored hair" stumbling from her quickie
wedding on the arm of her "baby Crosby" husband. She concludes with a longer, ironic example of a typical wedding celebration: the bored waiter pouring pallid pink champagne; the
bride's father and his new son-in-law exchanging ribald "ritual
jokes about the wedding night"; and the underage, visibly pregnant bride sobbing with pleasure that the wedding "was just as
nice as I hoped and dreamed it would be."

In "The Brown Wasps," naturalist Loren Eiseley philosophically explores the subtle thesis that all living creatures can
survive only if their homing instinct enables them either to find
their real home or create a substitute. To illustrate this he uses
examples of old men sleeping in train stations, surrogate homes,
like old brown wasps "creeping slowly over an abandoned wasp
nest" in search of remembered habitation. He offers equally
memorable anecdotes of the homing behavior of a slug, a dis-
placed field mouse, pigeons, and a blind beggar who continued
to beg on an abandoned corner, formerly the site of a busy train

station. The essay climaxes in a case history of Eiseley himself, who traveled two thousand miles in search of a tree he'd planted as a child, which "somehow stood for my father and the love I bore him." The common elements in these illustrations bridge the various species, uniting all living creatures to reinforce Eiseley's thesis.

Architect Minoru Yamasaki uses both positive and negative examples to illustrate his point that "the purpose of architecture is to create usable, livable areas where man can lead his life both productively and happily." Some types of architecture (such as Japanese) and specific buildings (England's Crystal Palace) exemplify these ideals; many of the "flat, glassy buildings" of recent years do not. In "The Cosmic Calendar," astronomer Carl Sagan uses an extended analogy as an illustration. On a hypothetical calendar for the month of December, he superimposes the relative dates of the formation of the major features of the universe. The first day of the month signals the development of a "significant oxygen atmosphere" on Earth; the thirty-first marks the passage of three geological epochs and the emergence of the first humans.

In Lai Man Lee's "My Bracelet," the student author uses an example itself, a Chinese jade bracelet, as the subject of her essay. To explain its significance, Lee treats this example in a number of typical ways. She describes its physical appearance, explains its cultural meaning, relates the history of her particular bracelet, and identifies its current status as a permanent part of her life, literally and symbolically.

When you're seeking examples for your own writing, as the motto of the State of Michigan advises, "look about you." Ask "What do I want to illustrate?" "Why?" "Is this a good illustration?" If someone throws an abstraction at you—"What is Truth? Beauty? Justice?"—you can toss it back, without striking out on the curve, if you examine your own experience. Who is the most beautiful person you ever knew? Was the beauty skin-deep? Internal? Or both? Why? What, in your view, is the most beautiful place on earth (including, perhaps, your own home, a favorite grandmother's kitchen, or . . .)? What makes it so attractive? Other examples might come from what you know about the lives of your family and friends; from conversations, reading, radio, and television. To control the illustrations (instead of leaving vague, general gaps for your readers to fill in) is to have your readers experience the subject your way. With revealing examples, you're in charge.

JOAN DIDION

> Much of Didion's writing deals with estrangement and aliena-
> tion—of people from each other, from religion, from their roots
> in geography, family, and society. She finds such lost souls in
> Las Vegas, where the unreal milieu provides an ironic contrast
> to the pseudo-sentimentality of "Marrying Absurd." (A bio-
> graphical sketch of Didion appears on page 4.)

Marrying Absurd

1   To be married in Las Vegas, Clark County, Nevada, a bride
     must swear that she is eighteen or has parental permission
and a bridegroom that he is twenty-one or has parental permission. Someone must put up five dollars for the license. (On
Sundays and holidays, fifteen dollars. The Clark County Courthouse issues marriage licenses at any time of the day or night
except between noon and one in the afternoon, between eight
and nine in the evening, and between four and five in the morning.) Nothing else is required. The State of Nevada, alone among
these United States, demands neither a premarital blood test nor
a waiting period before or after the issuance of a marriage license.
Driving in across the Mojave from Los Angeles, one sees the
signs way out on the desert, looming up from that moonscape
of rattlesnakes and mesquite, even before the Las Vegas lights
appear like a mirage on the horizon: "GETTING MARRIED? Free
License Information First Strip Exit." Perhaps the Las Vegas
wedding industry achieved its peak operational efficiency
between 9:00 p.m. and midnight of August 26, 1965, an otherwise unremarkable Thursday which happened to be, by Presidential order, the last day on which anyone could improve his
draft status merely by getting married. One hundred and sev-
enty-one couples were pronounced man and wife in the name
of Clark County and the State of Nevada that night, sixty-seven
of them by a single justice of the peace, Mr. James A. Brennan.
Mr. Brennan did one wedding at the Dunes and the other sixty-

six in his office, and charged each couple eight dollars. One bride lent her veil to six others. "I got it down from five to three minutes," Mr. Brennan said later of his feat. "I could've married them *en masse,* but they're people, not cattle. People expect more when they get married."

What people who get married in Las Vegas actually do 2 expect—what, in the largest sense, their "expectations" are—strikes one as a curious and self-contradictory business. Las Vegas is the most extreme and allegorical of American settlements, bizarre and beautiful in its venality and in its devotion to immediate gratification, a place the tone of which is set by mobsters and call girls and ladies' room attendants with amyl nitrite poppers in their uniform pockets. Almost everyone notes that there is no "time" in Las Vegas, no night and no day and no past and no future (no Las Vegas casino, however, has taken the obliteration of the ordinary time sense quite so far as Harold's Club in Reno, which for a while issued, at odd intervals in the day and night, mimeographed "bulletins" carrying news from the world outside); neither is there any logical sense of where one is. One is standing on a highway in the middle of a vast hostile desert looking at an eighty-foot sign which blinks "STARDUST" or "CAESAR'S PALACE." Yes, but what does that explain? This geographical implausibility reinforces the sense that what happens there has no connection with "real" life; Nevada cities like Reno and Carson are ranch towns, Western towns, places behind which there is some historical imperative. But Las Vegas seems to exist only in the eye of the beholder. All of which makes it an extraordinarily stimulating and interesting place, but an odd one in which to want to wear a candlelight satin Priscilla of Boston wedding dress with Chantilly lace insets, tapered sleeves and a detachable modified train.

And yet the Las Vegas wedding business seems to appeal 3 to precisely that impulse. "Sincere and Dignified Since 1954," one wedding chapel advertises. There are nineteen such wedding chapels in Las Vegas, intensely competitive, each offering better, faster, and, by implication, more sincere services than the next: Our Photos Best Anywhere, Your Wedding on A Phonograph Record, Candlelight with Your Ceremony, Honeymoon Accommodations, Free Transportation from Your Motel to

Courthouse to Chapel and Return to Motel, Religious or Civil
Ceremonies, Dressing Rooms, Flowers, Rings, Announcements,
Witnesses Available, and Ample Parking. All of these services,
like most others in Las Vegas (sauna baths, payroll-check cash-
ing, chinchilla coats for sale or rent) are offered twenty-four hours
a day, seven days a week, presumably on the premise that
marriage, like craps, is a game to be played when the table
seems hot.

4   But what strikes one most about the Strip chapels, with
their wishing wells and stained-glass paper windows and their
artificial bouvardia, is that so much of their business is by no
means a matter of simple convenience, of late-night liaisons
between show girls and baby Crosbys. Of course there is some
of that. (One night about eleven o'clock in Las Vegas I watched
a bride in an orange minidress and masses of flame-colored hair
stumble from a Strip chapel on the arm of her bridegroom, who
looked the part of the expendable nephew in movies like *Miami
Syndicate.* "I gotta get the kids," the bride whimpered. "I gotta
pick up the sitter, I gotta get to the midnight show." "What you
gotta get," the bridegroom said, opening the door of a Cadillac
Coupe de Ville and watching her crumple on the seat, "is so-
ber.") But Las Vegas seems to offer something other than "convenience"; it is merchandising "niceness," the facsimile of proper
ritual, to children who do not know how else to find it, how to
make the arrangements, how to do it "right." All day and evening long on the Strip, one sees actual wedding parties, waiting
under the harsh lights at a crosswalk, standing uneasily in the
parking lot of the Frontier while the photographer hired by The
Little Church of the West ("Wedding Place of the Stars") certifies
the occasion, takes the picture: the bride in a veil and white satin
pumps, the bridegroom usually in a white dinner jacket, and
even an attendant or two, a sister or a best friend in hot-pink
peau de soie, a flirtation veil, a carnation nosegay. "When I Fall
in Love It Will Be Forever," the organist plays, and then a few
bars of Lohengrin. The mother cries; the stepfather, awkward
in his role, invites the chapel hostess to join them for a drink at
the Sands. The hostess declines with a professional smile; she
has already transferred her interest to the group waiting outside.
One bride out, another in, and again the sign goes up on the
chapel door: "One moment please—Wedding."

I sat next to one such wedding party in a Strip restaurant 5 the last time I was in Las Vegas. The marriage had just taken place; the bride still wore her dress, the mother her corsage. A bored waiter poured out a few swallows of pink champagne ("on the house") for everyone but the bride, who was too young to be served. "You'll need something with more kick than that," the bride's father said with heavy jocularity to his new son-in-law; the ritual jokes about the wedding night had a certain Panglossian character, since the bride was clearly several months pregnant. Another round of pink champagne, this time not on the house, and the bride began to cry. "It was just as nice," she sobbed, "as I hoped and dreamed it would be."

Content

1. How does Didion's essay illustrate her observation that "there is no 'time' in Las Vegas, no night and no day and no past and no future" (¶ 2)?

2. What evidence does Didion supply to illustrate her point that in Las Vegas there is no "logical sense of where one is" (¶ 2)? Why is Las Vegas geographically implausible (¶ 2)?

3. Do you think that Didion agrees with the Las Vegas assumption that "marriage, like craps, is a game to be played when the table seems hot" (¶ 3)? What illustrations does she provide to demonstrate that the patrons of Las Vegas believe this?

4. Does the concluding illustration of the pregnant, underage bride sobbing with pleasure at the "niceness" of her wedding (¶ 5) support Didion's assertion that Las Vegas is "merchandising 'niceness,' the facsimile of proper ritual, to children who do not know how else to find it" (¶ 4)?

Strategies/Structures

1. Why does Didion emphasize so early in the essay the hasty weddings and the view of the justice of the peace who married sixty-seven couples in three hours, " 'I got it down from five to three mintues . . . I could've married them *en masse*, but they're people, not cattle' " (¶ 1).

2. What does the juxtaposition of the "moonscape of rattlesnakes and mesquite" with the "Getting Married" signs (¶ 1) indicate about the relation of the environment to a major activity performed there? Can you find other instances of comparable incongruities?

3. Why does Didion include "the stepfather, awkward in his role" (¶ 4) as a member of the wedding party? Whose place is he taking?

4. What does Didion illustrate in the vignette in paragraph 4 of the drunken showgirl bride in the "orange minidress and masses of flame-colored hair" and her bridegroom?

5. What is Didion's prevailing tone? Find some instances of it. Can she count on her readers to share her attitude toward Las Vegas weddings? Does Didion's intended audience include the kind of people who might get married in Las Vegas?

Language

1. What language is Didion imitating when she refers to "a candlelight satin Priscilla of Boston wedding dress with Chantilly lace insets, tapered sleeves and a detachable modified train" (¶ 2)? Why does she employ only one comma in this heavily modified sequence that might ordinarily use many more?

2. In paragraph 3 Didion quotes or paraphrases many advertising slogans. For what purposes? With what effects?

For Writing

1. Describe a place—either an entertainment spot, or college, or whole city or town, as Didion does Las Vegas, where through carefully selecting details you convey not only an impression of the place, but your attitude toward it, favorable or otherwise.

2. Connect two or three anecdotes or vignettes to illustrate a thesis, as Didion does with the sixty-seven speedy weddings (¶ 1), the wedding of the showgirl and the "expendable nephew" (¶ 4), and the wedding of the underage pregnant bride (¶ 5).

▶───◀

LOREN EISELEY

Eiseley (1907–1977) was an anthropoligist, historian of science, and academic administrator at the University of Pennsylvania from 1949 until his death. A prolific author known for his ability to clarify and illuminate complex phenomena for a general audience, Eiseley won the Phi Beta Kappa Science Award for *Darwin's Century* (1958). Among his other books are *The Immense Journey* (1957), *The Mind as Nature* (1962), *Francis Bacon and the Modern Dilemma* (1962), *The Invisible Pyramid* (1970), and *The Night Country* (1971), from which "The Brown Wasps" is reprinted below. Eiseley sensitively links all creatures, great and small, in a universe interpreted with scientific understanding and poetic insight.

The Brown Wasps

There is a corner in the waiting room of one of the great 1 Eastern stations where women never sit. It is always in the shadow and overhung by rows of lockers. It is, however, always frequented—not so much by genuine travelers as by the dying. It is here that a certain element of the abandoned poor seeks a refuge out of the weather, clinging for a few hours longer to the city that has fathered them. In a precisely similar manner I have seen, on a sunny day in midwinter, a few old brown wasps creep slowly over an abandoned wasp nest in a thicket. Numbed and forgetful and frost-blackened, the hum of the spring hive still resounded faintly in their sodden tissues. Then the temperature would fall and they would drop away into the white oblivion of the snow. Here in the station it is in no way different save that the city is busy in its snows. But the old ones cling to their seats as though these were symbolic and could not be given up. Now and then they sleep, their gray old heads resting with painful awkwardness on the backs of the benches.

Also they are not at rest. For an hour they may sleep in 2 the gasping exhaustion of the ill-nourished and aged who have to walk in the night. Then a policeman comes by on his round and nudges them upright.

"You can't sleep here," he growls. 3

A strange ritual then begins. An old man is difficult to 4 waken. After a muttered conversation the policeman presses a coin into his hand and passes fiercely along the benches prodding and gesturing toward the door. In his wake, like birds rising and settling behind the passage of a farmer through a cornfield, the men totter up, move a few paces and subside once more upon the benches.

5   One man, after a slight, apologetic lurch, does not move at all. Tubercularly thin, he sleeps on steadily. The policeman does not look back. To him, too, this has become a ritual. He will not have to notice it again officially for another hour.

6   Once in a while one of the sleepers will not awake. Like the brown wasps, he will have had his wish to die in the great droning center of the hive rather than in some lonely room. It is not so bad here with the shuffle of footsteps and the knowledge that there are others who share the bad luck of the world. There are also the whistles and the sounds of everyone, everyone in the world, starting on journeys. Amidst so many journeys somebody is bound to come out all right. Somebody.

7   Maybe it was on a like thought that the brown wasps fell away from the old paper nest in the thicket. You hold till the last, even if it is only to a public seat in a railroad station. You want your place in the hive more than you want a room or a place where the aged can be eased gently out of the way. It is the place that matters, the place at the heart of things. It is life that you want, that bruises your gray old head with the hard chairs; a man has a right to his place.

8   But sometimes the place is lost in the years behind us. Or sometimes it is a thing of air, a kind of vaporous distortion above a heap of rubble. We cling to a time and place because without them man is lost, not only man but life. This is why the voices, real or unreal, which speak from the floating trumpets at spiritualist seances are so unnerving. They are voices out of nowhere whose only reality lies in their ability to stir the memory of a living person with some fragment of the past. Before the medium's cabinet both the dead and the living revolve endlessly about an episode, a place, an event that has already been engulfed by time.

9   This feeling runs deep in life; it brings stray cats running over endless miles, and birds homing from the ends of the earth. It is as though all living creatures, and particularly the more intelligent, can survive only by fixing or transforming a bit of time into space or by securing a bit of space with its objects

immortalized and made permanent in time. For example, I once saw, on a flower pot in my own living room, the efforts of a field mouse to build a remembered field. I have lived to see this episode repeated in a thousand guises, and since I have spent a large portion of my life in the shade of a nonexistent tree, I think I am entitled to speak for the field mouse.

One day as I cut across the field which at that time extended on one side of our suburban shopping center, I found a giant slug feeding from a runnel of pink ice cream in an abandoned Dixie cup. I could see his eyes telescope and protrude in a kind of dim, uncertain ecstasy as his dark body bunched and elongated in the curve of the cup. Then, as I stood there at the edge of the concrete, contemplating the slug, I began to realize it was like standing on a shore where a different type of life creeps up and fumbles tentatively among the rocks and sea wrack. It knows its place and will only creep so far until something changes. Little by little as I stood there I began to see more of this shore that surrounds the place of man. I looked with sudden care and attention at things I had been running over thoughtlessly for years. I even waded out a short way into the grass and the wild-rose thickets to see more. A huge black-belted bee went droning by and there were some indistinct scurryings in the underbrush. 10

Then I came to a sign which informed me that this field was to be the site of a new Wanamaker suburban store. Thousands of obscure lives were about to perish, the spores of puff-balls would go smoking off to new fields, and the bodies of little white-footed mice would be crunched under the inexorable wheels of the bulldozers. Life disappears or modifies its appearances so fast that everything takes on an aspect of illusion— a momentary fizzing and boiling with smoke rings, like pouring dissident chemicals into a retort. Here man was advancing, but in a few years his plaster and bricks would be disappearing once more into the insatiable maw of the clover. Being of an archaeological cast of mind, I thought of this fact with an obscure sense of satisfaction and waded back through the rose thickets to the concrete parking lot. As I did so, a mouse scurried ahead of me, frightened of my steps if not of that ominous Wanamaker sign. I saw him vanish in the general direction of my apartment house, his little body quivering with fear in the great open sun on the 11 blazing concrete. Blinded and confused, he was running straight away from his field. In another week scores would follow him.

12   I forgot the episode then and went home to the quiet of my living room. It was not until a week later, letting myself into the apartment, that I realized I had a visitor. I am fond of plants and had several ferns standing on the floor in pots to avoid the noon glare by the south window.

13   As I snapped on the light and glanced carelessly around the room, I saw a little heap of earth on the carpet and a scrabble of pebbles that had been kicked merrily over the edge of one of the flower pots. To my astonishment I discovered a full-fledged burrow delving downward among the fern-roots. I waited silently. The creature who had made the burrow did not appear. I remembered the wild field then, and the flight of the mice. No house mouse, no *Mus domesticus,* had kicked up this little heap of earth or sought refuge under a fern root in a flower pot. I thought of the desperate little creature I had seen fleeing from the wild-rose thicket. Through intricacies of pipes and attics, he, or one of his fellows, had climbed to this high green solitary room. I could visualize what had occurred. He had an image in his head, a world of seed pods and quiet, of green sheltering leaves in the dim light among the weed stems. It was the only world he knew and it was gone.

14   Somehow in his flight he had found his way to this room with drawn shades where no one would come till nightfall. And here he had smelled green leaves and run quickly up the flower pot to dabble his paws in common earth. He had even struggled half the afternoon to carry his burrow deeper and had failed. I examined the hole, but no whiskered twitching face appeared. He was gone. I gathered up the earth and refilled the burrow. I did not expect to find traces of him again.

15   Yet for three nights thereafter I came home to the darkened room and my ferns to find the dirt kicked gaily about the rug and the burrow reopened, though I was never able to catch the field mouse within it. I dropped a little food about the mouth of the burrow, but it was never touched. I looked under beds or sat reading with one ear cocked for rustlings in the ferns. It was all in vain; I never saw him. Probably he ended in a trap in some other tenant's room.

But before he disappeared I had come to look hopefully 16
for his evening burrow. About my ferns there had begun to
linger the insubstantial vapor of an autumn field, the distilled
essence, as it were, of a mouse brain in exile fom its home. It
was a small dream, like our dreams, carried a long and weary
journey along pipes and through spider webs, past holes over
which loomed the shadows of waiting cats, and finally, desperately, into this room where he had played in the shuttered
daylight for an hour among the green ferns on the floor. Every
day these invisible dreams pass us on the street, or rise from
beneath our feet, or look out upon us from beneath a bush.

Some years ago the old elevated railway in Philadelphia 17
was torn down and replaced by a subway system. This ancient
El with its barnlike stations containing nut-vending machines
and scattered food scraps had, for generations, been the favorite
feeding ground of flocks of pigeons, generally one flock to a
station along the route of the El. Hundreds of pigeons were
dependent upon the system. They flapped in and out of its
stanchions and steel work or gathered in watchful little audiences about the feet of anyone who rattled the peanut-vending
machines. They even watched people who jingled change in
their hands, and prospected for food under the feet of the crowds
who gathered between trains. Probably very few among the
waiting people who tossed a crumb to an eager pigeon realized
that this El was like a food-bearing river, and that the life which
haunted its banks was dependent upon the running of the trains
with their human freight.

I saw the river stop. 18

The time came when the underground tubes were ready; 19
the traffic was transferred to a realm unreachable by pigeons. It
was like a great river subsiding suddenly into desert sands. For
a day, for two days, pigeons continued to circle over the El or
stand close to the red vending machines. They were patient
birds, and surely this great river which had flowed through the
lives of unnumbered generations was merely suffering from some
momentary drought.

They listened for the familiar vibrations that had always 20
heralded an approaching train; they flapped hopefully about the
head of an occasional workman walking along the steel runways.

They passed from one empty station to another, all the while growing hungrier. Finally they flew away.

21   I thought I had seen the last of them about the El, but there was a revival and it provided a curious instance of the memory of living things for a way of life or a locality that has long been cherished. Some weeks after the El was abandoned workmen began to tear it down. I went to work every morning by one particular station, and the time came when the demolition crews reached this spot. Acetylene torches showered passersby with sparks, pneumatic drills hammered at the base of the structure, and a blind man who, like the pigeons, had clung with his cup to a stairway leading to the change booth, was forced to give up his place.

22   It was then, strangely, momentarily, one morning that I witnessed the return of a little band of the familiar pigeons. I even recognized one or two members of the flock that had lived around this particular station before they were dispersed into the streets. They flew bravely in and out among the sparks and the hammers and the shouting workmen. They had returned— and they had returned because the hubbub of the wreckers had convinced them that the river was about to flow once more. For several hours they flapped in and out through the empty windows, nodding their heads and watching the fall of girders with attentive little eyes. By the following morning the station was reduced to some burned-off stanchions in the street. My bird friends had gone. It was plain, however, that they retained a memory for an insubstantial structure now compounded of air and time. Even the blind man clung to it. Someone had provided him with a chair, and he sat at the same corner staring sightlessly at an invisible stairway where, so far as he was concerned, the crowds were still ascending to the trains.

23   I have said my life has been passed in the shade of a non-existent tree, so that such sights do not offend me. Prematurely I am one of the brown wasps and I often sit with them in the great droning hive of the station, dreaming sometimes of a certain tree. It was planted sixty years ago by a boy with a bucket and a toy spade in a little Nebraska town. That boy was myself. It was a cottonwood sapling and the boy remembered it because of some words spoken by his father and because everyone died

or moved away who was supposed to wait and grow old under its shade. The boy was passed from hand to hand, but the tree for some intangible reason had taken root in his mind. It was under its branches that he sheltered; it was from this tree that his memories, which are my memories, led away into the world.

After sixty years the mood of the brown wasps grows heav- 24 ier upon one. During a long inward struggle I thought it would do me good to go and look upon that actual tree. I found a rational excuse in which to clothe this madness. I purchased a ticket and at the end of two thousand miles I walked another mile to an address that was still the same. The house had not been altered.

I came close to the white picket fence and reluctantly, with 25 great effort, looked down the long vista of the yard. There was nothing there to see. For sixty years that cottonwood had been growing in my mind. Season by season its seeds had been floating farther on the hot prairie winds. We had planted it lovingly there, my father and I, because he had a great hunger for soil and live things growing, and because none of these things had long been ours to protect. We had planted the little sapling and watered it faithfully, and I remembered that I had run out with my small bucket to drench its roots the day we moved away. And all the years since it had been growing in my mind, a huge tree that somehow stood for my father and the love I bore him. I took a grasp on the picket fence and forced myself to look again.

A boy with the hard bird eye of youth pedaled a tricycle 26 slowly up beside me.

"What'cha lookin' at?" he asked curiously. 27

"A tree," I said. 28

"What for?" he said. 29

"It isn't there," I said, to myself mostly, and began to walk 30 away at a pace just slow enough not to seem to be running.

"What isn't there?" the boy asked. I didn't answer. It was 31 obvious I was attached by a thread to a thing that had never been there, or certainly not for long. Something that had to be held in the air, or sustained in the mind, because it was part of my orientation in the universe and I could not survive without it. There was more than an animal's attachment to a place. There was something else, the attachment of the spirit to a grouping of events in time; it was part of our morality.

32   So I had come home at last, driven by a memory in the brain as surely as the field mouse who had delved long ago into my flower pot or the pigeons flying forever amidst the rattle of nut-vending machines. These, the burrow under the greenery in my living room and the red-bellied bowls of peanuts now hovering in midair in the minds of pigeons, were all part of an elusive world that existed nowhere and yet everywhere. I looked once at the real world about me while the persistent boy pedaled at my heels.

33   It was without meaning, though my feet took a remembered path. In sixty years the house and street had rotted out of my mind. But the tree, the tree that no longer was, that had perished in its first season, bloomed on in my individual mind, unblemished as my father's words. "We'll plant a tree here, son, and we're not going to move any more. And when you're an old, old man you can sit under it and think how we planted it here, you and me, together."

34   I began to outpace the boy on the tricycle.

35   "Do you live here, Mister?" he shouted after me suspiciously. I took a firm graps on airy nothing—to be precise, on the bole of a great tree. "I do," I said. I spoke for myself, one field mouse, and several pigeons. We were all out of touch but somehow permanent. It was the world that had changed.

Content

1. What is Eiseley's thesis? What do his principal illustrations—the old men in the train station, the field mouse, the pigeons at the El, and Eiseley's return to the imagined tree of his childhood—have in common? How do they bear on his thesis?

2. Eiseley continually compares the human and the natural worlds. In what ways can we better understand the old men in the train station through the analogy to brown wasps? How is the blind man begging at the Philadelphia El like the pigeons that flock around it? Is the human climate of the El appropriately compared to a "food-bearing river" (¶ 17) in its importance to the pigeons?

3. What is the real world for the creatures and men in Eiseley's essay?

4. Can Eiseley be certain that the fleeing white-footed mouse he saw in the field near his apartment (¶ 11) was the same as the mouse in his

apartment? Does it matter? Is Eiseley justified in interpreting the mouse among his apartment ferns in human terms (¶s 12–16)?

5. Explain the last two sentences of the essay: "We were all out of touch but somehow permanent. It was the world that had changed."

Strategies/Structures

1. Eiseley's perspective shifts as he moves from illustration to illustration. From whose point of view does he see the old men in the train station? The field mouse in his living room? The pigeons in the El? Himself as a child?

2. What is the function of the one-sentence paragraph (¶ 18)—"I saw the river stop."? What is the effect of that isolated sentence? Would it gain or lose effect if integrated with the preceding sentence?

3. What determines the order of the illustrations in Eiseley's essay?

Language

1. Why is the essay titled "The Brown Wasps" rather than "The White-Footed Mouse" or "The Pigeons"?

2. Does the language of paragraph 16 really describe a mouse's dream? Or is it a human's view of what a mouse's dream might be like? What is the relation between the mouse's Eden and the Eden of Eiseley's own imaginary boyhood tree?

For Writing

1. Pick an incident or phenomenon in your life and explain it in such a way that illustrates, by analogy or extension, a thesis applicable to other people or phenomena.

2. Write an extended analogy comparing a phenomenon of human behavior with a phenomenon of animal behavior or vice versa. (For an example, see Barry Lopez, "My Horse," pages 305–12.)

MINORU YAMASAKI

Yamasaki (b. 1912) earned a bachelor's degree in architecture from the University of Washington in 1934. He worked as a freelance designer, 1935–1945, and taught briefly at New York

University and Columbia during this time. From 1945 through
1959 he was designer and partner in various Michigan architectural firms; since 1959 he has headed his own firm in Birmingham, Michigan. Among his notable designs are the World
Trade Center in New York and the Irwin Library at Bulter University (Indianapolis). He is a member of the National Council
on the Arts, and has won numerous architectural honors, including two First Honor awards from the American Institute of
Architects and three honorary doctorates.

In the selection below from Yamasaki's autobiography,
A Life in Architecture, he illustrates what his own buildings
exemplify, the belief that "man is much happier when his
environment consists of delicate elements, beautifully proportioned. . . ."

The Aesthetics and Practice of Architecture

1   T he building[1] was for me the epitome of the Japanese architectural tradition, the embodiment of the standards of
beauty as defined by Emerson. In today's world, traditional Japanese architecture in its pure form is impossible, except in the
most special of circumstances. But I think it important to use
both its delicacy and the warmth of feeling it creates for the
individual as standards by which to design contemporary buildings. One is never overwhelmed in a traditional Japanese structure, and the same should be true of today's buildings, no matter
how large and imposing they may be. It is the human sense of
scale and detail that relates buildings to man. This also demands
that a building be created so that it has a certain warmth for the
people that will be involved in it. Today's structures are by
necessity built of steel, glass, and concrete, but the judicious use

---

[1] A "delightful" restaurant-garden where Yamasaki often dined during his visits
to Japan, which exhibited Ralph Waldo Emerson's concept of beauty as "the
result of perfect economy."

of texture and color, plus landscaping, artworks, and interior finishes, can turn these cold materials into building that people enjoy being in and around.

I feel very strongly that man is much happier when his [2] environment consists of delicate elements, beautifully proportioned, whether they are of wood or stone, concrete or steel. I thoroughly dislike being in the interiors of buildings that are made of cold, rough, and massive brick, concrete, or stone. I much prefer the softness of wood and plaster, and floors of carpet or, in Japan, tatami, because of the comfort these materials provide and the warm, human feeling that they impart. Obviously there have been successful spaces built in beautifully polished marbles and other stones, but I basically prefer softer materials for interiors, since this is where people spend most of their time. I have used polished marble in both residential and office interiors, but I have done so sparingly. I have also used these materials in more monumental areas, such as public lobbies, where polished or honed marble seems more appropriate to me. Rougher materials seem much more suitable for gardens and exterior walls, but not in interior spaces, where they are uncomfortable and abrasive when people come into contact with them. I enjoy materials delicately designed and pleasing to the touch as well as to the eye.

Whenever I am in Japan I try to make time to visit some [3] classic expression of its architectural tradition. Wandering through the structures or sitting in the gardens, I find myself renewed, once again determined to make these the standards by which I will develop my work. Modern man spends too much time thinking of ways to improvise and supposedly improve upon designs, usually to the detriment of true aesthetics. Objects and buildings become too overdone, too trendy, giving them no lasting meaning. It is this we must contemplate on and try to avoid.

A general assessment of what I have learned in my practice [4] is that the purpose of architecture is to create usable, livable areas where man can lead his life both productively and happily, doing the variety of activities in which he needs and wishes to be involved. We must also provide protection from the elements—wind, sun, rain, snow, cold, and heat—as well as from the more violent aspects of nature, such as fire, earthquakes, hurricanes, and so on. Beyond these basics, the architecture we design should give man an aesthetic, emotional fulfillment, so that when he goes from home to work or to other activities, he can anticipate with pleasure his arrival at his destination.

5   For the past few decades, the trend in architectural design has been to avoid tradition and history and to attempt to conceive a totally new style of architecture. My travels have thoroughly convinced me that, as in other endeavors of life, we can and should refer to the sensitive and thoughtful buildings and cities that men of the past designed in order to create a satisfying urban environment today. The development of contemporary architecture through the technology of the late eighteenth century, probably best exemplified by the Crystal Palace, was set back by the traditional architecture of the Chicago World's Fair in 1893. This fair influenced architects throughout the world. The opportunity to develop buildings more compatible with the materials and machinery of the day did not again present itself until after World War II.

6   The flat, glassy buildings that were contemporary man's early attempts to break away from the false "traditional" of the early nineteen hundreds have become the nuclei for many urban areas that are, as a result, devoid of the fine qualities that the architects of the past had instilled in their buildings. Traveling around the world, I have been able to see many of the treasures of man's architectural history. No matter who the architect or what the country, these masterpieces all had one common characteristic: each was designed so that the changes in light experienced from sunrise through to sunset created maximum impact, no matter at what time of the day. In each case, the silhouette of the structure was beautiful and exciting even against a cloudy sky, and much more so on a sunny day.

7   In the past, religious buildings, which rose upward toward the heavens, were the focal points of cities, other buildings being low and subdued in order to indicate the importance of these religious structures. Today, because of the much stronger building materials we have available to us, we make our buildings ever higher. But this means that, for structural reasons, these higher buildings must be simple in design, while lower ones are much more adaptable to varying forms and silhouettes. This

makes the contemporary city somewhat the opposite of those of the past. One of the greatest problems we have is the monotony of the facades used for the higher buildings. Whether they be all glass, mirror glass, or metal, the very flatness of these structures tends to make for dull facades. At the same time, the tendency to cluster the taller buildings because of the high cost of land only increases this problem. There is a need for a few buildings to be more interestingly treated so that man is surrounded by some richer, more varied structures.

How do we alleviate this problem? In the past, the stone 8 buildings in Europe and the delicate paper and wood buildings of Japan were beautifully ornamented. The handicraft of the past made the facades of structures more interesting, and, when exceptionally well done, as has been the case in Europe, each fine building imparted an extremely satisfying feeling of completeness to the more sensitive observer. Many still prefer these traditional structures against the dead simplicity of the present-day buildings.

The problem for the modern architect is, then, to try and 9 apply comparable ideals to today's world. How we achieve this, I do not know, except that sensitively done stamping and precasting of metal can give us more interesting surfaces. As our technology grows, there will be other means to achieve the richness that so delighted people in the past. Many sculptors of today are realizing the need for their works to enrich and make complete our contemporary environment. Though there are so far only a few examples of a style of sculpture that can be incorporated into facades of buildings, the spaces between and around them can be enriched by the presence of well-executed works of art. What I want to emphasize here, however, is that there has to be a totally new concept in designing buildings, for we must realize that we have to use contemporary materials and technology; we cannot return to the handicraft of the past.

Another important aspect is one that I feel Frank Lloyd 10 Wright discovered in the historical architecture of Japan and translated so beautifully in this country. This is the element of surprise. By this I mean that when going from space to space, the change is sudden and almost breathtaking. The best examples are in the wandering Japanese temples where one goes from a sunlit court of raked gravel and carefully placed stones through dark corridors to a courtyard filled with foliage that forms a particularly interesting and varying ceiling against the blue sky. This sense of surprise can be introduced into today's buildings. We can, for example, raise and lower ceiling heights and vary the openness and spaciousness of rooms. There are, in fact, numerous ways to make buildings less monotonous so that people experience changing aesthetic sensations as they move around within a single structure and its landscaped surroundings. The realization of this is, however, little evident in modern architecture. The challenge, I believe, is to discover and create means of providing new sensations of delight and pleasure in the surroundings man builds for himself.

11   I personally dislike the appearance of mirror glass, especially when it is used to face an entire building, covering the structure, spandrel areas, and even the parapets, and thus, because of its reflective quality, completely hiding the structure of the building and masking the human activity within it. At the same time, contrary to popular opinion, mirror glass is less efficient in terms of heating and cooling a building than is regular glass. I have tended to avoid the "all-glass" building, which is actually about sixty percent glass, for these reasons, and also because I have a very strong feeling of acrophobia, so that when I stand near a large pane of glass in a high building, I feel very uncomfortable, as though I were standing on a stationary but floating carpet. Experience has taught me that about thirty-percent glass area is enough to completely eliminate feelings of claustrophobia and still give the secure sense of being in a building. Though it is extremely important and pleasant for the occupants of a building to have the pleasure of seeing out of the windows, experiencing the outdoor elements and the view from the security of an inside environment, I believe that a building should be designed so that its occupants are very aware that they are actually within a structure enjoying its protection, rather than attempting to attain the sense of being outdoors by making the building all glass. Occasionally a glass house built with a lovely frame and set in a beautiful garden may be a delight, but I am convinced that such exposure in a building more than one or two stories high would be just as uncomfortable for its oc-

cupants as would be a totally enclosed space. The percentage of glass in the World Trade Center is about thirty, and many tenants have told me that they formerly occupied offices with much more glass, but they are completely comfortable with that proportion. Since the windows are shoulder width and floor-to-ceiling, one can lean against the frame of the windows and look down to the street below without any sense of fear.

Weathering steel is another instance of a new technology that was sold to many architects before its disadvantages were fully realized. This kind of steel rusts for three years to make its own permanent finish. However, too late it was seen that this rusting stained many beautiful pavements and adjacent walls beyond repair. Fortunately this material is now used mainly in bridges or on walls above grass or gravel. 12

What I am trying to say is that while change and development are important aspects of architecture, innovation purely for innovation's sake usually only results in unaesthetic and sometimes unsound structures. If an architect is to apply a new technology to a project, he must be sure of it and the results it will produce. Too often we have the attitude that today's buildings are impermanent, so that if a new technology is applied and fails on a particular structure, we rationalize it by saying the building will not be there for very long anyway. But, aside from the waste of money, energy, and resources inherent in such thinking, this attitude reflects a sense of irresponsibility that pervades many aspects of our society and culture. As architects, we must strive and innovate, but with a proper amount of proportion and common sense. No technique can be too unusual, as long as it is well thought out. 13

In architecture, the key to simplicity and aesthetic beauty lies in the structure of a building. The skeletal framework of birds, animals, or human beings has much to do with man's assessment of their beauty. When that framework disappears because of its covering, as in a hippopotamus or a pig, the impression is usually one of ugliness, regardless of how interesting the underlying form of the animal may be. Some years ago I went hunting for the first and only time in my life. I saw a deer passing not five feet away from me, but it was so beautiful that I did not even raise my rifle to shoot it. All I felt was a sense 14 of relief as I watched its lovely white tail bobbing away into the underbrush.

15   Buildings, too, must be designed so that the facade enhances the structure, rather than hiding or distorting it, for the latter usually results in something that is unpleasant both to look at and to be in.

Content

1. How does Yamasaki's essay illustrate his contention that "the purpose of architecture is to create usable, livable areas where man can lead his life both productively and happily" (¶ 4)?

2. What specific details throughout the essay does Yamasaki use to illustrate his belief that "It is the human sense of scale and detail that relates buildings to man" (¶ 1)?

3. Judging from Yamasaki's views on architecture, what do you suppose his buildings look like? If you have seen any of his buildings, such as the World Trade Center, do these illustrate the architectural principles he discusses here?

4. Does Yamasaki's essay contain any clues, other than his name, about his Japanese origin? Do you think that traditional Japanese architecture has influenced Yamasaki's sense of what is architecturally pleasing?

Strategies/Structures

1. How can you tell that Yamasaki is writing for a general audience rather than for an audience primarily of architects? What, if anything, do you as a reader need to know about architecture that the author doesn't tell you or imply in the context of the essay?

2. How does Yamasaki's reference to the deer that was too beautiful to shoot illustrate his assertion that when the skeletal "framework disappears because of its covering, as in a hippopotamous or pig, the impression is usually one of ugliness" (¶ 13)? How would a different choice of animals have affected his illustration? Of what relevance is this to architecture?

3. Yamasaki clearly feels passionately about his subject, which is the essence of his life and work. Yet his tone is dispassionate. Why? Would his views have been more or less convincing if he had employed a different tone?

Language

1. Should Yamasaki have explicitly defined such terms as "delicate elements" (¶ 2), "beautifully proportioned" (2), "usable, livable areas" (4), "an extremely satisfying feeling of completeness" (8)? Can you tell from context what these terms mean, or do you have to supply your own meaning?

2. If necessary, look up references so you can identify the Crystal Palace (¶ 5), Frank Lloyd Wright (10), acrophobia (11), and World Trade Center (11).

For Writing

1. Describe a building that you particularly like, preferably one in which you live or work or otherwise spend considerable time. In your description show how the building's architectural features enhance its functions, including the enjoyment and/or performance of people using it.

2. Analyze the architectural features of a building you particularly dislike, preferably one in which you live or work or otherwise spend considerable time, to show how these features inhibit or otherwise detract from its functions and from the enjoyment and/or performance of people using it.

CARL SAGAN

One of the most celebrated astronomers of the twentieth century, Sagan (b. 1934) was born in New York City and was educated at the University of Chicago and Indiana University. Presently a professor of Astronomy and Space Sciences at Cornell University, Sagan has received NASA Medals for Exceptional Scientific Achievement (1972) and Distinguished Public Service (1977) for his central role in the Mariner, Viking, and Voyager programs; the Joseph Priestly Award (1975) "for distinguished contributions to the welfare of mankind"; and the 1978 Pulitzer Prize for Literature for *The Dragons of Eden* (1977). Foremost among his other books are *The Cosmic Connection*

(1973) and *Cosmos* (1980). The following excerpt from *The Dragons of Eden* reveals how analogy may be particularly useful to
help sceintists or other specialists explain complex or technical
phenomena in terms their less specialized audience will understand. The points of correspondence enable the readers to use
what they have already learned to organize and interpret new
information. Analogies provide efficient shortcuts to
understanding.

The Cosmic Calendar

1   The world is very old, and human beings are very young.
Significant events in our personal lives are measured in
years or less; our lifetimes in decades; our family genealogies in
centuries; and all of recorded history in millennia. But we have
been preceded by an awesome vista of time, extending for prodigious periods into the past, about which we know little—both
because there are no written records and because we have real
difficulty in grasping the immensity of the intervals involved.

2   Yet we are able to date events in the remote past. Geological
stratification and radioactive dating provide information on archaeological, paleontological and geological events; and astro-
physical theory provides data on the ages of planetary surfaces,
stars, and the Milky Way Galaxy, as well as an estimate of the
time that has elapsed since that extraordinary event called the
Big Bang—an explosion that involved all of the matter and energy in the present universe. The Big Bang may be the beginning
of the universe, or it may be a discontinuity in which information
about the earlier history of the universe was destroyed. But it
is certainly the earliest event about which we have any record.

3   The most instructive way I know to express this cosmic
chronology is to imagine the fifteen-billion-year lifetime of the
universe (or at least its present incarnation since the Big Bang)
compressed into the span of a single year. Then every billion
years of Earth history would correspond to about twenty-four
days of our cosmic year, and one second of that year to 475 real

COSMIC CALENDAR
DECEMBER

SUNDAY	MONDAY	TUESDAY	WEDNESDAY	THURSDAY	FRIDAY	SATURDAY
	1 Significant oxygen atmosphere begins to develop on Earth.	**2**	**3**	**4**	**5** Extensive vulcanism and channel formation on Mars.	**6**
7	**8**	**9**	**10**	**11**	**12**	**13**
14	**15**	**16** First worms.	**17** Precambrian ends. Paleozoic Era and Cambrian Period begin. Invertebrates flourish.	**18** First oceanic plankton. Trilobites flourish.	**19** Ordovician Period. First fish, first vertebrates.	**20** Silurian Period. First vascular plants. Plants begin colonization of land.
21 Devonian Period begins. First insects. Animals begin colonization of land.	**22** First amphibians. First winged insects.	**23** Carboniferous Period. First trees. First reptiles.	**24** Permian Period begins. First dinosaurs.	**25** Paleozoic Era ends. Mesozoic Era begins.	**26** Triassic Period. First mammals.	**27** Jurassic Period. First birds.
28 Cretaceous Period. First flowers. Dinosaurs become extinct.	**29** Mesozoic Era ends. Cenozoic Era and Tertiary Period begin. First cetaceans. First primates.	**30** Early evolution of frontal lobes in the brains of primates. First hominids. Giant mammals flourish.	**31** End of the Pliocene Period. Quaternary (Pleistocene and Holocene) Period. First humans.			

PRE-DECEMBER DATES

Big Bang	January 1
Origin of the Milky Way Galaxy	May 1
Origin of the solar system	September 9
Formation of the Earth	September 14
Origin of life on Earth	~September 25
Formation of the oldest rocks known on Earth	October 2
Date of oldest fossils (bacteria and blue-green algae)	October 9
Invention of sex (by microorganisms)	~November 1
Oldest fossil photosynthetic plants	November 12
Eukaryotes (first cells with nuclei) flourish	November 15

$\sim$ = *approximately*

revolutions of the Earth about the sun. [In what follows,] I present the cosmic chronology in three forms: a list of some representative pre-December dates; a calendar for the month of December; and a closer look at the late evening of New Year's Eve. On this scale, the events of our history books—even books that make significant efforts to deprovincialize the present—are so compressed that it is necessary to give a second-by-second recounting of the last seconds of the cosmic year. Even then, we find events listed as contemporary that we have been taught to consider as widely separated in time. In the history of life, an equally rich tapestry must have been woven in other periods—for example, between 10:02 and 10:03 on the morning of April 6th or September 16th. But we have detailed records only for the very end of the cosmic year.

4   The chronology corresponds to the best evidence now available. But some of it is rather shaky. No one would be astounded if, for example, it turns out that plants colonized the land in the Ordovician rather than the Silurian Period; or that segmented worms appeared earlier in the Precambrian Period than indicated. Also, in the chronology of the last ten seconds of the cosmic year, it was obviously impossible for me to include all significant events; I hope I may be excused for not having explicitly mentioned advances in art, music and literature or the

DECEMBER 31

Origin of *Proconsul* and *Ramapithecus*, probable ancestors of apes and men	~1:30 P.M.
First humans	~10:30 P.M.
Widespread use of stone tools	11:00 P.M.
Domestication of fire by Peking man	11:46 P.M.
Beginning of most recent glacial period	11:56 P.M.
Seafarers settle Australia	11:58 P.M.
Extensive cave painting in Europe	11:59 P.M.
Invention of agriculture	11:59:20 P.M.
Neolithic civilization; first cities	11:59:35 P.M.
First dynasties in Sumer, Ebla and Egypt; development of astronomy	11:59:50 P.M.
Invention of the alphabet; Akkadian Empire	11:59:51 P.M.
Hammurabic legal codes in Babylon; Middle Kingdom in Egypt	11:59:52 P.M.
Bronze metallurgy; Mycenaean culture; Trojan War; Olmec culture: invention of the compass	11:59:53 P.M.
Iron metallurgy; First Assyrian Empire; Kingdom of Israel; founding of Carthage by Phoenicia	11:59:54 P.M.
Asokan India; Ch'in Dynasty China; Periclean Athens; birth of Buddha	11:59:55 P.M.
Euclidean geometry; Archimedean physics; Ptolemaic astronomy; Roman Empire; birth of Christ	11:59:56 P.M.
Zero and decimals invented in Indian arithmetic; Rome falls; Moslem conquests	11:59:57 P.M.
Mayan civilization; Sung Dynasty China; Byzantine empire; Mongol invasion; Crusades	11:59:58 P.M.
Renaissance in Europe; voyages of dicovery from Europe and from Ming Dynasty China; emergence of the experimental method in science	11:59:59 P.M.
Widespread development of science and technology; emergence of a global culture; acquisition of the means for self-destruction of the human species; first steps in spacecraft planetary exploration and the search for extraterrestrial intelligence	Now: The first second of New Year's Day

historically significant American, French, Russian and Chinese revolutions.

5   The construction of such tables and calendars is inevitably humbling. It is disconcerting to find that in such a cosmic year the Earth does not condense out of interstellar matter until early September; dinosaurs emerge on Christmas Eve; flowers arise on December 28th; and men and women originate at 10:30 P.M. on New Year's Eve. All of recorded history occupies the last ten seconds of December 31; and the time from the waning of the Middle Ages to the present occupies little more than one second. But because I have arranged it that way, the first cosmic year has just ended. And despite the insignificance of the instant we have so far occupied in cosmic time, it is clear that what happens on and near Earth at the beginning of the second cosmic year will depend very much on the scientific wisdom and the distinctly human sensitivity of mankind.

Content

1. What analogy does Sagan use to explain the cosmic calendar? Is a year a more appropriate basis for comparison than a decade or a century would be? Why or why not?

2. What other analogies does Sagan use in this explanation? For what purposes?

3. What information do the diagram (The Cosmic Calendar) and the chart of "Pre-December Dates" supply that is not apparent from Sagan's prose text? In what other ways do they help clarify and organize his explanation? In this case, is one diagram more eloquent than a lengthy prose explanation? How do the prose text and the diagram reinforce one another?

Strategies/Structures

1. Is the chronological progression from remote past to the present time the most useful way for Sagan to organize his material? How clear would have been an explanation that proceeded in the reverse order, from the present to the remote past?

2. Analogies have their limitations; at some point the correspondence

breaks down because of significant dissimilarities. What are the limitations of Sagan's analogy?

Language

1. To what extent do readers need to know the meaning of such phenomena as "geological stratification," "radioactive dating," and "the Big Bang" (all in ¶ 2)? Is Sagan's explanation of "the Big Bang" sufficient for his purposes here?
2. This essay discusses some difficult scientific concepts, and it contains some appropriately scientific polysyllabic words. Yet the first sentence is almost childishly simple. Why does Sagan begin so simply?

For Writing

1. Write an explanation of a scientific or technical phenomenon for an audience of nonspecialists. Use an analogy between your subject and something familiar to your audience to clarify your explanation.
2. Use a compression or an expansion of time as the basis for explaining a particularly memorable period in your life, happy, stressful, or otherwise.

◀───▶

LAI MAN LEE

Lee was born in Hong Kong in 1960, and moved to the Washington, D.C. area with her family in 1963, where she has lived ever since. She earned a B.S. in psychology from the College of William and Mary in 1982.

Lee wrote this essay to fulfill a freshman English assignment to explain the symbolic connotations of an object. Her explanation illustrates the meanings of the bracelet to Chinese women in general, and its complex significance to her in particular. The bracelet itself was later broken "into two clean pieces" during an accident in a volleyball class; Lee has saved them and awaits their repair. She says, "I don't think that I'm very superstitious but . . . that bracelet does seem to have brought me good luck."

❖ *My Bracelet*

1   W hen I stop to think about which possession of mine means the most to me, I find myself looking at my left wrist. Adorning my wrist is a simple solid jade bracelet. Its color is uneven, ranging from a pale green, almost-white, to a sea green, and it has a brown spot, an imperfection in the stone. There are tiny scratches on the bracelet, hardly noticeable, and a crack on one side—where the bracelet may eventually break completely. But in spite of its imperfections, the bracelet could not be any more perfect to me than it is because of the sentimental value it holds.

2   I will always remember the first time I saw a jade bracelet of this kind, when I was eight. It was in a museum collection of Chinese jewelry. I found it amazing that the bracelet could be a perfectly polished ring carved from one single piece of jade, and thought it must be very valuable.

3   I went home and told my mother, who explained to me that such bracelets were quite common among Chinese women, and varied greatly in expense and quality. Some women would get jade bracelets when they were very young and wear them until they died. Since jade is a soft stone, it can break very easily when treated roughly. My mother told me that if a bracelet did break, the woman would wrap all the fragments up in a handkerchief and save the pieces for the rest of her life, for even the pieces would bring good luck. This gave me an image of the Chinese woman, and having my bracelet will always remind me of my culture and the individual that I am.

4   I remember very clearly the night my parents gave me the bracelet. It was in my sophomore year of high school, and I had stayed out past my curfew of midnight. When I got home that night, my parents gave me a lecture on responsibility. I expected to be placed on restriction, but instead they gave me a jade bracelet. I was totally shocked . . . but when I went to bed that night I was supremely happy.

5   The next morning, my father told me that because they had gone shopping for the bracelet, he had not gone to the

racetrack and had missed out on winning $20,000 because of me. However, he said that I was worth it.

The bracelet will always remind me of those two days and the love that exists in my relationship with my parents, even though nothing is ever said. I know that no matter what I may do, my parents will always love me and accept me the way I am.   6

Since I got the bracelet, I have not taken it off—mostly because I don't want to, but also because my hand has outgrown the bracelet and therefore it is stuck on permanently. My bracelet means so much to me that if it should ever break I would be enormously upset. But then, I could always save the pieces for good luck.   7

Content

1. What does the jade bracelet symbolize to Chinese women in general?
2. What personal symbolism does the bracelet have for Lee? In what respects is this symbolism congruent with the bracelet's general symbolism?
3. Why did Lee's parents give her such a significant present on the night she stayed out past her midnight curfew?

Strategies/Structures

1. Why does Lee begin her essay with a description of the bracelet?
2. What pattern of organization does Lee use?
3. How can you tell that Lee assumes her audience is not Chinese?
4. Lee's seven paragraph essay contains two paragraphs of two sentences each (¶s 5, 6) and two of three sentences each (¶s 2, 7). Are any of them too short? Could any be combined for greater coherence? If so, which ones?

Language

1. Is it appropriate for Lee to express such complex and powerful symbolism in such simple and straightforward language?
2. Lee says her bracelet has great sentimental value (¶ 1). Is her tone or choice of language sentimental? Should it be?

For Writing

1. Pick an object or place that has symbolic connotations, to people in general or to you in particular, or both. In an essay on the subject, describe the object or place, if necessary, then illustrate the connotations so that their various meanings become apparent to readers, even if they are unfamiliar with it.

2. Whether you are a member of a minority or majority culture, select an object or phenomenon (such as the prevalence of fast-food restaurants, or the popularity of running or soccer), describe or explain it, and analyze it as an illustration of the culture to which you belong.

Strategies for Writing— Illustration and Example

1. Is my essay a single, extended illustration? Or a combination of several? What am I using the illustration(s) for—to clarify a point, to make an abstraction or a relationship concrete? To provide a definition? To imply an argument?

2. Is my audience familiar with my example(s) or not? How much detail and background information must I provide to be sure the audience understands what I'm saying? How many examples will make my point most effectively? When will they become redundant or boring?

3. What kinds of illustrations or examples am I using? Positive? Negative? Or both? Simple or complicated? What are the sources of my examples—my own or others' personal experiences, a knowledge of history or some other subject, reading? Are they to be interpreted literally, symbolically, or on multiple levels?

4. If I'm using more than one illustration or example, in what order will I arrange them? From the most to least memorable, or vice versa? From the simplest to the most elaborate, or the reverse? In the order in which they occur naturally, historically, or in which they are arranged spatially or geographically? Or by some other means?

5. Are the illustrations or examples self-evident? To what extent must I analyze them to explain their meaning? Will my language (sarcastic, nostalgic, sentimental, objective) help to provide an interpretation? Does the language fit the example?

Additional Writing Topics

Write an essay that illustrates one of the statements below, or your adaptation or variation on it.

1. Actions speak louder than words.
2. To err is human.
3. The only thing we have to fear is fear itself.
4. And you shall know the truth and the truth shall set you free.
5. Two heads are better than one.
6. A house divided against itself cannot stand.
7. You can lead a horse to water but you can't make him drink.
8. Time is money.
9. There never was a good war or a bad peace.
10. The style is the man.

11. Early to bed and early to rise, makes a man healthy, wealthy, and wise.
12. Without justice, courage is weak.
13. An ounce of prevention is worth a pound of cure.
14. Self-love is the greatest of all flatterers.
15. Those who can, do; those who can't, teach.
16. Vision is the art of seeing things invisible.
17. A little learning is a dangerous thing.
18. Some books are to be tasted, others to be swallowed, and some few to be chewed and digested.
19. Love is blind.
20. Knowledge is power.

9   *Comparison and Contrast*

Writers compare people, places, things, or qualities to identify their similarities, and contrast them to identify the differences. What you say about one subject usually helps to illuminate or explain the other; such explanations have the added advantage of answering questions that hinge on the similarities and differences under consideration. Your commentary can also provide the basis for judging the relative merits and demerits of the subject at hand.

For instance, comparison and contrast can help you determine whether to choose a liberal arts or a technical education, and what your future will be like with whichever you select. It can help you explain the resemblances between the works of Faulkner and Hemingway, and the differences—and to justify your preference for one author over the other. Comparison and contrast can help you decide whom to vote for, what movie to see (or avoid), where to spend your next vacation, what car to buy, what person to marry. A thoroughgoing, detailed comparison and contrast of the reasons for the quality of life with and without handguns, conservation of natural resources, or nuclear testing can provide a convincing argument for your choice.

But not everything will work. The subjects you select should have some obvious qualities in common to make the comparison and contrast fruitful. If you try to compare very dissimilar things, as the Mad Hatter does in *Alice in Wonderland* ("Why is a raven like a writing desk?"), you'll have to stretch for an answer ("Because they both begin with an *r* sound.") that may be either silly or irrelevant. Barry Lopez in the following essay, "My Horse," can easily compare his horse and his truck; both are modes of transportation with "heart." But if he tried to compare either with, say, a blood transfusion ("because they both provide energy"), the fragile basis for comparison would be too slight to hold up.

In writing an essay of comparison and contrast you'll need to justify your choice of subject, unless the basis for comparison is obvious. The very title of Bruce Catton's essay, "Grant and Lee," leads readers to expect a comparison of the two extraordinary Civil War leaders, and a contrast because one epitomized the North, the other the South. In "My Horse," however, after examining for seven paragraphs how the Indians regarded their horses, Lopez justifies the comparison with his truck by, "I do not own a horse. I am attached to a truck, however, and I have come to think of it in a similar way."

You'll also have to limit your comparison. It would take a book or more to compare and contrast all the relevant aspects of the People's Republic of China and Taiwan. In a short essay on the subject you could focus instead on their relative educational systems, on their relations with the United States, or on the everyday life of the average worker in each country. Likewise, in a short paper, you're better off to compare the relevant aspects of two entities. The more items you add, the more complicated the comparison becomes, as you try to deal with the political system in the People's Republic of China, and Taiwan, and Russia, and Poland, and East Germany, and. . . .

There are three common ways to organize an essay of comparison and contrast, such as of two very different houses, your own and your grandparents'. You could discuss all the relevant features first of house *A;* then those of house *B;* and then evaluate the similarities and differences. This works well for a very short paper, where readers can keep in mind everything you've said about house *A* while they're reading about house *B*. The longer the discussion, the less easy it is for readers to remember what they need to.

In a longer essay, therefore, it's preferable to compare and contrast one point at a time, alternating between subjects: the setting of house *A*, the setting of house *B*; the floor plan of house *A*, the floor plan of house *B*, and so on. If you've evaluated each point as you went along, the conclusion, having evolved naturally, might simply sum up the logical outcome of the comparison: "Although my grandparents' house is larger and has many attractive nooks and crannies, my smaller, newer house is more energy efficient and easier to maintain." Or you could group all the similarities of houses *A* and *B* in one section of a paper, and all the differences in another.

Whatever pattern of comparison and contrast you use, a topic outline can help you to organize such papers, and to make sure you've covered equivalent points for each item in the comparison. However you organize the paper, you don't have to give equal emphasis to the similarities and to the differences; some may simply be more important than others. In "That Lean and Hungry Look," Suzanne Britt Jordan intentionally focuses far more extensively on the differences between the temperaments and lifestyles of fat and thin people than she does on their similarities. But you do have to make your chosen points of comparison relevant. James Agee, in "Comedy's Greatest Era," concentrates on the comic essence of four great silent comedians, Charlie Chaplin, Harold Lloyd, Harry Langdon, and Buster Keaton (only three are covered in the excerpt on pp. 324–31). It would have been beside his point to examine the private life or financial status of one unless he had done so for all of them. Note that Agee's essay is atypical of the others in this section in that he presents information about more than two people, and although his points of discussion are roughly congruent, he lets the readers make most of the overt comparisons among the actors.

In writing an essary of comparison and contrast, it helps to ask: What are the major similarities in the items at hand?

What are their conspicuous differences? What pattern of organization will reflect my emphasis most clearly? As indicated, essays of comparison and contrast may include other types of writing, particularly description, narration, and analysis. Classification and division often determine the points to be covered in such essays. And essays of comparison and contrast themselves become, at times, illustrations or arguments, direct or indirect, overt or more subtle. Long live the differences and the zest they provide.

BARRY LOPEZ

Lopez was born in 1945 near New York City. He received a
B.A. from Notre Dame in 1966 and an M.A. in teaching in
1968, after which he studied at the University of Oregon
(1969–70). He now lives in Finn Rock, Oregon, where he is a
professional writer and free-lance photographer. Much of his
writing presents sympathetic, sometimes poetic, interpretations
of animal behavior in relation to other animals or humans.
Among his books are *Desert Notes: Reflections in the Eye of a
Raven* (1976); *River Notes: The Dance of the Herons* (1979); and *Of
Wolves and Men* (1979), illustrated with his own photographs.
That Lopez is a careful and perceptive observer of his subjects
is revealed in the multiple perspectives from which he regards
"My Horse," reprinted below from the *North American Review*.

My Horse

I t is curious that Indian warriors on the northern plains in   1
the nineteenth century, who were almost entirely dependent
on the horse for mobility and status, never gave their horses
names. If you borrowed a man's horse and went off raiding for
other horses, however, or if you lost your mount in battle and
then jumped on mine and counted coup on an enemy—well,
those horses would have to be shared with the man whose horse
you borrowed, and that coup would be mine, not yours. Because
even if I gave him no name, he was my horse.

If you were a Crow warrior and I a young Teton Sioux out   2
after a warrior's identity and we came over a small hill somewhere in the Montana prairie and surprised each other, I could
tell a lot about you by looking at your horse.

Your horse might have feathers tied in his mane, or in his   3
tail, or a medicine bag tied around his neck. If I knew enough
about the Crow, and had looked at you closely, I might make
some sense of the decoration, even guess who you were if you
were well-known. If you had painted your horse I could tell
even more, because we both decorated our horses with signs

that meant the same things. Your white handprints high on his flanks would tell me you had killed an enemy in a hand-to-hand fight. Small horizontal lines stacked on your horse's foreleg, or across his nose, would tell me how many times you had counted coup. Horse hoof marks on your horse's rump, or three-sided boxes, would tell me how many times you had stolen horses. If there was a bright red square on your horse's neck I would know you were leading a war party and that there were probably others out there in the coulees behind you.

4   You might be painted all over as blue as the sky and covered with white dots, with your horse painted the same way. Maybe hailstorms were your power—or if I chased you a hailstorm might come down and hide you. There might be lightning bolts on the horse's legs and flanks, and I would wonder if you had lightning power, or a slow horse. There might be white circles around your horse's eyes to help him see better.

5   Or you might be like Crazy Horse, with no decoration, no marks on your horse to tell me anything, only a small lightning bolt on your cheek, a piece of turquoise tied behind your ear.

6   You might have scalps dangling from your rein.

7   I could tell something about you by your horse. All this would come to me in a few seconds. I might decide this was my moment and shout my war cry—*Hoka hey!* Or I might decide you were like the grizzly bear: I would raise my weapon to you in salute and go my way, to see you again when I was older.

8   I do not own a horse. I am attached to a truck, however, and I have come to think of it in a similar way. It has no name; it never occurred to me to give it a name. It has little decoration; neither of us is partial to decoration. I have a piece of turquoise in the truck because I had heard once that some of the southwestern tribes tied a small piece of turquoise in a horse's hock to keep him from stumbling. I like the idea. I also hang sage in the truck when I go on a long trip. But inside, the truck doesn't look much different from others that look just like it on the outside. I like it that way. Because I like my privacy.

9   For two years in Wyoming I worked on a ranch wrangling horses. The horse I rode when I had to have a good horse was a quarter horse and his name was Coke High. The name came

with him. At first I thought he'd been named for the soft drink. I'd known stranger names given to horses by whites. Years later I wondered if some deviate Wyoming cowboy wise to cocaine had not named him. Now I think he was probably named after a rancher, an historical figure of the region. I never asked the people who owned him for fear of spoiling the spirit of my inquiry.

We were running over a hundred horses on this ranch. 10 They all had names. After a few weeks I knew all the horses and the names too. You had to. No one knew how to talk about the animals or put them in order or tell the wranglers what to do unless they were using the names—Princess, Big Red, Shoshone, Clay.

My truck is named Dodge. The name came with it. I don't 11 know if it was named after the town or the verb or the man who invented it. I like it for a name. Perfectly anonymous, like Rex for a dog, or Old Paint. You can't tell anything with a name like that.

The truck is a van. I call it a truck because it's not a car 12 and because "van" is a suburban sort of consumer word, like "oxford loafer," and I don't like the sound of it. On the outside it looks like any other Dodge Sportsman 300. It's a dirty tan color. There are a few body dents, but it's never been in a wreck. I tore the antenna off against a tree on a pinched mountain road. A boy in Midland, Texas, rocked one of my rear view mirrors off. A logging truck in Oregon squeeze-fired a piece of debris off the road and shattered my windshield. The oil pan and gas tank are pug-faced from high-centering on bad roads. (I remember a horse I rode for a while named Targhee whose hocks were scarred from tangles in barbed wire when he was a colt and who spooked a lot in high grass, but these were not like "dents." They were more like bad tires.)

I like to travel. I go mostly in the winter and mostly on 13 two-lane roads. I've driven the truck from Key West to Vancouver, British Columbia, and from Yuma to Long Island over the past four years. I used to ride Coke High only about five miles every morning when we were rounding up horses. Hard miles of twisting and turning. About six hundred miles a year. Then I'd turn him out and ride another horse for the rest of the day.

That's what was nice about having a remuda. You could do all you had to do and not take it all out on your best horse. Three car family.

14   My truck came with a lot of seats in it and I've never really known what to do with them. Sometimes I put the seats in and go somewhere with a lot of people, but most of the time I leave them out. I like riding around with that empty cavern of space behind my head. I know it's something with a history to it, that there's truth in it, because I always rode a horse the same way—with empty saddle bags. In case I found something. The possibility of finding something is half the reason for being on the road.

15   The value of anything comes to me in its use. If I am not using something it is of no value to me and I give it away. I wasn't always that way. I used to keep everything I owned—just in case. I feel good about the truck because it gets used. A lot. To haul hay and firewood and lumber and rocks and garbage and animals. Other people have used it to haul furniture and freezers and dirt and recycled newspapers. And to move from one house to another. When I lend it for things like that I don't look to get anything back but some gas (if we're going to be friends). But if you go way out in the country to a dump and pick up the things you can still find out there (once a load of cedar shingles we sold for $175 to an architect) I expect you to leave some of those things around my place when you come back—if I need them.

16   When I think back, maybe the nicest thing I ever put in that truck was timber wolves. It was a long night's drive from Oregon up into British Columbia. We were all very quiet about it; it was like moving clouds across the desert.

17   Sometimes something won't fit in the truck and I think about improving it—building a different door system, for example. I am forever going to add better gauges on the dash and a pair of driving lamps and a sunroof, but I never get around to doing any of it. I remember I wanted to improve Coke High once too, especially the way he bolted like a greyhound through patches of cottonwood on a river flat. But all I could do with him was to try to rein him out of it. Or hug his back.

Sometimes, road-stoned in a blur of country like south-   18
western Wyoming or North Dakota, I talk to the truck. It's like
wandering on the high plains under a summer sun, on plains
where, George Catlin wrote, you were "out of sight of land." I
say what I am thinking out loud, or point at things along the
road. It's a crazy, sun-stroked sort of activity, a sure sign it's
time to pull over, to go for a walk, to make a fire and have some
tea, to lie in the shade of the truck.

I've always wanted to pat the truck. It's basic to the rela-   19
tionship. But it never works.

I remember when I was on the ranch, just at sunrise, after   20
I'd saddled Coke High, I'd be huddled down in my jacket smoking a cigarette and looking down into the valley, along the river
where the other horses had spent the night. I'd turn to Coke
and run my hand down his neck and slap-pat him on the shoulder to say I was coming up. It made a bond, an agreement we
started the day with.

I've thought about that a lot with the truck, because we've   21
gone out together at sunrise on so many mornings. I've even
fumbled around trying to do it. But metal won't give.

The truck's personality is mostly an expression of two ideas: 22
"with-you" and "alone." When Coke High was "with-you" he
and I were the same animal. We could have cut a rooster out of
a flock of chickens, we were so in tune. It's the same with the
truck: rolling through Kentucky on a hilly two-lane road, three
in the morning under a full moon and no traffic. Picture it. You
roll like water.

There are other times when you are with each other but   23
there's no connection at all. Coke got that way when he was
bored and we'd fight each other about which way to go around
a tree. When the truck gets like that—"alone"—it's because it
feels its Detroit fat-ass design dragging at its heart and making
a fool out of it.

I can think back over more than a hundred nights I've slept   24
in the truck, sat in it with a lamp burning, bundled up in a
parka, reading a book. It was always comfortable. A good place
to wait out a storm. Like sleeping inside a buffalo.

The truck will go past 100,000 miles soon. I'll rebuild the   25 engine and put a different transmission in it. I can tell from magazine advertisements that I'll never get another one like it. Because every year they take more of the heart out of them. One thing that makes a farmer or a rancher go sour is a truck that isn't worth a shit. The reason you see so many old pickups in ranch country is because these are the only ones with any heart. You can count on them. The weekend rancher runs around in a new pickup with too much engine and not enough transmission and with the wrong sort of tires because he can afford anything, even the worst. A lot of them have names for their pickups too.

26   My truck has broken down, in out of the way places at the worst of times. I've walked away and screamed the foulness out of my system and gotten the tools out. I had to fix a water pump in a blizzard in the Panamint Mountains in California once. It took all day with the Coleman stove burning under the engine block to keep my hands from freezing. We drifted into Beatty, Nevada, that night with it jury-rigged together with—I swear—baling wire, and we were melting snow as we went and pouring it in to compensate for the leaks.

27   There is a dent next to the door on the driver's side I put there one sweltering night in Miami. I had gone to the airport to meet my wife, whom I hadn't seen in a month. My hands were so swollen with poison ivy blisters I had to drive with my wrists. I had shut the door and was locking it when the window fell off its runners and slid down inside the door. I couldn't leave the truck unlocked because I had too much inside I didn't want to lose. So I just kicked the truck a blow in the side and went to work on the window. I hate to admit kicking the truck. It's like kicking a dog, which I've never done.

28   Coke High and I had an accident once. We hit a badger hole at a full gallop. I landed on my back and blacked out. When I came to, Coke High was about a hundred yards away. He stayed a hundred yards away for six miles, all the way back to the ranch.

29   I want to tell you about carrying those wolves, because it was a fine thing. There were ten of them. We had four in the

truck with us in crates and six in a trailer. It was a five hundred mile trip. We went at night for the cool air and because there wouldn't be as much traffic. I could feel from the way the truck rolled along that its heart was in the trip. It liked the wolves inside it, the sweet odor that came from the crates. I could feel that same tireless wolf-lope developing in its wheels; it was like you might never have to stop for gas, ever again.

The truck gets very self-focused when it works like this; 30 its heart is strong and it's good to be around it. It's good to be *with* it. You get the same feeling when you pull someone out of a ditch. Coke High and I pulled a Volkswagen out of the mud once, but Coke didn't like doing it very much. Speed, not strength, was his center. When the guy who owned the car thanked us and tried to pat Coke, the horse snorted and swung away, trying to preserve his distance, which is something a horse spends a lot of time on.

So does the truck. 31

Being distant lets the truck get its heart up. The truck has 32 been cold and alone in Montana at 38 below zero. It's climbed horrible, eroded roads in Idaho. It's been burdened beyond overloading, and made it anyway. I've asked it to do these things because they build heart, and without heart all you have is a machine. You have nothing. I don't think people in Detroit know anything at all about heart. That's why everything they build dies so young.

One time in Arizona the truck and I came through one of 33 the worst storms I've ever been in, an outrageous, angry blizzard. But we went down the road, right through it. You couldn't explain our getting through by the sort of tires I had on the truck, or the fact that I had chains on, or was a good driver, or had a lot of weight over my drive wheels or a good engine, because it was more than this. It was a contest between the truck and the blizzard—and the truck wouldn't quit. I could have gone to sleep and the truck would have just torn a road down Interstate 40 on its own. It scared the hell out of me; but it gave me heart, too.

We came off the Mogollon Rim that night and out of the 34 storm and headed south for Phoenix. I pulled off the road to sleep for a few hours, but before I did I got out of the truck. It was raining. Warm rain. I tied a short piece of red avalanche cord into the grill. I left it there for a long time, like an eagle feather on a horse's tail. It flapped and spun in the wind. I could hear it ticking against the grill when I drove.

35   When I have to leave that truck I will just raise up my left arm—*Hoka hey!*—and walk away.

Content

1. What is the main subject of Lopez's essay, his truck or his horse? Why does he title the essay "My Horse," and what does he mean by the title?

2. In what ways does Lopez's truck resemble a horse—in functions, relationship with its owner, appearance, and other features? Which comparisons does Lopez make explicit? Which does he imply? To what else does he compare his truck?

3. How much does the reader have to know about horses and trucks in order to understand Lopez's comparison? How much does the comparison reveal about Lopez himself?

4. Why does Lopez refer twice to transporting "the nicest thing I ever put in that truck, timber wolves" (¶s 16, 29)? What does this incident reveal about Lopez? Illustrate about the truck? Why doesn't Lopez fully explain why he was moving the timber wolves?

Strategies/Structures

1. Why does Lopez begin this essay on his truck by describing the horses of 19th-century plains Indian warriors? What similarities are there between paragraph 7 and the concluding paragraph?

2. Lopez intentionally breaks a number of the conventional rules of writing. For instance, he uses numerous sentence fragments (¶ 13, for example). He begins and ends sentences with prepositions (¶s 25, 30). He addresses the reader as "you" (¶s 2, 29). He writes one-sentence paragraphs (¶ 31). What are the effects of this rule-breaking?

3. Lopez includes a number of narratives within his overall structure of comparison and contrast. What functions do they serve? What narrative technique does he employ?

4. In what respects are the horse and the truck different (¶s 15, 19, for instance)? Is it wise, in an extended comparison, to acknowledge differences as well as similarities? What is the effect of acknowledging,

as Lopez does in paragraphs 26–28, the problems he has had with his truck and his horse?

5. What does Lopez use Detroit to symbolize in this essay (¶ 32)?

Language

1. Why do people name their animals, or cars, or trucks? Why does Lopez like the anonymous name *Dodge* that came with his truck (¶ 11)? Why doesn't he give the truck a more individual name?

2. Lopez uses many similes in this essay, such as "like sleeping inside a buffalo" (¶ 24). Identify some of them and show what purposes they fulfill.

For Writing

1. Write an extended analogy comparing someone you know well to his or her pet or vehicle, such as a bicycle, car, motorcycle, boat, or plane.

2. Some responsibilities (such as having a paper route or other job, caring for a younger sibling, pet, vegetable garden, or vehicle) are regarded as aids to maturation. If you have participated regularly or over an extended period in such an activity, explain it as a symbol of your growing up.

◄──►

BRUCE CATTON

Catton (1889–1978), a Michigan native, attended Oberlin College. After a career as a newspaper reporter, he became the editor of *American Heritage* and a distinguished Civil War historian. *A Stillness at Appomattox* (1953) won the Pulitzer Prize and the National Book Award for history. Catton's numerous historical works include *Mr. Lincoln's Army* (1951), *The Hallowed Ground* (1956), *Never Call Retreat* (1965), and *Gettysburg: The Final Fury* (1974).

Catton has said that he was fascinated not by "the strategy or political meanings" of the Civil War, but by the "almost incomprehensible emotional experience which this war brought to our country." This essay emphasizes that focus, showing Grant and Lee as contrasting embodiments of their very different cultures, Western and Southern, yet in temperament and leadership styles, very much alike.

Grant and Lee: A Study in Contrasts

1   When Ulysses S. Grant and Robert E. Lee met in the parlor of a modest house at Appomattox Court House, Virginia, on April 9, 1865, to work out the terms for the surrender of Lee's Army of Northern Virginia, a great chapter in American life came to a close, and a great new chapter began.

2   These men were bringing the Civil War to its virtual finish. To be sure, other armies had yet to surrender, and for a few days the fugitive Confederate government would struggle desperately and vainly, trying to find some way to go on living now that its chief support was gone. But in effect it was all over when Grant and Lee signed the papers. And the little room where they wrote out the terms was the scene of one of the poignant, dramatic contrasts in American history.

3   They were two strong men, these oddly different generals, and they represented the strengths of two conflicting currents that, through them, had come into final collision.

4   Back of Robert E. Lee was the notion that the old aristocratic concept might somehow survive and be dominant in American life.

5   Lee was tidewater Virginia, and in his background were family, culture, and tradition . . . the age of chivalry transplanted to a New World which was making its own legends and its own myths. He embodied a way of life that had come down through the age of knighthood and the English country squire. America was a land that was beginning all over again, dedicated to nothing much more complicated than the rather hazy belief that all men had equal rights and should have an equal chance in the world. In such a land Lee stood for the feeling that it was

somehow of advantage to human society to have a pronounced inequality in the social structure. There should be a leisure class, backed by ownership of land; in turn, society itself should be keyed to the land as the chief source of wealth and influence. It would bring forth (according to this ideal) a class of men with a strong sense of obligation to the community; men who lived not to gain advantage for themselves, but to meet the solemn obligations which had been laid on them by the very fact that they were privileged. From them the country would get its leadership; to them it could look for the higher values—of thought, of conduct, of personal deportment—to give it strength and virtue.

Lee embodied the noblest elements of this aristocratic ideal. 6 Through him, the landed nobility justified itself. For four years, the Southern states had fought a desperate war to uphold the ideals for which Lee stood. In the end, it almost seemed as if the Confederacy fought for Lee; as if he himself was the Confederacy . . . the best thing that the way of life for which the Confederacy stood could ever have to offer. He had passed into legend before Appomattox. Thousands of tired, underfed, poorly clothed Confederate soldiers, long since past the simple enthusiasm of the early days of the struggle, somehow considered Lee the symbol of everything for which they had been willing to die. But they could not quite put this feeling into words. If the Lost Cause, sanctified by so much heroism and so many deaths, had a living justification, its justification was General Lee.

Grant, the son of a tanner on the Western frontier, was 7 everything Lee was not. He had come up the hard way and embodied nothing in particular except the eternal toughness and sinewy fiber of the men who grew up beyond the mountains. He was one of a body of men who owed reverence and obeisance to no one, who were self-reliant to a fault, who cared hardly anything for the past but who had a sharp eye for the future.

These frontier men were the precise opposites of the tide- 8 water aristocrats. Back of them, in the great surge that had taken people over the Alleghenies and into the opening Western country, there was a deep, implicit dissatisfaction with a past that had settled into grooves. They stood for democracy, not from any reasoned conclusion about the proper ordering of human society, but simply because they had grown up in the middle of democracy and knew how it worked. Their society might have privileges, but they would be privileges each man had won for himself. Forms and patterns meant nothing. No man was born to anything, except perhaps to a chance to show how far he could rise. Life was competition.

9   Yet along with this feeling had come a deep sense of belonging to a national community. The Westerner who developed a farm, opened a shop, or set up in business as a trader, could hope to prosper only as his own community prospered—and his community ran from the Atlantic to the Pacific and from Canada down to Mexico. If the land was settled, with towns and highways and accessible markets, he could better himself. He saw his fate in terms of the nation's own destiny. As its horizons expanded, so did his. He had, in other words, an acute dollars-and-cents stake in the continued growth and development of his country.

10   And that, perhaps, is where the contrast between Grant and Lee becomes most striking. The Virginia aristocrat, inevitably, saw himself in relation to his own region. He lived in a static society which could endure almost anything except change. Instinctively, his first loyalty would go to the locality in which that society existed. He would fight to the limit of endurance to defend it, because in defending it he was defending everything that gave his own life its deepest meaning.

11   The Westerner, on the other hand, would fight with an equal tenacity for the broader concept of society. He fought so because everything he lived by was tied to growth, expansion, and a constantly widening horizon. What he lived by would survive or fall with the nation itself. He could not possibly stand by unmoved in the face of an attempt to destroy the Union. He would combat it with everything he had, because he could only see it as an effort to cut the ground out from under his feet.

12   So Grant and Lee were in complete contrast, representing two diametrically opposed elements in American life. Grant was the modern man emerging; beyond him, ready to come on the stage, was the great age of steel and machinery, of crowded cities and a restless burgeoning vitality. Lee might have ridden down from the old age of chivalry, lance in hand, silken banner

fluttering over his head. Each man was the perfect champion of his cause, drawing both his strengths and his weaknesses from the people he led.

Yet it was not all contrast, after all. Different as they were— in background, in personality, in underlying aspiration—these two great soldiers had much in common. Under everything else, they were marvelous fighters. Furthermore, their fighting qualities were really very much alike. 13

Each man had, to begin with, the great virtue of utter tenacity and fidelity. Grant fought his way down the Mississippi Valley in spite of acute personal discouragement and profound military handicaps. Lee hung on in the trenches at Petersburg after hope itself had died. In each man there was an indomitable quality . . . the born fighter's refusal to give up as long as he can still remain on his feet and lift his two fists. 14

Daring and resourcefulness they had, too; the ability to think faster and move faster than the enemy. These were the qualities which gave Lee the dazzling campaigns of Second Manassas and Chancellorsville and won Vicksburg for Grant. 15

Lastly, and perhaps greatest of all, there was the ability, at the end, to turn quickly from war to peace once the fighting was over. Out of the way these two men behaved at Appomattox came the possibility of a peace of reconciliation. It was a possibility not wholly realized, in the years to come, but which did, in the end, help the two sections to become one nation again . . . after a war whose bitterness might have seemed to make such a reunion wholly impossible. No part of either man's life became him more than the part he played in this brief meeting in the McLean house at Appomattox. Their behavior there put all succeeding generations of Americans in their debt. Two great Americans, Grant and Lee—very different, yet under everything very much alike. Their encounter at Appomattox was one of the great moments of American history. 16

Content

1. According to Catton, in what ways did Robert E. Lee embody Southern values and culture before the Civil War? In what ways did Grant embody Western values and culture during the same period?

2. Explain, with reference to your answer in question 1, Catton's observation that "Each man was the perfect champion of his cause, drawing both his strengths and weaknesses from the people he led" (¶ 14).

3. What qualities does Catton identify to show that "these two great soldiers had much in common." How did these qualities contribute to their behavior at Appomattox, from which came "the possibility of a peace of reconciliation" (¶ 16)?

4. Catton does not discuss specific reasons for the defeat of the Confederacy in the Civil War. What reasons does he imply in identifying Lee with a particular region, a "static society which could endure almost anything except change" (¶ 10); and Grant with "The broader concept of society . . . tied to growth, expansion, and a constantly widening horizon" (¶ 11)?

Strategies/Structures

1. Why does Catton contrast Grant and Lee before he compares them. If he had compared them first, showing their similarities before discussing their differences, how would this have affected the essay?

2. How much space does Catton devote to the contrasts between the two men? How much to the comparison? Why doesn't he give the comparison and contrast equal emphasis?

3. In what ways does Catton treat Grant and Lee as symbols of their respective cultures? Do the readers receive a sense of them as individuals? Should they, in light of Catton's purpose?

4. Why does Catton begin and end his essay with references to the surrender at Appomattox?

Language

1. What does Catton mean by saying "Lee was tidewater Virginia" (¶ 5)? How does his use of the image "Lee might have ridden down from the old age of chivalry, lance in hand, silken banner fluttering over his head" (¶ 12) reinforce the sense that Lee embodies his tidewater culture? Is the chivalric image intended to be complimentary or derogatory?

2. Look up any of the following words if you're uncertain of their meanings: poignant (¶ 2), chivalry (as in age of chivalry) (5), obeisance (7), tenacity (11), burgeoning (12), indomitable (14). How do these words contribute to the tone of Catton's essay?

For Writing

1. Write an essay comparing and contrasting two other historical figures familiar to you, as embodiments of their time; for instance, John
F. Kennedy and Lyndon Johnson or Richard Nixon, Booker T. Washington and W. E. B. Du Bois, Eleanor Roosevelt and Phyllis Schlafly.
2. Does Catton's analysis of the dominant features of the South and
the West as embodied in Lee and Grant still hold true for either or both
of these regions today? Use representative people of either culture to
help explain your answer.

SUZANNE BRITT JORDAN

Jordan, born in 1946 in Winston-Salem, North Carolina and
educated at Salem College and Washington University, taught
English at Central Carolina Technical College and then at
North Carolina State University. She is presently a free-lance
writer with regular columns in the Raleigh *News and Observer*
and the European edition of *The Stars and Stripes;* her articles
and essays also appear in *Newsday,* the *New York Times,* the
Baltimore *Sun,* the Des Moines *Register and Tribune,* and several
other newspapers. Jordan, who describes herself as "stately,
plump," says, "I talk, eat, drink, walk around the block, read,
have a stream of company, and sit on the grass outside. I try
not to preach, do handicrafts, camp, bowl, argue, visit relatives, or serve on committees."

"That Lean and Hungry Look," below, is a contemporary
example of a classical form of literature, the "character," in
which the stereotypical features of a character type ("the angry
man") or role ("the schoolboy," "the housewife") are identified
and often satirized.

That Lean and Hungry Look

C aesar was right. Thin people need watching. I've been   1
watching them for most of my adult life, and I don't like
what I see. When these narrow fellows spring at me, I quiver

to my toes. Thin people come in all personalities, most of them menacing. You've got your "together" thin person, your mechanical thin person, your condescending thin person, your tsk-tsk thin person, your efficiency expert thin person. All of them are dangerous.

2   In the first place, thin people aren't fun. They don't know how to goof off, at least in the best, fat sense of the word. They've always got to be a doing. Give them a coffee break, and they'll jog around the block. Supply them with a quiet evening at home, and they'll fix the screen door and lick S&H green stamps. They say things like "there aren't enough hours in the day." Fat people never say that. Fat people think the day is too damn long already.

3   Thin people make me tired. They've got speedy little metabolisms that cause them to bustle briskly. They're forever rubbing their bony hands together and eying new problems to "tackle." I like to surround myself with sluggish, inert, easygoing fat people, the kind who believe that if you clean it up today, it'll just get dirty again tomorrow.

4   Some people say the business about the jolly fat person is a myth, that all of us chubbies are neurotic, sick, sad people. I disagree. Fat people may not be chortling all day long, but they're a hell of a lot *nicer* than the wizened and shriveled. Thin people turn surly, mean and hard at a young age because they never learn the value of a hot-fudge sundae for easing tension. Thin people don't like gooey soft things because they themselves are neither gooey nor soft. They are crunchy and dull, like carrots. They go straight to the heart of the matter while fat people let things stay all blurry and hazy and vague, the way things actually are. Thin people want to face the truth. Fat people know there is no truth. One of my thin friends is always staring at complex, unsolvable problems and saying, "The key thing is . . ." Fat people never say that. They know there isn't any such thing as the key thing about anything.

5   Thin people believe in logic. Fat people see all sides. The sides fat people see are rounded blobs, usually gray, always nebulous and truly not worth worrying about. But the thin person persists. "If you consume more calories than you burn," says one of my thin friends, "you will gain weight. It's that

simple." Fat people always grin when they hear statements like that. They know better.

Fat people realize that life is illogical and unfair. They know 6 very well that God is not in his heaven and all is not right with the world. If God was up there, fat people could have two doughnuts and a big orange drink anytime they wanted it.

Thin people have a long list of logical things they are always 7 spouting off to me. They hold up one finger at a time as they reel off these things, so I won't lose track. They speak slowly as if to a young child. The list is long and full of holes. It contains tidbits like "get a grip on yourself," "cigarettes kill," "cholesterol clogs," "fit as a fiddle," "ducks in a row," "organize" and "sound fiscal management." Phrases like that.

They think these 2,000-point plans lead to happiness. Fat 8 people know happiness is elusive at best and even if they could get the kind thin people talk about, they wouldn't want it. Wisely, fat people see that such programs are too dull, too hard, too off the mark. They are never better than a whole cheesecake.

Fat people know all about the mystery of life. They are the 9 ones acquainted with the night, with luck, with fate, with playing it by ear. One thin person I know once suggested that we arrange all the parts of a jigsaw puzzle into groups according to size, shape and color. He figured this would cut the time needed to complete the puzzle by at least 50 per cent. I said I wouldn't do it. One, I like to muddle through. Two, what good would it do to finish early? Three, the jigsaw puzzle isn't the important thing. The important thing is the fun of four people (one thin person included) sitting around a card table, working a jigsaw puzzle. My thin friend had no use for my list. Instead of joining us, he went outside and mulched the boxwoods. The three remaining fat people finished the puzzle and made chocolate, double-fudged brownies to celebrate.

The main problem with thin people is they oppress. Their 10 good intentions, bony torsos, tight ships, neat corners, cerebral machinations and pat solutions loom like dark clouds over the loose, comfortable, spread-out, soft world of the fat. Long after fat people have removed their coats and shoes and put their feet up on the coffee table, thin people are still sitting on the edge of the sofa, looking neat as a pin, discussing rutabagas. Fat people are heavily into fits of laughter, slapping their thighs and whooping it up, while thin people are still politely waiting for the punch line.

11 Thin people are downers. They like math and morality and reasoned evaluating of the limitations of human beings. They have their skinny little acts together. They expound, prognose, probe and prick.

12 Fat people are convivial. They will like you even if you're irregular and have acne. They will come up with a good reason why you never wrote the great American novel. They will cry in your beer with you. They will put your name in the pot. They will let you off the hook. Fat people will gab, giggle, guffaw, gallumph, gyrate and gossip. They are generous, giving and gallant. They are gluttonous and goodly and great. What you want when you're down is soft and jiggly, not muscled and stable. Fat people know this. Fat people have plenty of room. Fat people will take you in.

Content

1. Jordan is defining two categories of people, thin and fat. Does she stereotype them? If so, what does she gain from stereotyping? If not, how does she individualize each category?

2. Has she overlooked characteristics typical of either group—for instance, the effects on one's health of being either too fat or too thin? If so, why might she have chosen not to discuss such characteristics? Does she treat thin people fairly? Does she intend to do so?

3. Based on your knowledge of fat and thin people, would you say that Jordan's depiction of each is accurate? Why or why not?

4. For the purpose of contrast, Jordan has concentrated on the differences between fat and thin people. What similarities, if any, do they have? Are these related to their weight?

5. What would the effect on this essay have been if Jordan had inserted a discussion of another type of person and personality into the essay?

Strategies/Structures

1. Throughout, Jordan makes blanket generalizations about both thin and fat people. Does she support these? Is her evidence appropriate? Sufficiently comprehensive to make her case?

2. At what point in the essay do you realize that Jordan is being humorous? Does her humor reinforce or undermine her point? Explain your answer.

3. What is the point of the extended illustration of the jigsaw puzzle group in paragraph 9?

Language

1. Why does Jordan use so much alliteration (a device more often employed in poetry) in paragraph 12, her final paragraph?

2. Jordan's language is conversational, sometimes slangy: "Thin people are downers. . . . They have their skinny little acts together"(¶ 11). In what ways does the language reinforce what Jordan says about fat people?

For Writing

1. Jordan has depicted two extremes in body size—fat and thin people, with their attendant personality characteristics. Yet most people are somewhere else along the continuum from fat to thin. Write an essay in which you characterize a type of person different from the two discussed here.

2. Write a humorous essay in which you divide a larger category (such as students, parents, Southerners, Easterners, Californians) into subcategories as Jordan does in the first paragraph, and then characterize each subcategory through comparing and contrasting its parts (working students, athletes, grinds, partygoers).

JAMES AGEE

After graduation from Harvard in 1932, Agee, born in Knoxville in 1909, worked as a writer for *Fortune*, *Time*, and *The Nation*. His reputation as a writer of quiet force and poetic beauty began with the publication in 1942 of *Let Us Now Praise Famous Men*, with photographs by Walker Evans, a moving interpretation of Appalachian people during the Depression. After 1948 he concentrated on screenplays, including *The Quiet One* (1949) and *The African Queen* (1952). A novel, *A Death in the Family* (1957), was published after his death in 1955 and awarded the Pulitzer Prize for fiction. His film reviews and scripts were collected in *Agee on Film* (1958, 1960). His letters to a close friend, Father James H. Flye, were published in 1962, reinforcing the belated recognition of his importance as a major American writer. His praise of *Henry V*, that "those who made the film . . . have loved and served the language so well" might appropriately be said of the poetic Agee himself.

Comedy's Greatest Era

1   Had he done nothing else, [Mac] Sennett would be remembered for giving a start to three of the four comedians who now began to apply their sharp individual talents to this newborn language [of visual comedy]. The one whom he did not train (he was on the lot briefly but Sennett barely remembers seeing him around) wore glasses, smiled a great deal and looked like the sort of eager young man who might have quit divinity school to hustle brushes. That was Harold Lloyd. The others were grotesque and poetic in their screen characters in degrees which appear to be impossible when the magic of silence is broken. One, who never smiled, carried a face as still and sad as a daguerreotype through some of the most preposterously ingenious and visually satisfying physical comedy ever invented. That was Buster Keaton. One looked like an elderly baby and, at times, a baby dope fiend; he could do more with less than any other comedian. That was Harry Langdon [omitted in this text]. One looked like Charlie Chaplin, and he was the first man to give the silent language a soul.

2   When Charlie Chaplin started to work for Sennett he had chiefly to reckon with Ford Sterling, the reigning comedian. Their first picture together amounted to a duel before the assembled professionals. Sterling, by no means untalented, was a big man with a florid Teutonic style which, under this special pressure, he turned on full blast. Chaplin defeated him within a few minutes with a wink of the mustache, a hitch of the trousers, a quirk of the little finger.

With *Tillie's Punctured Romance*, in 1914, he became a major 3
star. Soon after, he left Sennett when Sennett refused to start a
landslide among the other comedians by meeting the raise Chaplin demanded. Sennett is understandably wry about it in retrospect, but he still says, "I was right at the time." Of Chaplin
he says simply, "Oh well, he's just the greatest artist that ever
lived." None of Chaplin's former rivals rates him much lower
than that; they speak of him no more jealously than they might
of God. We will try here only to suggest the essence of his
supremacy. Of all comedians he worked most deeply and most
shrewdly within a realization of what a human being is, and is
up against. The Tramp is as centrally representative of humanity,
as many-sided and as mysterious, as Hamlet, and it seems unlikely that any dancer or actor can ever have excelled him in
eloquence, variety or poignancy of motion. As for pure motion,
even if he had never gone on to make his magnificent feature-
length comedies, Chaplin would have made his period in movies
a great one singlehanded even if he had made nothing except
The Cure, or *One A.M.* In the latter, barring one immobile taxi
driver, Chaplin plays alone, as a drunk trying to get upstairs
and into bed. It is a sort of inspired elaboration on a soft-shoe
dance, involving an angry stuffed wildcat, small rugs on slippery
floors, a Lazy Susan table, exquisite footwork on a flight of stairs,
a contretemps with a huge, ferocious pendulum and the funniest
and most perverse Murphy bed in movie history—and, always
made physically lucid, the delicately weird mental processes of
a man ethereally sozzled.

Before Chaplin came to pictures people were content with 4
a couple of gags per comedy; he got some kind of laugh every
second. The minute he began to work he set standards—and
continually forced them higher. Anyone who saw Chaplin eating
a boiled shoe like brook trout in *The Gold Rush*, or embarrassed
by a swallowed whistle in *City Lights*, has seen perfection. Most
of the time, however, Chaplin got his laughter less from the
gags, or from milking them in any ordinary sense, than through
his genius for what may be called *inflection*—the perfect, change-
ful shading of his physical and emotional attitudes toward the
gag. Funny as his bout with the Murphy bed is, the glances
of awe, expostulation and helpless, almost whimpering desire

for vengeance which he darts at this infernal machine are even better.

5   A painful and frequent error among tyros is breaking the comic line with a too-big laugh, then a letdown; or with a laugh which is out of key or irrelevant. The masters could ornament the main line beautifully; they never addled it. In *A Night Out* Chaplin, passed out, is hauled along the sidewalk by the scruff of his coat by staggering Ben Turpin. His toes trail; he is as supine as a sled. Turpin himself is so drunk he can hardly drag him. Chaplin comes quietly to, realizes how well he is being served by his struggling pal, and with a royally delicate gesture plucks and savors a flower.

6   The finest pantomime, the deepest emotion, the richest and most poignant poetry were in Chaplin's work. He could probably pantomime Bryce's *The American Commonwealth* without ever blurring a syllable and make it paralyzingly funny into the bargain. At the end of *City Lights* the blind girl who has regained her sight, thanks to the Tramp, sees him for the first time. She has imagined and anticipated him as princely, to say the least; and it has never seriously occurred to him that he is inadequate. She recognizes who he must be by his shy, confident, shining joy as he comes silently toward her. And he recognizes himself, for the first time, through the terrible changes in her face. The camera just exchanges a few quiet close-ups of the emotions which shift and intensify in each face. It is enough to shrivel the heart to see, and it is the greatest piece of acting and the highest moment in movies.

7   Harold Lloyd worked only a little while with Sennett. During most of his career he acted for another major comedy producer, Hal Roach. He tried at first to offset Chaplin's influence and establish his own individuality by playing Chaplin's exact opposite, a character named Lonesome Luke who wore clothes much too small for him and whose gestures were likewise as un-Chaplinesque as possible. But he soon realized that an opposite in itself was a kind of slavishness. He discovered his own comic identity when he saw a movie about a fighting parson: a hero who wore glasses. He began to think about those glasses day and night. He decided on horn rims because they were youthful, ultravisible on the screen and on the verge of becoming

fashionable (he was to make them so). Around these large lense-less horn rims he began to develop a new character, nothing grotesque or eccentric, but a fresh, believable young man who could fit into a wide variety of stories.

Lloyd depended more on story and situation than any of the other major comedians (he kept the best stable of gagmen in Hollywood, at one time hiring six); but unlike most "story" comedians he was also a very funny man from inside. He had, as he has written, "an unusually large comic vocabulary." More particularly he had an expertly expressive body and even more expressive teeth, and out of this thesaurus of smiles he could at a moment's notice blend prissiness, breeziness and asininity, and still remain tremendously likable. His movies were more extroverted and closer to ordinary life than any others of the best comedies: the vicissitudes of a New York taxi driver; the unaccepted college boy who, by desperate courage and inspired ineptitude, wins the Big Game. He was especially good at put-ting a very timid, spoiled or brassy young fellow through dev-astating embarrassments. He went through one of his most uproarious Gethsemanes as a shy country youth courting the nicest girl in town in *Grandma's Boy*. He arrived dressed "strictly up to date for the Spring of 1862," as a subtitle observed, and found that the ancient colored butler wore a similar flowered waistcoat and moldering cut-away. He got one wandering, ner-vous forefinger dreadfully stuck in a fancy little vase. The girl began cheerfully to try to identify that queer smell which dilated from him; Grandpa's best suit was rife with mothballs. A te-nacious litter of kittens feasted off the goose grease on his home-shined shoes.

Lloyd was even better at the comedy of thrills. In *Safety Last*, as a rank amateur, he is forced to substitute for a human fly and to climb a medium-sized skyscraper. Dozens of awful things happen to him. He gets fouled up in a tennis net. Popcorn falls on him from a window above, and the local pigeons treat him like a cross between a lunch wagon and St. Francis of Assisi. A mouse runs up his britches leg, and the crowd below salutes his desperate dance on the window ledge with wild applause of the daredevil. A good deal of this full-length picture hangs thus by its eyelashes along the face of a building. Each new floor

is like a new stanza in a poem; and the higher and more horrifying it gets, the funnier it gets.

10   In this movie Lloyd demonstrates beautifully his ability to
do more than merely milk a gag, but to top it. (In an old, simple
example of topping, an incredible number of tall men get, one
by one, out of a small closed auto. After as many have clambered
out as the joke will bear, one more steps out: a midget. That
tops the gag. Then the auto collapses. That tops the topper.) In
Safety Last Lloyd is driven out to the dirty end of a flagpole by
a furious dog; the pole breaks and he falls, just managing to
grab the minute hand of a huge clock. His weight promptly pulls
the hand down from IX to VI. That would be more than enough
for any ordinary comedian, but there is further logic in the situation. Now, hideously, the whole clockface pulls loose and
slants from its trembling springs above the street. Getting out
of difficulty with the clock, he makes still further use of the
instrument by getting one foot caught in one of these obstinate
springs.

11   A proper delaying of the ultrapredictable can of course be
just as funny as a properly timed explosion of the unexpected.
As Lloyd approaches the end of his horrible hegira up the side
of the building in *Safety Last*, it becomes clear to the audience,
but not to him, that if he raises his head another couple of inches
he is going to get murderously conked by one of the four arms
of a revolving wind gauge. He delays the evil moment almost
interminably, with one distraction and another, and every delay
is a suspense-tightening laugh; he also gets his foot nicely en-
tangled in a rope, so that when he does get hit, the payoff of
one gag sends him careening head downward through the abyss
into another. Lloyd was outstanding even among the master
craftsmen at setting up a gag clearly, culminating and getting
out of it deftly, and linking it smoothly to the next. Harsh experience also taught him a deep and fundamental rule: Never
try to get "above" the audience.

12   Lloyd tried it in *The Freshman*. He was to wear an unfin-
ished, basted-together tuxedo to a college party, which would
gradually fall apart as he danced. Lloyd decided to skip the
pants, a low-comedy cliché, and lose just the coat. His gag men
warned him. A preview proved how right they were. Lloyd had

to reshoot the whole expensive sequence, build it around defective pants and climax it with the inevitable. It was one of the funniest things he ever did.

When Lloyd was still a very young man he lost about half 13 his right hand (and nearly lost his sight) when a comedy bomb exploded prematurely. But in spite of his artificially built-out hand he continued to do his own dirty work, like all of the best comedians. The side of the building he climbed in *Safety Last* did not overhang the street, as it appears to. But the nearest landing place was a roof three floors below him, as he approached the top, and he did everything, of course, the hard way, i.e., the comic way, keeping his bottom stuck well out, his shoulders hunched, his hands and feet skidding over perdition.

If great comedy must involve something beyond laughter, 14 Lloyd was not a great comedian. If plain laughter is any criterion—and it is a healthy counterbalance to the other—few people have equaled him, and nobody has ever beaten him. . . .

Buster Keaton started work at the age of three and a half 15 with his parents in one of the roughest acts in vaudeville ("The Three Keatons"); Harry Houdini gave the child the name Buster in admiration for a fall he took down a flight of stairs. In his first movies Keaton teamed with Fatty Arbuckle under Sennett. He went on to become one of Metro's biggest stars and earners; a Keaton feature cost about $200,000 to make and reliably grossed $2 million. Very early in his movie career friends asked him why he never smiled on the screen. He didn't realize he didn't. He had got the deadpan habit in variety; on the screen he had merely been so hard at work it had never occurred to him there was anything to smile about. Now he tried it just once and never again. He was by his whole style and nature so much the most deeply "silent" of the silent comedians that even a smile was as deafeningly out of key as a yell. In a way his pictures are like a transcendent juggling act in which it seems that the whole universe is in exquisite flying motion and the one point of repose is the juggler's effortless, uninterested face.

Keaton's face ranked almost with Lincoln's as an early 16 American archetype; it was haunting, handsome, almost beautiful, yet it was irreducibly funny; he improved matters by topping it off with a deadly horizontal hat, as flat and thin as a phonograph record. One can never forget Keaton wearing it, standing erect at the prow as his little boat is being launched. The boat goes grandly down the skids and, just as grandly, straight on to the bottom. Keaton never budges. The last you see of him, the water lifts the hat off the stoic head and it floats away.

17   No other comedian could do as much with the deadpan. He used this great, sad, motionless face to suggest various related things: a one-track mind near the track's end of pure insanity; mulish imperturbability under the wildest of circumstances; how dead a human being can get and still be alive; an awe-inspiring sort of patience and power to endure, proper to granite but uncanny in flesh and blood. Everything that he was and did bore out this rigid face and played laughs against it. When he moved his eyes, it was like seeing them move in a statue. His short-legged body was all sudden, machinelike angles, governed by a daft aplomb. When he swept a semaphorelike arm to point, you could almost hear the electrical impulse in the signal block. When he ran from a cop his transitions from accelerating walk to easy jog trot to brisk canter to headlong gallop to flogged-piston sprint—always floating, above this frenzy, the untroubled, untouchable face—were as distinct and as soberly in order as an automatic gearshift.

18   Keaton was a wonderfully resourceful inventor of mechanistic gags (he still spends much of his time fooling with Erector sets); as he ran afoul of locomotives, steamships, prefabricated and overelectrified houses, he put himself through some of the hardest and cleverest punishment ever designed for laughs. In *Sherlock Jr.*, boiling along on the handlebars of a motorcycle quite unaware that he has lost his driver, Keaton whips through city traffic, breaks up a tug-of-war, gets a shovelful of dirt in the face from each of a long line of Rockette-timed ditchdiggers, approaches at high speed a log which is hinged open by dynamite precisely soon enough to let him through and, hitting an obstruction, leaves the handlebars like an arrow leaving a bow, whams through the window of a shack in which the heroine is about to be violated, and hits the heavy feet first, knocking him through the opposite wall. The whole sequence is as clean in motion as the trajectory of a bullet.

Much of the charm and edge of Keaton's comedy, however, [19] lay in the subtle leverages of expression he could work against his nominal deadpan. Trapped in the side wheel of a ferryboat, saving himself from drowning only by walking, then desperately running, inside the accelerating wheel like a squirrel in a cage, his only real concern was, obviously, to keep his hat on. Confronted by Love, he was not as deadpan as he was cracked up to be, either; there was an odd, abrupt motion of his head which suggested a horse nipping after a sugar lump.

Keaton worked strictly for laughs, but his work came from [20] so far inside a curious and original spirit that he achieved a great deal besides, especially in his feature-length comedies. (For plain hard laughter his nineteen short comedies—the negatives of which have been lost—were even better.) He was the only major comedian who kept sentiment almost entirely out of his work, and he brought pure physical comedy to its greatest heights. Beneath his lack of emotion he was also uninsistently sardonic; deep below that, giving a disturbing tension and grandeur to the foolishness, for those who sensed it, there was in his comedy a freezing whisper not of pathos but of melancholia. With the humor, the craftsmanship and the action there was often, besides, a fine, still and sometimes dreamlike beauty. Much of his Civil War picture *The General* is within hailing distance of Mathew Brady. And there is a ghostly, unforgettable moment in *The Navigator* when, on a deserted, softly rolling ship, all the pale doors along a deck swing open as one behind Keaton and, as one, slam shut, in a hair-raising illusion of noise.

Perhaps because "dry" comedy is so much more rare and [21] odd than "dry" wit, there are people who never much cared for Keaton. Those who do cannot care mildly.

As soon as the screen began to talk, silent comedy was [22] pretty well finished.

Content

1. What are some of the major characteristics of the comic styles of the comedians Agee analyzes: Chaplin, Lloyd, Keaton?
2. How do Agee's illustrations successfully explain Buster Keaton's funniness, although he "never smiled on screen"?
3. Agee does not provide much explicit comparison and contrast among

the comic styles of these comedians. What contrasts do you find among them?

4. How has Agee tried to demonstrate the accuracy of his thesis implied by his title, that comedy's greatest era was during the period of silent films? Are you convinced? Agee's essay was written before the film prominence of Woody Allen, Peter Sellers, John Belushi, and Mel Brooks. Explain whether you think that the comic styles of some or any of these actors would cause Agee to change his mind.

5. To what extent, if any, does your understanding of Agee's illustrations depend on whether or not you've seen any of the actors or films he's discussing?

Strategies/Structures

1. Agee's illustrations of the comedians' styles involve considerable description and narration. Identify examples of each.

2. In explaining the actors' comic styles, Agee provides definitions of various aspects of comic technique. For instance, "topping a gag" is overtly defined and illustrated in paragraph 10. Since "milking a gag" has been illustrated in paragraphs 3, 4, 5, and 9, why doesn't Agee label this technique until paragraph 10? What illustration does he provide for the rule, "Never try to get 'above' the audience" (¶ 12)? How is this single example sufficient to make his point?

3. Why does Agee discuss Buster Keaton last in this series of comedians? What evidence does Agee employ to illustrate Keaton's deadpan (¶s 15–17)?

4. Why is it fitting that so many of Agee's explanations are visual? Why does his last explanation, about *The Navigator*, hint at sound, expressed in terms of sight (¶ 20)?

5. The rhythm and cadence of Agee's sentences reflect the rhythm and emphasis of the actions they describe. A conspicuous example is the sentence in paragraph 18 beginning, "In *Sherlock Jr.* . . . ." Find others and show how they work.

Language

1. If necessary, look up the following words or phrases in a dictionary or other reference book: "florid teutonic style" (¶ 2), Murphy bed (3), tyro (5), "supine as a sled" (5), asininity (8), "Gethsemane" (8), tenacious (8), archetype (16), imperturbability (17), Rockette (18), Mathew Brady (20).

2. Agee uses many figures of speech, including similes ("a face as still and sad as a daguerreotype," ¶ 1), and metaphors ("thesaurus of smiles," ¶ 8). Identify others and show how they provide pictorial illustrations of his points.

3. Most of Agee's sentences end with a strong verb or phrase. Identify such sentences. If this order were varied, how would this affect the verbal impact?

For Writing

1. Compare and contrast the distinctive features of the comic style of two of your favorite film or television comedians, either in characteristic roles or in particular shows. Imagine that your audience has never seen the people you're discussing.

2. Debate Agee's claim that the period of silent films was "comedy's greatest era" by analyzing one of your favorite comedians whose humor depends on sound as well as sight.

Strategies for Writing— Comparison and Contrast

1. Will my essay focus on the similarities between two or more things (comparison) or the differences (contrast), or will I be discussing both similarities and differences? Why do I want to make the comparison or contrast? To find, explore, or deny overt or less apparent resemblances among the items? To decide which one of a pair or group is better or preferable? Or to use the comparison or contrast to argue for my preference?

2. Are my readers familiar with one or more of the objects of my comparison? If they are familiar with them all, then can I concentrate on the unique features of my analysis? (If they are familiar with only one item, start with the known before discussing the unknown. If they are unacquainted with everything, for purposes of explanation you might wish to begin with a comparison that focuses on the common elements among the items under discussion.)

3. How global or minute will my comparison be (i.e., Do I want to make only a few points of comparison or contrast, or many)? Will my essay make more sense to my readers if I present each subject as a complete unit before discussing the next? Or will the comparison or contrast be more meaningful if I proceed point-by-point?

4. Have I ruled out trivial and irrelevant comparisons? Does each point have a counterpart that I have treated in an equivalent manner, through comparable analysis or illustration, length, and language?

5. Suppose I like or favor one item of the comparison or contrast over the others? Am I obliged to treat every item equally in language and tone, or can my tone vary to reinforce my interpretation?

Additional Writing Topics

Write an essay that compares and contrasts any of the following pairs:

1. Two people with a number of relevant characteristics in common (two of your teachers, roommates, friends, relatives playing the same role—i.e., two of your sisters or brothers, two of your grandparents, a father or mother and a stepparent)

2. Two cities or regions of the country you know well, or two neighborhoods you have lived in

3. Two comparable historical figures with similar positions, such as two presidents, two senators, two generals (see "Grant and Lee"), two explorers, or others

4. The styles of two performers—musicians, actors or actresses, dancers, athletes participating in the same sport, comedians
5. The work of two writers, painters, theater or film directors; or two (or three) works by the same writer or painter
6. Two religions or two sects or churches within the same religion
7. Two political parties, campaigns, or machines, past or present
8. Two colleges or universities (or programs or sports teams within them) that you know well
9. Two styles of friendship, courtship, marriage, or family (both may be contemporary, or you may compare and contrast past and present styles)
10. Two academic majors, professions, or other careers
11. Your ideal life (present or future) and your actual life
12. Two utopian communities (real or imaginary)
13. Two explanations or interpretations of the same scientific, economic, religious, psychological, or political phenomenon (for instance, Creationism vs. Darwinism; Freudian vs. Skinnerian theory of behavior)
14. The cuisine of two different countries or two or more parts of a country (Greek vs. French cooking; Sezchuan, Cantonese, and Peking Chinese food)

PART IV

Arguing: Directly and Indirectly

$\blacktriangleright$ ──────────────────────── $\blacktriangleleft$

10 *Appealing to Reason: Deductive and Inductive Arguments*

When you write persuasively you're trying to move your readers to either belief or action or both. You can do this through appealing to their reasons, their emotions, or their sense of ethics, as you know if you've ever tried to prove a point on an exam or change an attitude in a letter to the editor. The next section discusses appeals to emotion and ethics; here we'll concentrate on argumentation.

An argument, as we're using the term here, does not mean a knockdown confrontation over an issue: "Philadelphia is the most wonderful place in the world to live!" "No it's not. Social snobbery has ruined the City of Brotherly Love." Nor is an argument hard-sell brainwashing that admits of no alternatives:

"America—love it or leave it!" When you write an argument, however, as a reasonable writer you'll present a reasonable proposition that states what you believe, and you'll offer logic, evidence, and perhaps emotional appeals, to try to convince your readers of the merits of what you say. Sometimes, but not always, you'll also argue that they should adopt a particular course of action.

Unless you're writing an indirect argument that makes its point through satire, irony, or some other oblique means, you'll probably want to identify the issue at hand and justify its significance early in the essay. If it's a touchy subject, you may wish at this point to demonstrate good will toward readers likely to disagree with you by showing the basis for your common concern: "Most Americans would agree that it's always important for our population to be well educated and resourceful." You could follow this by acknowledging the merits of their valid objections: "And it's also true that there's a limit as to how much private citizens can be taxed to support public education." You'd probably want to follow this with an explanation of why, nevertheless, your position is better: "But it's unconstitutional to permit tuition tax credits for private education."

There are a number of suitable ways to organize the body of your argument. If your audience is inclined to agree with much of what you say, you might want to put your strongest point first and provide the most evidence for that, before proceeding to the lesser points, arranged in order of descending importance. For an antagonistic audience you could do the reverse, beginning with the points easiest to accept or agree with and concluding with the most difficult. Or you could work from the most familiar to the least familiar points.

No matter what organizational pattern you choose, you'll need to provide supporting evidence—through specific examples, facts and figures, the opinions of experts, case histories, narratives, analogies, considerations of cause and effect. Any or all of these techniques can be employed in either *inductive* or *deductive* reasoning. Chances are that most of your arguments will proceed by induction, using a set of specific examples to prove a general proposition. Research scientists and detectives, among others, often work this way, gathering evidence, interpreting it, and formulating conclusions based on what they've found. In "Ethnic Bias in Textbooks," Frances FitzGerald analyzes the changing treatment of minorities through numerous examples from 20th-century American history textbooks. In "E.R.A.—R.I.P.," Andrew Hacker likewise reasons inductively to demonstrate that "women who needed the security" of their conventional marriages "defeated the ERA because it jeopardized the way of life they had entered in good faith." He supports this with an analysis of examples, legal cases, quotations from experts and housewives, and with a long and ingenious reinterpretation of statistics to show that women's liberation isn't what the figures make it out to be.

In an essay of deductive reasoning, you'll be working the other way around, proceeding from a general proposition to a specific conclusion. The model for a deductive argument is the syllogism, a three-part sequence that begins with a major premise, is followed by a minor premise, and leads to a conclusion. Aristotle's classic example of this basic logical pattern is:

> Major premise: All men are mortal.
> Minor premise: Socrates is a man.
> Conclusion: Therefore, Socrates is mortal.

Thomas Jefferson, principal author of "The Declaration of Independence," explores the consequences of the proposition that "all men are created equal" and that their "unalienable Rights" cannot be abridged. In "Letter from Birmingham Jail," Martin Luther King, Jr. argues for the proposition that "one has not only a legal but a moral responsibility to disobey unjust laws." You'll want to avoid *logical fallacies* in your reasoning, as they do. The Glossary provides examples of these, and Max Shulman's "Love is a Fallacy" (pp. 410–20) furnishes humorous illustrations of misapplied logic.

After you've written a logical argument, have someone who disagrees with you read it critically to look for loopholes. Your critic's guidelines could be the same questions you might ask yourself while writing the paper: What do I want to prove? How do I want my readers to react? What is my strongest evidence? My weakest? Does my organizational pattern strengthen the argument? Have I anticipated opposing points of view? If you can satisfy yourself and a critic, you can take on the world. Or is that a logical fallacy?

THOMAS JEFFERSON

Politician, philosopher, architect, inventor, and writer, Jefferson (1743–1826) was born near Charlottesville, Virginia, and was educated at the College of William and Mary. He served as a delegate to the Continental Congress in 1775, as Governor of the Commonwealth of Virginia, and as third President of the United States. With help from Benjamin Franklin and John Adams, he wrote *The Declaration of Independence* in mid-June 1776, and after further revision by the Continental Congress in Philadelphia, it was signed on July 4. Frequently called "an expression of the American mind," Jefferson's Declaration is based on his acceptance of democracy as the ideal form of government, a belief also evidenced in his refusal to sign the Constitution until the Bill of Rights was added. Jefferson died at Monticello, his home in Charlottesville, on July 4, 1826, the fiftieth anniversary of the signing of the Declaration.

The Declaration of Independence

1   When in the course of human events, it becomes necessary for one people to dissolve the political bands which have connected them with another, and to assume among the Powers of the earth, the separate and equal station to which the Laws of Nature and of Nature's God entitle them, a decent respect to the opinions of mankind requires that they should declare the causes which impel them to the separation.

2   We hold these truths to be self-evident, that all men are created equal, that they are endowed by their Creator with certain unalienable Rights, that among these are Life, Liberty and the pursuit of Happiness. That to secure these rights, Governments are instituted among Men deriving their just powers from the consent of the governed. That whenever any Form of Government becomes destructive of these ends, it is the Right of the People to alter or to abolish it, and to institute new Government,

laying its foundation on such principles and organizing its powers in such form, as to them shall seem most likely to effect their Safety and Happiness. Prudence, indeed, will dictate that Governments long established should not be changed for light and transient causes; and accordingly all experience hath shown, that mankind are more disposed to suffer, while evils are sufferable, than to right themselves by abolishing the forms to which they are accustomed. But when a long train of abuses and usurpations pursuing invariably the same Object evinces a design to reduce them under absolute Despotism, it is their right, it is their duty, to throw off such government, and to provide new Guards for their future security. Such has been the patient sufferance of these Colonies; and such is now the necessity which constrains them to alter their former Systems of Government. The history of the present King of Great Britain is a history of repeated injuries and usurpations, all having in direct object the establishment of an absolute Tyranny over these States. To prove this, let Facts be submitted to a candid world.

He has refused his Assent to Laws, the most wholesome 3 and necessary for the public good.

He has forbidden his Governors to pass Laws of immediate 4 and pressing importance, unless suspended in their operation till his Assent should be obtained; and when so suspended, he has utterly neglected to attend them.

He has refused to pass other Laws for the accommodation 5 of large districts of people, unless those people would relinquish the right of Representation in the Legislature, a right inestimable to them and formidable to tyrants only.

He has called together legislative bodies at places unusual, 6 uncomfortable, and distant from the depository of their Public Records, for the sole purpose of fatiguing them into compliance with his measures.

He has dissolved Representative Houses repeatedly, for 7 opposing with manly firmness his invasions on the rights of the people.

He has refused for a long time, after such dissolutions, to 8 cause others to be elected; whereby the Legislative Powers, incapable of Annihilation, have returned to the People at large for their exercise; the State remaining in the mean time exposed to all the dangers of invasion from without, and convulsions within.

9   He has endeavoured to prevent the population of these States; for that purpose obstructing the Laws of Naturalization of Foreigners; refusing to pass others to encourage their migration hither, and raising the conditions of new Appropriations of Lands.

10   He has obstructed the Administration of Justice, by refusing his Assent to Laws for establishing Judiciary Powers.

11   He has made Judges dependent on his Will alone, for the tenure of their offices, and the amount and payment of their salaries.

12   He has erected a multitude of New Offices, and sent hither swarms of Officers to harass our People, and eat out their substance.

13   He has kept among us, in time of peace, Standing Armies without the Consent of our Legislature.

14   He has affected to render the Military independent of and superior to the Civil Power.

15   He has combined with others to subject us to jurisdictions foreign to our constitution, and unacknowledged by our laws; giving his Assent to their acts of pretended Legislation:

16   For quartering large bodies of armed troops among us:

17   For protecting them, by a mock Trial, from Punishment for any Murders which they should commit on the Inhabitants of these States:

18   For cutting off our Trade with all parts of the world:

19   For imposing Taxes on us without our Consent:

20   For depriving us in many cases, of the benefits of Trial by Jury:

21   For transporting us beyond Seas to be tried for pretended offenses:

22   For abolishing the free System of English Laws in a Neighbouring Province, establishing therein an Arbitrary government, and enlarging its boundaries so as to render it at once an example and fit instrument for introducing the same absolute rule into these Colonies:

23   For taking away our Charters, abolishing our most valuable Laws, and altering fundamentally the Forms of our Governments:

24   For suspending our own Legislatures, and declaring themselves invested with Power to legislate for us in all cases whatsoever.

He has abdicated Government here, by declaring us out of 25 his Protection and waging War against us.

He has plundered our seas, ravaged our Coasts, burnt our 26 towns and destroyed the Lives of our people.

He is at this time transporting large Armies of foreign Mer- 27 cenaries to compleat works of death, desolation and tyranny, already begun with circumstances of Cruelty & perfidy scarcely paralleled in the most barbarous ages, and totally unworthy the Head of a civilized nation.

He has constrained our fellow Citizens taken Captive on 28 the high Seas to bear Arms against their Country, to become the executioners of their friends and Brethren, or to fall themselves by their Hands.

He has excited domestic insurrections amongst us, and has 29 endeavoured to bring on the inhabitants of our frontiers, the merciless Indian Savages, whose known rule of warfare, is an undistinguished destruction of all ages, sexes and conditions.

In every stage of these Oppressions We Have Petitioned 30 for Redress in the most humble terms: Our repeated petitions have been answered only by repeated injury. A Prince, whose character is thus marked by every act which may define a Tyrant, is unfit to be the ruler of a free People.

Not have We been wanting in attention to our British breth- 31 ren. We have warned them from time to time of attempts by their legislature to extend an unwarrantable jurisdiction over us. We have reminded them of the circumstances of our emigration and settlement here. We have appealed to their native justice and magnanimity and we have conjured them by the ties of our common kindred to disavow these usurpations, which would inevitably interrupt our connections and correspondence. They too have been deaf to the voice of justice and of consanguinity. We must, therefore acquiesce in the necessity, which denounces our Separation, and hold them, as we hold the rest of mankind, Enemies in War, in Peace Friends.

We, therefore, the Representatives of the United States of 32 America, in General Congress, Assembled, appealing to the Su-preme Judge of the world for the rectitude of our intentions, do, in the Name, and by Authority of the good People of these Colonies, solemnly publish and declare, That these United Col-onies are, and of Right ought to be Free and Independent States;

that they are Absolved from all Allegiance to the British Crown, and that all political connection between them and the State of Great Britain, is and ought to be totally dissolved; and that as Free and Independent States, they have full power to levy War, conclude Peace, contract Alliances, establish Commerce, and to do all other Acts and Things which Independent States may of right do. And for the support of this Declaration, with a firm reliance on the protection of Divine Providence, we mutually pledge to each other our lives, our Fortunes and our sacred Honor.

Content

1. What are "the Laws of Nature and of Nature's God" to which Jefferson refers in paragraph 1? Why doesn't he specify what they are? Is a brief allusion to them in the first paragraph sufficient support for the fundamental premise of the second paragraph?

2. What is Jefferson's fundamental premise (¶ 2)? Does he ever prove it? Does he need to?

3. In paragraphs 3–30 the Declaration states a series of the American colonists' grievances against the British King, George III. What are some of these grievances? Can they be grouped into categories related to the "unalienable rights" Jefferson has specified at the outset, the rights to "Life, Liberty and the pursuit of Happiness"?

4. From the nature of the grievances Jefferson identifies, what ideal of government does he have in mind? Can such a government exist among colonial peoples, or only in an independent nation?

5. Is the conclusion (¶ 34) the inevitable consequence of the reasoning that precedes it? Are there any feasible alternatives?

Strategies/Structures

1. Why has Jefferson listed the grievances in the order in which they appear?

2. Is the Declaration of Independence written primarily for an audience of the British King and his advisors? Who else would be likely to be vitally involved?

3. Could the American colonists have expected the British simply to agree with what they said? Or is the Declaration of Independence in effect a declaration of war?

Language

1. What is the tone of this document? How would Jefferson have expected this tone to have affected King George III and associates? How might the same tone have affected the American patriots of 1776?
2. Look up in a good college dictionary the meanings of any problematic words, such as: station (¶ 1), unalienable (2), despotism (2), usurpations (2), abdicated (16), perfidy (18), redress (21), magnanimity (22), rectitude (23).

For Writing

1. Write an essay in which you discuss the extent to which the federal government of the United States exhibits the ideals of government that Jefferson promoted in "The Declaration of Independence."
2. Write your own "declaration of independence," in which you justify setting yourself (or yourself as a member of a particular social, occupational, economic, ethnic, or cultural group) free from an oppressor or oppressive group.
3. Is colonialism ever justified? In an essay on this issue, supplement your knowledge of history with "The Declaration of Independence" and Orwell's "Shooting an Elephant" (pp. 47–55), bearing in mind that each was written from the viewpoint of considerable sympathy with the colonized people.

▶───◀

MARTIN LUTHER KING, JR.

King (1929–1968), a clergyman from Atlanta, became a national spokesman for civil rights after he led a successful boycott of Montgomery, Alabama's segregated bus system in 1955. In 1956 the Supreme Court declared Alabama's segregation laws unconstitutional after Dr. King had brought the issue to national attention. Under King's forceful and at times charismatic influence, the activities for civil rights and racial equality increased throughout the country, and culminated in a march on Washington, D.C. where King delivered his famous "I Have a Dream . . ." speech. In 1964, he was awarded the Nobel Peace Prize for his civil rights leadership. Ironically, his life ended violently: he was assassinated in 1968 in Memphis while supporting striking sanitation workers.

In 1963, King wrote the letter reprinted below while imprisoned for "parading without a permit," replying to eight clergymen who feared violence in the Birmingham desegregation demonstrations. Warning that America had more to fear from passive moderates ("the appalling silence of good people") than from extremists, King defended his policy of "nonviolent direct action" and explained why he was compelled to disobey "unjust laws." Though ostensibly addressed to the eight clergymen, King's letter was actually intended for the worldwide audience his civil rights activities commanded.

Letter from Birmingham Jail

April 16, 1963

My Dear Fellow Clergymen:

1   While confined here in the Birmingham city jail, I came across your recent statement calling my present activities "unwise and untimely." Seldom do I pause to answer criticism of my work and ideas. If I sought to answer all the criticisms that cross my desk, my secretaries would have little time for anything other than such correspondence in the course of the day, and I would have no time for constructive work. But since I feel that you are men of genuine good will and that your criticisms are sincerely set forth, I want to try to answer your statement in what I hope will be patient and reasonable terms.

AUTHOR'S NOTE: This response to a published statement by eight fellow clergymen from Alabama (Bishop C. C. J. Carpenter, Bishop Joseph A. Durick, Rabbi Hilton L. Grafman, Bishop Paul Hardin, Bishop Holan B. Harmon, the Reverend George M. Murray, the Reverend Edward V. Ramage and the Reverend Earl Stallings) was composed under somewhat constricting circumstances. Begun on the margins of the newspaper in which the statement appeared while I was in jail, the letter was continued on scraps of writing paper supplied by a friendly Negro trusty, and concluded on a pad my attorneys were eventually permitted to leave me. Although the text remains in substance unaltered, I have indulged in the author's prerogative of polishing it for publication.

I think I should indicate why I am here in Birmingham, 2
since you have been influenced by the view which argues against
"outsiders coming in." I have the honor of serving as president
of the Southern Christian Leadership Conference, an organization operating in every southern state, with headquarters in
Atlanta, Georgia. We have some eighty-five affiliated organizations across the South, and one of them is the Alabama Christian Movement for Human Rights. Frequently we share staff,
educational and financial resources with our affiliates. Several
months ago the affiliate here in Birmingham asked us to be on
call to engage in a nonviolent direct-action program if such were
deemed necessary. We readily consented, and when the hour
came we lived up to our promise. So I, along with several members of my staff, am here because I was invited here. I am here
because I have organizational ties here.

But more basically, I am in Birmingham because injustice 3
is here. Just as the prophets of the eighth century B.C. left their
villages and carried their "thus saith the Lord" far beyond the
boundaries of their home towns, and, just as the Apostle Paul
left his village of Tarsus and carried the gospel of Jesus Christ
to the far corners of the Greco-Roman world, so am I compelled
to carry the gospel of freedom beyond my own home town. Like
Paul, I must constantly respond to the Macedonian call for aid.

Moreover, I am cognizant of the interrelatedness of all com- 4
munities and states. I cannot sit idly by in Atlanta and not be
concerned about what happens in Birmingham. Injustice anywhere is a threat to justice everywhere. We are caught in an
inescapable network of mutuality, tied in a single garment of
destiny. Whatever affects one directly, affects all indirectly. Never
again can we afford to live with the narrow, provincial "outside
agitator" idea. Anyone who lives inside the United States can
never be considered an outsider anywhere within its bounds.

You deplore the demonstrations taking place in Birming- 5
ham. But your statement, I am sorry to say, fails to express a
similar concern for the conditions that brought about the demonstrations. I am sure that none of you would want to rest
content with the superficial kind of social analysis that deals
merely with effects and does not grapple with underlying causes.
It is unfortunate that demonstrations are taking place in Bir-

mingham, but it is even more unfortunate that the city's white power structure left the Negro community with no alternative.

6   In any nonviolent campaign there are four basic steps: collection of the facts to determine whether injustices exist; negotiation; self-purification; and direct action. We have gone through all these steps in Birmingham. There can be no gainsaying the fact that racial injustice engulfs this community. Birmingham is probably the most thoroughly segregated city in the United States. An ugly record of brutality is widely known. Negroes have experienced grossly unjust treatment in the courts. There have been more unsolved bombings of Negro homes and churches in Birmingham than in any other city in the nation. These are the hard brutal facts of the case. On the basis of these conditions, Negro leaders sought to negotiate with the city fathers. But the latter consistently refused to engage in good-faith negotiation.

7   Then, last September, came the opportunity to talk with leaders of Birmingham's economic community. In the course of the negotiations, certain promises were made by the merchants—for example, to remove the stores' humiliating racial signs. On the basis of these promises, the Reverend Fred Shuttlesworth and the leaders of the Alabama Christian Movement for Human Rights agreed to a moratorium on all demonstrations. As the weeks and months went by, we realized that we were the victims of a broken promise. A few signs, briefly removed, returned; the others remained.

8   As in so many past experiences, our hopes had been blasted, and the shadow of deep disappointment settled upon us. We had no alternative except to prepare for direct action, whereby we would present our very bodies as a means of laying our case before the conscience of the local and the national community. Mindful of the difficulties involved, we decided to undertake a process of self-purification. We began a series of workshops on nonviolence, and we repeatedly asked ourselves: "Are you able to accept blows without retaliating?" "Are you able to endure the ordeal of jail?" We decided to schedule our direct-action program for the Easter season, realizing that except for Christmas, this is the main shopping period of the year. Knowing that a strong economic-withdrawal program would be the by-product of direct action, we felt that this would be the best time to bring pressure to bear on the merchants for the needed change.

Then it occurred to us that Birmingham's mayoralty election was coming up in March, and we speedily decided to postpone action until after election day. When we discovered that the Commissioner of Public Safety, Eugene "Bull" Connor, had piled up enough votes to be in the run-off, we decided again to postpone action until the day after the run-off so that the demonstrations could not be used to cloud the issues. Like many others, we waited to see Mr. Connor defeated, and to this end we endured postponement after postponement. Having aided in this community need, we felt that our direct-action program could be delayed no longer.

You may well ask: "Why direct action? Why sit-ins, marches and so forth? Isn't negotiation a better path?" You are quite right in calling for negotiation. Indeed, this is the very purpose of direct action. Nonviolent direct action seeks to create such a crisis and foster such a tension that a community which has constantly refused to negotiate is forced to confront the issue. It seeks so to dramatize the issue that it can no longer be ignored. My citing the creation of tension as part of the work of the nonviolent-resister may sound rather shocking. But I must confess that I am not afraid of the word "tension." I have earnestly opposed violent tension, but there is a type of constructive nonviolent tension which is necessary for growth. Just as Socrates felt that it was necessary to create a tension in the mind so that individuals could rise from the bondage of myths and half-truths to the unfettered realm of creative analysis and objective appraisal, so must we see the need for nonviolent gadflies to create the kind of tension in society that will help men rise from the dark depths of prejudice and racism to the majestic heights of understanding and brotherhood.

The purpose of our direct-action program is to create a situation so crisis-packed that it will inevitably open the door to negotiation. I therefore concur with you in your call for negotiation. Too long has our beloved Southland been bogged down in a tragic effort to live in monologue rather than dialogue.

One of the basic points in your statement is that the action that I and my associates have taken in Birmingham is untimely. Some have asked: "Why didn't you give the new city administration time to act?" The only answer that I can give to this query is that the new Birmingham administration must be prodded about as much as the outgoing one, before it will act. We are sadly mistaken if we feel that the election of Albert Boutwell as mayor will bring the millennium to Birmingham. While Mr. Boutwell is a much more gentle person than Mr. Connor, they are both segregationists, dedicated to maintenance of the status quo. I have hope that Mr. Boutwell will be reasonable enough to see the futility of massive resistance to desegregation. But he will not see this without pressure from devotees of civil rights. My friends, I must say to you that we have not made a single gain in civil rights without determined legal and nonviolent pressure. Lamentably, it is an historical fact that privileged groups seldom give up their privileges voluntarily. Individuals may see the moral light and voluntarily give up their unjust posture; but, as Reinhold Niebuhr has reminded us, groups tend to be more immoral than individuals.

13   We know through painful experience that freedom is never voluntarily given by the oppressor; it must be demanded by the oppressed. Frankly, I have yet to engage in a direct-action campaign that was "well timed" in the view of those who have not suffered unduly from the disease of segregation. For years now I have heard the word "Wait!" It rings in the ear of every Negro with piercing familiarity. This "Wait" has almost always meant "Never." We must come to see, with one of our distinguished jurists, that "justice too long delayed is justice denied."

14   We have waited for more than 340 years for our constitutional and Godgiven rights. The nations of Asia and Africa are moving with jetlike speed toward gaining political independence, but we still creep at horse-and-buggy pace toward gaining a cup of coffee at a lunch counter. Perhaps it is easy for those who have never felt the stinging darts of segregation to say, "Wait." But when you have seen vicious mobs lynch your mothers and fathers at will and drown your sisters and brothers at whim; when you have seen hate-filled policemen curse, kick and even kill your black brothers and sisters; when you see the vast majority of your twenty million Negro brothers smothering in an airtight cage of poverty in the midst of an affluent society; when you suddenly find your tongue twisted and your speech stammering as you seek to explain to your six-year-old daughter why she can't go to the public amusement park that has just

been advertised on television, and see tears welling up in her eyes when she is told that Funtown is closed to colored children, and see ominous clouds of inferiority beginning to form in her little mental sky, and see her beginning to distort her personality by developing an unconscious bitterness toward white people; when you have to concoct an answer for a five-year-old son who is asking: "Daddy, why do white people treat colored people so mean?"; when you take a cross-country drive and find it necessary to sleep night after night in the uncomfortable corners of your automobile because no motel will accept you; when you are humiliated day in and day out by nagging signs reading "white" and "colored"; when your first name becomes "nigger," your middle name becomes "boy" (however old you are) and your last name becomes "John," and your wife and mother are never given the respected title "Mrs."; when you are harried by day and haunted by night by the fact that you are a Negro, living constantly at tiptoe stance, never quite knowing what to expect next, and are plagued with inner fears and outer resentments; when you are forever fighting a degenerating sense of "nobodiness"—then you will understand why we find it difficult to wait. There comes a time when the cup of endurance runs over, and men are no longer willing to be plunged into the abyss of despair. I hope, sirs, you can understand our legitimate and unavoidable impatience.

You express a great deal of anxiety over our willingness to 15 break laws. This is certainly a legitimate concern. Since we so diligently urge people to obey the Supreme Court's decision of 1954 outlawing segregation in the public schools, at first glance it may seem rather paradoxical for us consciously to break laws. One may well ask: "How can you advocate breaking some laws and obeying others?" The answer lies in the fact that there are two types of laws: just and unjust. I would be the first to advocate obeying just laws. One has not only a legal but a moral responsibility to obey just laws. Conversely, one has a moral responsibility to disobey unjust laws. I would agree with St. Augustine that "an unjust law is no law at all."

Now, what is the difference between the two? How does 16 one determine whether a law is just or unjust? A just law is a man-made code that squares with the moral law or the law of

God. An unjust law is a code that is out of harmony with the moral law. To put it in the terms of St. Thomas Aquinas: An unjust law is a human law that is not rooted in eternal law and natural law. Any law that uplifts human personality is just. Any law that degrades human personality is unjust. All segregation statutes are unjust because segregation distorts the soul and damages the personality. It gives the segregator a false sense of superiority and the segregated a false sense of inferiority. Segregation, to use the terminology of the Jewish philosopher Martin Buber, substitutes an "I-it" relationship for an "I-thou" relationship and ends up relegating persons to the status of things. Hence segregation is not only politically, economically and sociologically unsound, it is morally wrong and sinful. Paul Tillich has said that sin is separation. Is not segregation an existential expression of man's tragic separation, his awful estrangement, his terrible sinfulness. Thus it is that I can urge men to obey the 1954 decision of the Supreme Court, for it is morally right; and I can urge them to disobey segregation ordinances, for they are morally wrong.

17   Let us consider a more concrete example of just and unjust laws. An unjust law is a code that a numerical or power majority group compels a minority group to obey but does not make binding on itself. This is *difference* made legal. By the same token, a just law is a code that a majority compels a minority to follow and that it is willing to follow itself. This is *sameness* made legal.

18   Let me give another explanation. A law is unjust if it is inflicted on a minority that, as a result of being denied the right to vote, had no part in enacting or devising the law. Who can say that the legislature of Alabama which set up that state's segregation laws was democratically elected? Throughout Alabama all sorts of devious methods are used to prevent Negroes from becoming registered voters, and there are some counties in which even though Negroes constitute a majority of the population, not a single Negro is registered. Can any law enacted under such circumstances be considered democratically structured?

19   Sometimes a law is just on its face and unjust in its application. For instance, I have been arrested on a charge of parading without a permit. Now, there is nothing wrong in having an

ordinance which requires a permit for a parade. But such an ordinance becomes unjust when it is used to maintain segregation and to deny citizens the First-Amendment privilege of peaceful assembly and protest.

I hope you are able to see the distinction I am trying to point out. In no sense do I advocate evading or defying the law, as would the rabid segregationist. That would lead to anarchy. One who breaks an unjust law must do so openly, lovingly, and with a willingness to accept the penalty. I submit that an individual who breaks a law that conscience tells him is unjust, and who willingly accepts the penalty of imprisonment in order to arouse the conscience of the community over its injustice, is in reality expressing the highest respect for law.

Of course, there is nothing new about this kind of civil disobedience. It was evidenced sublimely in the refusal of Shadrach, Meshach and Abednego to obey the laws of Nebuchadnezzar, on the ground that a higher moral law was at stake. It was practiced superbly by the early Christians, who were willing to face hungry lions and the excruciating pain of chopping blocks rather than submit to certain unjust laws of the Roman Empire. To a degree, academic freedom is a reality today because Socrates practiced civil disobedience. In our own nation, the Boston Tea Party represented a massive act of civil disobedience.

We should never forget that everything Adolf Hitler did in Germany was "legal" and everything the Hungarian freedom fighters did in Hungary was "illegal." It was "illegal" to aid and comfort a Jew in Hitler's Germany. Even so, I am sure that, had I lived in Germany at the time, I would have aided and comforted my Jewish brothers. If today I lived in a Communist country where certain principles dear to the Christian faith are suppressed, I would openly advocate disobeying that country's antireligious laws.

I must make two honest confessions to you, my Christian and Jewish brothers. First, I must confess that over the past few years I have been gravely disappointed with the white moderate. I have almost reached the regrettable conclusion that the Negro's great stumbling block in his stride toward freedom is not the White Citizen's Counciler or the Ku Klux Klanner, but the white moderate, who is more devoted to "order" than to justice; who prefers a negative peace which is the absence of tension to a positive peace which is the presence of justice; who constantly says: "I agree with you in the goal you seek, but I cannot agree with your methods of direct action"; who paternalistically believes he can set the timetable for another man's freedom; who lives by a mythical concept of time and who constantly advises the Negro to wait for a "more convenient season." Shallow understanding from people of good will is more frustrating than absolute misunderstanding from people of ill will. Lukewarm acceptance is much more bewildering than outright rejection.

24   I had hoped that the white moderate would understand that law and order exist for the purpose of establishing justice and that when they fail in this purpose they become the dangerously structured dams that block the flow of social progress. I had hoped that the white moderate would understand that the present tension in the South is a necessary phase of the transition from an obnoxious negative peace, in which the Negro passively accepted his unjust plight, to a substantive and positive peace, in which all men will respect the dignity and worth of human personality. Actually, we who engage in nonviolent direct action are not the creators of tension. We merely bring to the surface the hidden tension that is already alive. We bring it out in the open, where it can be seen and dealt with. Like a boil that can never be cured so long as it is covered up but must be opened with all its ugliness to the natural medicines of air and light, injustice must be exposed, with all the tension its exposure creates, to the light of human conscience and the air of national opinion before it can be cured.

25   In your statement you assert that our actions, even though peaceful, must be condemned because they precipitate violence. But is this a logical assertion? Isn't this like condemning a robbed man because his possession of money precipitated the evil act of robbery? Isn't this like condemining Socrates because his unswerving commitment to truth and his philosophical inquiries precipitated the act by the misguided populace in which they made him drink hemlock? Isn't this like condemning Jesus because his unique God-consciousness and never-ceasing devotion to God's will precipitated the evil act of crucifixion? We must come to see that, as the federal courts have consistently affirmed,

it is wrong to urge an individual to cease his efforts to gain his basic constitutional rights because the quest may precipitate violence. Society must protect the robbed and punish the robber.

I had also hoped that the white moderate would reject the myth concerning time in relation to the struggle for freedom. I have just received a letter from a white brother in Texas. He writes: "All Christians know that the colored people will receive equal rights eventually, but it is possible that you are in too great a religious hurry. It has taken Christianity almost two thousand years to accomplish what it has. The teachings of Christ take time to come to earth." Such an attitude stems from a tragic misconception of time, from the strangely irrational notion that there is something in the very flow of time that will inevitably cure all ills. Actually, time itself is neutral; it can be used either destructively or constructively. More and more I feel that the people of ill will have used time much more effectively than have the people of good will. We will have to repent in this generation not merely for the hateful words and actions of the bad people but for the appalling silence of the good people. Human progress never rolls in on wheels of inevitability; it comes through the tireless efforts of men willing to be co-workers with God, and without this hard work, time itself becomes an ally of the forces of social stagnation. We must use time creatively, in the knowledge that the time is always ripe to do right. Now is the time to make real the promise of democracy and transform our pending national elegy into a creative psalm of brotherhood. Now is the time to lift our national policy from the quicksand of racial injustice to the solid rock of human dignity.

You speak of our activity in Birmingham as extreme. At first I was rather disappointed that fellow clergymen would see my nonviolent efforts as those of an extremist. I began thinking about the fact that I stand in the middle of two opposing forces in the Negro community. One is a force of complacency, made up in part of Negroes who, as a result of long years of oppression, are so drained of self-respect and a sense of "somebodiness" that they have adjusted to segregation; and in part of a few middle-class Negroes who, because of a degree of academic and economic security and because in some ways they profit by segregation, have become insensitive to the problems of the masses. The other force is one of bitterness and hatred, and it comes perilously close to advocating violence. It is expressed in the various black nationalist groups that are springing up across the nation, the largest and best-known being Elijah Muhammad's Muslim movement. Nourished by the Negro's frustration over the continued existence of racial discrimination, this movement is made up of people who have lost faith in America, who have absolutely repudiated Christianity, and who have concluded that the white man is an incorrigible "devil."

28   I have tried to stand between these two forces, saying that we need emulate neither the "do-nothingism" of the complacent nor the hatred and despair of the black nationalist. For there is the more excellent way of love and nonviolent protest. I am grateful to God that, through the influence of the Negro church, the way of nonviolence became an integral part of our struggle.

29   If this philosophy had not emerged, by now many streets of the South would, I am convinced, be flowing with blood. And I am further convinced that if our white brothers dismiss as "rabble-rousers" and "outside agitators" those of us who employ nonviolent direct action, and if they refuse to support our nonviolent efforts, millions of Negroes will, out of frustration and despair, seek solace and security in black-nationalist ideologies—a development that would inevitably lead to a frightening racial nightmare.

30   Oppressed people cannot remain oppressed forever. The yearning for freedom eventually manifests itself, and that is what has happened to the American Negro. Something within has reminded him of his birthright of freedom, and something without has reminded him that it can be gained. Consciously or unconsciously, he has been caught up by the *Zeitgeist*, and with his black brothers of Africa and his brown and yellow brothers of Asia, South America and the Caribbean, the United States Negro is moving with a sense of great urgency toward the promised land of racial justice. If one recognizes this vital urge that has engulfed the Negro community, one should readily understand why public demonstrations are taking place. The Negro has many pent-up resentments and latent frustrations, and he must release them. So let him march; let him make prayer pilgrimages to the city hall; let him go on freedom rides—and try

to understand why he must do so. If his repressed emotions are not released in nonviolent ways, they will seek expression through violence; this is not a threat but a fact of history. So I have not said to my people: "Get rid of your discontent." Rather, I have tried to say that this normal and healthy discontent can be channeled into the creative outlet of nonviolent direct action. And now this approach is being termed extremist.

But though I was initially disappointed at being categorized   31
as an extremist, as I continued to think about the matter I gradually gained a measure of satisfaction from the label. Was not Jesus an extremist for love: "Love your enemies, bless them that curse you, do good to them that hate you, and pray for them which despitefully use you, and persecute you." Was not Amos an extremist for justice: "Let justice roll down like waters and righteousness like an ever-flowing stream." Was not Paul an extremist for the Christian gospel: "I bear in my body the marks of the Lord Jesus." Was not Martin Luther an extremist: "Here I stand; I cannot do otherwise, so help me God." And John Bunyan: "I will stay in jail to the end of my days before I make a butchery of my conscience." And Abraham Lincoln: "This nation cannot survive half slave and half free." And Thomas Jefferson: "We hold these truths to be self-evident, that all men are created equal. . . ." So the question is not whether we will be extremists, but what kind of extremists we will be. Will we be extremists for hate or for love? Will we be extremists for the preservation of injustice or for the extension of justice? In that dramatic scene on Calvary's hill three men were crucified. We must never forget that all three were crucified for the same crime—the crime of extremism. Two were extremists for immorality, and thus fell below their environment. The other, Jesus Christ, was an extremist for love, truth and goodness, and thereby rose above his environment. Perhaps the South, the nation and the world are in dire need of creative extremists.

I had hoped that the white moderate would see this need.   32
Perhaps I was too optimistic; perhaps I expected too much. I suppose I should have realized that few members of the oppressor race can understand the deep groans and passionate yearnings of the oppressed race, and still fewer have the vision to see that injustice must be rooted out by strong, persistent and

determined action. I am thankful, however, that some of our white brothers in the South have grasped the meaning of this social revolution and committed themselves to it. They are still all too few in quantity, but they are big in quality. Some—such as Ralph McGill, Lillian Smith, Harry Golden, James McBride Dabbs, Ann Braden and Sarah Patton Boyle—have written about our struggle in eloquent and prophetic terms. Others have marched with us down nameless streets of the South. They have languished in filthy, roach-infested jails, suffering the abuse and brutality of policemen who view them as "dirty nigger-lovers." Unlike so many of their moderate brothers and sisters, they have recognized the urgency of the moment and sensed the need for powerful "action" antidotes to combat the disease of segregation.

33   Let me take note of my other major disappointment. I have been so greatly disappointed with the white church and its leadership. Of course, there are some notable exceptions. I am not unmindful of the fact that each of you has taken some significant stands on this issue. I commend you, Reverend Stallings, for your Christian stand on this past Sunday, in welcoming Negroes to your worship service on a nonsegregated basis. I commend the Catholic leaders of this state for integrating Spring Hill College several years ago.

34   But despite these notable exceptions, I must honestly reiterate that I have been disappointed with the church. I do not say this as one of those negative critics who can always find something wrong with the church. I say this as a minister of the gospel, who loves the church; who was nurtured in its bosom; who has been sustained by its spiritual blessings and who will remain true to it as long as the cord of life shall lengthen.

35   When I was suddenly catapulted into the leadership of the bus protest in Montgomery, Alabama, a few years ago, I felt we would be supported by the white church. I felt that the white ministers, priests and rabbis of the South would be among our strongest allies. Instead, some have been outright opponents, refusing to understand the freedom movement and misrepresenting its leaders; all too many others have been more cautious than courageous and have remained silent behind the anesthetizing security of stained-glass windows.

In spite of my shattered dreams, I came to Birmingham 36
with the hope that the white religious leadership of this community would see the justice of our cause and, with deep moral
concern, would serve as the channel through which our just
grievances could reach the power structure. I had hoped that
each of you would understand. But again I have been
disappointed.

I have heard numerous southern religious leaders admon- 37
ish their worshipers to comply with a desegregation decision
because it is the law, but I have longed to hear white ministers
declare: "Follow this decree because integration is morally right
and because the Negro is your brother." In the midst of blatant
injustices inflicted upon the Negro, I have watched white
churchmen stand on the sideline and mouth pious irrelevancies
and sanctimonious trivialities. In the midst of a mighty struggle
to rid our nation of racial and economic injustice, I have heard
many ministers say: "Those are social issues, with which the
gospel has no real concern." And I have watched many churches
commit themselves to a completely other-worldly religion which
makes a strange, un-Biblical distinction between body and soul,
between the sacred and the secular.

I have traveled the length and breadth of Alabama, Mis- 38
sissippi and all the other southern states. On sweltering summer
days and crisp autumn mornings I have looked at the South's
beautiful churches with their lofty spires pointing heavenward.
I have beheld the impressive outlines of her massive religious-
education buildings. Over and over I have found myself asking:
"What kind of people worship here? Who is their God? Where
were their voices when the lips of Governor Barnett dripped
with words of interposition and nullification? Where were they
when Governor Wallace gave a clarion call for defiance and
hatred? Where were their voices of support when bruised and
weary Negro men and women decided to rise from the dark
dungeons of complacency to the bright hills of creative protest?"

Yes, these questions are still in my mind. In deep disap- 39
pointment I have wept over the laxity of the church. But be
assured that my tears have been tears of love. There can be no
deep disappointment where there is not deep love. Yes, I love

the church. How could I do otherwise? I am in the rather unique position of being the son, the grandson and the great-grandson of preachers. Yes, I see the church as the body of Christ. But, oh! How we have blemished and scarred that body through social neglect and through fear of being nonconformists.

40   There was a time when the church was very powerful—in the time when the early Christians rejoiced at being deemed worthy to suffer for what they believed. In those days the church was not merely a thermometer that recorded the ideas and principles of popular opinion; it was a thermostat that transformed the mores of society. Whenever the early Christians entered a town, the people in power became disturbed and immediately sought to convict the Christians for being "disturbers of the peace" and "outside agitators." But the Christians pressed on, in the conviction that they were "a colony of heaven," called to obey God rather than man. Small in number, they were big in commitment. They were too God-intoxicated to be "astronomically intimidated." By their effort and example they brought an end to such ancient evils as infanticide and gladiatorial contests.

41   Things are different now. So often the contemporary church is a weak, ineffectual voice with an uncertain sound. So often it is an archdefender of the status quo. Far from being disturbed by the presence of the church, the power structure of the average community is consoled by the church's silent—and often even vocal—sanction of things as they are.

42   But the judgment of God is upon the church as never before. If today's church does not recapture the sacrificial spirit of the early church, it will lose its authenticity, forfeit the loyalty of millions, and be dismissed as an irrelevant social club with no meaning for the twentieth century. Every day I meet young people whose disappointment with the church has turned into outright disgust.

43   Perhaps I have once again been too optimistic. Is organized religion too inextricably bound to the status quo to save our nation and the world? Perhaps I must turn my faith to the inner spiritual church, the church within the church, as the true *ekklesia* and the hope of the world. But again I am thankful to God that some noble souls from the ranks of organized religion have broken loose from the paralyzing chains of conformity and joined

us as active partners in the struggle for freedom. They have left their secure congregations and walked the streets of Albany, Georgia, with us. They have gone down the highways of the South on tortuous rides for freedom. Yes, they have gone to jail with us. Some have been dismissed from their churches, have lost the support of their bishops and fellow ministers. But they have acted in the faith that right defeated is stronger than evil triumphant. Their witness has been the spiritual salt that has preserved the true meaning of the gospel in these troubled times. They have carved a tunnel of hope through the dark mountain of disappointment.

I hope the church as a whole will meet the challenge of this decisive hour. But even if the church does not come to the aid of justice, I have no despair about the future. I have no fear about the outcome of our struggle in Birmingham, even if our motives are at present misunderstood. We will reach the goal of freedom in Birmingham and all over the nation, because the goal of America is freedom. Abused and scorned though we may be, our destiny is tied up with America's destiny. Before the pilgrims landed at Plymouth, we were here. Before the pen of Jefferson etched the majestic words of the Declaration of Independence across the pages of history, we were here. For more than two centuries our forebears labored in this country without wages; they made cotton king; they built the homes of their masters while suffering gross injustice and shameful humiliation—and yet out of a bottomless vitality they continued to thrive and develop. If the inexpressible cruelties of slavery could not stop us, the opposition we now face will surely fail. We will win our freedom because the sacred heritage of our nation and the eternal will of God are embodied in our echoing demands.

Before closing I feel impelled to mention one other point in your statement that has troubled me profoundly. You warmly commended the Birmingham police force for keeping "order" and "preventing violence." I doubt that you would have so warmly commended the police force if you had seen its dogs sinking their teeth into unarmed, nonviolent Negroes. I doubt that you would so quickly commend the policemen if you were to observe their ugly and inhumane treatment of Negroes here in the city jail; if you were to watch them push and curse old

Negro women and young Negro girls; if you were to see them slap and kick old Negro men and young boys; if you were to observe them as they did on two occasions, refuse to give us food because we wanted to sing our grace together. I cannot join you in your praise of the Birmingham police department.

46   It is true that the police have exercised a degree of discipline in handling the demonstrators. In this sense they have conducted themselves rather "nonviolently" in public. But for what purpose? To preserve the evil system of segregation. Over the past few years I have consistently preached that nonviolence demands that the means we use must be as pure as the ends we seek. I have tried to make clear that it is wrong to use immoral means to attain moral ends. But now I must affirm that it is just as wrong, or perhaps even more so, to use moral means to preserve immoral ends. Perhaps Mr. Connor and his policemen have been rather nonviolent in public, as was Chief Pritchett in Albany, Georgia, but they have used the moral means of nonviolence to maintain the immoral end of racial injustice. As T. S. Eliot has said: "The last temptation is the greatest treason: To do the right deed for the wrong reason."

47   I wish you had commended the Negro sit-inners and demonstrators of Birmingham for their sublime courage, their willingness to suffer and their amazing discipline in the midst of great provocation. One day the South will recognize its real heroes. They will be the James Merediths, with the noble sense of purpose that enables them to face jeering and hostile mobs, and with the agonizing loneliness that characterizes the life of the pioneer. They will be old, oppressed, battered Negro women, symbolized in a seventy-two-year-old woman in Montgomery, Alabama, who rose up with a sense of dignity and with her people decided not to ride segregated buses, and who responded with ungrammatical profundity to one who inquired about her weariness: "My feet is tired, but my soul is at rest." They will be the young high school and college students, the young ministers of the gospel and a host of their elders, courageously and nonviolently sitting in at lunch counters and willingly going to jail for conscience' sake. One day the South will know that when these disinherited children of God sat down at lunch counters, they were in reality standing up for what is best in the American

dream and for the most sacred values in our Judaeo-Christian heritage, thereby bringing our nation back to those great wells of democracy which were dug deep by the founding fathers in their formulation of the Constitution and the Declaration of Independence.

Never before have I written so long a letter. I'm afraid it 48 is much too long to take your precious time. I can assure you that it would have been much shorter if I had been writing from a comfortable desk, but what else can one do when he is alone in a narrow jail cell, other than write long letters, think long thoughts and pray long prayers?

If I have said anything in this letter that overstates the truth 49 and indicates an unreasonable impatience, I beg you to forgive me. If I have said anything that understates the truth and indicates my having a patience that allows me to settle for anything less than brotherhood, I beg God to forgive me.

I hope this letter finds you strong in the faith. I also hope 50 that circumstances will soon make it possible for me to meet each of you, not as an integrationist or a civil-rights leader but as a fellow clergyman and a Christian brother. Let us all hope that the dark clouds of racial prejudice will soon pass away and the deep fog of misunderstanding will be lifted from our fear-drenched communities, and in some not too distant tomorrow the radiant stars of love and brotherhood will shine over our great nation with all their scintillating beauty.

Yours for the cause of Peace and Brotherhood,
Martin Luther King, Jr.

Content

1. In paragraph 4 King makes several assertions on which he bases the rest of his argument. What are they? Does he ever prove them, or does he assume that readers will take them for granted?

2. In paragraph 5 King asserts that Birmingham's "white power structure left the Negro community with no alternative" but to commit civil disobedience. Does he ever prove this? Does he need to? Is it a debatable statement?

3. What, according to King, are the "four basic steps" in "any non-

violent campaign" (¶ 6)? What is the goal of "nonviolent direct action" (¶ 10)? What is the "constructive, nonviolent tension" (¶ 10) King favors?

4. Why has King been disappointed by white moderates (¶s 23–32)? By the white church (¶s 33–44)? What does he want white moderates to do? What does he claim that the church should do?

5. How does King deal with the argument that civil rights activists are too impatient, that they should go slow because " 'It has taken Christianity almost two thousand years to accomplish what it has' " (¶ 26)? How does he refute the argument that he is an extremist (¶ 27)?

Strategies/Structures

1. How does King establish, in the salutation and first paragraph, his reasons for writing? The setting in which he writes? His intended audience? A sensitive, reasonable tone?

2. King's letter ostensibly replies to that of the eight clergymen. Find passages in which he addresses them, and analyze the voice he uses. In what relation to the clergymen does King see himself? He also has a secondary audience; who are its members? Locate passages that seem especially directed to this second audience. In what relation to this audience does King see himself?

3. Why does King cite the theologians Aquinas (a Catholic), Buber (a Jew), and Tillich (a Protestant) in paragraph 16? What similarities link the three?

4. After defending his actions against the criticisms of the clergymen, King takes the offensive in paragraphs 23–44. How does he signal this change?

5. Which parts of King's letter appeal chiefly to reason? To emotion? How are the two types of appeals interrelated?

6. King uses large numbers of rhetorical questions throughout this essay (see ¶s 18, 25, 31, 38, 39). Why? With what effects?

Language

1. How does King define a "just law" (¶s 16, 17)? An "unjust law" (¶s 16, 17)? Why are these definitions crucial to the argument that follows?

2. Consult your dictionary, if necessary, for the meanings of the following words or others you do not understand: cognizant (¶ 4), gainsaying (6), moratorium (7), gadflies (10), harried (14), degenerating (14), abyss (14), incorrigible (27), *Zeitgeist* (30), scintillating (47).

For Writing

1. Under what circumstances, if any, is breaking the law justifiable? If you use Dr. King's definition of just and unjust law (¶s 15–20), or make any distinction, say, between moral law and civil law, be sure to explain what you mean. You may, if you wish, use examples with which you are personally familiar. Or you may elaborate on some of the examples King uses (¶ 22) or on examples from King's own civil rights activities, such as the boycotts in the early 1950s of the legally segregated Montgomery bus system (¶ 35).

2. If you are a member of a church, or attend church regularly, what, if any, commitment do you think your church should make to the betterment of minorities, the poor, or other groups who do not attend that church?

3. Would you ever be willing to go to jail for a cause? What cause? Under what circumstances? If you knew that a prison record might bar you from some privileges in some states (such as practicing law or medicine), would you still be willing to take such a risk?

▶━━━◀

Frances FitzGerald

Among FitzGerald's (b.1940) public-spirited ancestors are a number of energetic, intelligent, attractive women, including the Peabody sisters of Salem, Massachusetts: Sophia, wife of author Nathaniel Hawthorne; Mary, married to educator Horace Mann; and Elizabeth, a notable abolitionist and educator. Other relatives include Mary Parkman Peabody, FitzGerald's grandmother, active in community work and once jailed for civil rights activities, and two of her children: Endicott Peabody, FitzGerald's uncle and the former governor of Massachusetts; and Marietta Tree, FitzGerald's mother, appointed by President Kennedy as the United States representative to the Human Rights Commission of the United Nations Economic and Social Council. This activist heritage has doubtless contributed to FitzGerald's career of investigative journalism; her work has appeared in *Atlantic, The New Yorker, The Village Voice,* and the *New York Times Magazine.* She won both a Pulitzer Prize for contemporary affairs writing and a National Book Award in 1973 for *Fire in the Lake: the Vietnamese and Americans in Vietnam.* Her most recent book is *America Revised: History Schoolbooks in the Twentieth Century* (1979), an investigation of how history books have been written—and rewritten— to promote what politicians and publishers believe is the national interest, irrespective of the facts, as the chapter reprinted below reveals.

Ethnic Bias in Textbooks

1   The [history] textbooks made many discoveries about Americans during the nineteen-sixties. The country they had conceived as male and Anglo-Saxon turned out to be filled with blacks, "ethnics," Indians, Asians, and women. (The history texts have not actually found many women in America, but they have replaced their pictures of Dolley Madison with photographs of Susan B. Anthony.) The country also turned out to be filled with Spanish-speaking people who had come from Mexico, Puerto Rico, and other countries of the Caribbean basin. This last of their discoveries was—at least, to judge from the space they gave it—the most important one next to the discovery of the blacks. In books of the early seventies, there were two- and four-page color spreads on Puerto Rico and on "The Mexican Heritage" and "Mexican Americans Today," these featuring pictures of Toltec statues, César Chávez, and Anthony Quinn. The sudden eruption of Latinos was, of course, the publishers' response to pressure from the powerful school boards of Texas, California, and New York—states that harbored a great percentage of the new immigrants from the south. The pressures were apparently unexpected, for the photographs of César Chávez and the Toltec statues stand out as uncomfortably in

these books as the photographs of George Washington Carver and the civil-rights marches do in the books of the mid-sixties. There is little actual history behind them. The previous editions of these texts had contained some history of Latin America, but it had had to be cut, because of its condescending tone.

The textbook tradition, in fact, served the newest immi- [2] grant population rather worse than it served any other group. In the first place, the Spanish colonizers of the New World had always been American history's villains par excellence. In the early nineteenth century, the Reverend Jedidiah Morse had devoted heartfelt efforts to a defamation of the Spanish character. This was just a start; his successors throughout the nineteenth century reserved their most vitriolic prose for the Spanish and their doings, going on at great length about gold lust, cruelty to Indians, and crazed searchings for the Fountain of Youth. The sturdy tradition of Hispanophobia continued undiluted until the nineteen-twenties. At that point, a small minority of texts began to make concessions. The Spanish, these texts said, lacked "moral and ethical character," but they had made certain contributions to the New World; they had, after all, discovered it, and they had brought it Christianity, mission architecture, and domestic animals. As time went on, this "balanced" approach gradually took over the books, and by the nineteen-thirties it was the conventional wisdom; it continued as such until the late sixties. The tone, however, remained distinctly jaundiced. One book that was published in 1967 and is still in use in some schools summarizes the whole subject of the Spanish colonization in two short sections entitled "Spain Monopolizes Much of the World" and "Spain Makes Many Contributions But Permits Few Freedoms." In this very capitalistic and Cold War book, the word "monopoly" is as much anathema as "effeminacy" or "luxury" was in the Reverend Mr. Morse's text, and the permission of "few freedoms" is the moral equivalent of papism. The typical text of the late sixties and early seventies takes a slightly less dogmatic attitude. A good example is to be found in the 1973 revised printing of an older text, *The Adventure of the American People*, by Henry F. Graff and John A. Krout. The text makes some effort to describe Spanish feudalism as a system and goes on to list the "contributions" of the Spanish—most of which are crops. The Spanish section concludes:

> Although we can see after four hundred years what things were of enduring significance in the Spanish settlements, at the time only gold seemed worthwhile. In fact, the Spanish conquerors never took on the tasks of taming the forests and rivers of America and colonizing the land.
>
> Finding gold so easily and so early drove them madly on to look for more. They never found it, but the search left its mark on Spanish culture in the New World, and in its turn it also affected the mother country. . . .
>
> At home, the Spaniards failed to reinvest the gold and silver drawn from the mines of the New World. When they had used it up, Spain lived only on memories of its past. Gambling always on "hitting the jackpot," it left to others the richest prize of all—what later became the United States. How different our history might have been if our own abundant gold and silver deposits had been found first by the Spaniards!

3   A number of the mid-seventies books have broken the tradition of two centuries by making no reference to gold, slavery, or massacres of Indians in connection with the Spanish. (The principle that lies behind textbook history is that the inclusion of nasty information constitutes bias even if the information is true.) But this bowdlerization has not really brought the books any closer to the truth, for the real distortion of the texts lay less in what they said about the Spanish than in what they did not say. The students of Graff and Krout might be shocked to learn, as they could from Howard Mumford Jones, in *O Strange New World*, that while the "forlorn little band of Englishmen were trying to stick it out on Roanoke Island three hundred poets were competing for a prize in Mexico City," and that when Jefferson was President the great scientist Alexander von Humboldt declared that, of all the cities in the Western Hemisphere, Mexico City had the most solid scientific institutions.

That textbook historians detested the Spanish colonizers 4
did not mean that they therefore sympathized with the colonized
peoples. The same writers who were eloquent on the subject of
Spanish gold lust also tended to revel in the gory details of Aztec
human sacrifices. Montezuma, it seemed, deserved Cortés. About
the other native peoples of the region the texts said little or
nothing. And when they dropped the Spanish they dropped
the whole history of Latin America. In 1848, "the Mexicans"
would crop up in the context of a border war; in 1898, "the
Cubans" and "the Puerto Ricans" would make an appearance
as the grateful beneficiaries of the Spanish-American War. Who
these people were remained mysterious, for the texts, whether
or not they justified these wars per se, never credited the Mexicans or the Cubans with having any views. The Latin-American
nations were, it appeared, nothing more than the objects of
United States foreign policy.

Having cut out most of these offending passages, the text 5
publishers may now be on the verge of rewriting history backward to accommodate the new population of Spanish-speaking
Americans. If so, the histories of the future will be interesting
to see, for the rewriting will affect not only domestic social history but the whole textbook notion of the space that the United
States has occupied in the New World.

Only in the nineteen-sixties did the textbooks finally end 6
their rear-guard action on behalf of a Northern European America. The civil-rights movement had shattered the image of a
homogeneous American society and, for the first time in the
twentieth century, raised profound questions about the national
identity. The answer given by that movement and accepted as
orthodoxy by most state and big city school boards was that the
United States is a multiracial, multicultural society. This formula,
however, raised as many questions as it answered. Was the
United States really like Yugoslavia—a country held together
only by a delicate balance among ethnic and cultural groups?
Or was there some integration of these groups? Was there a
dominant culture—and was that a good thing? Was there some
principle of unity that Americans ought to support apart from
that of the state? The current texts show signs of struggle with

these questions. The struggle has had no clear outcome, for the social portrait drawn by the texts remains divided and confused.

7   The current texts represent the United States as a multiracial society to the extent that they include some material on all the large racial and ethnic groups, and that their photographs show people of all colors (also of all ages and both sexes) and suggest that even white Americans come from different ethnic backgrounds. The books contain a good deal of social history on these groups. Most texts assert that the early settlers had African as well as European roots, and virtually all of them have sections on Aztec, Mayan, and North American Indian cultures. In one text, the account of colonization begins with the settlement of Puerto Rico by Ponce de León. Another text begins with a chapter on immigrants and includes a discussion of the migration of blacks from South to North after the Second World War. The texts also describe certain of the "problems" that minorities have faced in the United States, such as the internment of Japanese-Americans during the Second World War. But it's on the subject of these "problems" that the texts are still confused. They have succeeded in including all groups, but they have not succeeded in treating them all equally. There is, for instance, a remarkable disparity between their treatment of European ethnic groups and their treatment of all other ethnic minorities.

8   Most current texts discuss the European ethnic groups in two separate places—in their chapters on immigration and industrialization in the nineteenth century, and again in their chapters on modern-day life. Their nineteenth-century social history now includes a good deal of material that would have been labelled "too controversial" a decade ago. In place of the brief dismissive passages about toiling masses arriving in the land of liberty, the texts now describe in some painful detail the difficulties so many of the immigrants faced when they got off the boats: brutalizing labor in factories and mines, slum conditions in the cities, prejudice against them, and the shock of entering another culture. The so-called "inquiry," or "discovery," texts—which focus on a few topics and illustrate them with documents from primary and secondary sources—include

portions of diaries or books by the newly arrived Europeans which present the experience from a perspective that was heretofore unthinkable: that of the immigrants themselves. In the sections on modern-day life, the texts make some attempt at consistency with this point of view. They describe not individual artists but working-class families that came originally from Poland, Greece, or Russia, and they contend that the European culture of these families has not melted away—that they still have strong religious, culinary, and other traditions. But here the discussion ends. With two exceptions, they do not discuss the assimilation of European ethnic groups; they do not discuss the washout of European traditions in America or the fusion of various cultures. They insist—following Nathan Glazer and Daniel P. Moynihan's sociological study *Beyond the Melting Pot*—that the "ethnics" have not been assimilated but have separately added to the wonderful variety of life in America. There is some irony in this. The very fact that the texts can depict the horrors of life for the immigrants in the eighteen-eighties shows that some assimilation has occurred; otherwise, the texts would be accused of offending group sensibilities. A further proof is that a number of the authors of these American-history books are the children or grandchildren of such immigrants.

Still, even with this overstatement of the Glazer-Moynihan thesis, the treatment of European minorities is far more realistic than that of non-European minorities, whose sensibilities the publishers are anxious not to offend. The photographs in the mass-market texts rarely show a non-white person who is brutalized, dirty, or even poor—unless the photograph specifically illustrates "pockets of poverty in America." There are almost no pictures of black sharecroppers, or black laborers of any kind unless they are in integrated groups wearing hard hats. Except for Stokely Carmichael, other black militants, and the hardhat laborers, blacks pictured in current texts wear business suits or lab coats. The same goes for other non-white people. Most of them are smiling. You can find pictures of Chicano farmworkers, but the workers are always clean and look as if they're enjoying their work. They're always smiling at César Chávez. The Puerto Ricans are smiling and healthy. The Chinese are smiling at healthy-looking vegetable stands. Indeed, everyone is smiling so hard you would think that all non-white people in the United States took happy pills. (The Russians, by contrast, appear to be a sombre lot. Their grimness dates from a time in the fifties when a group of right-wing organizations made an enormous fuss about a photograph of smiling Russian children.) There are a few exceptions to this rule. But there are no exceptions to the rule of art. Many of the current texts overflow with examples of art by non-white people. In the first chapters, there are pages on which the printed word makes a few ant trails around huge color pictures of folk art: Mayan temples or Aztec masks, Iroquois blankets, Pueblo pottery (but no feather headdresses, for these are thought to be stereotypical). Later on, there are pictures of modern Mexican murals and disquisitions on black painters and writers, and occasionally on one or two black musicians. (One book includes a half-page reproduction of a painting in Hudson River school style that happens to have been painted by a black.) Apparently the publishers have yet to find a Puerto Rican landscape painter or a Chinese-American poet, but one imagines that they are trying hard, since artists must now come from everywhere except Europe. In addition to artists, the non-white minorities seem to have hero figures and "leaders," while the European groups do not; and all of them are always said to be struggling to achieve full rights.

10   The publishers have mentioned the struggles of non-white peoples, but in order to sell books to a majority they sometimes refrain from mentioning what these groups are struggling against. Though most books delineate the social and economic institutions that made life so hard for the nineteenth-century immigrants, they do not always do the same for the non-white Americans in modern times. The Chicano farmworkers are struggling, but some texts fail to mention the growers. The American Indians are struggling in a void, there being no mention of the historical arrangements between private corporations and the Bureau of Indian Affairs for the exploitation of natural resources on the tribal lands. In regard to the civil-rights movement, there is often no discussion of institutionalized racism— not even that which was contained in the Southern school systems before Little Rock. The books report at length on reform movements and reform measures but rarely tot up the results,

thus giving little or no indication that many of the attempts at reform have failed. This is hardly surprising, since they usually fail to explain in any detail how or why the injustices came into being in the first place. As one critic has pointed out, the texts report that blacks fought in the Revolutionary War but not that the Framers of the Constitution, with the three-fifths compromise, among other provisions, made slavery a part of the political system. Furthermore, only the most sophisticated of the inquiry books report any of the "struggles to achieve full rights" from the point of view of the strugglers.

The current version of the history of racial minorities in 11 America represents the compromise that the publishers have made among the conflicting demands of a variety of pressure groups, inside and outside the school systems. The compromise is an unhappy one, and it is bound to change in the future, if only because its inconsistencies are so obvious. However, it is interesting to ask at this point what a truly "multiracial, multicultural" history text would look like. The question is an academic one, admittedly, but there are certain organizations, such as the Council on Interracial Books for Children, that do argue it, in an academic way, and that do give certain answers through their criticisms of current texts. To look at the council's very detailed and sophisticated criticism of the texts is to see that somewhere—far from where the texts are now—there is a real dilemma in the very notion of a "multiracial, multicultural" history. Let us take an example. In its list of twenty-six "stereotypes, distortions and omissions" that the history texts generally make about "native Americans," the council points to a passage from one of the more näive of the texts—*America: Its People and Values*, by Leonard C. Wood, Ralph H. Gabriel, and Edward L. Biller. The passage reads:

> A friendly Indian named Squanto helped the colonists. He showed them how to plant corn and how to live on the edge of the wilderness. A soldier, Captain Miles Standish, taught the Pilgrims how to defend themselves against unfriendly Indians.

The council's objection to this passage is that it is Eurocentric to characterize native Americans as either "friendly" or "unfriendly." Squanto was actually assisting invaders, whereas the "unfriendly" Indians were defending their communities. "All nations define a 'patriot' as one whose allegiance is toward his or her own people," the council report continues. "Consequently, true Native American heroes are those who fought to preserve and protect their people's freedom and land."

12   The implications of that objection are far-reaching. To begin with, if the texts were really to consider American history from the perspective of the American Indians, they would have to conclude that the continent had passed through almost five hundred years of unmitigated disaster, beginning with the epidemics spread by the Europeans and continuing on most fronts today. Then, if the texts were really to consider the Indian point of view, they could not simply say this but would have to take the position of Squanto—if not that of his more patriotic fellows—and categorize Miles Standish as friendly or unfriendly. And ditto for the next four hundred years—while making sure, of course, to portray the diverse views of all the Indian nations, and their diverse relations with the white settlers. When you add to this, as the council would, the Chicano, Asian-American, African-American, Puerto Rican, and women's perspectives on events, American history becomes unbelievably complicated— as does the whole issue of what constitutes balance and fairness. But the inclusion of other perspectives is crucial to a multiracial or multiethnic history. Add to that the notion "multicultural" and there is yet another level of complexity involved, for culture, of course, is not the same as race, and (to raise a problem that neither the text writers nor their critics seem to have considered) some of the greatest cultural differences in the United States lie between Anglo-Saxon Protestant males. Conceivably, the publishers could make a book that would include all these perspectives—or, more realistically, they could produce different texts for the different sections of society. But in either case the message of the texts would be that Americans have no common history, no common culture, and no common values, and that membership in a racial or cultural group constitutes the most fundamental experience of each individual. The message would be that the center cannot, and should not, hold.

13   The logical extreme of the "multiracial, multicultural" position is worth considering, if only because it clarifies the tra-

ditional ideology of the texts. At least since the eighteen-nineties, the school histories have focussed more or less narrowly on the development of the nation-state. To the extent that they dealt with social history, they have assumed a fairly homogeneous society, in which all differences could be justly compromised to suit all parties. In practice, this has meant taking the position of the ruling groups—whoever they happened to be at any given time—and suppressing the views of others. Since the nineteen-thirties, text writers have been lecturing children on the need for tolerance and respect for differences, but they have at the same time continued to minimize social conflicts and emphasize the similarities between Americans. The conflicts of the ninteen-sixties jolted only a small percentage of the texts out of this approach. The inquiry books, for extremely literate—and thus largely white, upper-middle-class—children, present cultural diversity and social conflict. The mass-market texts, for the less literate, picture people with "foreign-sounding" names and different-colored skin, but the message remains the traditional one: Americans are all alike, no matter what their color or their background.

Content

1. What changes have occurred in the presentation of Hispanic peoples in American history textbooks during the nineteenth and twentieth centuries (see ¶s 1–5, especially ¶ 2)? Why does FitzGerald treat them in such detail? Does she explain why the earlier textbook writers treated the Spanish so harshly?

2. How, in FitzGerald's opinion, have history textbooks since the 1960s attempted to show the United States as a "multiracial, multicultural society" (¶s 6–9)? What problems does she say this has presented (see ¶ 6 and those following)?

3. Why do textbooks intended for a wide audience ("mass-market texts") "rarely show a non-white person who is brutalized, dirty, or even poor" (¶ 9)?

4. Why, according to FitzGerald, do textbook publishers "mention the struggles of non-white peoples . . . but refrain from mentioning what these groups are struggling against (¶ 10)? Does she identify exceptions to this policy?

5. FitzGerald appears to be measuring the textbooks she discusses

against an ideal standard of how such books should treat ethnic minorities. What is her standard? How well does she think "mass market" textbooks meet her criteria? Do "inquiry books" fare any better?

Strategies/Structures

1. Typical of an inductive argument, FitzGerald presents new evidence in nearly every paragraph. Does the evidence become progressively more convincing as it becomes more and more abundant? Why or why not?

2. FitzGerald summarizes her main point in the last sentence. Does all the evidence she presents lead up to this point? By what place in this essay is her thesis apparent?

3. FitzGerald points out numerous instances of the presentation of certain kinds of evidence and the withholding of other evidence to convey a particular impression of a given ethnic minority at a particular time period of textbook publication. Does she appear to be using the same techniques in her representation of the history books she discusses? Explain your answer.

Language

1. Be sure you know the meaning of vitriolic (¶ 2), Hispanophobia (2—if you can't find the blend, try *Hispano* and *phobia*), bowdlerization (3), orthodoxy (6), rear-guard action (6), academic question (11).

2. Identify some of the words and phrases that FitzGerald uses to slant her analysis in favor of her argument. Would you characterize her tone throughout as objective? Or does this language contribute to another, more critical tone? If so, show where this tone is present.

For Writing

1. Examine an American history textbook that you have used, either in high school or college (or borrow a copy of such a book commonly used in your school) to determine its presentation of Hispanics, blacks, American Indians, some other ethnic minority; or women. Write a paper in which you identify and explain your findings, as FitzGerald has done (you may compare your evidence with hers, if you wish). Among the dimensions you might consider are the following:

   a. Does it provide photographs of members of this group? If so, of what people—and what are they doing in the photographs (working—at what; playing—at what)? Are they smiling? What other illustrations does it provide concerning this group?

b. Does the book identify the group's contributions to American culture? If so, what are they?
c. Does the book specify what, if any, difficulties this group, or portions of it, had in settling, surviving, or otherwise becoming part of American culture?
d. From whose point of view is this information presented? That of the dominant white majority? The minority? Or some other perspective?

2. Write an essay in which, on the basis of evidence from two history textbooks published a decade or more apart, you attack or defend the thesis, "The facts of history do not change, only the interpretations."

ANDREW HACKER

Hacker (b. 1929) was educated at Amherst, Oxford, and Princeton, and taught government at Cornell until 1971, when he became a professor of government at Queens College of the City University of New York. Hacker is a contributor to many periodicals, including *The Atlantic, Harper's, New York Review of Books,* and *The New York Times Magazine.* He has also written a number of books on politics and government, among them *Political Theory: Philosophy, Ideology, Science* (1961), *Congressional Districting* (1963), *The End of the American Era* (1970), and *The New Yorkers* (1975). In the essay below, Hacker blames the failure of the Equal Rights Amendment on its presumed beneficiaries—women. Although the thesis of this essay is stated in the first paragraph, to make his point Hacker inductively assembles evidence through an overview of the changing situation of women between 1972 and 1980.

"E.R.A.——R.I.P."

T he Equal Rights Amendment expired in the final stretch, three states short of the finish line. And before the postmortems begin, it would be well to scotch one myth. The Equal

Rights Amendment was never a battle between the sexes, with men having the final say. Ronald Reagan notwithstanding, few men cared much either way. On the contrary, a crucial reason for the ERA's defeat was opposition from women.

2   Legislators who voted against it could point to their negative mail, which came mainly from women. For them that was excuse enough. Even the polls were deceptive, for they failed to show the depth of feeling on the against side. It would be well to understand why so many women ended up opposing a measure intended for their benefit.

3   As originally proposed, the Equal Rights Amendment seemed altogether innocuous. Its two dozen words ("Equality of rights under the law shall not be denied or abridged by the United States or by any state on account of sex") simply summarized a principle accepted by the courts and embodied in legislation. The amendment cleared Congress in March of 1972, with only eight dissents in the Senate and 24 in the House. Before the year was over, no fewer than 22 state legislatures had ratified the ERA. The 16 others needed for its adoption were expected to follow suit in 1973.

4   As everyone now knows, however, it did not turn out that way. Over the ensuing five years, only 13 more states added their approval, with Indiana the last, in 1977. Not only that, five of the ratifying states moved to rescind their passage—an unusual step now facing legal challenge.

5   And if only five went on record as changing their minds, soundings show that at least as many more would not repeat their ratifications were they to vote today.

6   In 1978 an embarrassed Congress—this time with 225 dissenting votes—gave the amendment 39 more months to muster three more states. But when, this June, Illinois' moderately liberal legislature failed to act favorably, it became clear that the amendment had reached the end of its road. (Anyone inclined to believe that ratification is still possible is invited to identify three candidates for conversion among the 15 holdouts: Alabama, Arkansas, Arizona, Florida, Georgia, Illinois, Louisiana, Mississippi, Missouri, Nevada, North Carolina, Oklahoma, South Carolina, Utah, and Virginia.) Principle apart, the Republicans' repudiation of the ERA can be seen as a refusal to align with a lost cause.

What happened is that early in its course, the ERA lost its   7
innocent status. In fact, this change occurred during the nine
months after the amendment had left Congress and while it was
winning quick approval from half the necessary states. Stirred
by this success, women who had worked for the ERA began to
talk as if, quite literally, it signaled a new era. What began as a
request for equal rights merged into the more militant cause of
women's liberation. Guarantees purposely left vague in the
wording of the amendment were now being discussed in concrete terms.

One such guarantee was that women, no less than men,   8
should be free to choose what to do with whatever might happen
to grow within their bodies. Needless to say, such an interpretation had serious implications. It was not as if women were
demanding the right to decide about having their adenoids removed. In addition, much began to be said about what property
rights women should be able to claim, either at the breakup of
a marriage or even prior to the wedding. Here the hidden message seemed to be that divorce was an eventuality every woman
could expect.

There was also the whole "Ms." phenomenon, which was   9
part of a more generalized attack on all the disabilities inhering
in the double standard. (And at the same time it was easy to
imply that the title "Mrs." showed passive acquiescence to a
subordinate condition.) Thus the passage of the ERA would be
a sign that women were gaining not only legal rights but the
power and the sanction to lead lives of their own choosing. Nor
could its supporters imagine how any rational woman could
object to these goals.

Still, the main impetus for the amendment arose from ine-   10
quities in employment—in particular, the obstacles women encountered in entering certain fields, obtaining equal pay, and
getting merited promotions. At its simplest, equal rights would
mean that fire departments could not refuse to consider a certain
application because of the candidate's sex.

But those in the vanguard of the ERA appeared also to be   11
saying that for real emancipation to come about, women must
begin filling the positions hitherto held by men. While there
were polite murmurings about how other avenues were acceptable, the word was that you had better get out of the house

and into something serious. Nor was it legitimate to settle for being a secretary or stewardess; little girls were reprimanded for playing at being nurses.

12   Given this expanded outlook, the last letter in the ERA came to stand for more than the amendment. It signified an atmosphere and an attitude that could cut across class lines. Women could be miners or state troopers as well as executives or attorneys. To the aim of equality was jointed the spirit of independence.

13   It was at this point that Phyllis Schlafly gave form to a following that in fact was waiting for her. It is too easy to say that those for whom she spoke misunderstood the amendment. Allusions to unisex toilets and frontline combat duty were good for getting attention, but they weren't the central concern. The women who responded to Schlafly were under no illusions about the impetus for the ERA

14   More than that, they were aware of how they would be affected, and, at the same time, were hesitant to air their underlying anxieties, at least in a public forum. So instead they spoke as if their chief concern were to preserve the family. But in so doing they were talking about themselves. For the women who felt most threatened by the ERA were housewives—and their number should not be underestimated even in 1980.

15   There has been a great deal of talk about how housewives are a disappearing species. Betty Friedan, for example, likes to cite the statistic that among American households only 17 percent remain with a father as the wage earner, the mother a full-time homemaker, and one or more resident children. In fact, the figures tell a different story.

16   But before examining them, it would be well to realize that this country still has many millions of women for whom caring for a home has been their lifetime calling. Moreover, most of them remember when the vocation of housewife was an honored estate. Some are old enough to recall when on radio or television a woman was asked her occupation, if she answered "housewife" the rafters rang with applause. Now, when asked what they do, they find themselves saying "just a housewife" in apologetic tones. And from this grows an edge of anger over being made to feel outmoded.

Quite clearly, there are many women who feel that with a   17
fair chance they will end up among the winners. Other women,
however, would rather not be tested. But the issue is not whether
they are afraid of competing with men alone, as the working
world already contains many ambitious women. Nor should it
be assumed that all younger women are committed to careers.
Students at my college tell me that many women in high school
set having a home and a husband as their overriding aim. Even
today most marriages take place before the bride is 22, and
children are born soon thereafter.

What of reports that more married women are employed   18
than ever before, and thus take a stake in a better deal at work?
Here it would be well to see just what the figures say. To begin
with, the Labor Department regards as having a job anyone who
works ("for pay or profit") one hour or more during a given
week. Under this generous interpretation, it is not surprising
that so many women are classed as being in the labor force. The
school crossing guard who goes on duty for 10 hours a week
gets the same statistical weight as an advertising executive who
puts in a 10-hour day.

The Census Bureau also has tables showing that of all mar-   19
ried women currently living with their husbands, fewer than a
third have full-time jobs. Among mothers with children under
6, three-quarters do not work at all or take only part-time jobs.
And with wives whose children are all over 18, two-thirds either
have not chosen employment or have limited themselves to part-
time work. In fact, the majority of married women choose not
to go to work once their children have left home.

Thus, in the typical two-income marriage, the wife con-   20
stributes less than 22 percent of the family's total earnings, a
fraction owing less to discrimination than to her supplemental
schedule. Even for those who can say that they are more than
"just a housewife," their obligations at home still take priority.
At every class level the full-time working wife remains relatively
rare. Cases where one spouse is an urban planner and the other
a financial analyst, with their 2-year old at a super day-care
center, are not yet common enough to weight the statistical
columns.

One of the more compelling arguments for the ERA ad-   21

dressed itself to women who must support themselves because of divorce or desertion or early widowhood. When circumstances require women to make it on their own, they discover just how limited their rights and opportunities are. Even now no one is entirely sure what claims a wife can make after 20 years of marriage. While alimony is less and less granted to a spouse, it has yet to be settled whether a husband must pay the bills while his former wife tries to equip herself for a gainful occupation. As indicated earlier, these are rights any number of women may someday wish to assert.

22   Yet therein lies the rub. It is not that women who have stayed at home see themselves as second-class creatures deserving a lesser set of rights. Rather they look on themselves as having entered into a complementary contract. In return for caring for a husband and raising their children, what the wife expects in return is love and companionship, of course, but also a status of some honor and a measure of protection. To put the matter even more bluntly, she does not want to be divorced; nor does she even wish to contemplate how she would survive were that situation ever to come about. This may be a foolish attitude, but to label it as such is not the way to win converts to the ERA.

23   The typical wife is shrewd enough to realize that the more women assert their rights, the more controls loosen over men. Until recently, men acquiesced to the moral and cultural pressures that kept marriages intact. Men may have stayed married out of duty; but at least they stayed. It is in this sense that the ERA atmosphere threatens family life. Moral obligations that once bound partners cannot be provisos and demands.

24   Germaine Greer once offered a two-word solution to a wife unhappy with her husband: "Leave him." Yet it would be well to acknowledge that as the middle years approach there are not that many marriages where the woman wants to pack her bags. Her situation may seem pathetic, especially if he wants out and she still wants to keep him. Or so it may appear to liberated women on whom years have yet to take a toll. At this point there is still one unfairness even the ERA will not remedy: In our society women depreciate faster than men. Divorce can spell

opportunities for a husband. For a wife it often means the end of the road she chose.

At this point we come to a phase of the ERA no one really wants to discuss. The divorce rate is not only rising, but is now hitting marriages once believed immune. Increasingly husbands in their 40s are deciding they want another time around and are seeking this rejuvenation with a younger second wife. 25

Of course, this situation is not entirely new. In the past, however, the other woman tended to be a manicurist or a chorus girl, a plot line more for the movies than for actual life. Now husbands are increasingly apt to have as colleagues high-powered younger women who understand their professional problems in ways a wife never can. These affinities can emerge as easily in a patrol car as in planning a marketing campaign. Shared work, particularly under pressure, has aphrodisiac effects. 26

For wives who mainly stay at home, the ERA stands for new relationships at work that can lead to losing a husband. Even if the wife at home has never seen the statistics, she knows that if she finds herself divorced at the age of 40, her own chances for remarriage are less than 1 in 3. This realization is hardly one to align her with women who seem ready to give their husbands a second stab at life. It is difficult to support an amendment that consigns you to the shelf. 27

With Phyllis Schafly always in the limelight, many people concluded that opposition to the ERA was a one-woman operation. In fact, the rank and file were always there, but their support never took the form of a coherent movement. Women anxious about the ERA were not the sort to go on marches or bare their souls in public. Yet in countless informal ways they got their feelings across: in coffee hours, at country clubs, even over dinner at home. This was especially apparent at July's [1980] Republican convention, where close to a quarter of the delegates were women. 28

When a party aspiring to the presidency takes a stand against an amendment thought to have strong support, it should not be dismissed as an impulsive act. It could just be that the Republicans have been studying the political statistics over the 29 past few years. They know that the people who count in politics are those who actually go to the polls. And as it turns out, among married women, close to two-thirds vote in most elections, whereas fewer than half of single women do.

30   In addition, the median age of the American electorate is fast approaching 50. Of persons between the ages of 45 and 64, about 60 percent usually vote, while for those from 25 to 34 the figure is less than 40 percent. Ronald Reagan may hope to reap rewards by showing that he cares about citizens most likely to cast ballots.

31   The ERA was definitely a "woman's issue," with women dominating both sides of the struggle. If the amendment's supporters erred, it was in ignoring the sensibilities of women not avid for careers or for whom that option appears to come too late. Women opposed the ERA because it jeopardized a way of life they had entered in good faith. And their legislators listened.

Content

1. According to Hacker, why did the passage of the ERA initially seem assured (¶ 3)?

2. What does Hacker mean by "early in its course, the ERA lost its innocent status" (¶ 7)? Why should a merger with "the more militant cause of women's liberation" have tainted this status?

3. Is Hacker himself for or against the ERA? Cite some of the evidence that enables you to tell. At what point in the essay, if at all, are you certain of his stance?

4. Who does Hacker claim feel most threatened by the ERA (¶ 14)? What does Hacker think of the views of the women who oppose ERA?

5. Does Hacker make any assumptions about men's attitudes toward the ERA? If so, what are they? Or does he assume that men share the views of women toward the ERA—pro and con? If so, is this assumption justified?

Strategies/Structures

1. Show how Hacker uses statistics and interprets them to make his point (¶s 15–20, 27). Could these be interpreted in other ways less supportive of Hacker's argument? Could different statistics or other types of evidence be used to dispute his point?

2. Hacker's intended audience was originally the readers of *Harper's*, a group fairly well educated, liberal, above college age, and moderately affluent. Are such people likely to be convinced by his argument? Would any other types of readers be likely to be convinced by his argument? If so, specify some of their major characteristics. If not, explain why not.

Language

1. Hacker wrote this essay in 1980, two years before the time limit to extend ratification of the ERA was up. Why, at that time, should he have written of the ERA in the past tense instead of the present?

2. In arguing a debatable and emotional issue, is it a desirable strategy to do as Hacker does and maintain an objective tone? Are there any places where Hacker's tone is less than objective? If so, where do they occur? What is his tone there? Does it reinforce his argument?

For Writing

1. Write an essay in which you attack or defend the thesis "The ERA deserved to die." In presenting your argument, be sure that you acknowledge and counter the reasons of your potential opponents.

2. Write an essay in which you defend a woman's right to be a housewife, or a man's right to be a househusband. If you would allow part of one group—say mothers or fathers of preschool children, but not the entire group—this right, explain why you are restricting your defense to some people and not others.

Strategies for Writing— Appealing to Reason: Deductive and Inductive Arguments

1. Do I want to convince my audience of the truth of a particular matter? Do I want essentially to raise their consciousness of an issue? Do I want to promote a belief or refute a theory? Or do I want to move my readers to action? If action, what kind? To change their minds, attitudes or behavior? To right a wrong, or alter a situation?

2. At the outset, do I expect my audience to agree with my ideas? To be neutral about the issues at hand? Or to be opposed to my views? Can I build into my essay responses to my readers' anticipated reactions, such as rebuttals to their possible objections? Do I know enough about my subject to be able to do this?

3. What is my strongest (and presumably most controversial) point, and where should I put it? At the beginning, if my audience agrees with my views? At the end, after a gradual build-up, for an antagonistic audience? How much development (and consequent emphasis) should each point have? Will a deductive or inductive format (see pp. 338–39) best express my thesis?

4. What will be my best sources of evidence? My own experience? The experiences of people I know? Common sense or common knowledge? Opinion from experts in a relevant field? Scientific evidence? Historic records? Economic, anthropological, or statistical data?

5. What tone will best reinforce my evidence? Will my audience also find this tone appealing? Convincing? Would an appropriate tone be sincere? Straightforward? Objective? Reassuring? Confident? Placating? What language can I use to most appropriately convey this tone?

Additional Topics for Writing

Write a logical, clearly reasoned, well-supported argument appropriate in organization, language, and tone to the subject and appealing to your designated audience.

1. Even (or especially) with today's rates of unemployment and underemployment, a college education is still (or is not) worth the effort.
2. Smoking is (is not) hazardous to your health.
3. Economic recovery is (is not) more important to our country than conservation and preservation of our country's resources.

4. The Social Security system should (should not) be preserved at all costs.
5. Everyone should (should not) be entitled to comprehensive medical care (supply one: from the cradle to the grave; in early childhood; while a student; in old age).
6. Drunk drivers should (should not) be jailed, even for a first offense.
7. Auto safety belts should (should not) be mandatory.
8. Companies manufacturing products that may affect consumers' health or safety (such as food, drugs, liquor, automobiles, pesticides) should (should not) have consumer representatives on their boards of directors.
9. The civil rights, women's liberation, gay liberation, or some comparable movement has (has not) accomplished major and long-lasting benefits for the group it represents.
10. Despite some advances in recent years, women (or members of a particular minority) are (are not) economically handicapped and should (should not) be offered extra help to enable them to gain equality.
11. Intercollegiate athletic teams that are big business should (should not) hire their players; intercollegiate athletics should (should not) have professional status.
12. Our generation has correctly (incorrectly) been labeled as the "me" generation, selfish and self-centered.

11 Appealing to Emotion and Ethics

◄━━━━━━━━━━━━━━━━━━━━━━━━►

The essence of an emotional appeal is passion. You write from passion, and you expect your readers to respond with equal fervor. "I have a dream." "The only thing we have to fear is fear itself." "We have nothing to offer but blood, sweat, and tears." "The West wasn't won with a loaded gun!" "We shall overcome."

You can't incite your readers, either to agree with you or to take action on behalf of the cause you favor, by simply bleeding all over the page. The process of writing and rewriting and revising again (see pp. 431–45) will act to cool your red-hot emotion, and will enable you to modulate in subsequent drafts what you might have written the first time just to get out of your system. "Hell, no! We won't go!" As the essays in this section and elsewhere reveal, writers who appeal most effectively to their readers' emotions themselves exercise considerable control over the organization and examples they use to make their points.

They also keep particularly tight rein over the tone and connotations of their language, crucial in an emotional appeal. Tone, the prevailing mood of the essay, like a tone of voice conveys your attitude toward your subject, and toward the evidence you present in support of your point. In "Marrakech," George Orwell protests the indifference that white colonials have for the humanity of the brown- and black-skinned people they govern and exploit: "People with brown skins are next door to invisible." Yet his tone is measured, reasonable, matter-of-fact, almost objective:

> Even [their] graves themselves soon fade back into the soil. Sometimes, out for a walk, as you break your way through the prickly pear, you notice that it is rather bumpy underfoot, and only a certain regularity in the bumps tells you that you are walking over skeletons.

There is nothing grisly, nothing ghoulish, nothing macabre in this description: no death's heads or bones protruding through the dirt. Only Orwell's ironic questions, asking what his white readers have never thought to ask, "Are they really the same flesh as yourself? Do they even have names?"

If you are appealing to your readers' emotions through irony, the tone of your words, their music, is likely to be at variance with their overt message—and to intentionally undermine it. Thus the narrator of Swift's "A Modest Proposal" can, with an impassive face, advocate that year-old children of the poor Irish peasants be sold for "a most delicious, nourishing, and wholesome food, whether stewed, roasted, baked, or broiled; and," in an additional inhumane observation, "I make no doubt that it will equally serve in a fricassee or a ragout."

The connotations, overtones of the language, are equally significant in emotional appeals, as they subtly (or not so subtly) reinforce the overt, literal meanings of the words. Swift's narrator always calls the children *it*, with an impersonal connotation, and never employs the humanizing terms of *he, she,* or *baby*. The *it* emphasizes the animalistic connotations of the narrator's references to a newborn as "a child just dropped from its dam," further dehumanizing both mother and child.

Language, tone, and message often combine to present an *ethical appeal*—a way of impressing your readers that you as the author (and perhaps as a character in your own essay) are a knowledgeable person of good moral character, good will, and good sense. Consequently, you are a person of integrity, and to be believed as a credible, reasonable advocate of the position you take in your essay. In "None of This Is Fair," Richard Rodriguez explains that as a Mexican-American he benefited considerably from Affirmative Action programs to gain financial aid in college, and to get highly competitive job offers afterward. Having thus established his fitness to discuss the subject, Rodriguez agrees with the critics of Affirmative Action, that "None of this is fair." His actions reinforce his words. Not only does he decide to reject all the job offers obtained by this "unfair" means; he turns his attention, at the conclusion, to the "seriously disadvantaged," irrespective of color, the poor on whom he wishes us all to focus our best efforts.

The possibility always exists, of course, that a charlatan could so cleverly pass himself off as ethical that people would fall for his lies and his line. Max Shulman's "Love Is a Fallacy" explores this possibility in the character of the unethical Dobie Gillis, a law student trying to win the fair and thoroughly illogical Polly Espy by teaching her to think logically and thereby transforming her into a mate fit to match his "giant intellect." Fortunately, Dobie blows his cover in the first line, "Cool was I and logical." He is neither, as we learn in this spoof on logical fallacies, where an emotional appeal ultimately prevails.

Appeals to emotion and ethics are often intertwined. Such appeals are everywhere, for example, in the connotations of descriptions and definitions. Furthermore, if your readers like and trust you they're more likely to believe what you say, and to be moved to agree with your point of view. The evidence in a scientific report, however strong in itself, is buttressed by the credibility of the researcher. The sense of realism, the truth of a narrative, is enhanced by the credibility of the narrator; we believe Thurber when he says he couldn't see cells under a microscope and flunked botany; we believe that E.B. White spent a memorable week at a lake in Maine with his son, and we accept and respect what he learned there.

Hearts compel agreement where minds hesitate. Don't hesitate to make ethical use of this understanding.

◄───►

GEORGE ORWELL

In "Marrakech," written in 1939, as in most of his other
writings, Orwell exemplifies the principles he set forth in
"Why I Write": "Every line of serious work that I have written
since 1936 has been written, directly or indirectly, against total-
itarianism. . . . My starting point is always a feeling of parti-
sanship, a sense of injustice. . . . I write because there is some
lie that I want to expose, some fact to which I want to draw
attention, and my initial concern is to get a hearing." Orwell's
profound concern for the condition of the poor is manifested in
his illustrations that help readers who are presumably not poor
to see people and conditions of living and working that were
previously invisible: the bumps in the desert land that are skeletons of people too poor to be buried with dignity; the starving
worker begging food in the zoo; old women silently carrying
heavier loads than pack animals. These visual images combine
to present a silent but eloquent plea not only for attention but
for social change. (A biographical sketch of Orwell appears on
page 47.)

Marrakech

As the corpse went past the flies left the restaurant table in   1
a cloud and rushed after it, but they came back a few
minutes later.

The little crowd of mourners—all men and boys, no   2
women—threaded their way across the market-place between
the piles of pomegranates and the taxis and the camels, wailing
a short chant over and over again. What really appeals to the
flies is that the corpses here are never put into coffins, they are
merely wrapped in a piece of rag and carried on a rough wooden
bier on the shoulders of four friends. When the friends get to
the burying-ground they hack an oblong hole a foot or two deep,

dump the body in it and fling over it a little of the dried-up, lumpy earth, which is like broken brick. No gravestone, no name, no identifying mark of any kind. The burying-ground is merely a huge waste of hummocky earth, like a derelict building-lot. After a month or two no one can even be certain where his own relatives are buried.

3   When you walk through a town like this—two hundred thousand inhabitants, of whom at least twenty thousand own literally nothing except the rags they stand up in—when you see how the people live, and still more how easily they die, it is always difficult to believe that you are walking among human beings. All colonial empires are in reality founded upon that fact. The people have brown faces—besides, there are so many of them! Are they really the same flesh as yourself? Do they even have names? Or are they merely a kind of undifferentiated brown stuff, about as individual as bees or coral insects? They rise out of the earth, they sweat and starve for a few years, and then they sink back into the nameless mounds of the graveyard and nobody notices that they are gone. And even the graves themselves soon fade back into the soil. Sometimes, out for a walk, as you break your way through the prickly pear, you notice that it is rather bumpy underfoot, and only a certain regularity in the bumps tells you that you are walking over skeletons.

4   I was feeding one of the gazelles in the public gardens.

5   Gazelles are almost the only animals that look good to eat when they are still alive, in fact, one can hardly look at their hindquarters without thinking of mint sauce. The gazelle I was feeding seemed to know that this thought was in my mind, for though it took the piece of bread I was holding out it obviously did not like me. It nibbled rapidly at the bread, then lowered its head and tried to butt me, then took another nibble and then butted again. Probably its idea was that if it could drive me away the bread would somehow remain hanging in mid-air.

6   An Arab navvy working on the path nearby lowered his heavy hoe and sidled towards us. He looked from the gazelle to the bread and from the bread to the gazelle, with a sort of quiet amazement, as though he had never seen anything quite

like this before. Finally he said shyly in French:

"*I could eat some of that bread.*"   7

I tore off a piece and he stowed it gratefully in some secret place under his rags. This man is an employee of the Municipality.

When you go through the Jewish quarters you gather some   8 idea of what the medieval ghettoes were probably like. Under their Moorish rulers the Jews were only allowed to own land in certain restricted areas, and after centuries of this kind of treatment they have ceased to bother about overcrowding. Many of the streets are a good deal less than six feet wide, the houses are completely windowless, and sore-eyed children cluster everywhere in unbelievable numbers, like clouds of flies. Down the centre of the street there is generally running a little river of urine.

In the bazaar huge families of Jews, all dressed in the long   9 black robe and little black skull-cap, are working in dark fly-infested booths that look like caves. A carpenter sits cross-legged at a prehistoric lathe, turning chair-legs at lightning speed. He works the lathe with a bow in his right hand and guides the chisel with his left foot, and thanks to a lifetime of sitting in this position his left leg is warped out of shape. At his side his grandson, aged six, is already starting on the simpler parts of the job.

I was just passing the coppersmiths' booths when some-   10 body noticed that I was lighting a cigarette. Instantly, from the dark holes all round, there was a frenzied rush of Jews, many of them old grandfathers with flowing grey beards, all clamouring for a cigarette. Even a blind man somewhere at the back of one of the booths heard a rumour of cigarettes and came crawling out, groping in the air with his hand. In about a minute I had used up the whole packet. None of these people, I suppose, works less than twelve hours a day, and every one of them looks on a cigarette as a more or less impossible luxury.

As the Jews live in self-contained communities they follow   11 the same trades as the Arabs, except for agriculture. Fruitsellers, potters, silversmiths, blacksmiths, butchers, leatherworkers, tailors, water-carriers, beggars, porters—whichever way you look you see nothing but Jews. As a matter of fact there are thirteen thousand of them, all living in the space of a few acres. A good job Hitler isn't here. Perhaps he is on his way, however. You hear the usual dark rumours about the Jews, not only from the Arabs but from the poorer Europeans.

12   "Yes, *mon vieux*, they took my job away from me and gave it to a Jew. The Jews! They're the real rulers of this country, you know. They've got all the money. They control the banks, finance—everything."

13   "But," I said, "isn't it a fact that the average Jew is a labourer working for about a penny an hour?"

14   "Ah, that's only for show! They're all moneylenders really. They're cunning, the Jews."

15   In just the same way, a couple of hundred years ago, poor old women used to be burned for witchcraft when they could not even work enough magic to get themselves a square meal.

16   All people who work with their hands are partly invisible, and the more important the work they do, the less visible they are. Still, a white skin is always fairly conspicuous. In northern Europe, when you see a labourer ploughing a field, you probably give him a second glance. In a hot country, anywhere south of Gibraltar or east of Suez, the chances are that you don't even see him. I have noticed this again and again. In a tropical landscape one's eye takes in everything except the human beings. It takes in the dried-up soil, the prickly pear, the palm-tree and the distant mountain, but it always misses the peasant hoeing at his patch. He is the same colour as the earth, and a great deal less interesting to look at.

     It is only because of this that the starved countries of Asia and Africa are accepted as tourist resorts. No one would think of running cheap trips to the Distressed Areas. But where the human beings have brown skins their poverty is simply not noticed. What does Morocco mean to a Frenchman? An orange-grove or a job in government service. Or to an Englishman? Camels, castles, palm-trees, Foreign Legionnaires, brass trays and bandits. One could probably live here for years without noticing that for nine-tenths of the people the reality of life is an endless, back-breaking struggle to wring a little food out of an eroded soil.

Most of Morocco is so desolate that no wild animal bigger 18 than a hare can live on it. Huge areas which were once covered with forest have turned into a treeless waste where the soil is exactly like broken-up brick. Nevertheless a good deal of it is cultivated, with frightful labour. Everything is done by hand. Long lines of women, bent double like inverted capital Ls, work their way slowly across the field, tearing up the prickly weeds with their hands, and the peasant gathering lucerne for fodder pulls it up stalk by stalk instead of reaping it, thus saving an inch or two on each stalk. The plough is a wretched wooden thing, so frail that one can easily carry it on one's shoulder, and fitted underneath with a rough iron spike which stirs the soil to a depth of about four inches. This is as much as the strength of the animals is equal to. It is usual to plough with a cow and a donkey yoked together. Two donkeys would not be quite strong enough, but on the other hand two cows would cost a little more to feed. The peasants possess no harrows, they merely plough the soil several times over in different directions, finally leaving it in rough furrows, after which the whole field has to be shaped with hoes into small oblong patches, to conserve water. Except for a day or two after the rare rainstorms there is never enough water. Along the edges of the fields channels are hacked out to a depth of thirty or forty feet to get at the tiny trickles which run through the subsoil.

Every afternoon a file of very old women passes down the 19 road outside my house, each carrying a load of firewood. All of them are mummified with age and the sun, and all of them are tiny. It seems to be generally the case in primitive communities that the women, when they get beyond a certain age, shrink to the size of children. One day a poor old creature who could not have been more than four feet tall crept past me under a vast load of wood. I stopped her and put a five-sou piece (a little more than a farthing) into her hand. She answered with a shrill wail, almost a scream, which was partly gratitude but mainly surprise. I suppose that from her point of view, by taking any notice of her, I seemed almost to be violating a law of nature.

She accepted her status as an old woman, that is to say as a beast of burden. When a family is travelling it is quite usual to see a father and a grown-up son riding ahead on donkeys, and an old woman following on foot, carrying the baggage.

20   But what is strange about these people is their invisibility. For several weeks, always at about the same time of day, the file of old women had hobbled past the house with their firewood, and though they had registered themselves on my eyeballs I cannot truly say that I had seen them. Firewood was passing—that was how I saw it. It was only that one day I happened to be walking behind them, and the curious up-and-down motion of a load of wood drew my attention to the human being underneath it. Then for the first time I noticed the poor old earth-coloured bodies, bodies reduced to bones and leathery skin, bent double under the crushing weight. Yet I suppose I had not been five minutes on Moroccan soil before I noticed the overloading of the donkeys and was infuriated by it. There is no question that the donkeys are damnably treated. The Moroccan donkey is hardly bigger than a St Bernard dog, it carries a load which in the British army would be considered too much for a fifteen-hands mule, and very often its pack-saddle is not taken off its back for weeks together. But what is peculiarly pitiful is that it is the most willing creature on earth, it follows its master like a dog and does not need either bridle or halter. After a dozen years of devoted work it suddenly drops dead, whereupon its master tips it into the ditch and the village dogs have torn its guts out before it is cold.

21   This kind of thing makes one's blood boil, whereas—on the whole—the plight of the human beings does not. I am not commenting, merely pointing to a fact. People with brown skins are next door to invisible. Anyone can be sorry for the donkey with its galled back, but it is generally owing to some kind of accident if one even notices the old woman under her load of sticks.

22   As the storks flew northward the Negroes were marching southward—a long, dusty column, infantry, screw-gun batteries

and then more infantry, four or five thousand men in all, winding up the road with a clumping of boots and a clatter of iron
wheels.

They were Senegalese, the blackest Negroes in Africa, so   23
black that sometimes it is difficult to see whereabouts on their
necks the hair begins. Their splendid bodies were hidden in
reach-me-down khaki uniforms, their feet squashed into boots
that looked like blocks of wood, and every tin hat seemed to be
a couple of sizes too small. It was very hot and the men had
marched a long way. They slumped under the weight of their
packs and the curiously sensitive black faces were glistening with
sweat.

As they went past a tall, very young Negro turned and   24
caught my eye. But the look he gave me was not in the least
the kind of look you might expect. Not hostile, not contemp-
tuous, not sullen, not even inquisitive. It was the shy, wide-
eyed Negro look, which actually is a look of profound respect.
I saw how it was. This wretched boy, who is a French citizen
and has therefore been dragged from the forest to scrub floors
and catch syphilis in garrison towns, actually has feelings of
reverence before a white skin. He has been taught that the white
race are his masters, and he still believes it.

But there is one thought which every white man (and in   25
this connection it doesn't matter twopence if he calls himself a
Socialist) thinks when he sees a black army marching past. "How
much longer can we go on kidding these people? How long
before they turn their guns in the other direction?"

It was curious, really. Every white man there has this   26
thought stowed somewhere or other in his mind. I had it, so
had the other onlookers, so had the officers on their sweating
chargers and the white NCOs marching in the ranks. It was a
kind of secret which we all knew and were too clever to tell;
only the Negroes didn't know it. And really it was almost like
watching a flock of cattle to see the long column, a mile or two
miles of armed men, flowing peacefully up the road, while the
great white birds drifted over them in the opposite direction,
glittering like scraps of paper.

Content

1. What is the thesis of Orwell's essay? Is it implicit or explicit?
2. Does Orwell's thesis apply to poor people anywhere, including the United States in the 1980s? Or is it restricted to people of a particular color, in a particular locale?
3. What ethical values does Orwell manifest in this essay? Does he expect his readers to share these values at the outset of the essay? Or is he trying to persuade his readers throughout the essay to believe as he does?
4. What do Orwell's illustrations reveal about the relation between poverty and powerlessness? Why does he conclude the essay with the illustration of the marching, respectful Senegalese soldiers and ask "How long before they turn their guns in the other direction?"

Strategies/Structures

1. Writers are often cautioned against writing one-sentence paragraphs. Yet Orwell begins "Marrakech" with such a paragraph. Why does he do so? With what effect?
2. Writers are also advised to begin their essays with opening paragraphs that are appealing or otherwise compelling enough to attract the readers' interest. Does Orwell follow this advice, by beginning his essay with an image of flies at an outdoor restaurant table "rushing after" a corpse that is being carried past the diners, an account of the funeral, and a description of the burial ground? How do these details reinforce the thesis of his essay?
3. Why has Orwell placed the illustrations in the order in which they appear? He develops some more fully than others; what is the relation between the amount of development and the order in which these examples appear? Why are most of these illustrations visual?
4. Identify, as specifically as you can, the audience for whom Orwell is writing. Does it include the poor? Jews? Blacks? People laboring with their hands? Or does it include only people oblivious to these groups and their individual members?

Language

1. What is Orwell's definition of poverty? How do his examples reinforce his overt statements about the condition of the poor?
2. Why does Orwell use an essentially matter-of-fact tone to make case for a subject that is obviously laden with emotion?

For Writing

1. Write an essay in which you expand on or disagree with Orwell's observation that "All people who work with their hands are partly invisible, and the more important the work they do, the less visible they are." To illustrate your point, use examples from your own experiences as a blue-collar worker or manual laborer or your knowledge of others with menial jobs.

   Or write an essay, using similar techniques, in which you discuss the invisibility or powerlessness of the poor. Your thesis should reflect your attitude toward their situation.

2. Make a case for or against an emotionally-charged subject about which you feel strongly (such as stiff penalties for drunken drivers, or the drafting of women), but conduct your argument, as Orwell does, in an unemotional tone. Use one or two extended examples, as Orwell does, to illustrate your point.

▶━━◀

JONATHAN SWIFT

Jonathan Swift (1667–1745), born and reared in Dublin by his English parents, obtained a degree from Trinity College, Dublin in 1685 only by "special grace." In England, actively involved in literature and English politics, Swift's support of the Tory party was ironically rewarded in 1713 with an appointment he detested, as Dean of St. Patrick's Cathedral in Dublin. Although he regarded Dublin as "exile," he remained there the rest of his life, beloved by the Irish, whose part he took in opposition to the English government. Swift composed various memorable satires in verse and prose, including the *Battle of the Books* (1704) and the perenially popular classic, *Gulliver's Travels* (1726). The latter begins with a good natured satire on religion and politics, proceeds to a modulated attack on the foibles of scientific invention, and concludes with a savage indictment of a mankind lacking in reason, ethics, and virtue.

Swift wrote "A Modest Proposal" with his characteristically "savage indignation" in the summer of 1729, after three years of drought and crop failure had forced over 35,000 peasants to leave their homes and wander the countryside looking for work, food, and shelter for their starving families. The absentee owners of much of the land, living in England to avoid taxes and church fees, remained insensitive to their tenants' problems. This essay, issued in Dublin as a pamphlet, was intended to reach an English audience as well as Irish readers who could act to alleviate the suffering of the people depicted. The victims themselves, largely illiterate, would probably have been unaware of this forceful plea on their behalf.

A Modest Proposal

1   I t is a melancholy object to those who walk through this great town or travel in the country, when they see the streets, the roads, and cabin doors, crowded with beggars of the female sex, followed by three, four, or six children, all in rags and importuning every passenger for an alms. These mothers, instead of being able to work for their honest livelihood, are forced to employ all their time in strolling to beg sustenance for their helpless infants: who as they grow up either turn thieves for want of work, or leave their dear native country to fight for the pretender in Spain, or sell themselves to the Barbadoes.

2   I think it is agreed by all parties that this prodigious number of children in the arms, or on the backs, or at the heels of their mothers, and frequently of their fathers, is in the present deplorable state of the kingdom a very great additional grievance; and, therefore, whoever could find out a fair, cheap, and easy method of making these children sound, useful members of the commonwealth, would deserve so well of the public as to have his statue set up for a preserver of the nation.

3   But my intention is very far from being confined to provide only for the children of professed beggars; it is of a much greater extent, and shall take in the whole number of infants at a certain age who are born of parents in effect as little able to support them as those who demand our charity in the streets.

4   As to my own part, having turned my thoughts for many years upon this important subject, and maturely weighed the

several schemes of our projectors, I have always found them grossly mistaken in their computation. It is true, a child just dropped from its dam may be supported by her milk for a solar year, with little other nourishment; at most not above the value of two shillings, which the mother may certainly get, or the value in scraps, by her lawful occupation of begging; and it is exactly at one year old that I propose to provide for them in such a manner as instead of being a charge upon their parents or the parish, or wanting food and raiment for the rest of their lives, they shall on the contrary contribute to the feeding, and partly to the clothing, of many thousands.

There is likewise another great advantage in my scheme, that it will prevent those voluntary abortions, and that horrid practice of women murdering their bastard children, alas! too frequent among us! sacrificing the poor innocent babes I doubt more to avoid the expense than the shame, which would move tears and pity in the most savage and inhuman breast.

The number of souls in this kingdom being usually reckoned one million and a half, of these I calculate there may be about two hundred thousand couple whose wives are breeders; from which number I subtract thirty thousand couple who are able to maintain their own children (although I apprehend there cannot be so many, under the present distress of the kingdom); but this being granted, there will remain an hundred and seventy thousand breeders. I again subtract fifty thousand for those women who miscarry, or whose children die by accident or disease within the year. There only remain an hundred and twenty thousand children of poor parents annually born. The question therefore is, how this number shall be reared and provided for? which, as I have already said, under the present situation of affairs, is utterly impossible by all the methods hitherto proposed. For we can neither employ them in handicraft or agriculture; we neither build houses (I mean in the country) nor cultivate land; they can very seldom pick up a livelihood by stealing, till they arrive at six years old, except where they are of towardly parts; although I confess they learn the rudiments much earlier; during which time they can, however, be properly looked upon only as probationers; as I have been informed by a principal gentleman in the country of Cavan, who protested to me that he never knew above one or two instances under the age of six, even in a part of the kingdom so renowned for the quickest proficiency in that art.

7   I am assured by our merchants, that a boy or a girl before twelve years old is no saleable commodity; and even when they come to this age they will not yield above three pounds, or three pounds and half a crown at most on the Exchange; which cannot turn to account either to the parents or kingdom, the charge of nutriment and rags having been at least four times that value.

8   I shall now therefore humbly propose my own thoughts, which I hope will not be liable to the least objection.

9   I have been assured by a very knowing American of my acquaintance in London, that a young healthy child well nursed is at a year old a most delicious, nourishing, and wholesome food, whether stewed, roasted, baked, or broiled; and I make no doubt that it will equally serve in a fricassee or a ragout.

10   I do therefore humbly offer it to public consideration that of the hundred and twenty thousand children already computed, twenty thousand may be reserved for breed, whereof only one-fourth part to be males; which is more than we allow to sheep, black cattle, or swine; and my reason is, that these children are seldom the fruits of marriage, a circumstance not much regarded by our savages; therefore one male will be sufficient to serve four females. That the remaining hundred thousand may, at a year old, be offered in sale to the persons of quality and fortune through the kingdom; always advising the mother to let them suck plentifully in the last month, so as to render them plump and fat for a good table. A child will make two dishes at an entertainment for friends; and when the family dines alone, the fore or hind quarter will make a reasonable dish, and seasoned with a little pepper or salt will be very good boiled on the fourth day, especially in winter.

11   I have reckoned upon a medium that a child just born will weigh twelve pounds, and in a solar year, if tolerably nursed, will increase to twenty-eight pounds.

12   I grant this food will be somewhat dear, and therefore very proper for landlords, who, as they have already devoured most of the parents, seem to have the best title to the children.

13   Infant's flesh will be in season throughout the year, but more plentiful in March, and a little before and after: for we are

told by a grave author, an eminent French physician, that fish being a prolific diet, there are more children born in Roman Catholic countries about nine months after Lent than at any other season; therefore, reckoning a year after Lent, the markets will be more glutted than usual, because the number of popish infants is at least three to one in this kingdom: and therefore it will have one other collateral advantage, by lessening the number of papists among us.

I have already computed the charge of nursing a beggar's 14 child (in which list I reckon all cottagers, laborers, and four-fifths of the farmers) to be about two shillings per annum, rags included; and I believe no gentleman would repine to give ten shillings for the carcass of a good fat child, which, as I have said, will make four dishes of excellent nutritive meat, when he has only some particular friend or his own family to dine with him. Thus the squire will learn to be a good landlord, and grow popular among the tenants; the mother will have eight shillings net profit, and be fit for work till she produces another child.

Those who are more thrifty (as I must confess the times 15 require) may flay the carcass; the skin of which artificially dressed will make admirable gloves for ladies, and summer boots for fine gentlemen.

As to our city of Dublin, shambles may be appointed for 16 this purpose in the most convenient parts of it, and butchers we may be assured will not be wanting: although I rather recommend buying the children alive, and dressing them hot from the knife as we do roasting pigs.

A very worthy person, a true lover of his country, and 17 whose virtues I highly esteem, was lately pleased in discoursing on this matter to offer a refinement upon my scheme. He said that many gentlemen of this kingdom, having of late destroyed their deer, he conceived that the want of venison might be well supplied by the bodies of young lads and maidens, not exceeding fourteen years of age nor under twelve; so great a number of both sexes in every country being now ready to starve for want of work and service; and these to be disposed of by their parents, if alive, or otherwise by their nearest relations. But with due deference to so excellent a friend and so deserving a patriot, I cannot be altogether in his sentiments; for as to the males, my

American acquaintance assured me from frequent experience that their flesh was generally tough and lean, like that of our schoolboys by continual exercise, and their taste disagreeable; and to fatten them would not answer the charge. Then as to the females, it would, I think, with humble submission be a loss to the public, because they soon would become breeders themselves: and besides, it is not improbable that some scrupulous people might be apt to censure such a practice (although indeed very unjustly), as a little bordering upon cruelty; which, I confess, has always been with me the strongest objection against any project, how well soever intended.

18   But in order to justify my friend, he confessed that this expedient was put into his head by the famous Psalmanazar, a native of the island Formosa, who came from thence to London about twenty years ago: and in conversation told my friend, that in his country when any young person happened to be put to death, the executioner sold the carcass to persons of quality as a prime dainty; and that in his time the body of a plump girl of fifteen, who was crucified for an attempt to poison the emperor, was sold to his imperial majesty's prime minister of state, and other great mandarins of the court, in joints from the gibbet, at four hundred crowns. Neither indeed can I deny, that if the same use were made of several plump young girls in this town, who without one single groat to their fortunes cannot stir abroad without a chair, and appear at the playhouse and assemblies in foreign fineries which they never will pay for, the kingdom would not be the worse.

19   Some persons of a desponding spirit are in great concern about that vast number of poor people, who are aged, diseased, or maimed, and I have been desired to employ my thoughts what course may be taken to ease the nation of so grievous an encumbrance. But I am not in the least pain upon that matter, because it is very well known that they are every day dying and rotting by cold and famine, and filth and vermin, as fast as can be reasonably expected. And as to the young laborers, they are now in as hopeful a condition: they cannot get work, and consequently pine away for want of nourishment, to a degree that if at any time they are accidentally hired to common labor, they have not strength to perform it; and thus the country and themselves are happily delivered from the evils to come.

I have too long digressed, and therefore shall return to my 20 subject. I think the advantages by the proposal which I have made are obvious and many, as well as of the highest importance.

For first, as I have already observed, it would greatly lessen 21 the number of papists, with whom we are yearly overrun, being the principal breeders of the nation as well as our most dangerous enemies; and who stay at home on purpose to deliver the kingdom to the Pretender, hoping to take their advantage by the absence of so many good Protestants, who have chosen rather to leave their country than stay at home and pay tithes against their conscience to an Episcopal curate.

Secondly, The poor tenants will have something valuable 22 of their own, which by law may be made liable to distress and help to pay their landlord's rent, their corn and cattle being already seized, and money a thing unknown.

Thirdly, Whereas the maintenance of an hundred thousand 23 children from two years old and upward, cannot be computed at less than ten shillings a piece per annum, the nation's stock will be thereby increased fifty thousand pounds per annum, beside the profit of a new dish introduced to the tables of all gentlemen of fortune in the kingdom who have any refinement in taste. And the money will circulate among ourselves, the goods being entirely of our own growth and manufacture.

Fourthly, The constant breeders beside the gain of eight 24 shillings sterling per annum by the sale of their children, will be rid of the charge of maintaining them after the first year.

Fifthly, This food would likewise bring great custom to taverns, where the vintners will certainly be so prudent as to procure the best receipts for dressing it to perfection, and consequently have their houses frequented by all the fine gentlemen, who justly value themselves upon their knowledge in good 25 eating; and a skillful cook who understands how to oblige his guests, will contrive to make it as expensive as they please.

Sixthly, This would be a great inducement to marriage, 26 which all wise nations have either encouraged by rewards or enforced by laws and penalties. It would increase the care and tenderness of mothers toward their children, when they were sure of a settlement for life to the poor babes, provided in some sort by the public, to their annual profit instead of expense. We should see an honest emulation among the married women, which of them would bring the fattest child to the market. Men would become as fond of their wives during the time of their pregnancy as they are now of their mares in foal, their cows in calf, their sows when they are ready to farrow; nor offer to beat or kick them (as is too frequent a practice) for fear of a miscarriage.

27   Many other advantages might be enumerated. For instance, the addition of some thousand carcasses in our exportation of barreled beef, the propagation of swine's flesh, and improvement in the art of making good bacon, so much wanted among us by the great destruction of pigs, too frequent at our table; which are no way comparable in taste or magnificence to a well-grown, fat, yearling child, which roasted whole will make a considerable figure at a lord mayor's feast or any other public entertainment. But this and many others I omit, being studious of brevity.

28   Supposing that one thousand families in this city would be constant customers for infants' flesh, besides others who might have it at merry-meetings, particularly at weddings and christenings, I compute that Dublin would take off annually about twenty thousand carcasses; and the rest of the kingdom (where probably they will be sold somewhat cheaper) the remaining eighty thousand.

29   I can think of no one objection that will possibly be raised against this proposal, unless it should be urged that the number of people will be thereby much lessened in the kingdom. This I freely own, and it was indeed one principal design in offering it to the world. I desire the reader will observe, that I calculate my remedy for this one individual kingdom of Ireland and for no other that ever was, is, or I think ever can be upon earth. Therefore let no man talk to me of other expedients; of taxing our absentees at five shillings a pound: of using neither clothes nor household furniture except what is of our own growth and manufacture: of utterly rejecting the materials and instruments that promote foreign luxury: of curing the expensiveness of pride, vanity, idleness, and gaming in our women: of introducing a vein of parsimony, prudence, and temperance: of learning to love our country, in the want of which we differ even from Laplanders and the inhabitants of Topinamboo: of quitting our animosities and factions, nor acting any longer like the Jews,

who were murdering one another at the very moment their city
was taken: of being a little cautious not to sell our country and
conscience for nothing: of teaching landlords to have at least
one degree of mercy toward their tenants: lastly, of putting a
spirit of honesty, industry, and skill into our shopkeepers; who,
if a resolution could now be taken to buy only our native goods,
would immediately unite to cheat and exact upon us in the price,
the measure, and the goodness, nor could ever yet be brought
to make one fair proposal of just dealing, though often and
earnestly invited to it.

Therefore I repeat, let no man talk to me of these and the   30
like expedients, till he has at least some glimpse of hope that
there will be ever some hearty and sincere attempts to put them
in practice.

But as to myself, having been wearied out for many years   31
with offering vain, idle, visionary thoughts, and at length utterly
despairing of success, I fortunately fell upon this proposal; which,
as it is wholly new, so it has something solid and real, of no
expense and little trouble, full in our own power, and whereby
we can incur no danger in disobliging England. For this kind of
commodity will not bear exportation, the flesh being of too tender
a consistence to admit a long continuance in salt, although perhaps I could name a country which would be glad to eat up our
whole nation without it.

After all, I am not so violently bent upon my own opinion   32
as to reject any offer proposed by wise men, which shall be
found equally innocent, cheap, easy, and effectual. But before
something of that kind shall be advanced in contradiction to my
scheme, and offering a better, I desire the author or authors will
be pleased maturely to consider two points. First, as things now
stand, how they will be able to find food and raiment for an
hundred thousand useless mouths and backs. And secondly,
there being a round million of creatures in human figure
throughout this kingdom, whose subsistence put into a common
stock would leave them in debt two millions of pounds sterling,
adding those who are beggars by profession to the bulk of farmers, cottagers, and laborers, with the wives and children who
are beggars in effect; I desire those politicians who dislike my
overture, and may perhaps be so bold as to attempt an answer,

that they will first ask the parents of these mortals, whether they would not at this day think it a great happiness to have been sold for food at a year old in the manner I prescribe, and thereby have avoided such a perpetual scene of misfortunes as they have since gone through by the oppression of landlords, the impossibility of paying rent without money or trade, the want of common sustenance, with neither house nor clothes to cover them from the inclemencies of the weather, and the most inevitable prospect of entailing the like or greater miseries upon their breed for ever.

33   I profess, in the sincerity of my heart, that I have not the least personal interest in endeavoring to promote this necessary work, having no other motive than the public good of my country, by advancing our trade, providing for infants, relieving the poor, and giving some pleasure to the rich. I have no children by which I can propose to get a single penny; the youngest being nine years old, and my wife past child-bearing.

Content

1. What is the overt thesis of Swift's essay. What is its implied (and real) thesis? In what ways do these theses differ?
2. What are the primary aims and values of the narrator of the essay? Identify the economic advantages of his proposal that he offers in paragraphs 9–16. How do the narrator's alleged aims and values differ from the aims and values of Swift as the essay's author?
3. What do the advantages that the narrator offers for his proposal (¶s 21–26) reveal about the social and economic conditions of Ireland when Swift was writing?
4. Why is it a "very knowing *American*" who has assured the narrator of the suitability of year-old infants for food (¶ 9)?
5. Swift as the author of the essay expects his readers to respond to the narrator's cold economic arguments on a humane, moral level. What might such an appropriate response be?

Strategies/Structures

1. What persona (a created character) does the speaker of Swift's essay have? How are readers to know that this character is not Swift himself?
2. Why does the narrator use so many mathematical computations throughout? How do they reinforce his economic argument? How do they enhance the image of his cold-bloodedness?

3. Why did Swift choose to present his argument indirectly rather than overtly? What advantages does this indirect, consistently ironic technique provide? What disadvantages does it have (for instance, do you think Swift's readers are likely to believe he really advocated eating babies)?

Language

1. What is the prevailing tone of the essay? How does it undermine what the narrator says? How does the tone reinforce Swift's implied meaning?
2. Why does Swift say "a child just dropped from its dam" (¶ 4) instead of "just born from his mother"? What other language reinforces the animalistic associations (see, for instance, "breeders" in paragraph 17)?
3. In paragraph 21 Swift refers to Roman Catholics by the common term "Papists." What clues does the context provide as to whether this usage is complimentary or derogatory? How does this emphasize the sense of a split between the English Episcopalian landowners and the Irish Catholic tenants that prevails throughout the essay?

For Writing

1. Write a modest proposal of your own. Pick some problem that you think needs to be solved, and propose a radical solution—perhaps a dramatic way to bring about world peace, preserve endangered species, dispose of chemical or nuclear waste.
2. Write an essay in which a created character, a narrative persona, speaks ironically (as Swift's narrator does) about your subject. The character's values should be at variance with the values you and your audience share. For instance, if you want to propose stiff penalties for drunk driving, your narrator could be a firm advocate of drinking, and of driving without restraint, and could be shown driving unsafely while under the influence of alcohol, indifferent to the dangers.

MAX SHULMAN

Born (1919) in Minnesota and educated at the University of Minnesota (B.A., 1942), Shulman is the author of several Broadway plays and such nonsensical novels as *Barefoot Boy*

With Cheek (1943), *Sleep Till Noon* (1950), and *Rally Round the Flag, Boys!* (1957). His humorous newspaper column "On Campus" appeared in the 1950s in over three hundred and fifty college newspapers. His collection of short stories *The Many Loves of Dobie Gillis* (1953), from which "Love Is a Fallacy" is reprinted below, was successfully adapted for television. "Love is a Fallacy" exemplifies the humor that made Shulman a favorite with America's college students, and at the same time argues the sometimes painful reality of human relationships. The insufferable narrator, Dobie Gillis, believes he possesses a "giant intellect"; he has an ego to match. Dobie tries to teach logic to a dazzlingly beautiful co-ed, Polly Espy, who responds to his pompous instruction with batting eyelashes and exclamations of "This is marvy. Do more! Do more!" But she learns her lesson well in this essay that provides an amusing explanation of logic and illogic for Shulman's readers and, through a clever reversal, puts Dobie in his rightful place.

Love Is a Fallacy

1   C ool was I and logical. Keen, calculating, perspicacious, acute and astute—I was all of these. My brain was as powerful as a dynamo, as precise as a chemist's scales, as penetrating as a scalpel. And—think of it!—I was only eighteen.

2   It is not often that one so young has such a giant intellect. Take, for example, Petey Bellows, my roommate at the university. Same age, same background, but dumb as an ox. A nice enough fellow, you understand, but nothing upstairs. Emotional type. Unstable. Impressionable. Worst of all, a faddist. Fads, I submit, are the very negation of reason. To be swept up in every new craze that comes along, to surrender yourself to idiocy just because everybody else is doing it—this, to me, is the acme of mindlessness. Not, however, to Petey.

3   One afternoon I found Petey lying on his bed with an expression of such distress on his face that I immediately diagnosed appendicitis. "Don't move," I said. "Don't take a laxative. I'll get a doctor."

"Raccoon," he mumbled thickly.   4

"Raccoon?" I said, pausing in my flight.   5

"I want a raccoon coat," he wailed.   6

I perceived that his trouble was not physical, but mental.   7
"Why do you want a raccoon coat?"

"I should have known it," he cried, pounding his temples.   8
"I should have known they'd come back when the Charleston
came back. Like a fool I spent all my money for textbooks, and
now I can't get a raccoon coat."

"Can you mean," I said incredulously, "that people are   9
actually wearing raccoon coats again?"

"All the Big Men on Campus are wearing them. Where've   10
you been?"

"In the library," I said, naming a place not frequented by   11
Big Men on Campus.

He leaped from the bed and paced the room. "I've got to   12
have a raccoon coat," he said passionately. "I've got to!"

"Petey, why? Look at it rationally. Raccoon coats are un-   13
sanitary. They shed. They smell bad. They weigh too much.
They're unsightly. They—"

"You don't understand," he interrupted impatiently. "It's   14
the thing to do. Don't you want to be in the swim?"

"No," I said truthfully.   15

"Well, I do," he declared. "I'd give anything for a raccoon   16
coat. Anything!"

My brain, that precision instrument, slipped into high gear.   17
"Anything?" I asked, looking at him narrowly.

"Anything," he affirmed in ringing tones.   18

I stroked my chin thoughtfully. It so happened that I knew   19
where to get my hands on a raccoon coat. My father had had
one in his undergraduate days; it lay now in a trunk in the attic
back home. It also happened that Petey had something I wanted.
He didn't *have* it exactly, but at least he had first right on it. I
refer to his girl, Polly Espy.

I had long coveted Polly Espy. Let me emphasize that my   20
desire for this young woman was not emotional in nature. She
was, to be sure, a girl who excited the emotions, but I was not
one to let my heart rule my head. I wanted Polly for a shrewdly
calculated, entirely cerebral reason.

21   I was a freshman in law school. In a few years I would be out in practice. I was well aware of the importance of the right kind of wife in furthering a lawyer's career. The successful lawyers I had observed were, almost without exception, married to beautiful, gracious, intelligent women. With one omission, Polly fitted these specifications perfectly.

22   Beautiful she was. She was not yet of pin-up proportions, but I felt sure that time would supply the lack. She already had the makings.

23   Gracious she was. By gracious I mean full of graces. She had an erectness of carriage, an ease of bearing, a poise that clearly indicated the best of breeding. At table her manners were exquisite. I had seen her at the Kozy Kampus Korner eating the specialty of the house—a sandwich that contained scraps of pot roast, gravy, chopped nuts, and a dipper of sauerkraut—without even getting her fingers moist.

24   Intelligent she was not. In fact, she veered in the opposite direction. But I believed that under my guidance she would smarten up. At any rate, it was worth a try. It is, after all, easier to make a beautiful dumb girl smart than to make an ugly smart girl beautiful.

25   "Petey," I said, "are you in love with Polly Espy?"

26   "I think she's a keen kid," he replied, "but I don't know if you'd call it love. Why?"

27   "Do you," I asked, "have any kind of formal arrangement with her? I mean are you going steady or anything like that?"

28   "No. We see each other quite a bit, but we both have other dates. Why?"

29   "Is there," I asked, "any other man for whom she has a particular fondness?"

30   "Not that I know of. Why?"

31   I nodded with satisfaction. "In other words, if you were out of the picture, the field would be open. Is that right?"

32   "I guess so. What are you getting at?"

33   "Nothing, nothing," I said innocently, and took my suitcase out of the closet.

34   "Where you going?" asked Petey.

35   "Home for the week end." I threw a few things into the bag.

"Listen," he said, clutching my arm eargerly, "while you're 36
home, you couldn't get some money from your old man, could
you, and lend it to me so I can buy a raccoon coat?"

"I may do better than that," I said with a mysterious wink 37
and closed my bag and left.

"Look," I said to Petey when I got back Monday morning. 38
I threw open the suitcase and revealed the huge, hairy, gamy
object that my father had worn in his Stutz Bearcat in 1925.

"Holy Toledo!" said Petey reverently. He plunged his hands 39
into the raccoon coat and then his face. "Holy Toledo!" he repeated fifteen or twenty times.

"Would you like it?" I asked. 40

"Oh yes!" he cried, clutching the greasy pelt to him. Then 41
a canny look came into his eyes. "What do you want for it?"

"Your girl," I said, mincing no words. 42

"Polly?" he said in a horrified whisper. "You want Polly?" 43

"That's right." 44

He flung the coat from him. "Never," he said stoutly. 45

I shrugged. "Okay. If you don't want to be in the swim, I 46
guess it's your business."

I sat down in a chair and pretended to read a book, but 47
out of the corner of my eye I kept watching Petey. He was a
torn man. First he looked at the coat with the expression of a
waif at a bakery window. Then he turned away and set his jaw
resolutely. Then he looked back at the coat, with even more
longing in his face. Then he turned away, but with not so much
resolution this time. Back and forth his head swiveled, desire
waxing, resolution waning. Finally he didn't turn away at all;
he just stood and stared with mad lust at the coat.

"It isn't as though I was in love with Polly," he said thickly. 48
"Or going steady or anything like that."

"That's right," I murmured. 49

"What's Polly to me, or me to Polly?" 50

"Not a thing," said I. 51

"It's just been a casual kick—just a few laughs, that's all." 52

"Try on the coat," said I. 53

He complied. The coat bunched high over his ears and 54
dropped all the way down to his shoe tops. He looked like a
mound of dead raccoons. "Fits fine," he said happily.

55   I rose from my chair. "Is it a deal?" I asked, extending my hand.

56   He swallowed. "It's a deal," he said and shook my hand.

57   I had my first date with Polly the following evening. This was in the nature of a survey; I wanted to find out just how much work I had to do to get her mind up to the standard I required. I took her first to dinner. "Gee, that was a delish dinner," she said as we left the restaurant. Then I took her to a movie. "Gee, that was a marvy movie," she said as we left the theater. And then I took her home. "Gee, I had a sensaysh time," she said as she bade me good night.

58   I went back to my room with a heavy heart. I had gravely underestimated the size of my task. This girl's lack of information was terrifying. Nor would it be enough merely to supply her with information. First she had to be taught to *think*. This loomed as a project of no small dimensions, and at first I was tempted to give her back to Petey. But then I got to thinking about her abundant physical charms and about the way she entered a room and the way she handled a knife and fork, and I decided to make an effort.

59   I went about it, as in all things, systematically. I gave her a course in logic. It happened that I, as a law student, was taking a course in logic myself, so I had all the facts at my finger tips. "Polly," I said to her when I picked her up on our next date, "tonight we are going over to the Knoll and talk."

60   "Oo, terrif," she replied. One thing I will say for this girl: you would go far to find another so agreeable.

61   We went to the Knoll, the campus trysting place, and we sat down under an old oak, and she looked at me expectantly. "What are we going to talk about?" she asked.

62   "Logic."

63   She thought this over for a minute and decided she liked it. "Magnif," she said.

64   "Logic," I said, clearing my throat, "is the science of thinking. Before we can think correctly, we must first learn to recognize the common fallacies of logic. These we will take up tonight."

65   "Wow-dow!" she cried, clapping her hands delightedly.

66   I winced, but went bravely on. "First let us examine the fallacy called Dicto Simpliciter."

"By all means," she urged, batting her lashes eagerly.   67

"Dicto Simpliciter means an argument based on an un-   68
qualified generalization. For example: Exercise is good. Therefore everybody should exercise."

"I agree," said Polly earnestly. "I mean exercise is won-   69
derful. I mean it builds the body and everything."

"Polly," I said gently, "the argument is a fallacy. *Exercise*   70
is good is an unqualified generalization. For instance, if you have
heart disease, exercise is bad, not good. Many people are ordered
by their doctors not to exercise. You must *qualify* the generalization. You must say exercise is *usually* good, or exercise is good
for most people. Otherwise you have committed a Dicto Simpliciter. Do you see?"

"No," she confessed. "But this is marvy. Do more! Do   71
more!"

"It will be better if you stop tugging at my sleeve," I told   72
her, and when she desisted, I continued. "Next we take up a
fallacy called Hasty Generalization. Listen carefully: You can't
speak French. I can't speak French. Petey Bellows can't speak
French. I must therefore conclude that nobody at the University
of Minnesota can speak Franch."

"Really?" said Polly, amazed. *"Nobody?"*   73

I hid my exasperation. "Polly, it's a fallacy. The general-   74
ization is reached too hastily. There are too few instances to
support such a conclusion."

"Know any more fallacies?" she asked breathlessly. "This   75
is more fun than dancing even."

I fought off a wave of despair. I was getting nowhere with   76
this girl, absolutely nowhere. Still, I am nothing if not persistent.
I continued. "Next comes Post Hoc. Listen to this: Let's not take
Bill on our picnic. Every time we take him out with us, it rains."

"I know somebody just like that," she exclaimed. "A girl   77
back home—Eula Becker, her name is. It never fails. Every single
time we take her on a picnic—"

"Polly," I said sharply, "it's a fallacy. Eula Becker doesn't   78
cause the rain. She has no connection with the rain. You are
guilty of Post Hoc if you blame Eula Becker."

"I'll never do it again," she promised contritely. "Are you   79
mad at me?"

I sighed. "No, Polly, I'm not mad."   80

81   "Then tell me some more fallacies."

82   "All right. Let's try Contradictory Premises."

83   "Yes, let's," she chirped, blinking her eyes happily.

84   I frowned, but plunged ahead. "Here's an example of Contradictory Premises: If God can do anything, can He make a stone so heavy that He won't be able to lift it?"

85   "Of course," she replied promptly.

86   "But if He can do anything, He can lift the stone," I pointed out.

87   "Yeah," she said thoughtfully. "Well, then I guess He can't make the stone."

88   "But He can do anything." I reminded her.

89   She scratched her pretty, empty head. "I'm all confused," she admitted.

90   "Of course you are. Because when the premises of an argument contradict each other, there can be no argument. If there is an irresistible force, there can be no immovable object. If there is an immovable object, there can be no irresistible force. Get it?"

91   "Tell me some more of this keen stuff," she said eagerly.

92   I consulted my watch. "I think we'd better call it a night. I'll take you home now, and you go over all the things you've learned. We'll have another session tomorrow night."

93   I deposited her at the girls' dormitory, where she assured me that she had had a perfectly terrif evening, and I went glumly home to my room. Petey lay snoring in his bed, the raccoon coat huddled like a great hairy beast at his feet. For a moment I considered waking him and telling him that he could have his girl back. It seemed clear that my project was doomed to failure. The girl simply had a logic-proof head.

94   But then I reconsidered. I had wasted one evening; I might as well waste another. Who knew? Maybe somewhere in the extinct crater of her mind a few embers still smoldered. Maybe somehow I could fan them into flame. Admittedly it was not a prospect fraught with hope, but I decided to give it one more try.

95   Seated under the oak the next evening I said, "Our first fallacy tonight is called Ad Misericordiam."

96   She quivered with delight.

"Listen closely," I said. "A man applies for a job. When   97
the boss asks him what his qualifications are, he replies that he
has a wife and six children at home, the wife is a helpless cripple,
the children have nothing to eat, no clothes to wear, no shoes
on their feet, there are no beds in the house, no coal in the cellar,
and winter is coming."

A tear rolled down each of Polly's pink cheeks. "Oh, this   98
is awful, awful," she sobbed.

"Yes, it's awful," I agreed, "but it's no argument. The man   99
never answered the boss's question about his qualifications. Instead he appealed to the boss's sympathy. He committed the
fallacy of Ad Misericordiam. Do you understand?"

"Have you got a handkerchief?" she blubbered.   100

I handed her a handkerchief and tried to keep from scream-   101
ing while she wiped her eyes. "Next," I said in a carefully controlled tone, "we will discuss False Analogy. Here is an example:
Students should be allowed to look at their textbooks during
examinations. After all, surgeons have X rays to guide them
during an operation, lawyers have briefs to guide them during
a trial, carpenters have blueprints to guide them when they are
building a house. Why, then, shouldn't students be allowed to
look at their textbooks during an examination?"

"There now," she said enthusiastically, "is the most marvy   102
idea I've heard in years."

"Polly," I said testily, "the argument is all wrong. Doctors,   103
lawyers, and carpenters aren't taking a test to see how much
they have learned, but students are. The situations are altogether
different, and you can't make an analogy between them."

"I still think it's a good idea," said Polly.   104

"Nuts," I muttered. Doggedly I pressed on. "Next we'll   105
try Hypothesis Contrary to Fact."

"Sounds yummy," was Polly's reaction.   106

"Listen: If Madame Curie had not happened to leave a   107
photographic plate in a drawer with a chunk of pitchblend,
the world today would not know about radium."

"True, true," said Polly, nodding her head. "Did you see   108
the movie? Oh, it just knocked me out. That Walter Pidgeon is
so dreamy. I mean he fractures me."

"If you can forget Mr. Pidgeon for a moment," I said coldly,   109

"I would like to point out that the statement is a fallacy. Maybe Madame Curie would have discovered radium at some later date. Maybe somebody else would have discovered it. Maybe any number of things would have happened. You can't start with a hypothesis that is not true and then draw any supportable conclusions from it."

110   "They ought to put Walter Pidgeon in more pictures," said Polly. "I hardly ever see him any more."

111   One more chance, I decided. But just one more. There is a limit to what flesh and blood can bear. "The next fallacy is called Poisoning the Well."

112   "How cute!" she gurgled.

113   "Two men are having a debate. The first one gets up and says, 'My opponent is a notorious liar. You can't believe a word that he is going to say.' . . . Now, Polly, think. Think hard. What's wrong?"

114   I watched her closely as she knit her creamy brow in con-centration. Suddenly a glimmer of intelligence—the first I had seen—came into her eyes. "It's not fair," she said with indig-nation. "It's not a bit fair. What chance has the second man got if the first man calls him a liar before he even begins talking?"

115   "Right!" I cried exultantly. "One hundred per cent right. It's not fair. The first man has *poisoned the well* before anybody could drink from it. He has hamstrung his opponent before he could even start. . . . Polly, I'm proud of you."

116   "Pshaw," she murmured, blushing with pleasure.

117   "You see, my dear, these things aren't so hard. All you have to do is concentrate. Think—examine—evaluate. Come now, let's review everything we have learned."

118   "Fire away," she said with an airy wave of her hand.

119   Heartened by the knowledge that Polly was not altogether a cretin, I began a long, patient review of all I had told her. Over and over and over again I cited instances, pointed out flaws, kept hammering away without letup. It was like digging a tun-nel. At first everything was work, sweat, and darkness. I had no idea when I would reach the light, or even *if* I would. But I persisted. I pounded and clawed and scraped, and finally I was rewarded. I saw a chink of light. And then the chink got bigger and the sun came pouring in and all was bright.

Five grueling nights this took, but it was worth it. I had 120 made a logician out of Polly; I had taught her to think. My job was done. She was worthy of me at last. She was a fit wife for me, a proper hostess for my many mansions, a suitable mother for my well-heeled children.

It must not be thought that I was without love for this girl. 121 Quite the contrary. Just as Pygmalion loved the perfect woman he had fashioned, so I loved mine. I decided to acquaint her with my feelings at our very next meeting. The time had come to change our relationship from academic to romantic.

"Polly," I said when next we sat beneath our oak, "tonight 122 we will not discuss fallacies."

"Aw, gee," she said, disappointed. 123

"My dear," I said, favoring her with a smile, "we have 124 now spent five evenings together. We have gotten along splendidly. It is clear that we are well matched."

"Hasty Generalization," she repeated. "How can you say 125 that we are well matched on the basis of only five dates?"

I chuckled with amusement. The dear child had learned 126 her lessons well. "My dear," I said, patting her hand in a tolerant manner, "five dates is plenty. After all, you don't have to eat a whole cake to know that it's good."

"False Analogy," said Polly promptly. "I'm not a cake. I'm 127 a girl."

I chuckled with somewhat less amusement. The dear child 128 had learned her lessons perhaps too well. I decided to change tactics. Obviously the best approach was a simple, strong, direct declaration of love. I paused for a moment while my massive brain chose the proper words. Then I began:

"Polly, I love you. You are the whole world to me, and 129 the moon and the stars and the constellations of outer space. Please, my darling, say that you will go steady with me, for if you will not, life will be meaningless. I will languish. I will refuse my meals. I will wander the face of the earth, a shambling, hollow-eyed hulk."

There, I thought, folding my arms, that ought to do it. 130

"Ad Misericordiam," said Polly. 131

I ground my teeth. I was not Pygmalion; I was Franken- 132 stein, and my monster had me by the throat. Frantically I fought back the tide of panic surging through me. At all costs I had to keep cool.

133   "Well, Polly," I said, forcing a smile, "you certainly have learned your fallacies."

134   "You're darn right," she said with a vigorous nod.

135   "And who taught them to you, Polly?"

136   "You did."

137   "That's right. So you do owe me something, don't you, my dear? If I hadn't come along you never would have learned about fallacies."

138   "Hypothesis Contrary to Fact," she said instantly.

139   I dashed perspiration from my brow. "Polly," I croaked, "you mustn't take all these things so literally. I mean this is just classroom stuff. You know that the things you learn in school don't have anything to do with life."

140   "Dicto Simpliciter," she said, wagging her finger at me playfully.

141   That did it. I leaped to my feet, bellowing like a bull. "Will you or will you not go steady with me?"

142   "I will not," she replied.

143   "Why not?" I demanded.

144   "Because this afternoon I promised Petey Bellows that I would go steady with him."

145   I reeled back, overcome with the infamy of it. After he promised, after he made a deal, after he shook my hand! "The rat!" I shrieked, kicking up great chunks of turf. "You can't go with him, Polly. He's a liar. He's a cheat. He's a rat."

146   "Poisoning the Well," said Polly, "and stop shouting. I think shouting must be a fallacy too."

147   With an immense effort of will, I modulated my voice. "All right," I said. "You're a logician. Let's look at this thing logically. How could you choose Petey Bellows over me? Look at me—a brilliant student, a tremendous intellectual, a man with an assured future. Look at Petey—a knothead, a jitterbug, a guy who'll never know where his next meal is coming from. Can you give me one logical reason why you should go steady with Petey Bellows?"

148   "I certainly can," declared Polly. "He's got a raccoon coat."

Content

1. Shulman's character, Dobie Gillis, explains a number of logical fallacies to Polly Espy: Dicto Simpliciter (¶s 66–70); Hasty Generalization (¶s 72–74); Post Hoc (¶s 76–78); Contradictory Premises (¶s 84–90); Ad Misericordiam (¶s 95–99); False Analogy (¶s 101–103); Hypothesis Contrary to Fact (¶ 105–109); and Poisoning the Well (¶s 111–115). Explain each of these fallacies in your own words and give an example of each.

2. Will wearing a raccoon coat make Petey Bellows a Big Man on Campus? What logical fallacy does this imply? Could he become a Big Man on Campus without wearing a raccoon coat?

3. Is Dobie accurate in assuming that if Polly learns logic she will automatically be intelligent? What logical fallacies does he demonstrate in his relationship with Polly?

4. Why has Shulman created and used stereotypes as characters—the irritating pseudo-intellectual law student; the co-ed, beautiful but dumb; the loutish roommate who lusts after the status symbol of a raccoon coat? Does Shulman alter any or all of the stereotypes during the course of the narrative?

Strategies/Structures

1. Why has Shulman created such an obnoxious character, Dobie Gillis, as the narrator? Why would people want to continue reading this narrative about such an unpleasant character?

2. Is a humorous narrative a good way to teach a serious subject like logic? Why or why not? Can Shulman, using this format, explain enough about each fallacy to make it clear? Comprehensive?

3. Would you expect this narrative to end as it does? Why or why not?

Language

1. Identify the typical features of Dobie's and Polly's language, including vocabulary, use of slang, and repeated expressions. How does their speech help to characterize the speakers?

2. Shulman makes fun of his characters through parodying their language and their behavior. Give some examples. How do these parodies influence the readers' reactions to the characters?

For Writing

1. Pick one or two logical fallacies and write an essay using a narrative or extended illustration to explain the problems such fallacious reasoning can cause. It does not have to be humorous. For instance, you might discuss how stereotyping of a person or group by race, social class, educational level, or occupation has resulted in hasty generalizations prejudicial to your subject.

2. Write a humorous dialogue in which the speakers are characterized by their use—or abuse—of slang and clichés.

RICHARD RODRIGUEZ

Rodriguez, the son of Mexican-Americans, was born in San Francisco in 1944, and didn't learn English until he started grammar school. He has since learned it very well indeed, earning a B.A. at Stanford, an M.A. at Columbia, and a Ph.D. in Renaissance literature from the University of California at Berkeley. In addition to a career as a writer, Rodriguez at times teaches college English on the West Coast. In *The Hunger of Memory* (1982), he explores in six elegantly written autobiographical essays the internal self-division "over language, complexion, heritage or religion" that results from a dual culture. In "None of This Is Fair," reprinted below, Rodriguez explores some undesirable aspects of being a minority "scholarship boy"—not the least of which is the guilt he feels because of reverse discrimination in employment opportunities.

None of This Is Fair

1   My plan to become a professor of English—my ambition during long years in college at Stanford, then in graduate school at Columbia and Berkeley—was complicated by feelings of embarrassment and guilt. So many times I would see other Mexican-Americans and know we were alike only in race. And

yet, simply because our race was the same, I was, during the last years of my schooling, the beneficiary of their situation. Affirmative Action programs had made it all possible. The disadvantages of others permitted my promotion; the absence of many Mexican-Americans from academic life allowed my designation as a "minority student."

For me opportunities had been extravagant. There were   2
fellowships, summer research grants, and teaching assistantships. After only two years in graduate school, I was offered teaching jobs by several colleges. Invitations to Washington conferences arrived and I had the chance to travel abroad as a "Mexican-American representative." The benefits were often, however, too gaudy to please. In three published essays, in conversations with teachers, in letters to politicians and at conferences, I worried the issue of Affirmative Action. Often I proposed contradictory opinions. Though consistent was the admission that— because of an early, excellent education—I was no longer a principal victim of racism or any other social oppression. I said that but still I continued to indicate on applications for financial aid that I was a Hispanic-American. It didn't really occur to me to say anything else, or to leave the question unanswered.

Thus I complied with and encouraged the odd bureaucratic   3
logic of Affirmative Action. I let government officials treat the disadvantaged condition of many Mexican-Americans with my advancement. Each fall my presence was noted by Health, Education, and Welfare department statisticians. As I pursued advanced literary studies and learned the skill of reading Spenser and Wordsworth and Empson, I would hear myself numbered among the culturally disadvantaged. Still, silent, I didn't object.

But the irony cut deep. And guilt would not be evaded by   4
averting my glance when I confronted a face like my own in a crowd. By late 1975, nearing the completion of my graduate studies at Berkeley, I was so wary of the benefits of Affirmative Action that I feared my inevitable success as an applicant for a teaching position. The months of fall—traditionally that time of academic job-searching—passed without my applying to a single school. When one of my professors chanced to learn this in late November, he was astonished, then furious. He yelled at me: Did I think that because I was a minority student jobs would

just come looking for me? What was I thinking? Did I realize that he and several other faculty members had already written letters on my behalf? Was I going to start acting like some other minority students he had known? They struggled for success and then, when it was almost within reach, grew strangely afraid and let it pass. Was that it? Was I determined to fail?

5   I did not respond to his questions. I didn't want to admit to him, and thus to myself, the reason I delayed.

6   I merely agreed to write to several schools. (In my letter I wrote: "I cannot claim to represent disadvantaged Mexican-Americans. The very fact that I am in a position to apply for this job should make that clear.") After two or three days, there were telegrams and phone calls, invitations to interviews, then airplane trips. A blur of faces and the murmur of their soft questions. And, over someone's shoulder, the sight of campus buildings shadowing pictures I had seen years before when I leafed through Ivy League catalogues with great expectations. At the end of each visit, interviewers would smile and wonder if I had any questions. A few times I quietly wondered what advantage my race had given me over other applicants. But that was an impossible question for them to answer without embarrassing me. Quickly, several persons insisted that my ethnic identity had given me no more than a "foot inside the door"; at most, I had a "slight edge" over other applicants. "We just looked at your dossier with extra care and we like what we saw. There was never any question of having to alter our standards. You can be certain of that."

7   In the early part of January, offers arrived on stiffly elegant stationery. Most schools promised terms appropriate for any new assistant professor. A few made matters worse—and almost more tempting—by offering more: the use of university housing; an unusually large starting salary; a reduced teaching schedule. As the stack of letters mounted, my hesitation increased. I started calling department chairmen to ask for another week, then 10 more days—"more time to reach a decision"—to avoid the decision I would need to make.

8   At school, meantime, some students hadn't received a single job offer. One man, probably the best student in the department, did not even get a request for his dossier. He and I

met outside a classroom one day and he asked about my opportunities. He seemed happy for me. Faculty members beamed.
They said they had expected it. "After all, not many schools are
going to pass up getting a Chicano with a Ph.D. in Renaissance
literature," somebody said laughing. Friends wanted to know
which of the offers I was going to accept. But I couldn't make
up my mind. February came and I was running out of time and
excuses. (One chairman guessed my delay was a bargaining ploy
and increased his offer with each of my calls.) I had to promise
a decision by the 10th; the 12th at the very latest.

On the 18th of February, late in the afternoon, I was in the   9
office I shared with several other teaching assistants. Another
graduate student was sitting across the room at his desk. When
I got up to leave, he looked over to say in an uneventful voice
that he had some big news. He had finally decided to accept a
position at a faraway university. It was not a job he especially
wanted, he admitted. But he had to take it because there hadn't
been any other offers. He felt trapped, and depressed, since his
job would separate him from his young daughter.

I tried to encourage him by remarking that he was lucky   10
at least to have found a job. So many others hadn't been able
to get anything. But before I finished speaking I realized that I
had said the wrong thing. And I anticipated his next question.

"What are your plans?" he wanted to know. "Is it true   11
you've gotten an offer from Yale?"

I said that it was. "Only, I still haven't made up my mind."   12

He stared at me as I put on my jacket. And smiling, then   13
unsmiling, he asked if I knew that he too had written to Yale.
In his case, however, no one had bothered to acknowledge his
letter with even a postcard. What did I think of that?

He gave me no time to answer.   14

"Damn!" he said sharply and his chair rasped the floor as   15
he pushed himself back. Suddenly, it was to *me* that he was
complaining. "It's just not right, Richard. None of this is fair.
You've done some good work, but so have I. I'll bet our records
are just about equal. But when we look for jobs this year, it's a
different story. You get all of the breaks."

To evade his criticism, I wanted to side with him. I was   16
about to admit the injustice of Affirmative Action. But he went

on, his voice hard with accusation. "It's all very simple this year. You're a Chicano. And I am a Jew. That's the only real difference between us."

17   His words stung me: there was nothing he was telling me that I didn't know. I had admitted everything already. But to hear someone else say these things, and in such an accusing tone, was suddenly hard to take. In a deceptively calm voice, I responded that he had simplified the whole issue. The phrases came like bubbles to the tip of my tongue: "new blood"; "the importance of cultural diversity"; "the goal of racial integration." These were all the arguments I had proposed several years ago— and had long since abandoned. Of course the offers were unjustifiable. I knew that. All I was saying amounted to a frantic self-defense. I tried to find an end to a sentence. My voice faltered to a stop.

18   "Yeah, sure," he said. "I've heard all that before. Nothing you say really changes the fact that Affirmative Action is unfair. You see that, don't you? There isn't any way for me to compete with you. Once there were quotas to keep my parents out of certain schools; now there are quotas to get you in and the effect on me is the same as it was for them."

19   I listened to every word he spoke. But my mind was really on something else. I knew at that moment that I would reject all of the offers. I stood there silently surprised by what an easy conclusion it was. Having prepared for so many years to teach, having trained myself to do nothing else, I had hesitated out of practical fear. But now that it was made, the decision came with relief. I immediately knew I had made the right choice.

20   My colleague continued talking and I realized that he was simply right. Affirmative Action programs *are* unfair to white students. But as I listened to him assert his rights, I thought of the seriously disadvantaged. How different they were from white, middle-class students who come armed with the testimony of their grades and aptitude scores and self-confidence to complain about the unequal treatment they now receive. I listen to them. I do not want to be careless about what they say. Their rights are important to protect. But inevitably when I hear them or their lawyers, I think about the most seriously disadvantaged, not simply Mexican-Americans, but of all those who do not ever

imagine themselves going to college or becoming doctors: white, black, brown. Always poor. Silent. They are not plaintiffs before the court or against the misdirection of Affirmative Action. They lack the confidence (my confidence!) to assume their right to a good education. They lack the confidence and skills a good primary and secondary education provides and which are prerequisites for informed public life. They remain silent.

The debate drones on and surrounds them in stillness. 21 They are distant, faraway figures like the boys I have seen peering down from freeway overpasses in some other part of town.

Content

1. What does Rodriguez mean by his fundamental premise, "None of this is fair" (¶ 15)?

2. What is Affirmative Action? What is reverse discrimination? What does Rodriguez's comparison of his job-seeking experience with those of his white male classmates illustrate about these terms?

3. Does Rodriguez intend that his readers generalize on the basis of the job-seeking experiences of himself and his two white male classmates, one Jewish?

4. What sorts of people does Rodriguez claim are currently benefiting from Affirmative Action programs? What sorts of people are the victims of reverse discrimination?

5. In Rodriguez's opinion, which people truly need Affirmative Action (¶ 20)? Why aren't they getting what they need? Why does he wait so long to get to this point?

Strategies/Structures

1. Does Rodriguez present himself as an attractive character in his personal narrative? How does he expect readers' reactions to his personality to affect their reactions to his point?

2. If Rodriguez believes that Affirmative Action doesn't benefit the "most seriously disadvantaged" of all races (¶ 20), why doesn't he illustrate the point with an example of such people?

Language

1. Why does Rodriguez use indirect discourse in paragraphs 4–10 and direct conversation in paragraphs 11–18? What would the effects of the

argument have been if he had used indirect discourse instead of direct conversation in paragraphs 11–18?

2. What is the point of the simile in the last line (¶ 21)? What is the effect of ending an essay with such a figure of speech?

For Writing

1. If you or someone you know has either benefited from Affirmative Action or experienced reverse discrimination, write an essay about that experience to illustrate a general point about it.

2. Rodriguez has been attacked as an Uncle Juan (a Chicano Uncle Tom) for claiming that he and other middle class minority students improperly benefit from Affirmative Action programs that do not aid "all those who never imagined themselves going to college or becoming doctors: white, black, brown. Always poor. Silent" (¶ 20). Write an essay in which you agree either with Rodriguez or with his critics.

Strategies for Writing— Appealing to Emotion and Ethics

1. Do I want to appeal primarily to my readers' emotions (and which emotions) or to their ethical sense of how people ought to behave? (Remember that in either case the appeals are intertwined with reason— see Chapter 10.)

2. To what kinds of readers am I making these appeals? What ethical or other personal qualities should I as an author exhibit? How can I lead my readers to believe that I am a person of sound character and good judgment?

3. What evidence can I choose to reinforce my appeals and my authorial image? Examples from my own life? The experiences of others? References to literature or scientific research? What order of arrangement would be most convincing? From the least emotionally moving or involving to the most? Or vice versa?

4. How can I interpret my evidence to move my readers to accept it? Should I explain very elaborately, or should I let the examples speak for themselves? (If you decide on the latter, try out your essay on someone unfamiliar with the examples to see if they are in fact self-evident.)

5. Do I want my audience to react with sympathy? Pity? Anger? Fear? Horror? To accomplish this, should I use much emotional language? Should my appeal be overt, direct? Or would indirection, understatement, be more effective? Would irony, saying the opposite of what I really mean (as Swift did), be more appropriate than a direct approach?

Additional Writing Topics

Write an essay that attempts to persuade one of the following audiences through a combination of appeals to reason, emotion, and ethics.

1. To someone you'd like for a friend, date, fiance(e), or spouse: Love me.
2. To an athlete, or to an athletic coach: Play according to the rules, even when the referee (umpire, or other judge) isn't looking.
3. To a prospective employer: I'm the best person for the job.
4. To a police officer: I shouldn't receive this traffic ticket. Or, to a judge or jury: I am innocent of the crime of which I'm accused.
5. To the voters: Vote for me (or for a candidate of my choice).
6. To admissions officers of a particular college, university, or of a

program within that institution (such as a medical or law school, graduate program, or a division with a special undergraduate degree): Let me in.

7. To the prospective buyer of a something you want to sell or a service you can perform: Buy this.

8. To your representative or senator: Save the environment/whales/ poor people/draft resisters/Social Security system (or another topic of your choice).

9. To an audience prejudiced against a particular group: X is beautiful. (X may be black, yellow, Hispanic, female, a member of a particular national or religious group . . .)

10. To people engaging in behavior that threatens their lives or their health: Stop doing X (or Stop doing X to excess)—smoking, drinking, overeating, undereating, or using drugs. Or Start doing X— exercising regularly, using seatbelts, planning for the future through getting an education, a stable job, an investment plan, a retirement plan. . . .

11. Pick a work of fiction or nonfiction whose content intrigues you and whose style you admire and write a brief parody (probably involving considerable exaggeration) of it to show your understanding of the content and your appreciation of the style. (See "The Allen Notebooks," pp. 13–17.)

12. Write a satire to argue implicitly for a point, as Swift does in "A Modest Proposal" (pp. 399–408). Use whatever techniques seem appropriate, such as creating a character who does the talking for you; setting a scene (such as of pathos or misery) that helps make your point; using a tone involving understatement, irony, or exaggeration. Be sure to supply enough clues to enable your readers to understand what you really mean.

PART V

Revising and Editing

12 *Revision*

Revision means, literally, "to see again." When you take a second, careful look at what you wrote as free writing or a first draft, chances are you'll decide to change it. As Donald Murray observes in "The Maker's Eye: Revising Your Own Manuscripts," "Rewriting isn't virtuous. It isn't something that ought to be done. It is simply something that most writers find they have to do to discover what they have to say and how to say it. It is a condition of the writer's life."

Many people think that revision means correcting the spelling and punctuation of a first—and only—draft. Writers who care about their work know that such changes, though necessary, are editorial matters remote from the heart of real revising. For to revise is to rewrite. And rewrite. Even if you're only making a grocery list, you might add and subtract material. Or change the organization. If your original list identified the items in the order they occurred to you, as lists often do, you could regroup them by categories of similar items, easier to shop for: produce, staples, meat, dairy products. You might provide specially detailed emphasis on the essentials, "a pound of Milagro

super-hot green chilies," and "a half gallon of double chocolate
extra fudge swirl ice cream."

The common concerns of revision, identified below, are
adapted from the essays by Murray, Zinsser, and Peterson in
this section.

1. Does your text contain sufficient *information?* What
   have you said? What does it *mean?*
2. Who is your intended *audience?* Will they understand
   what you've said? Do you need to supply any background information? Will you meet them, as Richard
   Wright had to decide, as allies or antagonists? How
   will this relationship determine what you say? And
   how you say it?
3. Do the *form* and *structure* of your writing suit the subject? Will these appeal to your audience? Would a
   commentary on fast-food restaurants, for instance, be
   more effective in an essay of description, comparison
   and contrast, or analysis—or some combination of the
   three?
4. Is the writing *developed* sufficiently? Or do you need to
   provide additional information, steps in an argument,
   or analysis of what you've already said? Does the *proportioning* reinforce your emphasis? Or do you need to
   expand some aspects and condense others?
5. Is the writing recognizably yours, in *style, voice,* and
   point of view? Do you like what you've said? If not, are
   you willing to change it? Is the body of your prose
   like that of an experienced runner: tight and taut, vigorous, self-contained, and supple?

Donald Murray's three revised versions of "The Maker's
Eye" show by example what he explains in his essay. Linda
Peterson analyzes, with examples from the original texts, an
outline and six successive drafts of Richard Wright's brief (ultimately one and three-fourths pages, cut down from three and
one-half) "statement explaining what he considered important
about *Black Boy* as an autobiographical book." Freshman Angela
Bowman moves from a first draft, free-association personal narrative on "Freddie the Fox and My Fifth Christmas" to, in the

revised version, a sharply honed analysis of the complex symbolic meanings of her subject.

Some parts of this brief introductory essay have been rewritten twice; other parts four, five, and six times. One sticky sentence, about grocery lists, has been revised a dozen times and is still in the process of change as this book goes to press. A favorite sentence that didn't quite seem to fit under question 5 has been included, thrown out, re-inserted, fished out of the wastebasket, scrutinized close up and farther off. Here it is: If your writing doesn't satisfy you, are you willing to change it to approach what you see in your inward vision, hear in your inward ear? Even as this is being written, it's being changed. *Approach* was originally *come closer to*, then *approximate;* both were rejected as too long. *Inward* vision isn't as pleasing as *inner* vision, but the phrase had to parallel *inward* ear—and *inner* ear sounded too anatomical. The entire metaphor seemed excessive in a paragraph dominated by another metaphor about trim body of prose. One image or the other had to be jettisoned. Will this discussion itself survive a censorious editor? The published version of this book will tell.

Ernest Heminway has said that he "rewrote the ending of *A Farewell to Arms,* the last page of it, thirty-nine times before I was satisfied."

"Was there some technical problem?" asked an interviewer. "What had you stumped?"

"Getting the words right," said Hemingway.

That is the essence of revision.

DONALD M. MURRAY

Murray (b. 1924), a Bostonian, was educated at the University of New Hampshire (A.B., 1948) and Boston University. He wrote editorials for the *Boston Herald* (1948–54), for which he was awarded the Pulitzer Prize in 1954, and was an editor for *Time* (1954–56). Murray has taught English at the University of New Hampshire since 1963, and has written numerous essays, books of short stories, poetry, and a novel, *The Man Who Had Everything* (1964). *A Writer Teaches Writing* (1968), an explanation of how people really write, has been highly influential in persuading writing teachers to teach their students to focus on the process of writing, rather than on the finished product.

Murray sees revising as central to the composing processes of many students and professional writers. He explains why in the following essay, whose own history illustrates his points. Murray completely rewrote the essay twice before it was first published in *The Writer* in 1973. Then, for an anthology, Murray "re-edited, re-revised, re-read, re-re-edited" it again. A draft of the first twelve paragraphs of the "re-edited, re-revised" version, with numerous changes, is reprinted below. As you examine both versions, note that many changes appear in the final ("re-re-edited") version that are not in the "re-revised" draft. Murray's careful practice reveals the truth of his own dictum, that "the words on a page are never finished."

*THE MAKER'S EYE: REVISING YOUR OWN MANUSCRIPTS** by DONALD M. MURRAY

1   When ~~the beginning writer~~ _{A STUDENTS} complete_s ~~his~~ ^A first draft, ~~he~~ ^{they} ~~usually reads it through to correct typographical errors and~~ consider_s the job of writing done_∧ ^{— — AND their teachers too OFTEN AGREE.} When ~~the~~ professional writer_s complete_s ~~his~~ ^{the} first draft, ~~he~~ ^{they} usually feel_s ~~he is~~ ^{they are} at the

---

**A different version of this article was published in *The Writer*, October 1973.

start of the writing process. ~~Now that he has~~ **When** a draft ~~he can~~
~~begin~~ writing, **can begin.** **is completed, the job OF**

That difference in attitude is the difference between amateur   2
and professional, inexperience and experience, journeyman and
craftsman. Peter F. Drucker, the prolific business writer, for
example, calls his first draft "the zero draft"--after that he
can start courting. Most ~~productive~~ writers share the feeling
~~that~~ the first draft, **ALL** and ~~most of those~~ which follow, ~~is an~~ **ARE**
opportunit**ies** to discover what they have to say and how they can
best say it.

~~Detachment and caring~~

To produce a progression of drafts, each of which says more   3
and says it better, the writer has to develop a special **KIND OF** reading
skill. In school we are taught to ~~read~~ **decode** what ~~is~~ **APPEARS** on the page **AS FINISHED WRITING.**
~~We try to comprehend what the author has said, what he meant,~~
~~and what are the implications of his words.~~

Writers, however, face a different category of possibility   4
and responsibility. To them, the words are never finished
on the page. Each can be changed, re-arranged, set off
a chain reaction of confusion or clarified meaning. This
is a different kind of reading, possibly more difficult
and certainly more exciting.

~~The~~ writer**s** ~~of such drafts~~ must **LEARN TO** be ~~his~~ own best enemy. ~~He~~ **Writers**   5
must accept the criticism of others, **their** and be suspicious of it; ~~he~~ **they**
—especially teachers—
must accept the praise of others, and be even more suspicious of
—especially teachers—
it. ~~He~~ **Writers** cannot depend on others. ~~He~~ **They** must detach himself from ~~his~~ **their**

own page*s* so that ~~he~~ *they* can apply both ~~his~~ *their* caring and ~~his~~ *their* craft to ~~his~~ *their* own work.

6   Detachment is not easy. Science fiction writer Ray Bradbury supposedly puts each manuscript away for a year and then rereads it as a stranger. Not many writers can afford the time to do this. We must read when our judgment may be at its worst, when we are close to the euphoric moment of creation. The writer "should be critical of everything that seems to him most delight-ful in his style," advises novelist Nancy Hale. "He should excise what he most admires, because he wouldn't thus admire it if he weren't . . . in a sense protecting it from criticism."

7   ~~The writer must learn to protect himself from his own ego, when it takes the form of uncritical pride or uncritical self-destruction.~~ *A*~~As~~ poet John Ciardi points out, ". . . the last act of the writing must be to become one's own reader. It is, I suppose, a schizophrenic process, to begin passionately and to end critically, to begin hot and to end cold; and, more important, to be passion-hot and critic-cold at the same time."

     ~~Just as~~ *unproductive* ~~dangerous~~ as the protective writer ~~is the despairing one, who thinks everything he does is terrible, dreadful, awful. If he is to publish, he must save what is effective on his page while he cuts away what doesn't work.~~ ⌐The writer must hear and respect his own voice.⌐

9   Remember ~~how each~~ *how the* craftsman ~~you have seen~~*s*--the carpenter *LOOKING AT THE LIE* ~~eyeing the level~~ of a shelf, the mechanic listening to the motor-- takes the instinctive step back. This is what ~~the~~ writer*s* ~~has to~~

do when they read ~~his~~ their own work. "The writer must survey his work critically, coolly, and as though he were a stranger to it," says children's book writer Eleanor Estes. "He must be willing to prune, expertly and hard-heartedly. At the end of each revision, a manuscript may look like a battered old hive, worked over, torn apart, pinned together, added to, deleted from, words changed and words changed back. Yet the book must maintain its original freshness and spontaneity."

¶ We are aware of ~~the~~ writers who think everything   8
they have written is literature but a more ~~serious~~
frequent and serious problem ~~is the~~ are writers ~~is~~ who
are ~~could~~ overly critical of each page, tear up
each page and never complete a draft. The ~~out~~
writer must cut what is bad to ~~save~~ reveal what
is good

~~It is far easier for most beginning writers to understand~~   10
~~the need for rereading and rewriting than it is to understand~~
~~how to go about it. The publishing writer doesn't necessarily~~
~~break down the various stages of rewriting and editing; he~~
~~just goes ahead and does it.~~ ¶ ~~One of our most~~ prolific ~~fiction~~
in the English speaking world,
writer, (Anthony Burgess,) says, "I might revise a page twenty
times." Short story and children's writer Roald Dahl states,
"By the time I'm nearing the end of a story, the first part
will have been reread and altered and corrected at least 150
times. . . . Good writing is essentially rewriting. I am
positive of this."

~~There is nothing virtuous in~~ ~~itself about~~ the rewriting process. It is   11
isn't virtuous.

simply an essential condition of life for most writers. There
a few
are writers who do very little rewriting, mostly because they
∧
have the capacity and experience to create and review a large

number of invisible drafts in their minds before they get to

Some   who slowly produce finished pages, performing
the page. And ~~many~~ writers ~~perform~~ all ~~of~~ the tasks of revision

simultaneously, page by page, rather than draft by draft. But

it is still possible to break down the process of rereading

one's own work into the sequence most published writers follow
MOST OF THE TIME .
~~as he studies his own page.~~

~~Seven elements~~

12   Many writers ~~at first just~~ scan their manuscript, reading as
To catch the larger   They TAKE THE
quickly as possible ~~for~~ problems of subject and form. ∧ ~~In this~~
CRAFTSMAN'S STEP BACK   SUPERFICIAL
~~way, they stand~~ back from the more ~~technical~~ details of language
the larger problems in writing .
so they can spot ~~any weaknesses in content or in organization.~~

Then as they reread — and reread and ~~the reread~~ RELEAD — they
~~When the writer reads his manuscript, he is usually looking~~
move in closer in a logical sequence which usually ~~was~~ INVOLVES
~~for~~ (seven elements.

13   The first is subject. As a writer
~~Do you have anything to say? If you~~
Sometimes writers are lucky, they   Writers LOOK FIRST TO DISCOVER IF THEY HAVE
~~are lucky, you will~~ find ~~that~~ indeed ~~you do~~ have something to
THAT they   ~~anything to say~~ SAID
say, perhaps a little more than you expected. If the subject   ANYTHING
writers know they CAN'T
is not clear, or if it is not yet limited or defined enough   WRITE
NOTHING,
for you to handle, don't go on. What you have to say is   SAVE

always more important than how you say it.

NOVELIST ELIZABETH JANEWAY SAYS, "I think there's A NICE
COOKING WORD ~~which~~ that Explains A little OF WHAT happens
while (the MANUSCRIPT is) STANDING. It CLARIFIES, LIKE
A CONSOMMÉ, perhaps."

The Maker's Eye: Revising Your Own Manuscripts

When students complete a first draft, they consider the job of writing done—and their teachers too often agree. When professional writers complete the first draft, they usually feel they are at the start of the writing process. When a draft is completed, the job of writing can begin.

That difference in attitude is the difference between amateur and professional, inexperience and experience, journeyman and craftsman. Peter F. Drucker, the prolific business writer, calls his first draft "the zero draft"—after that he can start counting. Most writers share the feeling the first draft, and all which follow, are opportunities to discover what they have to say and how they can best say it.

To produce a progression of drafts, each of which says more and says it more clearly, the writer has to develop a special kind of reading skill. In school we are taught to decode what appears on the page as finished writing. Writers, however, face a different category of possibility and responsibility when they read their own drafts. To them the words on the page are never finished. Each can be changed and rearranged, can set off a chain reaction of confusion or clarified meaning. This is a different kind of reading which is possibly more difficult and certainly more exciting.

Writers must learn to be their own best enemy. They must accept the criticism of others and be suspicious of it; they must accept the praise of others and be even more suspicious of it. Writers cannot depend on others. They must detach themselves from their own pages so that they can apply both their caring and their craft to their own work.

Such detachment is not easy. Science fiction writer Ray Bradbury supposedly puts each manuscript away for a year to the day and then rereads it as a stranger. Not many writers have the discipline or the time to do this. We must read when our judgment may be at its worst, when we are close to the euphoric moment of creation.

6   Then the writer, counsels novelist Nancy Hale, "should be critical of everything that seems to him most delightful in his style. He should excise what he most admires, because he wouldn't thus admire it if he weren't . . . in a sense protecting it from citicism." John Ciardi, the poet, adds, "The last act of the writing must be to become one's own reader. It is, I suppose, a schizophrenic process, to begin passionately and to end critically, to begin hot and to end cold; and, more important, to be passion-hot and critic-cold at the same time."

7   Most people think that the principal problem is that writers are too proud of what they have written. Actually, a greater problem for most professional writers is one shared by the majority of students. They are overly critical, think everything is dreadful, tear up page after page, never complete a draft, see the task as hopeless.

8   The writer must learn to read critically but constructively, to cut what is bad, to reveal what is good. Eleanor Estes, the children's book author, explains: "The writer must survey his work critically, coolly, as though he were a stranger to it. He must be willing to prune, expertly and hard-heartedly. At the end of each revision, a manuscript may look . . . worked over, torn apart, pinned together, added to, deleted from, words changed and words changed back. Yet the book must maintain its original freshness and spontaneity."

9   Most readers underestimate the amount of rewriting it usually takes to produce spontaneous reading. This is a great disadvantage to the student writer, who sees only a finished product and never watches the craftsman who takes the necessary step back, studies the work carefully, returns to the task, steps back, returns, steps back, again and again. Anthony Burgess, one of the most prolific writers in the English-speaking world, admits, "I might revise a page twenty times." Roald Dahl, the popular children's writer, states, "By the time I'm nearing the end of a story, the first part will have been reread and altered and corrected at least 150 times. . . . Good writing is essentially rewriting. I am positive of this."

10   Rewriting isn't virtuous. It isn't something that ought to be done. It is simply something that most writers find they have to do to discover what they have to say and how to say it. It is a condition of the writer's life.

There are, however, a few writers who do little formal 11
rewriting, primarily because they have the capacity and experience to create and review a large number of invisible drafts in
their minds before they approach the page. And some writers
slowly produce finished pages, performing all the tasks of revision simultaneously, page by page, rather than draft by draft.
But it is still possible to see the sequence followed by most writers
most of the time in rereading their own work.

Most writers scan their drafts first, reading as quickly as 12
possible to catch the larger problems of subject and form, then
move in closer and closer as they read and write, reread and
rewrite.

The first thing writers look for in their drafts is *information*. 13
They know that a good piece of writing is built from specific,
accurate, and interesting information. The writer must have an
abundance of information from which to construct a readable
piece of writing.

Next writers look for *meaning* in the information. The spe- 14
cifics must build to a pattern of significance. Each piece of specific
information must carry the reader toward meaning.

Writers reading their own drafts are aware of *audience*. They 15
put themselves in the reader's situation and make sure that they
deliver information which a reader wants to know or needs to
know in a manner which is easily digested. Writers try to be
sure that they anticipate and answer the questions a critical
reader will ask when reading the piece of writing.

Writers make sure that the *form* is appropriate to the subject 16
and the audience. Form, or genre, is the vehicle which carries
meaning to the reader, but form cannot be selected until the
writer has adequate information to discover its significance and
an audience which needs or wants that meaning.

Once writers are sure the form is appropriate, they must 17
then look at the *structure,* the order of what they have written.
Good writing is built on a solid framework of logic, argument,
narrative, or motivation which runs through the entire piece of
writing and holds it together. This is the time when many writers
find it most effective to outline as a way of visualizing the hidden
spine by which the piece of writing is supported.

The element on which writers may spend a majority of 18
their time is *development*. Each section of a piece of writing must

be adequately developed. It must give readers enough information so that they are satisfied. How much information is enough? That's as difficult as asking how much garlic belongs in a salad. It must be done to taste, but most beginning writers underdevelop, underestimating the reader's hunger for information.

19   As writers solve development problems, they often have to consider questions of *dimension*. There must be a pleasing and effective proportion among all the parts of the piece of writing. There is a continual process of subtracting and adding to keep the piece of writing in balance.

20   Finally, writers have to listen to their own voices. *Voice* is the force which drives a piece of writing forward. It is an expression of the writer's authority and concern. It is what is between the words on the page, what glues the piece of writing together. A good piece of writing is always marked by a consistent, individual voice.

21   As writers read and reread, write and rewrite, they move closer and closer to the page until they are doing line-by-line editing. Writers read their own pages with infinite care. Each sentence, each line, each clause, each phrase, each word, each mark of punctuation, each section of white space between the type has to contribute to the clarification of meaning.

22   Slowly the writer moves from word to word, looking through language to see the subject. As a word is changed, cut, or added, as a construction is rearranged, all the words used before that moment and all those that follow that moment must be considered and reconsidered.

23   Writers often read aloud at this stage of the editing process, muttering or whispering to themselves, calling on the ear's experience with language. Does this sound right—or that? Writers edit, shifting back and forth from eye to page to ear to page. I find I must do this careful editing in short runs, no more than fifteen or twenty minutes at a stretch, or I become too kind with myself. I begin to see what I hope is on the page, not what actually is on the page.

24   This sounds tedious if you haven't done it, but actually it is fun. Making something right is immensely satisfying, for writers begin to learn what they are writing about by writing. Language leads them to meaning, and there is the joy of discovery, of

understanding, of making meaning clear as the writer employs the technical skills of language.

Words have double meanings, even triple and quadruple meanings. Each word has its own potential for connotation and denotation. And when writers rub one word against the other, they are often rewarded with a sudden insight, an unexpected clarification.

The maker's eye moves back and forth from word to phrase to sentence to paragraph to sentence to phrase to word. The maker's eye sees the need for variety and balance, for a firmer structure, for a more appropriate form. It peers into the interior of the paragraph, looking for coherence, unity, and emphasis, which make meaning clear.

I learned something about this process when my first bi-focals were prescribed. I had ordered a larger section of the reading portion of the glass because of my work, but even so, I could not contain my eyes within this new limit of vision. And I still find myself taking off my glasses and bending my nose towards the page, for my eyes unconsciously flick back and forth across the page, back to another page, forward to still another, as I try to see each evolving line in relation to every other line.

When does this process end? Most writers agree with the great Russian writer Tolstoy, who said, "I scarcely ever reread my published writings, if by chance I come across a page, it always strikes me: all this must be rewritten; this is how I should have written it."

The maker's eye is never satisfied, for each word has the potential to ignite new meaning. This article has been twice written all the way through the writing process, and it was published four years ago. Now it is to be republished in a book. The editors made a few small suggestions, and then I read it with my maker's eye. Now it has been re-edited, re-revised, re-read, re-re-edited, for each piece of writing to the writer is full of potential and alternatives.

A piece of writing is never finished. It is delivered to a deadline, torn out of the typewriter on demand, sent off with a sense of accomplishment and shame and pride and frustration. If only there were a couple more days, time for just another run at it, perhaps then. . . .

Content

1. Why does Murray say that when a first "draft is completed, the job of writing can begin" (¶ 1)? Do you agree or disagree? If you thought before you read the essay that one draft was enough, has Murray's essay convinced you otherwise?

2. How does Murray explain John Ciardi's analysis of the "schizo-phrenic process" of becoming one's own reader, "to be passion-hot and critic-cold at the same time" (¶ 6)? Why does he consider it so important for writers to be both?

3. What are writers looking for when they revise? Is Murray's list (¶s 13–20) realistic? Comprehensive?

4. How can writers be sure that their "makers' eye" has in revision an accurate perception of the "need for variety and balance, for a firmer structure, for a more appropriate form . . . for coherence, unity, and emphasis" (¶ 26)? How do you, as a writer, know whether your writing is good or not? Does Murray's essay provide sufficient information to enable you to be an accurate judge of your own work? Why or why not?

Strategies/Structures

1. Many of Murray's revisions are for greater conciseness. For ex-ample, the first sentence of paragraph 11 initially read, "There is noth-ing virtuous in the rewriting process." Murray then revised it to "The rewriting process isn't virtuous." The published version says, "Re-writing isn't virtuous." What are the effects of these successive changes? And of other comparable changes?

2. Compare and contrast the deleted paragraph 8 of the original ver-sion and the rewritten paragraphs 8 and 9 of the typescript with para-graphs 7 and 8 in the printed version. Why did Murray delete the original paragraph 8? Which ideas did he salvage? Why did he delete the first two sentences of the original paragraph 9? Why did he delete "like a battered old hive" from Estes's remark (¶ 9)? Are the longer paragraphs of the printed version preferable to the shorter paragraphs of the original?

Language

1. In many places in the revision typescript (see ¶s 1, 5) Murray has changed masculine pronouns (he, his) to the plural, (they, their). What is the effect of these changes? What occurred in America between 1973,

when the essay was first written, and 1980, when it was again revised, to affect this usage?

2. The typescript contains comparisons of craftsmen at work to writers revising their manuscripts. Is the single, longer reference in the published version (¶ 9) preferable to the two shorter versions of the same metaphor in the typescript (¶s 9, 12)? Why or why not?

3. In the typescript Murray has added references to students and teachers which were not in the original published version. For whom was the original version intended? What do the additions reveal about the intended readers of the revision? (Note that in the published revision Murray has kept the references to student writers but deleted those to teachers.)

For Writing

Prepare a checklist of the points Murray says that writers look for in revising a manuscript: information, meaning, audience, form, structure, development, dimension, voice (¶s 13–20). Add others appropriate to your writing, and use the checklist as a guide in revising your own papers.

◄──

LINDA PETERSON

Peterson, born in 1948 in Saginaw, Michigan, was educated at Wheaton College (A.B., 1969), the University of Rhode Island (M.A., 1973), and Brown University (Ph.D., 1978). Since 1978, she has been an Assistant Professor of English and Director of Expository Writing at Yale University, where she is also a Branford College Fellow. She has published several scholarly articles on autobiography, and is currently at work on a book-length study of Victorian autobiography and several research projects in composition.

In this essay Peterson shows how Richard Wright revised the original text of his commentary on the significance of *Black Boy*. In the course of six successive drafts he moved from writing for himself and for readers who, like himself, had been victimized by the "scalding experiences" of racial prejudice, to writing for a very different audience. Thus his strategy in the later drafts became one of "making allies of his antagonists and finding common ground upon which author and audience can meet." Peterson analyzes the rhetorical and revision strategies that Wright used to accomplish this aim.

From Egocentric Speech to Public Discourse: Richard Wright Composes His Thoughts on Black Boy

1   After the publication of *Black Boy* in 1945, Richard Wright was frequently asked to discuss—and sometimes to defend—the truthfulness of his portrayal of Southern black life. In the year and a half following, he gave many radio and newspaper interviews, patiently repeating his facts and answering questions, many of them naive, about racial relations in the United States. Wright came to believe that interviewers usually asked the wrong questions and never asked the right ones— questions about the significance of *Black Boy* to himself as a man and as a writer, questions about the significance of the book to its readers, whether black or white. For one brief interview, however, Wright decided quite on his own to prepare a statement explaining what he considered important about *Black Boy* as an autobiographical book.

2   We know from the outline and six drafts of this interview statement that Wright found his topic difficult. Although neatly typed, the drafts show all the marks of a writer's frustration: some are torn and wrinkled, with whole paragraphs crossed out in pencil and other sections scribbled in pen; one draft even contains three pages slashed and then patched from behind with paper and tape to allow further revisions. No doubt Wright found the statement difficult precisely because he considered it so important. In only 500 words, he wanted to discuss the influence of other autobiographical works upon his own life, de-

scribe his place within a tradition of literary autobiography, and convince even his hostile readers that such autobiographical writing, including *Black Boy*, was relevant to their own lives.

For those who want to learn to write, however, these many 3 drafts offer a lesson in craftsmanship. Following Wright through his drafts becomes much like watching a master sculptor transform rough clay into a final product. We learn how to compose, how to shape, and how to judge when the product is ready to present to the public.

Before he begins his first draft, Wright compiles a list of 4 twelve items he wants to include in the interview statement. Except in its general sense of order, this list bears little resemblance to an outline: it makes no distinctions between main points and sub-points; it attempts no balance between sections; nor does it even suggest a line of argument. What is important about the list is that it gives Wright a chance to set down on paper some points about *Black Boy* and other autobiographies that he doesn't want to forget—without worrying about precise organization or word choice. Though not an outline, this list works as a starting technique. By the final item, Wright is actually composing, no longer just making a list or jotting down phrases but explaining his point in full, coherent sentences.

As Wright moves from list to first draft, he expands upon 5 his points freely and continues to suspend critical judgment about his style. In the first part of the draft, as in the list, he follows a simple narrative arrangement to get underway: "I've been interviewed many times. . . . But I've never had a chance to say what I wanted to say. . . . What I have to say about *Black Boy* does not concern the facts. . . . When I left the South in my 18–19th year" and so on [see pp. 455–59]. At this stage, Wright is literally talking to himself, not so much about circumstances in the past that led him to compose *Black Boy*, but about the specific writing task that confronts him now. The narrative serves as a self-starter, as a reminder of why he wants to write the statement and what he wants to include in it.

In the second part of the draft, Wright expands upon the 6 final eight items of his list, allowing himself to digress when he remembers an important connection. In the list Wright named four books he considered influential—Dostoevsky's *The House of the Dead*, Moore's *Confessions of a Young Man*, Joyce's *The Portrait of the Artist as a Young Man*, and Lawrence's *Sons and Lovers*—and a few points he wanted to make about them. As we might expect, these points were vague and undeveloped, and Wright's language was often obscure, its meaning unclear to anyone but himself. In the draft these points are considerably less vague, but they are now more repetitive. For each book Wright allows a full paragraph, in each one repeating his point that the book was true or that the book allowed him to see with new eyes.

7   This outline and the early drafts contain almost classic examples of what a rhetorician named Linda Flower calls writer-based prose: they are egocentric in focus; they use a rudimentary narrative framework or a list as a substitute for analytic thinking; they include words saturated with meaning that only the writer can understand, complexes of ideas assembled without apparent logical or causal connections, and highly elliptical language that leaves the reader without an interpretive context. In other words, they represent a stage in composing during which the writer is so immersed in the process of writing itself that he forgets his audience and sometimes even loses track of his subject.

8   Far from representing a failure, this egocentric or writer-based prose is a useful and sometimes necessary stage for both the professional and the student writer. In a draft it can function, in Flower's words, as a "medium for thinking," allowing the writer to transfer stored information from the brain to the page and to manipulate that information into a pattern of meaning. If it occurs in a draft, moreover, such writer-based prose will never confuse a reader; it is for the writer's eyes only. Failure occurs only when a writer submits a piece of writer-based prose to public eyes as if it were a finished piece of discourse. Unable to read the writer's mind, the public is likely to become confused, disgruntled, or even hostile.

9   Wright's drafts are useful because in them we can watch him revise his thoughts from egocentric, writer-based prose into effective public writing. In revision Wright uses four strategies, all of them adaptable by other writers. Two allow him to clarify his ideas for himself; two others allow him to communicate those ideas persuasively to his audience.

10   The first strategy—eliminating or altering first-person constructions—helps Wright shift his mode of expression from writer-

based narrative to audience-conscious exposition. There is certainly nothing wrong with using the first-person pronoun "I" or "me," particularly in an interview statement about an auto-biography. But Wright's initial draft contains an excessive number of "I's," "me's," and "my's," many of them obscuring the true subject of the sentence and diminishing the effectiveness of the true "I." (Like the little boy who cried "Wolf," the writer who says "I" too often may lose his audience.) Apparently, as Wright edited his manuscript, he realized that these unnecessary first-person constructions blocked his own understanding of his subject and that he sometimes used the "I" merely to narrate or list events, rather than to explain their significance. As a corrective, in the middle and late drafts, Wright shifted away from the narrative "I," signaling a shift from the action itself to the meaning of the action.

In the first draft, for example, the construction "The life 11 depicted *so touched me* that it formed an insight into the Negro life *that I had seen and lived in the South*" contains two personal references.

Wright cancels one in the first draft and the other in the 12 second; then, in the third draft he omits the sentence entirely, leaving only the essential point: a description of what that insight was. Similarly, a sentence that begins in the third draft with "When *I lived* in the South, *I was doomed* to look always through the eyes which *the South had given me*" changes in succeeding drafts to become "Living in the South doomed me." The revised version not only reduces the number of "I's," but more important, it places the true subject ("Living in the South") in the subject position.

Such revisions as these may seem slight, but cognitive psy- 13 chologists tell us that a shift in the grammatical subject of the sentence often accompanies a shift in thinking or perceiving and that we can discern progress in writing, at least in part, by watching grammatical shifts. Wright's drafts suggest that a writer can self-consciously encourage shifts in his thinking. If a writer wants to clarify his thoughts, he might try re-writing the sentence without an "I"; if a writer wants to discover her meaning, she might ask herself if another word or phrase in the sentence is its real subject.

Wright's second strategy—eliminating repetitious phrases— 14 sounds much like the common textbook rule, *Be concise*, but for him it is less a rule of style than a method for understanding his subject. Wright first allows himself to record what he remembers as significant about each autobiography. Then, as he revises, he uses his repetitions to discover and formulate his thesis.

15   In the first draft, for instance, he repeatedly mentions that the autobiographies he read were "true" or "meaningful," and he repeatedly comments that they allowed him to see things anew:

> It was through looking at the experiences of the Negro in the South *through alien eyes* that those experiences cast themselves into *meaningful forms.* I knew that THE HOUSE OF THE DEAD was *a true book,* for I had already lived certain aspects of it in the South.

> I knew while reading that book that it was *a true book,* for I [too] had grown up amidst what would sound very strange to many whites, a black Puritanical environment in the South. Once again, *through the eyes of George Moore,* I was able, in looking back *through alien eyes,* to see *something meaningful* in my life, to understand and grasp it for the first time.

> . . . here again I had a chance to grasp the meaning of phases of my own environment by looking at them *through the eyes of an alien artist,* by seeing them in the guises of another life. Joyce's THE PORTRAIT OF THE ARTIST AS A YOUNG MAN was particularly *meaningful to me* for it depicted a double revolt.

> I knew too that that book [SONS AND LOVERS] was *true,* for I had lived some phases of it in the South [see pp. 456–57].

Wright cuts many of these repetitious comments as he moves from one draft to the next and, as he does, he must focus instead on *why* the books were true and *what* they allowed him to see. But the very fact that he has given himself the freedom to record whatever he thinks about each book, without worrying about rules of form or style, makes the process of discovery easier. By the third draft he is able to formulate his thesis: that autobiographical literature supplies its readers with new perspectives from which to view and interpret experience. In the margin of that draft he scribbles this insight: "When I lived in the South, I was doomed to look always at life thru the eyes which the South had given me, and bewilderment and fear made me mute and afraid. But after I had left the South, luck gave me new eyes, borrowed eyes, with which to look back and see the meaning of what I had lived through." In the fourth draft this thesis statement becomes the second paragraph, and Wright places it, as he should, before the discussion of the four autobiographical novels that influenced him.

These two strategies—eliminating or altering first-person constructions and eliminating repetitious phrases—are appropriate for early stages of the composing process, for they allow a writer to use his natural patterns of grammar and syntax to discover what it is he wants to say. Once a writer discovers what he wants to say, however, he must then consider how he can say it persuasively. In this interview statement, Wright manages to persuade because he practices two rhetorical strategies: imagining an audience and creating a voice that is his own.

We know from interviews given before the publication of Black Boy that Wright expected his audience to be resistant, perhaps hostile to the views presented in the autobiography: "When this book, BLACK BOY, is published," he said in the New York Post, "there'll be plenty of sticks in it for everybody, from Communists to Fascists, with which to beat me over the head." We also know from reviews of Black Boy that Wright's predictions came true. Many white readers, astonished by the harshness of the life the book portrays, insisted that Wright's experiences were unusual rather than representative of black life; many black readers, afraid that the book would confirm white prejudice against blacks, refused to admit that Wright's story was factually accurate. Rhetorically, then, the task facing Wright in this interview was very difficult: he must convince his audience, whatever their response to Black Boy, that reading and thinking about his autobiography would help them understand not only black life in America but their own lives as well. Should he treat his

16

audience as antagonists, or should he imagine them, whatever their actual feelings, as allies or, at least, as neutral parties?

17   Wright's initial impulse—probably the one most of us have when someone challenges our veracity—was to meet that challenge head on. We can almost feel his fists clench as he refers in the first draft to the facts of Southern life, "facts which in my opinion are quite obvious, facts which really constitute a tremendous understatement." But Wright suppresses his impulse to confront his audience fists first. Wisely, he cancels his references to the contested facts of the autobiography, for he realizes that he has too little space to dispute the facts and that such a dispute would only take him away from his purpose and lead him into a rhetorical quagmire. Instead, his strategy becomes one of making allies of his antagonists and finding common ground upon which author and audience can meet.

18   Wright makes two attempts to create common ground— one false, the other effective. Falsely, at the end of the first draft he tries to suggest that his audience can discern the truth of the experiences recorded in *Black Boy* by recalling similar experiences of struggle and conflict in their own lives: "Ask yourselves as you read how often in your own lives have you had to grapple with the kind of problems depicted there." At this point Wright is trying to imagine his audience as comprising people *like* himself. By the completion of the sentence, however, he realizes the faultiness of this strategy and quickly cancels this well-intentioned but naive attempt, acknowledging that most of his audience is in fact *different* from himself: "I know that the broad masses of the American people are not compelled to live through experiences as scalding as those described in BLACK BOY."

19   After a false start, Wright finds a legitimate way to create common ground. In the second draft, he begins to think about people who may have had experiences similar to his own, and his answers—Jews during World War II, immigrant groups during the nineteenth and twentieth centuries—lead him to see *Black Boy's* place in history.

> Yet, BLACK BOY is an American story, and to those
> who care to let their minds drift back to the early days in
> this land when their forefathers struggled for freedom,

> BLACK BOY cannot be a strange story, an astonishing
> story. It cannot be an alien story to Jews who came to
> this land from the Old World, or to the Irish, the Poles,
> the Italians . . . Surely it cannot be alien to the teeming,
> homeless millions who roam ravaged Europe this hour!

The common ground becomes, then, the ground of American history, which all American readers of *Black Boy* share as a part of their heritage. Although every reader may not have experienced personally the conflicts that Wright describes in the book, as Americans they can understand and identify with the narrative of Wright's struggle for freedom. It is to them as Americans that Wright appeals.

Imagining an audience represents an important rhetorical strategy in most writing assignments, but Wright's strategy here— treating his audience as allies—may not work for every writer on every occasion. In *Black Boy* itself, Wright imagined his readers as alien, even hostile—a tactic suitable for a book about a black boy in a white world. In this statement about *Black Boy*, however, Wright chooses to imagine his audience as similar, perhaps sympathetic—a tactic suitable for an interview that stresses the universality of the American experience. The point is that writers are seldom bound to a single, fixed conception of an audience. They can alter their conception as they move from one draft to another, and they can adapt their conception to fit their subject or rhetorical purpose. 20

So, too, can a writer use his or her personal voice as a powerful rhetorical strategy. It may seem contradictory to speak here of using the first person when earlier we discussed reasons for eliminating it, but a writer must distinguish between the ineffective use of "I" and the effective use of his or her own voice. In early drafts Wright eliminates first-person pronouns when they obscure his subject or the development of his argument. But as he revises, he also uses them as a skillful means of persuading his audience and making his point. 21

Compare, for instance, the first and final versions of the paragraph that introduces the books which led Wright to believe that his life's story was worth telling. In the first version, Wright's voice—his "I"—gets lost, crowded out by a chorus of inconse- 22 quential "I's" that clutter the paragraph. In the final version, Wright's "I" controls the paragraph, carrying the conviction of a narrator who has lived through experiences worth recording: "I came North. . . . Books were the windows. . . . I read Dostoevsky's THE HOUSE OF THE DEAD. . . . It made me remember. . . . To me reading was a kind of remembering."

Wright continues to use his own voice effectively as he narrates the events that contributed to the composition of *Black Boy,* but his most powerful use of this technique comes at the end of the interview statement. There, in the final paragraph, he merges his individual voice with the voices of other black men and women in America and with the voices of the oppressed "all over this war-ravaged earth today." Addressing his audience as "you," he identifies his "I" with the "they" of the oppressed and creates, in effect, a "we":

> Because the hunger for freedom fills the hearts of men all over this war-ravaged earth today, I feel that Negroes in America have a moral duty, a sacred obligation to remind the nation constantly of their plight, their claim, their problem. And when you hear the voice of the submerged Negro in America, remember that it is but one of a world-wide chorus of voices sounding for freedom everywhere [see p. 461].

By calling his audience "you," Wright implicitly challenges them to choose between staying aloof or joining "the world-wide chorus of voices sounding for freedom." He challenges the "you's" to join the "we's."

This conclusion combines all the rhetorical strategies we have seen before: Wright uses no ineffective first-person pronouns or repetitions, he keeps his audience clearly in mind, and he speaks powerfully with his own voice. Most important, his strategies serve his original intention. With them he expresses his conviction that autobiographical books, his own *Black Boy* included, speak not for one man alone but for numberless masses, past and present, who struggle for personal freedom.

First Draft of Richard Wright's Interview Comments on Black Boy*

Since my book, BLACK BOY, has been published, I've been   1
interviewed many times by the press and radio; but almost always
I was called upon to answer questions which I did not personally
consider important. And I never had a chance to say what I
wanted to say.

And strangely enough, what I do have to say about BLACK BOY   2
does not concern the facts contained in that book. facts which
in my opinion are quite obvious, facts which really constitute
a tremendous understatement. What I do want to talk about is
how I came to feel that the facts recorded in BLACK BOY had for
me sufficient importance to warrant my writing about them, how
it was possible for me, born and bred in a seperate Jim Crow
culture, to feel that my life possessed a meaning which my
environment denied. That sense came slowly, bit by bit.

When I left the South in my 18-19th year, my head and heart   3
were full of a jumble of confused impressions and memories.
I wondered dimly about the meaning of the life I had lived, the
experiences I had had. Then, far away from the South, in another
city and in another culture, I read Dostoeevsky's THE HOUSE OF
THE DEAD, a descrption of the lives of political prisoners in
exile in Siberia. The life depicted so toughed me that it formed

---

*Note that this draft shows typographical errors and strikeovers, just as Wright composed it at the typewriter.

an insight into the Negro life that I had seen and lived in the
South. Dostoevsky described how prisoners living in close contact
vented their hostility upon each other rather than upon the Czar
or his officers who had sent them there. That strange pattern
of conduct made me remember how Negroes in the South had vented
their hostility upon each other rather than upon the whites
above them who shaped and ruled their lives. Reading, to me, was
a kind of remembering.

4   It was through looking at the experiences of the Negro in the
South through alien eyes that those experiences cast themselves
into meaningful forms. I knew that THE HOUSE OF THE DEAD was a
true book, for I had already lived certain aspects of it in the
South.

5   Another book that impressed me a great deal after I had left
the South was George Moore's CONFESSIONS OF A YOUNG MAN; this
book delt with the struggles of a young man against the restricting
influences of an English Victorian enviroment. I knew while
reading that book that it was a true book, for I had grown up
amidst what would sound very strange to many whites, a black
Puritanical enivroment in the South. Once again, through the
eyes of George Moore, I was able, in looking back through alien
eyes to see something meaningful in my life, to understand and
grasp it for the first time. Still another book yielded something
to me, James Joyce's THE PORTRAIT OF THE ARTIST AS A YOUNG MAN;
here again I had a chance to to grasp the meaning of phases of
my own environment by looking at them through the eyes of an
alien artist, by seeing them in the guises of another life.
Joyce's THE PORTRAIT OF THE ARTIST AS A YOUNG MAN was particularly

meaningful to me, for it depicted a double revolt. Joyce's hero
revolted against the Catholic Church and the life of Dublin of
his day; and also it must be remembered that Ireland was at grips,
as she seems always to be, with imperialistic England. The Negro
in the South, he is is to live in and breathe the culture of his
times, must wrench himself free of his southern environment and
while doing so he knows that that environment is at war is warred
upon by the white environment above it. I'll mention one more
book, D. H. Lawrence's SONS AND LOVERS, which dealt with the
experiences of a son of an English mining family; this son sought
to claim himself and be himself against the claims and demands of
his family and environment. I knew too that that book was true,
for I had lived some phases of it in the South.

    I've mentioned these books more or less at ramdom. I did not   6
have in mind any of these books when I wrote BLACK BOY. The point
of this is simple: I do not beliebe that it is possible for a
Negro boy growing up in the South, clinging simply to the bleak,
prejudice -ridden suothern enviroment, to develop that sense of
distance, objectivity that would enable him to see it and
understand it. All too often he is claimed by it completely.
The experiences described in BLACK BOY, nine hundred and xxxxx
ninty-nine times out of a thousand, usually crush the people who
undergo them. What the southern envornment offers a young Negro
is utterly lacking in that xxxxxxxxxx nourishment to make him live
enable him to livs and develop as a man.

    Lynching is a terrible thing. But there are many forms of   7
lynching. There is a lynching of men's xpixinx spirits as well
as their bodies. Physical lynching occurs rather infrewuently.

Spirutual lynching occurs every day, every hours, and every moment of the day in the South for the Negro.

8   BLACK BOY is an attempt to describe how one person grappled with that lynch atmosphere, to secape it, to become conscious of it and its tremendous and devasting effects upon Negro personality. The theme of BLACK BOY is not unique; it's the them, I feel, of any honest American, white or black. But Negro life is channled
         the experiences so harsh and intense,
into such narrow waters/ that these experiences assume a qualitatively different value, for they are a way of life for millions.

9   This brings me to something rather interesting. Those of you you read BLACK BOY can know the truth of what is contained in the book in a very simple way. Ask yourselvies as you read how often in your own lives have you had to grapple with the kind of problems depicted there. I'm not naive when I make this suggestion: I realize that ~~then~~ the~~m~~ ~~has~~ broad masses of the American people are not compelled to live through experiences as scalding as those described in BLACK BOY. Hence, merely because the experiences are alien to sons and daughters of American middle class families, to whom ~~new~~ education is a matter of course, food something to be taken for granted, freedom a heritage, there might be some doubt about the truthfulness about such experiences as those contained in BLACK BOY. If there is any doubt, then I'd suggest that they broaden~~ed~~ and educate themselves by reading the literaute of other nations, the books written by men beyond the boundaries of our own country, to read the literature of other people who have been compelled to meet and try to master such experiences. That nought ~~hem~~ not to be a difficult task today,

for Europe is full of such people, the world is full of them.
The majority of men on earth today live such lives. The job of
trying to be free, is the xxxx fact that fills the consciousness
of mankind all over the world today. Maybe some of us in America
has for gotten that. The nation that remembers it will be the
nation xxxxxxxxxx whose word will be law and hope for billions of
people.

Hence, I feel that Negroes in America have a duty for beyond   10
themselves in reminding the nation of their plight. The voice of
the submerged Negro is but one of the chorus of voices sounding
for freedom everywhere today.

Final (sixth) Draft of Richard Wright's Interview Comments on Black Boy

Since my book, BLACK BOY, was published, I've been interviewed   1
many times, but I've yet to say what I really want to say about
it. I don't want to discuss the events described there, but I
do want to tell how I came to feel that those events possessed
enough importance to compel me to write about them; how it was
possible for me to feel that my life had a meaning which my Jim
Crow, southern environment denied.

Living in the South doomed me to look always through eyes   2
which the South had given me, and bewilderment and fear made me
mute and afraid. But after I had left the South, luck gave me
other eyes, new eyes with which to look at the meaning of what
I'd lived through.

I came North in my 19th year, filled with the hunger to know.   3

Books were the windows through which I looked at the world., I
read Dostoevsky's THE HOUSE OF THE DEAD, an autobiographical
novel depicting the lives of exiled prisoners in Siberia, how
they lived in crowded barracks and vented their hostility upon
one another. It made me remember how Negroes in the South,
crowded into their Black Belts, vented their hostility upon one
another, forgetting that their lives were conditioned by the
whites above them. To me reading was a kind of remembering.

Another book shed light for me, George Moore's CONFESSIONS
OF A YOUNG MAN, which described how an English youth resisted
the restrictions of a Victorian environment; and at once I was
able, in looking back through alien eyes, to see my own life.
There was another book, James Joyce's THE PORTRAIT OF THE ARTIST
AS A YOUNG MAN, which depicted the double revolt of an Irish
youth against the oppressive religious life of Ireland, an Ireland
which England was seeking to strangle. I was reminded of the
stifling Negro environment in the South, an environment that is
exploited by the whites above it. I'll mention one more book,
D. H. Lawrence's SONS AND LOVERS, which dealt with the
experiences of a son of an English coal mining family, a son
who sought to escape the demands of a bleak environment.

4   I had in mind none of these books I've mentioned when I
wrote BLACK BOY. But books like these endlessly modified my
attitude. The point is this: I do not believe that it is
possible for a Negro boy growing up in the environment of the
South today to develop that sense of objectivity that will enable
him to grasp the meaning of his life. If he is to learn to live,
he needs help from the outside. Lynching is a terror that has

many forms; there is the lynching of men's spirits as well as their bodies, and spiritual lynching occurs every day for the Negro in the South.

I know that the scalding experiences of BLACK BOY are alien to most Americans to whom education is a matter of course thing, to whom food is something to be taken for granted, to whom freedom is a heritage. Yet to those whites who recall how, in the early days of this land, their forefathers struggled for freedom, BLACK BOY cannot be a strange story. Neither can it be a strange story to the Jews, the Poles, the Irish, and the Italians who came hopefully to this land from the Old World. Because the hunger for freedom fills the hearts of men all over this war-ravaged earth today, I feel that Negroes in America have a moral duty, a sacred obligation to remind the nation constantly of their plight, their claim, their problem. And when you hear the voice of the submerged Negro in America, remember that it is but one of the world-wide chorus of voices sounding for freedom everywhere.

Content

1. Whether or not you have read *Black Boy,* can you infer its subject from either version of Wright's essay? Explain why or why not with reference to one or both versions.

2. What writing process does Peterson demonstrate that Wright used in writing the first draft of his essay on *Black Boy?* In what ways does your writing process resemble this practice or differ from it?

3. Why did Wright revise his original essay? Why did he take six drafts to accomplish his purpose to his satisfaction?

4. Explain, with reference to Wright's two versions, Peterson's assertion (¶ 20) that "writers are seldom bound to a single, fixed conception of an audience. They can alter their conception as they move from one

draft to another, and they can adapt their conception to fit their subject or rhetorical purpose."

Strategies/Structures

1. Peterson shows how Wright used four principal rhetorical strategies in moving from the first to the sixth version of his statement about "what he considered important about *Black Boy* as an autobiographical book":

  a. Elimination of ineffective first-person pronouns
  b. Elimination of ineffective repetitions
  c. A changed conception of audience as similar to himself to a view of the audience as very different from himself
  d. An increasing use of his own "personal voice"

Through comparing the first and final versions of Wright's text, show, with reference to Peterson's analysis, where necessary, how Wright accomplished these changes.

2. What does Wright gain by reducing his initial essay to half its size in the final version? What, if anything, does he lose?

3. What authorial personality (persona) does Wright project in his first draft? In what ways does the persona of the sixth draft differ? What is Peterson's authorial persona? How does this persona reinforce the credibility of her analysis?

Language

1. Peterson's title uses "Egocentric Speech" and "Public Discourse." Explain the meaning of each term as illustrated in her essay.

2. In her essay Peterson quotes extensively from Wright's text. How closely does her language resemble Wright's in choice of vocabulary and images? In sentence construction and rhythm? How closely should the person who quotes make his or her language conform to the language of the person quoted? What is lost or gained by so doing?

For Writing

1. Examine two drafts of one of your papers to identify the changes you made. Do any of your changes eliminate ineffective first-person pronouns or inappropriate repetitions? Indentify any such instances. Did you make any of the changes to adapt your writing to your intended readers' interests or views? Explain.

2. After you have written the first draft of an essay, perhaps just to get the ideas down on paper, identify what you ultimately want that essay to accomplish and revise it accordingly.

◀──▶

WILLIAM ZINSSER

Born in New York City in 1922 and educated at Princeton University (A.B., 1944), Zinsser prepared early to become a journalist. During the 1940s and 1950s he wrote features, drama and film criticism, and editorials for the *New York Herald Tribune;* during the next decade he was a columnist for *Life* and *Look* and wrote *Any Old Place With You* (1966) and *The Lunacy Boom* (1970). In 1970, he began teaching expository writing at Yale University, an experience which led to his low-key, humorous, practical book of advice for writers, *On Writing Well* (1976, 1980). In the following chapter from that book, Zinsser demonstrates how style will follow naturally if writers believe in their own identity, their own opinions, "proceeding with confidence, generating it, if necessary, by pure willpower." For some writers the flexible, easy style Zinsser advocates may appear in the first draft. For many others, a smooth, natural-sounding final draft will result from numerous revisions.

Style

S o much for early warnings about the bloated monsters that   1
lie in ambush for the writer trying to put together a clean English sentence.

"But," you may say, "if I eliminate everything that you   2
think is clutter and strip every sentence to its barest bones, will there be anything left of me?"

The question is a fair one and the fear entirely natural.   3
Simplicity carried to its extreme might seem to point to a style

where the sentences are little more sophisticated than "Dick likes Jane" and "See Spot run."

4   I'll answer the question first on the level of mere carpentry. Then I'll get to the larger issue of who the writer is and how to preserve his or her identity.

5   Few people realize how badly they write. Nobody has shown them how much excess or murkiness has crept into their style and how it obstructs what they are trying to say. If you give me an article that runs to eight pages and I tell you to cut it to four, you'll howl and say it can't be done. Then you will go home and do it, and it will be infinitely better. After that comes the hard part: cutting it to three.

6   The point is that you have to strip down your writing before you can build it back up. You must know what the essential tools are and what job they were designed to do. If I may labor the metaphor of carpentry, it is first necessary to be able to saw wood neatly and to drive nails. Later you can bevel the edges or add elegant finials, if that is your taste. But you can never forget that you are practicing a craft that is based on certain principles. If the nails are weak, your house will collapse. If your verbs are weak and your syntax is rickety, your sentences will fall apart.

7   I'll admit that various nonfiction writers like Tom Wolfe and Norman Mailer and Hunter Thompson have built some remarkable houses. But these are writers who spent years learning their craft, and when at last they raised their fanciful turrets and hanging gardens, to the surprise of all of us who never dreamed of such ornamentation, they knew what they were doing. Nobody becomes Tom Wolfe overnight, not even Tom Wolfe.

8   First, then, learn to hammer in the nails, and if what you build is sturdy and serviceable, take satisfaction in its plain strength.

9   But you will be impatient to find a "style"—to embellish the plain words so that readers will recognize you as someone special. You will reach for gaudy similes and tinseled adjectives, as if "style" were something you could buy at a style store and drape onto your words in bright decorator colors. (Decorator colors are the colors that decorators come in.) Resist this shopping expedition: there is no style store.

Style is organic to the person doing the writing, as much   10
a part of him as his hair, or, if he is bald, his lack of it. Trying
to add style is like adding a toupee. At first glance the formerly
bald man looks young and even handsome. But at second
glance—and with a toupee there is always a second glance—he
doesn't look quite right. The problem is not that he doesn't look
well groomed; he does, and we can only admire the wigmaker's
almost perfect skill. The point is that he doesn't look like himself.

This is the problem of the writer who sets out deliberately   11
to garnish his prose. You lose whatever it is that makes you
unique. The reader will usually notice if you are putting on airs.
He wants the person who is talking to him to sound genuine.
Therefore a fundamental rule is: be yourself.

No rule, however, is harder to follow. It requires the writer   12
to do two things which by his metabolism are impossible. He
must relax and he must have confidence.

Telling a writer to relax is like telling a man to relax while   13
being prodded for a possible hernia, and, as for confidence, he
is a bundle of anxieties. See how stiffly he sits at his typewriter,
glaring at the paper that awaits his words, chewing the eraser
on the pencil that is so sharp because he has sharpened it so
many times. A writer will do anything to avoid the act of writing.
I can testify from my newspaper days that the number of trips
made to the water cooler per reporter-hour far exceeds the body's
known need for fluids.

What can be done to put the writer out of these miseries?   14
Unfortunately, no cure has yet been found. I can only offer the
consoling thought that you are not alone. Some days will go
better than others; some will go so badly that you will despair
of ever writing again. We have all had many of these days and
will have many more.

Still, it would be nice to keep the bad days to a minimum,   15
which brings me back to the matter of trying to relax.

As I said earlier, the average writer sets out to commit an   16
act of literature. He thinks that his article must be of a certain
length or it won't seem important. He thinks how august it will
look in print. He thinks of all the people who will read it. He
thinks that it must have the solid weight of authority. He thinks
that its style must dazzle. No wonder he tightens: he is so busy
thinking of his awesome responsibility to the finished article

that he can't even start. Yet he vows to be worthy of the task. He will do it—by God!—and, casting about for heavy phrases that would never occur to him if he weren't trying so hard to make an impression, he plunges in.

17   Paragraph 1 is a disaster—a tissue of ponderous generalities that seem to have come out of a machine. No *person* could have written them. Paragraph 2 is not much better. But Paragraph 3 begins to have a somewhat human quality, and by Paragraph 4 the writer begins to sound like himself. He has started to relax.

18   It is amazing how often an editor can simply throw away the first three or four paragraphs of an article and start with the paragraph where the writer begins to sound like himself. Not only are the first few paragraphs hopelessly impersonal and ornate; they also don't really say anything. They are a self-conscious attempt at a fancy introduction, and none is necessary.

19   A writer is obviously at his most natural and relaxed when he writes in the first person. Writing is, after all, a personal transaction between two people, even if it is conducted on paper, and the transaction will go well to the extent that it retains its humanity. Therefore I almost always urge people to write in the first person—to use "I" and "me" and "we" and "us." They usually put up a fight.

20   "Who am I to say what *I* think?" they ask. "Or what *I* feel?"

21   "Who are you *not* to say what you think?" I reply. "There's only one you. Nobody else thinks or feels in exactly the same way."

22   "But no one cares about my opinions," they say. "It would make me feel conspicuous."

23   "They'll care if you tell them something interesting," I say, "and tell them in words that come naturally."

24   Nevertheless, getting writers to use "I" is seldom easy. They think they must somehow earn the right to reveal their emotions or their deepest thoughts. Or that it is egotistical. Or that it is undignified—a fear that hobbles the academic world. Hence the professorial use of "one" ("One finds oneself not wholly in accord with Dr. Maltby's view of the human condition") and of the impersonal "it is" ("It is to be hoped that Professor Felt's essay will find the wider audience that it most

assuredly deserves"). These are arid constructions. "One" is a pedantic fellow—I've never wanted to meet him. I want a professor with a passion for his subject to tell me why it fascinates *him*.

I realize that there are vast regions of writing where "I" is 25 not allowed. Newspapers don't want "I" in their news stories; many magazines don't want it in their articles and features; businesses and institutions don't want it in the annual reports and pamphlets that they send so profusely into the American home. Colleges don't want "I" in their term papers or dissertations, and English teachers in elementary and high schools have been taught to discourage any first-person pronoun except the literary "we" ("We see in Melville's symbolic use of the white whale . . . ").

Many of these prohibitions are valid. Newspaper articles 26 should consist of news, reported as objectively as possible. And I sympathize with schoolteachers who don't want to give students an easy escape into opinion—"I think Hamlet was stupid"—before the students have grappled with the discipline of assessing a work on its merits and on external sources. "I" can be a self-indulgence and a cop-out.

Still, we have become a society fearful of revealing who 27 we are. We have evolved a national language of impersonality. The institutions that seek our support by sending us their brochures tend to sound remarkably alike, though surely all of them—hospitals, schools, libraries, museums—were founded and are still sustained by men and women with different dreams and visions. Where are these people? It is hard to glimpse them among all the passive sentences that say "initiatives were undertaken" and "priorities have been identified."

Even when "I" is not permitted, it's still possible to convey 28 a sense of I-ness. James Reston and Red Smith, for instance, don't use "I" in their columns; yet I have a good idea of what kind of people they are, and I could say the same of other essayists and reporters. Good writers are always visible just behind their words. If you aren't allowed to use "I," at least think "I" while you write, or write the first draft in the first person and then take the "I"s out. It will warm up your impersonal style.

Style, of course, is ultimately tied to the psyche, and writ- 29 ing has deep psychological roots. The reasons why we express ourselves as we do, or fail to express ourselves because of "writer's block," are buried partly in the subconscious mind. There are as many different kinds of writer's block as there are kinds of writers, and I have no intention of trying to untangle them here. This is a short book, and my name isn't Sigmund Freud.

30   But I'm struck by what seems to be a new reason for avoiding "I" that runs even deeper than what is not allowed or what is undignified. Americans are suddenly uncertain of what they think and unwilling to go out on a limb—an odd turn of events for a nation famous for the "rugged individualist." A generation ago our leaders told us where they stood and what they believed. Today they perform the most strenuous verbal feats to escape this fate. Watch them wriggle through *Meet the Press* or *Face the Nation* without committing themselves on a single issue.

31   President Ford, trying to assure a group of visiting businessmen that his fiscal policies would work, said: "We see nothing but increasingly brighter clouds every month." I took this to mean that the clouds were still fairly dark. Ford's sentence, however, was just misty enough to say nothing and still sedate his constituents.

32   But the true champ is Elliot Richardson, who held four major Cabinet positions in the 1970s—Attorney General and Secretary of Defense, Commerce and H.E.W. It's hard to know even where to begin picking from his vast trove of equivocal statements, but consider this one: "And yet, on balance, affirmative action has, I think, been a qualified success." A thirteen-word sentence with five hedging words. I give it first prize as the most wishy-washy sentence of the decade, though a close rival would be Richardson's analysis of how to ease boredom among assembly-line workers: "And so, at last, I come to the one firm conviction that I mentioned at the beginning: it is that the subject is too new for final judgments."

33   That's a firm conviction? Leaders who bob and weave like aging boxers don't inspire confidence—or deserve it. The same thing is true of writers. Sell yourself, and your subject will exert its own appeal. Believe in your own identity and your own opinions. Proceed with confidence, generating it, if necessary, by pure willpower. Writing is an act of ego and you might as well admit it. Use its energy to keep yourself going.

Content

1. What qualities does Zinsser consider the essence of good style? Does your own writing possess these qualities? If not, does either Zinsser or Murray (pp. 434–43) show you how to develop such qualities?

2. Why in Zinsser's opinion, is style "organic to the person doing the writing" (¶ 10)? Can you identify your favorite writers by their style? Does your writing have a style that is recognizably yours?

3. What does Zinsser mean by committing "an act of literature" (¶ 16)? Why are attempts to do so almost certain to result in bad style?

4. Why does Zinsser advocate writing in the first person (¶s 19–29)? Given the "vast regions of writing where 'I' is not allowed" (¶ 25), in what kinds of writing is "I" appropriate?

Strategies/Structures

1. Does Zinsser's style show that he practices what he preaches? Is it concise? Lively? Personable? Natural? Explain your answer.

2. Zinsser spends nearly one-third of this essay discussing first person (¶s 19–29). Does this emphasis reflect its importance to good style or simply Zinsser's preference?

Language

1. Zinsser uses many similes and metaphors to explain what he means by style. In what ways is Zinsser's discussion of the writing process illuminated by explaining it in terms of carpentry (¶s 4, 6–8)? The extended comparison of the wearing of a toupee with style as deliberate but unorganic embellishment of prose (¶s 10, 11) is unusual. Is it appropriate? Effective?

2. Does Zinsser's writing in the first person provide the stylistic benefits he attributes to first-person writing (¶s 19–29)?

3. Although Zinsser doesn't provide an overt self portrait, what kind of authorial image and personality emerges from the images, tone, and choice of language in this essay?

For Writing

1. Make a list of the features of your style you particularly like, such as *vigorous verbs, strong sentence structure, clarity, conciseness, first-person pronouns, vivid language, naturalness, its ability to convey a sense of your personality*. Make another list of features of your style you dislike, perhaps the opposite of some of the above. Use these lists as guidelines to write or revise successive drafts of your papers.

2. Write a brief essay evaluating the style of a writing you particularly enjoy (perhaps an essay in this book) according to Zinsser's criteria for good style (italicized in Exercise 1 immediately above).

◀──▶

ANGELA BOWMAN

Bowman is from Charles City, Virginia. She graduated in 1982 from the College of William and Mary with a major in psychology. She wrote and revised this essay for her freshman English class there.

The original draft of Bowman's essay had considerable interest, but is a confusing mixture of the meanings of Santa Claus, Freddie the fox, and the black doll. To revise this, Bowman outlined the first draft so she could pick out the main topics. She realized that in her paper she wanted to show how over the years Freddie had come to symbolize a cluster of events, ideas, and understandings that were triggered by her fifth Christmas.

With this in mind, Bowman made a new outline that grouped her ideas according to three major points: her father's explanation of Santa Claus (revision, paragraph 2); her present of a black doll (revision, paragraph 3); and the beginning of her life pattern of independence of mind (revision, paragraph 4). She also realized that her attitudes toward Santa as a Christmas spirit, and toward her own blackness had changed greatly as she had matured. In her revision she decided to emphasize these changes from past to present.

❖ *Freddie the Fox and My Fifth Christmas: Past and Present*

First Draft

1   I am fond of my collection of stuffed animals. I received one of my first stuffed animals for Christmas when I was five

years old. Stuffed animals did not mean very much to me then. My first stuffed animal was a red and white fox. I named him Freddie. He was just another toy under the Christmas tree. There was something different about my fifth Christmas. It was a confusing time. The night before Christmas my father had told me about the legend of Saint Nicholas and tried to explain who Santa Claus really was. I did not understand what he was talking about. It was confusing for me. Freddie helps me to remember that event. As time went by I realized what my father was trying to explain to me. Freddie also helps me to remember when the realization of who Santa was was not clear to me and the fact that it did become clearer.

When I look at Freddie now I remember that Christmas. I 2 also remember some of the thoughts and feelings that I felt when I woke up on Christmas morning and saw the tree. The first toy under the tree that I noticed was a doll. I hated the doll because she was black, and I was angry about it. I could not understand why Santa had left me that ugly doll. When I look at Freddie now, I remember that exact moment and I am ashamed. Freddie represents the fact that now I realize that at that age I had been brain-washed to think that only white dolls were pretty.

Freddie helps me to remember the ideas and feelings that 3 I experienced on my fifth Christmas morning. Yet the day and the items involved are not what are important. What is important is that I remember it as a confusing time which caused me to think and question what was going on around me. This can perhaps be seen in the instance when my father told me about Santa. Even though I did not understand what he was explaining I did not accept it either. I just listened to him politely and thought about it later. I still do not accept half truths and must research everything for myself.

Although Freddie is old, torn and perhaps worthless to 4 most people who see him, he means a lot to me. He has grown up with me. He was with me in the past when certain ideas were confusing to me. Since those confusing ideas have become clearer to me, Freddie represents my ability to search for answers that will satisfy my curiosities.

◆ Freddie the Fox and My Fifth Christmas: Past and Present

Final Version

1   On my fifth Christmas I was given Freddie, a stuffed toy fox that has since come to symbolize several important phenomena of that day: my having to cope with Santa Claus as a symbol rather than as a person; my initial rejection and later acceptance of a black doll—and pride in my race; and the beginning of my growing independence of mind.

2   On Christmas Eve my father told me about the legend of St. Nicholas and tried to explain that Santa represented the spirit of Christmas but was not a real person. I became confused and rejected his explanation, though secretly I felt that my father was right. He had never lied to me. I was so upset that I jumped down from his lap, stomped off, and hid in my room. Later I understood what I hadn't wanted to admit at the time. I had felt that if there wasn't a flesh-and-blood Santa I might not get any presents, but I couldn't tell my father this because that would have ignored his explanation of the true spirit of Christmas, generous and loving. Only when I was older and could express the genuine Christmas spirit myself was I able to fully understand what my father had meant.

3   The next morning I tiptoed to the Christmas tree, fearful that I'd find nothing after what my father had said the day before. What I saw was worse than nothing—an ugly black doll. I hated the doll because she was black. At that age I had been brain-washed to think that only white dolls were pretty. Maybe I'd been given the doll as punishment for rebelling against my father's explanation of Santa Claus. Now when I remember that moment I feel ashamed. With plenty of encouragement from my parents and others I have grown to be very proud of my blackness, symbolized by the doll. It's painful to think that I could ever have hated that doll.

4   Both events caused me to question ideas that I had previously taken for granted. I stopped accepting everything I was

told, though the realization that white skin wasn't prettier than black didn't come overnight. I started finding out things for myself, investigating and questioning. I must have driven my parents, teachers, and the local librarian wild because I never stopped asking questions. I still haven't, because I like to make important discoveries and decisions for myself.

Freddie the fox has been my mascot during the whole time. 5
We've grown up together. His presence symbolizes not only my fifth Christmas but the changes I've experienced since then. He links past and present.

Content

1. What is the thesis of the first version? Of the revision? At what point in each version is the thesis apparent?
2. Does Freddie the fox have any literal connection with what he symbolizes for Bowman? Does he need to? In which version is the symbolic connection clearer?
3. At what point in each version is it apparent that the author is black? Why is her race important in this essay? Given its importance, where should this information be presented?

Strategies/Structures

1. What revisions contributed to greater clarity in the second version?
2. Identify some of the unnecessary repetitions in the first version. Have they been eliminated in the revision? With what effect?
3. Every paragraph in the first version begins with a reference to Freddie the fox. Where do references in the revision occur? What function do they serve in each version?
4. Explain how Bowman uses past and present as a means of explaining each point in the revision. How does the motif control the organization of each paragraph? Of the whole paper? Is this also true in the original version?

Language

1. Identify some words present in the revision that are not in the original essay. What do they contribute to the essay?
2. The revision is about twenty words longer than the original, yet it seems shorter. Why?

For Writing

1. If you have written a draft of a paper that is unclear or badly organized, try revising it according to the process suggested in the introduction to this essay.

2. To write an essay about one or more symbols, see the suggestions on p. 298, with regard to Lai Man Lee's essay, "My Bracelet," and those on p. 79 concerning Tim Payne's analysis of "On the Beach at Bar Harbor."

GLOSSARY

Abstract refers to qualities, ideas, or states of being that exist but which our senses cannot perceive. What we perceive are the concrete by-products of abstract ideas. No single object or action can be labeled *love,* but a warm embrace or a passionate kiss is a visible, concrete token of the abstraction we call "love." In many instances abstract words such as *beauty, hatred, stupidity,* or *kindness* are more clearly understood if illustrated with **concrete** examples (*see* **Concrete** *and* **General/Specific**).

Allusion is a writer's reference to a person, place, thing, literary character, or quotation which the reader is expected to recognize. Because the reader supplies the meaning and the original context, such references are economical; writers don't have to explain them. By alluding to a young man as a *Romeo, Don Juan,* or *Casanova,* a writer can present the subject's amorous nature without needing to say more. To make sure that references will be understood, writers have to choose what their readers can reasonably be expected to recognize.

Analogy is a comparison made between two things, qualities, or ideas that have certain similarities although the items themselves may be very different. For example, Barry Lopez makes an analogy between his horse Coke High and his Dodge van in the essay "My Horse" (Chapter 9) that shows the similarities between animal and machine. Despite their obvious differences, Lopez stresses their likeness in function, response, and importance to him. The emphasis is on the objects' similarities; dissimilarities significant in number and kind would have weakened the analogy. Metaphors and similies are two figures of speech that are based on analogies, and such comparisons are often used in argumentation (*see* **Figures of Speech** *and* **Argumentation**).

Appeal to Emotion is one of several ways writers can move their readers to accept what they say. As a means of persuasion, the writer's appeal to emotion allows words and examples to affect readers in ways that advertisements sometimes affect consumers. Orwell's powerful essay "Marrakech" (Chapter 11) engages the readers' emotions as he describes the deplorable life and death circumstances of the natives. As momentary eyewitnesses, we are moved by the descriptions and convinced of Orwell's truthfulness. When a writer presents himself as a person of integrity, intelligence, and good will, he appeals to the reader's sense of ethics, as Martin Luther King, Jr. does in "Letter from Birmingham Jail" (Chapter 10). While one approach touches the heart and the other the mind, these appeals are not mutually exclusive and, indeed, are often intertwined (*see* Chapter 11).

Argument, in a specialized literary sense, is a prose summary of the plot, main idea, or subject of a prose or poetic work.

Argumentation is one of the four modes of discourse (*see* **Description, Exposition,** *and* **Narration**). It seeks to convince the reader of the truth or falseness of an idea. Writers sometimes accomplish this by appealing to readers' emotions as Orwell does in "Marrakech" or by appealing to readers' ethics as is the case in "None of This Is Fair" by Richard Rodriguez (*see* Chapter 11). Others, such as Andrew Hacker in "E.R.A.—R.I.P.," can argue for or against a volatile issue by appealing to the readers' sense of reason (*see* Chapter 10), though often in an argument these appeals are interrelated.

Audience consists of the readers of a given writing. Writers may write some pieces solely for themselves; others for their peers, teachers, or supervisors; others for people with special interest in and knowledge of the subject. Writers aware of some of the following dimensions can adapt the level of their language and the details of their presentation to different sorts of readers. What is the age range of the intended readers? The educational level? Their national, regional, or local background? Have they relevant biases, beliefs? How much do they know about the subject? Why should they be interested in it or in the writer's views? Gertrude Stein once observed, "I write for myself and strangers." By answering some of the questions above, the writer can perhaps convert strangers into friends.

Cause and Effect writing examines in detail the relationship between the *why* (cause) and *what* (effect) of an incident, phenomenon, or event. A writer could focus on the causes of a particular social, medical, or fictional occurrence (the Depression, psychotic depression in general, or Hamlet's depression in particular), or she might emphasize the effects of one or a combination of causes, such as the consequences of excessive indulgence in drugs, alcohol, or video games. In "Who's Afraid of Math, and Why?" (Chapter 4) Sheila Tobias explains the cultural causes of math anxiety, and its unfortunate effects—particularly on girls and women. As the poet William Butler Yeats observed, "Who can tell the dancer from the dance?"

Classification groups items or concepts to emphasize their similarities, and then, through division, breaks down the larger category into its separate components or subgroups to show their distinguishing features. For example, a writer attempting to classify a school's population might categorize the students as jocks, eggheads, preppies, and campus politicos. The writer who classifies information first determines the overall features of the forest and then identifies the specific trees it contains (*see* Chapter 7).

Cliché is a commonplace expression that reveals the writer's lack of imagination to use fresher, more vivid language. If a person finds himself *between a rock and a hard place,* he might decide to use a cliché, *come hell or high water,* in hopes that it will hit his reader *like a ton of bricks.* Such expressions, though, *fall on deaf ears* and roll off the reader *like water off a duck's back.* A cliché is *as dead as a mackerel;* its excessive familiarity dulls the reader's responses.

Coherence indicates an orderly relationship among the parts in a whole essay or other literary work. Writing is coherent when the interconnections among clauses, sentences, and paragraphs are clearly and logically related to the main subject under discussion. The writer may establish and maintain coherence through the use of transitional words or phrases (however; likewise), a consistent point of view, an ordered chronological or spatial presentation of information, appropriate pronoun references for nouns, or strategic repetition of important words or sentence structures.

Colloquial Expressions (*see* **Diction**)

Colloquialism (*see* **Diction**)

Comparison and Contrast aims to show the reader similarities and differences that exist between two or more things or ideas. Items that are alike (all apples) are compared while those that are dissimilar are contrasted (cherries, kumquats, passion fruit). *See* Chapter 9.

Conclusion refers to sentences, paragraphs, or longer sections of an essay that bring the work to a logical or psychologically satisfying end. Although a conclusion may (**a**) summarize or restate the essay's main point, and thereby refresh the reader's memory, it may also end with (**b**) the most important point, or (**c**) a memorable example, anecdote, or quotation, or (**d**) identify the broader implications or ultimate development of the subject. Stylistically, it's best to end with a bang, not a whimper; Lincoln's "Gettysburg Address" concludes with the impressive " . . . and that government of the people, by the people, and for the people, shall not perish from the earth." A vigorous conclusion grows organically from the material that precedes it and is not simply tacked on to get the essay over with.

Concrete terms give readers something specific to see, hear, touch, smell, or feel, while abstract terms are more general and intangible. Writers employ concrete words to show their subject or characters in action, rather than merely to tell about them. Yet a concrete word does not have to be hard, like cement; anything directly perceived by the senses is considered concrete, including an ostrich plume, the sound of a harp, a smile, or a cone of cotton candy (*see* **Abstract** *and* **General/Specific**).

Connotation and Denotation refer to two levels of interpreting the meanings of words. Denotation is the literal, explicit "core" meaning—the "dictionary" definition. Connotation refers to additional meanings implied or suggested by the word, or associated with it, depending on the user's or reader's personal experience, attitudes, and cultural conditioning. For example, the word *athlete* denotes a skilled participant in a sport. But to a sports enthusiast, *athlete* is likely to connote not just the phenomenon of one's participation in sports, but positive physical and moral qualities, such as robust physical condition, well-coordinated movements, a wholesome character, a love of the outdoors, and a concern with fair play. Those disenchanted with sports might regard an *athlete* as a marketable commodity for unscrupulous businessmen, an overpaid exploiter of the public, or someone who has developed every part of his anatomy but his brain—a "dumb jock."

Contrast (*see* **Comparison/Contrast**)

Deduction (*see* **Induction/Deduction**)

Deductive (*see* **Induction/Deduction**)

Definition explains the meaning of a word, identifying the essential properties of a thing or idea. Dictionaries furnish the various literal interpretations of individual words (*see* **Connotation/Denotation**), but a writer may provide extended or altered definitions, sometimes of essay length, to expand or supplement "core" meanings. "My Dog, Phydeaux" might be an extended personal definition of *dog*. Whether short or long, definitions may employ other strategies of exposition, such as classification ("Phydeaux, a collie"), comparison and contrast ("is better natured than Milo, my brother's bassett . . ."), description ("and has an unusual star-shaped marking on his forehead"). *See* Chapter 6.

Denotation (*see* **Connotation/Denotation**)

Description is a mode of discourse (*see* **Argumentation, Exposition,** *and* **Narration**) aimed at bringing something to life by telling how it looks, sounds, tastes, smells, feels, or acts. The writer tries to convey a sense impression, depict a mood, or both. Thus, the writer who conveys the heat of an August sidewalk; the sound, sight, and smell of the Atlantic breaking on the jagged coastline of Maine; or the bittersweetness of an abandoned love affair, enables readers to experience the situations. Description is a writer's spice; a little goes a long way. Except in extensively descriptive travel pieces, description is primarily used to enhance the other modes of discourse and is seldom an end in itself (*see* Chapter 5).

Diction is word choice. Hemingway was talking about diction when he explained that the reason he rewrote the last page of *Farewell to Arms* 39 times was because of problems in "getting the words right." Getting the words right means choosing, arranging, and using words appropriate to the purpose, audience, and sometimes the form of a particular piece of writing. Puns are fine in limericks and shaggy-dog stories ("I wouldn't send a knight out on a dog like this"), but they're out of place in technical reports and obituaries. Diction ranges on a continuum from highly formal (a *repast*) to informal writing and conversation (a *meal*) to slang (*eats*).

> *Formal English:* words and grammatical constructions used by educated native speakers of English in sermons, oratory, and in many serious books, scientific reports, and lectures.
> *Informal* (conversational or colloquial) *English:* ranges from the more relaxed but still standard usage in polite (but not stuffy) conversation or writing, as in much newspaper writing and in most of the essays in this book. In informal writing it's all right to use contractions ("I'll go to the wedding, but I won't wear tails") and some abbreviations, but not all (As Angela attached the IV bottle to the holder, she wondered whether the patient had OD'd on carbohydrates).
> *O.K.* is generally acceptable in conversation, but it's not O.K. in most formal or informal writing.
> *Slang:* highly informal (often figurative) word choice in speech or writing. It may be used by specialized groups

(pot, grass, uppers) or more general speakers to add vividness and humor (often derogatory) to their language ("Bluto, zoned out on brews, found booking for a rocks for jocks final really awesome."). Although some slang is old and sometimes even becomes respectable (cab), it often erupts quickly into the language and just as quickly disappears *(twenty-three skidoo)*; it's better to avoid all slang than to use outmoded slang.

Regionalisms: expressions used by people of a certain region of the country, often derived from the native languages of earlier settlers, such as *arroyo* for *deep ditch* used in the Southwest.

Dialect: the spoken (and sometimes written) language of a group of people that reflects their social, educational, economic, and geographic status ("My mama done tole me . . ."). Dialect may include regionalisms. In parts of the Northeast, *youse* is a dialect form of *you* while its counterpart in the South is *y'all.* Even some educated Southerners say *ain't,* but they don't usually write it, except to be humorous.

Technical Terms (jargon): words used by those in a particular trade, occupation, business, or specialized activity. For example, medical personnel use *stat* (immediately) and *NPO* (nothing by mouth); surfers' vocabularies include *shooting the curl, hot-dogging,* and *hang ten; hardware* has different meanings for carpenters and users of computers.

Division (*see* **Classification**)
Effect (*see* **Cause/Effect**)
Emphasis makes the most important ideas, characters, themes, or other elements stand out. The principal ways of achieving emphasis are through the use of

Proportion, saying more about the major issues and less about the minor ones.

Position, placing important material in the key spots, the beginning or ends of paragraphs or larger units. Arrangement in climactic order, with the main point of an argument or the funniest joke last, can be particularly effective.

Repetition, of essential words, phrases, and ideas (Jacques adored expensive women and fast cars—or was it fast women and expensive cars?).

Focus, pruning of verbal underbrush and unnecessary detail to accentuate the main features.

Mechanical devices, such as capitalization, underlining (italics), exclamation points, conveying enthusiasm and excitement, as well as emphasis, as advertisers and new journalists well know. Tom Wolfe's title, *Las Vegas (What ?) Las Vegas (Can't Hear You! Too Noisy) Las Vegas!!!!,* illustrates this practice, as well as the fact that nothing exceeds like excess.

Essay refers to a nonfiction composition on a central theme or subject, usually brief and written in prose. As the contents of this book reveal, essays come in varied modes—among them descriptive, narrative, analytic, argumentative—and moods, ranging from humorous to grim, whimsical to bitterly satiric. Essays are sometimes categorized as *formal* or *informal,* depending on the author's content, style, and organization. Formal essays, written in formal language, tend to focus on a single significant idea supported with evidence carefully chosen and arranged, such as the Lewis Thomas essay "The Technology of Medicine" (Chapter 7). Informal essays sometimes have a less obvious structure than formal essays; the subject may seem less significant, even ordinary; the manner of presentation casual, personal, or humorous. Yet these distinctions blur. Although E. B. White's "Once More to the Lake" (Chapter 2) discusses a personal experience in conversation and humorous language, its apparently trivial subject, the vacation of a boy and his father in the Maine woods, takes on universal, existential significance.

Etymology is information about the origin and history of words. Most dictionaries provide the etymologies of words in brackets or parentheses located before or after the definitions. In addition to furnishing clues about the current meanings of words, etymologies can show how the definitions have changed over time. Some words flaunt their origin: *denim* from its place of manufacture (Serge de Nîmes), *guy* from Guy Fawkes, who tried to blow up the British Parliament. Some have become more general (*kleenex* for any facial tissue), and others more specific (*corn* used to mean any grain). Some have taken a turn for the better and others for the worse: *housewife* and *hussy,* no longer sisters under the skin, have the same etymology. Consequently, etymologies give hints to the wondrous workings of the human mind, logical, psychological, quirky.

Evidence is supporting information that explains or proves a point. General comments or personal opinions that are not substantiated with evidence leave the reader wanting some proof of accuracy. Writers establish credibility by backing general statements with examples, facts, and figures that make evident their knowledge of the subject. We believe what Joan Didion says about Las Vegas weddings in "Marrying Absurd" (Chapter 8) because her specific examples show that she's been there and has understood the context.

Example (*see* **Illustration**)

Exposition is a mode of discourse that, as its name indicates, exposes information, through explaining, defining, or interpreting its subject. Expository prose is to the realm of writing what the Ford automobile has been historically to the auto industry—useful, versatile, accessible to the average person, and heavy duty, for it is the mode of most research reports, critical analyses, examination answers, case histories, reviews, and term papers. In exposition, writers employ a variety of techniques, such as definition, illustration, classification, comparison and contrast, analogy, and cause and effect reasoning. Exposition is not an exclusive mode; it is often blended with the other three (*see* **Argumentation, Description,** *and* **Narration**) to provide a more complete or convincing discussion of a subject.

Figures of Speech are used by writers who want to make their subject unique or memorable through vivid language. Literal language often lacks the connotations of figurative language. Instead of merely conveying information (The car was messy), a writer might use a figure of speech to attract attention (The car was a dumpster on wheels). Figures of speech enable the writer to play with words and with the reader's imagination. Some of the most frequently used figures of speech include the following:

> *Metaphor*—an implied comparison that equates two things or qualities without an explicit connecting word (Suzanne, a human dynamo, still throbbed with energy after four sets of tennis, a swim, and ten-mile bike ride).
> *Simile*—a direct comparison, usually with the connecting words *like* or *as* (He was as happy as a fly at a fruit market).
> *Personification*—the giving of human qualities to inanimate or nonhuman objects (This town dies every night at nine).
> *Hyperbole*—an elaborate exaggeration, often intended to be humorous or ironic (That guy will try to break about 300 of your fingers if he shakes your hand).
> *Understatement*—a deliberate downplaying of something's seriousness, like its antithesis, hyperbole, often for the sake of humor or irony (After losing his job, his wife, and his car within one hour's time, Marvin started to feel it wasn't going to be one of his best days).

Paradox—a contradiction that upon closer inspection is actually truthful (You never know what you've got until you lose it).

Rhetorical Question—a question asked for dramatic impact which demands no answer (How much more abuse are we supposed to endure from this tyrant?).

Metonymy—the representation of an object, public office, or concept by something associated with it (The White House announcement of world peace had the Hill rejoicing).

Dead Metaphor—a word or phrase, originally a figure of speech, that through constant use is treated literally (the *arm* of a chair, the *leg* of a table, the *head* of a bed).

Focus represents the writer's control and limitation of a subject to a specific aspect or set of features, determined in part by the subject under discussion (*what* the writer is writing about), the audience (to *whom* the writer is writing), and the purpose (*why* the writer is writing). Thus, instead of writing about food in general, someone writing for college students on limited budgets might focus on imaginative but economical meals.

General and Specific are the ends of a continuum that designates the relative degree of abstractness or concreteness of a word. General terms identify the class (*house*); specific terms restrict the class by naming its members (a *Georgian mansion*, a *Dutch colonial*, a *brick ranch*). To clarify relationships, words may be arranged in a series from general to specific: writers, twentieth-century authors, Southern novelists, William Faulkner (*see* **Abstract** *and* **Concrete**).

Generalization (*see* **Induction/Deduction** *and* **Logical Fallacies**)

Hyperbole (*see* **Figures of Speech**)

Illustration refers to providing an example, sometimes of essay length, that clarifies a broad statement or concept for the reader. This technique takes the reader from a general to a specific level of interpretation (*see* **General/Specific** *and* Chapter 8).

Induction and Deduction refer to two different methods of arriving at a conclusion. Inductive reasoning relies on examining specific instances, examples, or facts in an effort to arrive at a general conclusion. If you were to sample several cakes—chocolate, walnut, mocha, and pineapple upside-down—you might reach the general conclusion that all cakes are sweet. Conversely, deductive reasoning involves examining general principles in order to arrive at a specific conclusion. If you believe that all cakes are sweet, you would expect the next cake you encounter, say, lemon chiffon, to be sweet. Yet both of these types of reasoning can lead to erroneous generalizations if the reasoner or writer has not examined all of the relevant aspects of the issue. For instance, not all cakes are sweet—consider the biscuit cake in strawberry shortcake. Likewise, even if a writer cited five separate instances in which members of a particular ethnic group displayed criminal behavior, it would be incorrect to conclude that all members of this group are criminal. Beware, therefore, of using absolute words such as *always, never, everyone, no one, only,* and *none.*

Inductive (*see* **Induction/Deduction**)

Introduction is the beginning of a written work that is likely to present the author's subject, focus (perhaps including the thesis), attitude toward it, and possibly the plan for organizing supporting materials. The length of the introduction is usually proportionate to the length of what follows; short essays may be introduced by a sentence or two; a book may require an entire introductory chapter. In any case, an introduction should be sufficiently forceful and interesting to let readers know what is to be discussed and also entice them to continue reading. An effective introduction may

1. state the thesis or topic emphatically;
2. present a controversial or startling focus on the topic;
3. offer a witty or dramatic quotation, statement, metaphor, or analogy;
4. provide background information to help readers understand the subject, its history, or significance;
5. give a compelling anecdote or illustration from real life;
6. refer to an authority on the subject.

Irony is a technique that enables the writer to say one thing while meaning another, often with critical intention. Three types of irony are frequently used by writers: *verbal, dramatic,* and *situational.* Verbal irony is expressed with tongue in cheek, often implying the opposite of what is overtly stated. Thus, when said in the right tone, "That's baaad" means "That's extra good." The verbal ironist maintains tight control over tone, counting on the alert reader (or listener) to recognize the discrepancy between words and meaning, as did Jonathan Swift in "A Modest Proposal" (Chapter 11), where deadpan advocacy of cannibalism is really a monstrous proposal. Dramatic irony, found in plays, novels, and other forms of fiction, allows readers to see the wisdom or folly of characters' actions in light of information they have— the ace up their sleeve—that the characters lack. For example, readers know Desdemona is innocent of cheating on her husband,

Othello, but his ignorance of the truth leads him to murder her in a jealous rage. Situational irony, life's joke on life, entails opposition between what would ordinarily occur and what actually happens in a particular instance. In O. Henry's "The Gift of the Magi," the husband sells his watch to buy his wife combs for her hair, only to find out she has sold her hair to buy him a watch chain.

Jargon (*see* **Diction**)

Logical Fallacies are errors in reasoning and often occur in arguments.

Ad hominem: attacking a person's ideas or opinions by discrediting him as a person (Napoleon was too short to be a distinguished general).

Arguing from analogy: comparing only similarities between things, concepts, or situations while overlooking significant differences that might weaken the argument (Having a standing army is just like having a loaded gun in the house. If it's around, people will want to use it).

Begging the question: assuming that what is to be proven is already true without further proof, often through circular reasoning ("Rapists and murderers awaiting trial shouldn't be let out on bail" assumes that the suspects have already been proven guilty, which is the point of the impending trial).

Either/or reasoning: restricting the complex aspects of a difficult problem to only one of two solutions (Marry me or you'll end up single forever).

Non sequitur: making a conclusion that doesn't logically come from a cited instance (The Senator must be in cahoots with that shyster developer, Landphill. After all, they were fraternity brothers).

Hasty generalization: erroneously applying information or knowledge of one or a limited number of representative instances to an entire, much larger category (Poor people on welfare cheat. Why, just yesterday I saw a Cadillac parked in front of the tenement at 9th and Main).

Oversimplification: providing simplistic answers to complex problems (Ban handguns and stop organized crime).

Post hoc ergo propter hoc: erroneously citing a cause as an effect and vice versa (It always rains after I wash the car. Since I want to go to the beach, I won't wash it).

Metaphor (*see* **Figures of Speech**)

Metonomy (*see* **Figures of Speech**)

Modes of Discourse are traditionally identified as narration, description, argumentation, and exposition. In writing they are often intermingled. The *narration* of Orwell's "Marrakech" (Chapter 11), for instance, involves *description* of *characters* and settings, an explanation *(exposition)* of their motives, while the expression of its theme serves as an *argument*, direct and indirect. "Marrakech" argues through its characters, actions, and situations that for a white society to treat blacks as invisible is to violate their humanity.

Narration is one of four modes of discourse (*see* **Argumentation, Description**, *and* **Exposition**) that recounts an event or series of interrelated events. Jokes, fables, fairy tales, short stories, plays, novels, and other forms of literature are narrative if they tell a story. While some narrations provide only the basic *who, what, when, where*, and *why* of an occurrence in an essentially chronological arrangement, as in a newspaper account of a murder, others contain such features as plot, conflict, suspense, characterization, and description to intensify readers' interest. Whether as pared down as a nursery rhyme ("Lizzie Borden took an axe/ Gave her father forty whacks . . ."), of intermediate length such as Poe's "The Telltale Heart," or as full-blown as Melville's *Moby Dick*, the relaying of what happened to someone or something is a form of narration (*see* Chapter 2).

Narrative (*see* **Narration**)

Objective refers to the writer's presentation of information in a personally detached, unemotional way. The topic is stressed rather than the author's attitudes or feelings about it. Some process analyses, such as a manual on assembling a stereo, or directions on how to perform the Heimlich maneuver, are examples of objective writing; they aim to convey information about a particular subject, not the writer's feelings about it, as in subjective writing (*see* **Subjective**).

Paradox (*see* **Figures of Speech**)

Paragraph has a number of functions. Newspaper paragraphs, which are usually short and consist of a sentence or two, serve as punctuation—visual units to break up columns for ease of reading. A paragraph in most other prose is usually a single unified group of sentences that explain or illustrate a central idea, whether expressed overtly in a topic sentence, or merely implied. Paragraphs emphasize ideas; each new topic (or sometimes each important subtopic) demands a new paragraph. Short (sometimes even one-sentence) paragraphs can provide transitions from one major area of discussion to another, or indicate a change of speakers in dialogue.

Parallelism is the arrangement of two or more equally important ideas in similar grammatical form ("I came, I saw, I conquered"). Not only is it an effective method of presenting more than one thought at a time, it also makes reading more understandable and memorable for the reader because of the almost rhythmic quality it produces. Within a sentence parallel structure can exist between nouns that are paired (All work and no play made Jack a candidate for cardiac arrest), items in a series (His world revolved around debits, credits, cash flows, and profits), phrases (Reading books, preparing reports, and dictating interoffice memos—these were a few of his favorite things), and clauses (Most people only work to live; Jack lived only to work). Parallelism can also be established between sentences in a paragraph and between paragraphs in a longer composition, often through the repetition of key words and phrases, as Martin Luther King, Jr. did in his famous speech in which eight paragraphs in a row begin, "I have a dream . . ."

Parallel Structure (*see* **Parallelism**)

Paraphrase is putting someone else's ideas into your own words. Not to be confused with a summary, which condenses the original material, a paraphrase is a restatement that may be as long as the original or longer. For example, someone reading the following from Pope's *Essay on Criticism*, "True ease in writing comes from art, not chance, /As those move easiest who have learned to dance," might summarize the author's idea by saying: *Practice makes perfect*. A paraphrase of the same passage would demand further elaboration: *Writing is a skill acquired through training and practice, and luck has no part in successful composition*. Students writing research papers frequently find that paraphrasing information from their sources eliminates successive, lengthy quotations, and may clarify the originals. Be sure to acknowledge the source of either quoted or paraphrased material to avoid plagiarism (*see* **Summary**).

Person is a grammatical distinction made between the speaker (first person—I, we), the one spoken to (second person—you), and the one spoken about (third person—he, she, it, they). In an essay or fictional work the point of view is often identified by person. Thurber's "University Days" (Chapter 7) is written in the first person, while Catton's "Grant and Lee" (Chapter 9) is a third-person work (*see* **Point of View**).

Persona, literally a "mask," is a fictitious mouthpiece devised by a writer for the purpose of telling a story or making comments which may or may not relfect the author's feelings and attitudes. The persona may be a narrator, as in Swift's "A Modest Proposal" (Chapter 11), whose ostensibly humanitarian perspective advocates cannibalism and regards the poor as objects to be exploited. Swift as author emphatically rejects these views. In such cases the persona functions as a disguise for the highly critical author.

Personification (*see* **Figures of Speech**)

Persuasion, like argumentation, seeks to convince the reader or listener of an idea's truth or falseness. A persuasive argument can not only convince, but also arouse, or even move a reader to action (*see* **Argumentation, Appeal to Emotion,** *and* Part IV).

Plot is the cause-and-effect relationship between events that tell a story. Unlike narration, which is an ordering of events as they occur, a plot is a writer's plan for showing how the occurrence of these events actually brings about a certain effect. The plot lets the reader see how actions and events are integral parts of something much larger than themselves.

Point of View refers to the position—physical, mental, numerical—a writer takes when presenting information (*point*), and his attitude toward the subject (*view*). A writer sometimes adopts a point of view described as "limited," which restricts the inclusion of thoughts other than the narrator's. Conversely, the "omniscient" point of view allows the writer to know, see, and tell everything, not only about himself, but about others as well (*see* **Person**).

Prewriting is a writer's term for thinking about and planning what to say before the pen hits the legal pad. Reading, observing, reminiscing, and fantasizing can all be prewriting activities if they lead to writing something down. The most flexible stage in the writing process, prewriting enables writers to mentally formulate, compose, edit, and discard before they begin the physical act of putting words on paper.

Process Analysis is an expository explanation of how to do something or how something is done. Sometimes the writer provides directions that the reader can follow to achieve the desired results ("How to Cook Pasta," Chapter 3). Other discussions of a process explain how something was made or how it works; thus Rachel Carson helps us comprehend the earth's "Grey Beginnings" (Chapter 3). Sometimes a process analysis can provide more entertainment than instruction, as does Ann Upperco's "Learning to Drive" (Chapter 3).

Purpose identifies the author's reasons for writing. The purposes of a writing are many and varied. One can write to *clarify an issue for oneself,* or to *obtain self-understanding* ("Why I Like to Eat"). One can write to *tell a story, to narrate* ("My 1000-Pound Weight Loss"), or to *analyze a process* ("How to Make Quadruple Chocolate Cake"). Writing can explain *cause and effect* ("Obesity and Heart Attacks: The Fatal Connection"); it can *describe* ("The Perfect Meal"), *define* ("Calories"), *divide and classify* ("Fast Food, Slow Food, and Food that Just Sits There"). Writing can *illustrate* through examples ("McDonald's as a Symbol of American Culture"), and it can *compare and contrast* people, things, or ides (see Jordan's "That Lean and Hungry Look," Chapter 9). Writing can *argue*, *deductively or inductively* ("Processed Foods are Packaged Problems"), sometimes appealing more to emotions than to reason ("Anorexia! Beware!"). Writing can also provide *entertainment*, sometimes through parody or satire (*Real Men Don't Eat Quiche*).

Rhetoric, the art of using language effectively to serve the writer's purpose, originally referred to speech-making. Rhetoric now encompasses composition, and the information in this book is divided into rhetorical modes such as exposition, narration, description, and argumentation.

Rhetorical Question (*see* Figures of Speech).

Satire is humorous, witty criticism of people's foolish, thoughtless, or evil behavior. The satirist ridicules some aspect of human nature—or life in general—that should be changed. Depending on the severity of the author's attack, a satire can be mildly abrasive, such as Jordan's "That Lean and Hungry Look" (Chapter 9), or viciously scathing as Swift is in "A Modest Proposal" (Chapter 11). Usually (although not always), the satirist seeks to bring about reform through criticism.

Sentence, grammatically defined, is an independent clause containing a subject and verb, and may also include modifiers and related words. *Sentence structure* is another name for *syntax*, the arrangement of individual words in a sentence that shows their relationship to each other. Besides word choice (*diction*), writers pay special attention to the way their chosen words are arranged to form clauses, phrases, entire sentences. A *thesis sentence* (or *statement*) is the main idea in a written work that reflects the author's purpose. While experienced writers such as Thurber in "University Days" (Chapter 7) may only imply a thesis, student writers are frequently advised to provide an explicitly stated thesis in their essays, usually near the beginning, to help them organize subsequent paragraphs around this central thought. A *topic sentence* clearly reflects the major idea and unifying thought of a given paragraph. When it is placed near the beginning of a paragraph, a topic sentence provides the basis for other sentences in the paragraph. When the topic sentence comes at the end of a paragraph or essay, it may function as the conclusion of a logical argument, or the climax of an escalating emotional progression.

Simile (*see* Figures of Speech)

Slang (*see* **Diction**)

Specific (*see* **General/Specific**)

Style, the manner in which a writer says what he wants to say, is the result of the author's *diction* (word choice) and *syntax* (sentence structure), *arrangement of ideas, emphasis,* and *focus.* It is also a reflection of the author's *voice* (personality). While both Twain's "Uncle John's Farm" (Chapter 5) and McPhee's "The Pine Barrens" (Chapter 5) affectionately describe particular rural locations, the writers' styles differ considerably.

Subjective refers to writing that expresses the author's beliefs in and attitudes toward a particular subject. Although Catton in "Grant and Lee" (Chapter 9) explains the greatness of those Civil War leaders, he is less subjective and emotional than Lopez, who reveals the deep attachment he has for an old Dodge van in "My Horse" (Chapter 9). *See* **Objective.**

Summary is a condensation of main ideas from a given work that is usually much shorter than the original. Unlike a *paraphrase,* a summary seeks to reveal only the major points an author has made in a piece of writing (*see* **Paraphrase**).

Symbol refers to a person, place, thing, idea, or action that represents something other than itself. In Syfers's "I Want a Wife" (Chapter 6), "wife" symbolizes the combination roles of mother-mistress-servant that many men expect their wives to fulfill. In Jordan's "That Lean and Hungry Look" (Chapter 9), skinny people symbolize all that is dull, irritating, even sinister in the world, while fat people symbolize the good things in life.

Syntax (*see* **Sentence**)

Thesis Sentence (*see* **Sentence**)

Tone, the author's attitude toward a subject being discussed, can be serious (*see* Ellison's "Hidden Name and Complex Fate," Chapter 6), critical (*see* Brustein's "Reflections on Horror Movies," Chapter 7), laudatory (*see* Agee's "Comedy's Greatest Era," Chapter 9), mystical (*see* Dillard's "Transfiguration," Chapter 5), even sarcastic (*see* Syfers's "I Want a Wife," Chapter 6). Tone lets readers know how they are expected to react to what the writer is saying.

Topic Sentence (*see* **Sentence**)

Transition is the writer's ability to move the reader smoothly along the course of ideas. Abrupt changes in topics confuse the reader, but transitional words and phrases help tie ideas together. Stylistically, transition serves another purpose by adding fullness and body to otherwise short, choppy sentences and paragraphs. Writers use transition to show how ideas, things, and events are arranged chronologically (*first, next, after, finally*), spatially (*here, there, next to, behind*), comparatively (*like, just as, similar to*), causally (*thus,* *because, therefore*), and in opposition to each other (*unlike, but, contrary to*). Pronouns, connectives, repetition, and parallel sentence structure are other transitional vehicles that move the reader along.

Understatement (*see* **Figures of Speech**)

Voice refers to the extent to which the writer's personality is expressed in his or her work. In *personal voice*, the writer is on fairly intimate terms with the audience, referring to herself as "I" and the readers as "you." In *impersonal voice* the writer may refer to himself as "one" or "we," or try to eliminate personal pronouns when possible. Formal writings, such as speeches, research papers, and sermons, are more likely to use an impersonal voice than are more informal writings, such as personal essays. In grammar, *voice* refers to the *active* ("I *mastered* the word processor") or *passive* ("The word processor *was mastered* by me") form of a verb.